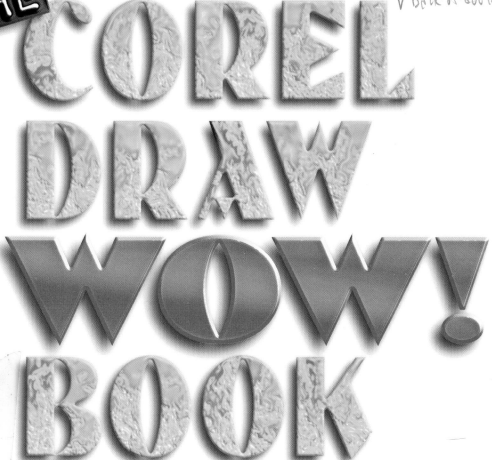

THE COREL DRAW WOW! BOOK

Linnea Dayton, Shane Hunt & Sharon Steuer

◯ Peachpit Press

The CorelDRAW Wow! Book

Linnea Dayton, Sharon Steuer, and Shane Hunt

Peachpit Press
1249 Eighth Street
Berkeley, CA 94710
(510) 524-2178
(510) 524-2221 (fax)

Find us on the World Wide Web at:

http://www.peachpit.com

Peachpit Press is a division of Addison Wesley Longman.

Cover: Jack Davis, from a design concept by Shane Hunt and Linnea Dayton
        Art shown on the cover (from the top): William Mogensen, Reed Fisher,
        Ceri Lines, Valerie Babb Krohn, David Brickley, Jolanta Romanowska

Book design: Jill Davis

Production and prepress: Jonathan Parker

ISBN 0-201-88632-4

0 9 8 7 6 5 4 3 2 1

Printed and bound in the United States of America

To Bullet

— Linnea Dayton

To my niece Tori, who at age 3 has somehow managed to balance her schedule with equal time drawing pictures on the computer and playing in the sandbox. She is my role model.

— Shane Hunt

To Linnea for persevering, and to Murphy for finally releasing us from his law

— Sharon Steuer

We would like to thank everyone who waited so patiently for this book. Topping our thank-you list have to be the many artists who so generously gave of their technical and design expertise, and of their time. Without them *The CorelDRAW Wow! Book* wouldn't have been possible.

We also owe heartfelt thanks to Bruce Wasserman, CorelDRAW consultant extraordinaire, whose schedule didn't permit him to act as an author of this book, but who contributed his extensive knowledge in consultation throughout its preparation.

We'd like to thank Jack Davis, not only for the artwork he contributed, but also for his remarkably deep, broad, and practical knowledge of computer graphics for print and screen, and for his clear thinking and kind diplomacy, all of which resources we called upon often.

We're very grateful to Jill Davis for her help in adapting her original robust *Wow!* book design to the particular needs of a volume that covers multiple versions of a graphics program.

We greatly appreciate the assistance of Joni Keele, Elizabeth Ryder, Peg Maskell Korn, and Robb Keele, who helped us collect and check information for the book.

Thank you to those at Corel Corporation who helped us all along with way. We'd particularly like to thank Fiona Rochester for her interest and support, and of course Michael Bellefeuille, Michelle Murphy, and Chip Maxwell.

Thanks to all of the individuals and companies who contributed samples and products for the CD-ROM (they're listed in Appendix E). And thanks to Tom Graney for testing the scripts generously donated by Colin MacNeil of Ur-Text.

We thank the multitalented Jonathan Parker — designer, production manager, and the world's best detail man — who once again did his magic, as he has for so many of the books in the Wow! series. And thanks to designer John Odam for conducting the press check.

And finally, additional thanks go to all the folks at Peachpit Press who have made completion of this book possible, with special thanks to Victor Gavenda, who mastered the CD-ROM, to production supervisor Cary Norsworthy, and to publisher Nancy Ruenzel.

CONTENTS

WELCOME TO *THE CORELDRAW WOW! BOOK*

IT WAS CORELDRAW™ THAT FIRST OPENED THE DOOR to producing professional-quality artwork on the DOS/Windows platform. And now, as more and more people put some version of the program to work— from the introductory version 3 (a powerful tool that had a tiny price-tag) all the way up to the 32-bit-optimized versions 7 and 8, and now even two Macintosh editions — CorelDRAW is easily the most popular drawing package on earth. With so many versions out there and such a broad range of experience among the folks who use them, it was a challenge to produce a book that could benefit everyone. But whether you're a beginner or a power user or somewhere in between, we guarantee *The CorelDRAW Wow! Book* will show you things you never knew about the program — techniques that will amaze and delight you.

What you'll find here are hundreds of pages of CorelDRAW knowledge, gleaned from experts. Art tips and techniques, design shortcuts, powerful guidelines for production, hardware and software tuning — all real-world insights into the potential and pitfalls of this powerful product. We've collected published artwork from CorelDRAW professionals and arranged it so you can walk through the specialized techniques revealed by each piece.

The book has been designed so that you can digest small chunks, in between your own hectic real-world demands, and take away techniques and skills that you can use immediately. You can read sequentially, skip around, research a specific topic, use the index to find the answer to a problem, dabble with the companion CD, whatever approach suits you. Our goal was to produce a book that helps you put the "Wow!" into your work.

HOW TO USE THIS BOOK

There are **five kinds of information** in the book: (1) basic information about how CorelDRAW's tools and functions work, (2) short tips for solving problems and making your work easier instantly, (3) step-by-step techniques for particular kinds of treatments and effects, (4) galleries showcasing other work by Corel-DRAW artists, with shorter descriptions than in the techniques sections, and (5) illustrated lists that make it easier to choose and apply CorelDRAW's built-in color schemes and special effects.

1

Basic information is found in results-oriented presentations at the beginnings of chapters.

1 In the **Basics** sections at the beginnings of the chapters we've gathered and condensed some of CorelDRAW's most important functions and organized them by goal rather than by palette or menu. In some cases we've done a little explaining about the design of the particular tool or function, with the idea that understanding exactly how something works can make it easier to remember how to use it. Our goal is to provide a "nuts-and-bolts" look at CorelDRAW that will help you maximize the program's potential and your own productivity.

Chapter 1 offers ideas for working efficiently; it's worth reading before you start in on the techniques. Reading the introductions to Chapters 2 and 3 should also be a priority, especially if you're not very experienced with CorelDRAW or some other Bezier-curve drawing program.

2 Tips are nuggets of information that can make you instantly more efficient. These have been arranged in the book to support the topic at hand, but you can also flip through and scan the tips on their own. They're easily identified by the gray title bar on top.

3 Each **Techniques** section, presented in a few pages, is designed to give you enough step-by-step information so you can carry out a similar project in CorelDRAW. Our goal was to provide enough written and pictorial instructions so you wouldn't have to hunt through the manual or use on-screen Help to follow the steps. This approach means you can jump in anywhere in the book and learn techniques that particularly interest you, without having to work sequentially through each previous chapter.

Much of the artwork in the techniques sections comes from real-world design or illustration projects, while the rest was created to demonstrate particularly useful effects. In either case, we've tried to make our examples as practical as possible. In some of the more complex projects we've focused on specific techniques rather than explaining every aspect of the art. Cross-references lead you to further explanations in other techniques sections.

CorelDRAW offers sometimes dozens of ways to arrive at a particular result. Our primary aim was to present the ones that produce the **best-looking artwork.** Given that criterion, there still might be several ways to achieve the goal. We've tried to choose the methods that take the **least time and effort.** Generally that means minimizing keystrokes, mouse clicks, and curve tweaking; reducing the opportunity for imprecision and misalignment that can come with unnecessary "hand-working" and "eyeballing"; and avoiding output problems, among other bugaboos.

In our instructions we've assumed that you can navigate through Windows or the Mac operating system and can work the CorelDRAW interface — you know how pull-down and fly-out menus work, for instance, and you understand how to click, drag,

2

QUICK COPIES

In any version of CorelDRAW from 3 on, there's a quick way to duplicate a selected object (or objects) exactly on top of the original: Select the object(s) with the Pick tool and **press the "+" key on the numeric keypad.** (You'll find this time-saving keystroke used in step-by-step instructions throughout the book.)

If you find yourself working on a computer **without a numeric keypad** — and in these days of laptops that could happen — another way to make a duplicate on top of the original is to select the object(s), copy them (Edit, Copy), and then paste (Edit, Paste). This, like the "+" shortcut, works in all versions.

Tips present small nuggets of CorelDRAW knowledge.

3a

Techniques are presented as numbered sets of instructions.

The importing, tracing, and blending that shaped the figure of the boy in *Late Afternoon* can be done in CorelDRAW 3 and all later versions, as can the exporting and

A version block at the beginning of each project tells which CorelDRAW versions can do the job and may suggest an alternative approach for other versions.

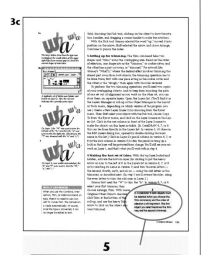

5

In CorelDRAW 5 both objects must be selected *before* you choose the Trim command, and the order of selection is all-important. The first

A work-around block tells how to do a particular step if the version you're using lacks a function needed for that step.

and double-click, and how to operate a two-button mouse if you're working in Windows.

Some of the step-by-step techniques covered in the book can't be done in all versions of CorelDRAW. The *version block* on the first page of each technique section tells you which versions make it practical to use the technique.

Instructions consist of numbered, illustrated steps. Where a particular step requires a different approach in some versions, a *work-around block* right in the text provides that information. If you need to know more about a process described in any step, check the index for references to other sections in the book.

We faced a dilemma in the techniques sections: In some cases putting down the click-and-drag detail for every command in every version would have made the instructions more complete but significantly longer and harder to read. So this is the approach we took:

- We made the instructions as short as they could be and still be accurate from version to version. For instance, if a keyboard shortcut works in all versions, like F11 for opening the Outline Pen dialog box, we used it in the instructions.

- But many keyboard shortcuts have changed over the years, partly to make CorelDRAW conform to the shortcut standards being used in other programs. So if there isn't a consistent keyboard shortcut, we listed a menu hierarchy. "Arrange, Transform, Scale & Mirror," for instance, means "in the Arrange menu choose Transform, and then choose Scale & Mirror in the resulting fly-out menu or dialog box."

- Some commands have changed slightly or moved from one menu to another. This is true for the palette that controls which layers of a CorelDRAW file can be seen and altered. The Layers roll-up has moved from the Arrange menu in version 3 to the Layout menu in later versions, and has become the Layers Manager in versions 6 and 7 and part of the Object Manager in version 8. In cases like this we get you as close as we can — for instance, "use the Layers list, from the Arrange or Layout menu, or the Object Manager in version 8."

4 The **"Gallery"** sections are for additional inspiration. Each "Gallery" page includes a description of how the featured artwork was produced, along with pertinent tips and tricks. Many of the techniques mentioned in the galleries are described in detail elsewhere in the book. Check the index if you need help finding a particular technique.

5 The **Resources** listings are useful visual references to some of CorelDRAW's harder-to-intuit features. Instead of having to scroll through a (sometimes poorly illustrated) on-screen list, you can spot what you're looking for on these pages. Fountain fills, Texture

4

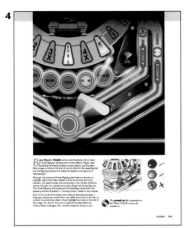

Many of the "Gallery" pages also include step-by-step illustrations.

5

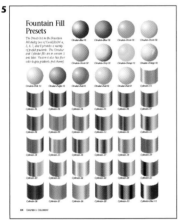

Resources "catalogs" let you see the effects of Lenses, Fountain Fill presets, and Texture Fills at a glance.

libraries, Lens effects, and plug-in filters, for instance, are shown for quick reference. In the Appendixes at the back of the book, you'll find other useful resources, such as a lists of CorelDRAW-friendly service bureaus, software suppliers, and contributing artists, and a description of how this book was produced.

Don't miss the Wow! CD-ROM. On the CD-ROM in the pocket at the back of this book you'll find demos of several versions of CorelDRAW, for both Mac and Windows, so you can try them out. Some of the artwork showcased in the book is also available on the CD for you to examine. (Remember that the artists retain all rights to this artwork. So unless you get written permission from the artist, you may not use the art in any other way.) You'll also find fonts, stock photos, and other software, including programs for preparing graphics for the World Wide Web, as well as a try-out version of Adobe Photoshop 5.

Experiment! Don't be afraid to try new things. The examples in this book are here to get you started if you're new to CorelDRAW, and to give you some new inspiration, insight, and ideas even if you're an old pro. But the tips and techniques presented here are just the beginning, and the sky's the limit!

Linnea Dayton
Shane Hunt
Sharon Steuer

April, 1999

PLEASE READ THIS FIRST

John Corkery used some of the same CorelDRAW shape-blending techniques to model the figures in this artwork for a vending machine as he used for the facial features of Hedy Lamarr, shown on the cover and on page 17.

IF YOU'RE NEW TO CORELDRAW, this chapter is designed to give you some general hints about how to use the program more easily and efficiently. We hope you'll read it before you start in on Chapters 2 and 3, which deal with the basics of using the program: how to draw and how to assign outlines and fills to the shapes you make. If you find you need a more comprehensive source of basic information, you can start with the tutorial that comes with the version of CorelDRAW you're using. For quick reference as you work, you can try the on-screen Help menu (though it may not always have the correct and complete information you're looking for). Or get an inexpensive, well-organized, and carefully indexed reference book like the *CorelDRAW Visual QuickStart Guide* (from Peachpit Press) for the version you use.

In this book we've covered all versions of CorelDRAW from the fast and reliable but rudimentary version 3 through the powerful and sophisticated version 8. At one time there were at least eight CorelDRAW versions on the market at once (five versions for Windows and a version each for the Mac, OS/2 and Unix), and all these versions still have devoted users all over the world. On the Wow! CD-ROM are working demos of version 5 for Windows and version 8 for Windows and Mac. So if you're currently using an older version, you can try new features firsthand.

KUDOS FOR CORELDRAW

With all of CorelDRAW's capabilities, before you get into the thick of the click-and-drag detail of CorelDRAW techniques presented in this book, we thought an overview of the program's comparative strengths and its development direction might be helpful.

From the beginning CorelDRAW has been fundamentally a vector-based art application like Adobe Illustrator or Macromedia Freehand, with its graphics information stored as mathematical curve descriptions. Its tools are designed to draw and color shapes and then to select and change them.

In some ways CorelDRAW can't be beat by any of the other popular drawing programs:

- When it comes to **blending** from one shape to another to create complex color changes or intermediate shapes, and then

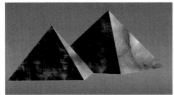

The fog illusion was created with Corel-DRAW's Interactive Transparency tool (available in versions 7 and 8). A transparency gradient was applied to each of the four triangles that make up the faces of the pyramids, allowing the background to show through.

FORCIER

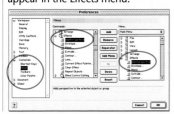
keeping the blend "live" so you can experiment with color, shape, and direction, CorelDRAW is outstanding, as you'll see in example after example throughout this book.

- In fact, one of CorelDRAW's high points is flexibility. It can keep both type and other objects **"live" and editable** as you apply all kinds of special effects and shape distortions, like the Lenses and Envelopes described in Chapter 4.

- The latest versions of the program provide sophisticated **transparency** so objects can be faded to allow the elements behind them to show through.

- Recent versions also allow you tremendous freedom to operate with **bitmaps** within the program, so that CorelDRAW now has some of the capabilities of raster-based programs like Adobe Photoshop or Corel PHOTO-PAINT, which create and store image information dot-by-dot instead of as curves.

- Every CorelDRAW version comes with more **extra software** by far than any other drawing program — not only clip art and fonts but other graphics programs as well. "Everything but the Kitchen Sink" on page 8 provides a quick overview of the extras.

To look at all the individual changes from one version of the program to the next could be overwhelming. In general, though, here are the trends:

- Succeeding versions have become **more powerful** drawing engines, with new ways to generate and combine the objects you draw.

- The trend has been to make the program **more "customizable,"** with roll-ups, palettes, and dockers, all of which are bits of interface that you can move around to suit your working style. You can also move commands from one menu to another, shorten or lengthen menus so they hold exactly the sets of commands you want, and change the keyboard shortcuts that save mousing to the menus.

- Another very important trend is that CorelDRAW has become **more "industry-standard"** — that is, more successful at exporting file formats (such as TIFFs and EPS's) that can be output successfully and that other graphics software and page layout programs can interpret and successfully incorporate into their own files.

Which Version Should I Use?

If you're happy with your current version of CorelDRAW, you may want to stick with it. Whatever version you use, you'll be able to follow along and create your own amazing artwork using the techniques outlined in this book.

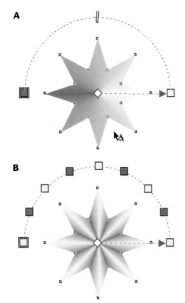

CorelDRAW's multicolor Fountain fills, introduced in version 4, allow sophisticated lighting effects that can add dimension. The addition of the Interactive Fill tool and drag-and-drop colors in version 7 make it possible to apply a Conical Fountain fill (A), then add colors (B), dragging them onto the curve of the Fountain fill from the on-screen palette, targeting them exactly where you want them.

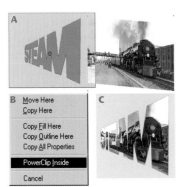

In CorelDRAW 7 and 8 running on a Windows-based system, holding down the right mouse button as you drag one object over another (A) opens a pop-up menu (B) that lets you assign the stationary object the outline and fill characteristics of the one you're dragging. You can even choose to mask (PowerClip) the dragged object inside the stationary one (C).

However, if you find from reading the step-by-step instructions in this book that later versions have features that will make your work easier and more efficient, we suggest an upgrade to CorelDRAW 8. If you have access to a university bookstore or another source that carries the academic version of CorelDRAW 8, you can get it for a very reasonable price. It comes without printed manuals, so you'll miss having a printed reference to the bonanza of clip art that has always come with the program, but the academic edition has all the functionality (and the bundled software) of the more expensive version.

If you're already working with CorelDRAW 8 or another relatively recent version, you may still learn some interesting techniques from the workarounds that we present for earlier versions — often the result is a little different, and that difference may be just what you're looking for (for instance, see the workarounds in "14-Carat Type" in Chapter 6).

Here are brief descriptions of the differences between the versions and the system requirements for each Windows and Mac edition of the program:

CorelDRAW 3 runs well on older computers. You can operate it on a 386-, 486-, or Pentium-based computer with only 4 MB of RAM; Windows 3.1 or later is required for TrueType fonts. It also runs on a long list of Unix platforms, requiring 24 MB of RAM.

CorelDRAW 4, also running on a 386-, 486-, or Pentium-based computer, can operate with 4 MB of RAM, but 8 MB was the recommended amount of memory. It added more fill options, including the Texture fills and multicolor *fountains*, or color gradients. (Texture fills and Fountain fills are covered in Chapter 3.). It introduced the Weld feature, for putting two or more objects together into a single shape. But it was a bit unpredictable and crash-prone.

CorelDRAW 5 was finally a solid, faster version that had the stability of 3 with features of 4 and more. It showed improved color output and added the ability to use shapes as "cookie cutters" to trim away parts of other shapes. And it introduced the Lens feature, which allowed for the creation of transparent objects directly in CorelDRAW. Version 5 runs on the Windows 3.1 386- or 486-based platform (the latter is recommended) with 8 MB of RAM (16 MB is recommended), and an optimized version blazes on Windows 95. CorelDRAW 5 and all subsequent versions require a CD-ROM drive and math coprocessor.

CorelDRAW 6 was the first version designed to run on a 486-based platform running Windows 95 (it also runs on Windows NT 3.51), with 16 MB of RAM (32 MB recommended). It was also the first version to run on the Mac, requiring a Power PC processor running Mac OS 7.5 or higher, 16 MB of RAM (32 MB recommended), and a CD-ROM drive. Version 6 had problems with printing, exporting, speed, and stability, some of which were fixed by the maintenance release. (If you're trying to run version 6 on the Mac, be sure to upgrade to 6.1.)

CorelDRAW 7, which requires a Pentium 60 with a minimum of 16 MB of RAM, runs better on the recommended Pentium 120 with 32 MB of RAM. It was the first version optimized to run on both Windows 95 and Windows NT. (This version was skipped on the Mac platform.) Drag-and-drop functions made it easier than ever to color objects and even mask them inside other shapes. And blends, Fountain fills, and even transparency effects were embodied in tools that could apply them interactively, without intermediary dialog boxes.

Version 7 added the ability to creatively manipulate bitmaps within CorelDRAW itself, using industry-standard Adobe Photoshop–compatible plug-in filters for special effects, and offering a powerful Convert To Bitmap feature for turning objects into bitmaps. It was also the first version to allow you to save files in previous CorelDRAW formats. It added an Internet Objects toolbar for preparing art for the World Wide Web, and the Property bar provided an interface that changes to show the options for the tool you're currently using.

CorelDRAW 8 runs on Windows 95 or Windows NT 4.0 with 16 MB of RAM (though 32 MB is strongly recommended) on a Pentium 90 (a Pentium 133 is recommended) or a Power PC–based Macintosh running Mac OS 7.6.1. Interface improvements included *dockers,* a kind of dialog box that can remain open so it's easy to get to when you need it, or be minimized to save screen space. Version 8 also added more interactive tools and improved the import and export filters that let you load files created by other programs and save CorelDRAW art in formats that other programs can successfully interpret. Other changes to the import procedure are the ability to import more than one file at a time and to specify where on the page you want the imported art to appear.

This version increased the program's interactivity, adding interactive Extrude, Distortion, Envelope, and even Drop Shadow tools. Assigning and changing outlines and fills became even easier: Each color swatch in the on-screen palette expands into a pop-up grid of closely related colors. You can open the appropriate dialog box for changing the outline or fill simply by double-clicking its color swatch on the Status bar. And the Uniform Fill and Outline Color dialog box offer a Color Harmonies option to help you choose pleasing combinations. These and other improvements to the way Corel-DRAW handles colors are described at the beginning of Chapter 3. A Publish To Internet Wizard and an HTML Conflict Analyzer were designed to help you through the process of preparing Web pages.

About Your System

When it comes to CorelDRAW (and most other graphics programs, for that matter), you can never have too much RAM, processing speed, or display power! The faster the processor and the more RAM

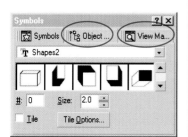

CorelDRAW 8's dockers can be minimized, so that several can share the same space on the screen. Click the "button" for an inactive docker to open it.

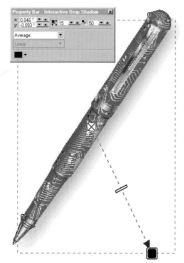

CorelDRAW 8 offers many interactive transformation tools. Here the Interactive Drop Shadow tool makes a group of objects seem to float above the page. Adjusting the midpoint slider controls how quickly the shadow fades out.

CorelDRAW has always shipped with a variety of support applications. The list changes from version to version Here are brief descriptions of some of the programs that have been included with CorelDRAW:

In earlier versions **Corel MOSAIC**™ was a nice visual file management tool, but it was made obsolete by Windows 95. **Corel MULTIMEDIA MANAGER**™ is the visual file-management utility that replaces MOSAIC in versions 7 and 8. In addition to helping with the organization and management of graphics files, MOSAIC and MANAGER can be used to browse the extensive clip art and photo libraries included with CorelDRAW.

Corel Color Manager™ is designed to help make your computer screen a better predictor of what your final output will look like. Getting predictable color is discussed in Chapter 3.

Corel PHOTO-PAINT™ is a powerful painting and photo-retouching application. It's designed for the kind of artwork that requires the look of natural media — brushes and paper — or the effects traditionally created in the darkroom. "CyberGoddess," in the Gallery section at the end of this chapter, and two other works by Sharon George in the Gallery at the end of Chapter 2 show the kind of "beyond–CorelDRAW" capabilities that PHOTO-PAINT can provide. Corel ARTISAN is the painting and image-editing program that came with CorelDRAW 6 on the Mac.

CorelDREAM 3D™ is a spline-based modeling and rendering package, with extensive tools for creating 3D objects (modelling), adding color and pattern to the models (texture mapping)., arranging models in a "scene," lighting the scene, positioning a "camera" (the viewpoint from with the scene will be "photographed"), and rendering (making a bitmap picture of the view seen by the camera).

CorelSCAN™ is a new "Wizard Driven" scanning utility designed to make it easier to scan images and to correct common problems found in scanned photos.

CorelTRACE™ (called Corel OCR-TRACE in later versions) is a bitmap-to-vector tracing utility. (Its use is discussed in Chapter 2.) The OCR (Optical Character Recognition) function can extract editable paragraph text from scanned documents.

Corel TEXTURE™ is a procedural texture-generation program that lets you create simulated natural textures like wood, stones, and marble.

CorelDEPTH™ helps create 3D logos and text, again using "Wizards" to set depth, color, angle and lighting effects.

CorelCAPTURE™ is a screen-capture utility, for taking pictures of what's on your computer screen.

Corel SCRIPT Editor™ allows users interested in programming to create macros, or "subprograms," that work within CorelDRAW or PHOTO-PAINT to automate complex tasks.

Thousands of **clip art** files in **.cdr** or **.cmx** format come with each version of CorelDRAW. Hundreds of **fonts** — some of them well-designed and others less so — also ship with the program. (Fonts are discussed at the beginning of Chapter 6.)

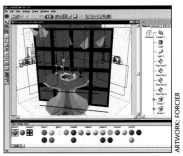

CorelDREAM 3D provides a "studio" where you can change the lighting and camera angle for rendering a scene you've arranged from the models you've built.

*A star shape inside a blue-filled circle (inset) was treated with the Circular Tiling Script available from Ur-Text, and a background rectangle of the same color was added behind the result. This script and others from Ur-Text, created with Corel SCRIPT Editor, are available for downloading from **http://tfts.i-us.com**.*

Along with an interface that lets you design your own textures, Corel TEXTURE provides presets that you can render to the dimensions and resolution you want. Shown here, left to right, are the presets Orange Banded Stone, Oak Floor, and Evening Sky.

In version 8 the knife tool can be used to make a freehand cut to divide an object in two. With the Shift key, the knife can be used like the Bezier tool to make smooth curves: Hold down the Shift key, position the tool on the path where you want to start the cut (make sure the icon is upright), click and drag to create the Bezier curve, position the knife on the path where you want the cut to end, and click. If you want to cut an imported bitmap (as shown here), you'll first have to PowerClip it within a path (Chapter 4 provides some examples of PowerClipping). A drop shadow was added to each of the two pieces above with the Interactive Drop Shadow tool.

GRAB THAT MEMORY!

To let CorelDRAW make the best use of memory in Windows 95/98 or on a Mac, open it *before* you open any other programs that you want to run at the same time.

USING SPACE WISELY

Since a page is typically vertical but the computer monitor is horizontal, storing palettes, toolbars, and other CorelDRAW "equipment" on the left or right side of the screen leaves more room for your artwork.

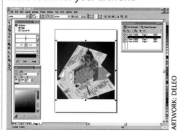

ARTWORK: DELEO

your computer has, the less your system need rely on *virtual memory*, a scheme it uses when all its working memory (RAM) is tied up and it's forced to swap information back and forth with your hard disk in order to get more working room. Reading and writing to your hard drive is much slower than operating strictly in RAM, so adding memory can dramatically increase CorelDRAW's speed, especially when you're working with large or complicated files. Get as fast a system as is practical, with 32 MB of RAM (or more), and with plenty of hard disk space.

Although you can get away with a standard 15-inch monitor, a 640 x 480 screen resolution is inadequate to display enough of the CorelDRAW workspace — especially the latest versions. With the addition of the Property bar, menu roll-ups, and dockers, desktop real estate for your artwork gets scarce. A video display card capable of 800 by 600 pixels in 16-bit color (thousands of colors) or 24-bit color (millions of colors) is what you'll want. With only 8-bit color (256 colors) the dithering (simulating the colors that aren't available by using patterns of dots of the available colors) is very harsh and the colors look flat, especially if you're working with bitmaps or photos. More video memory will give you more color options. If you can swing it, a 17-inch or larger monitor and 2MB or more of video RAM are well worth the expense.

WORKING SMART

Even after you've set up your computer with enough RAM and disk space to run Corel-DRAW effectively, there are more tricks to fine-tune the program's performance:

- **Don't overdo the fonts.** Try not to have more fonts installed and available than you really need, especially with Windows 3.1. If you really need more than a hundred fonts or so, consider getting a font utility to organize them into sets that you can turn on or off as you need them.

- **Adjust virtual memory.** Windows 95/98 does a good job managing virtual memory, but Windows 3.1 benefits from manual tweaking. From the Control Panel,

A PERFORMANCE TRICK

If your Windows 95- or 98-based system has over 24 MB of RAM, you can change the way the operating system uses the cache with a high-RAM system, and thus boost performance, as follows:

On the desktop, right-click on My Computer and select Properties. From the System Properties dialog, click the Performance tab and then the File System button. Change the Typical Role Of This Machine setting from Desktop Computer to Network Server. Then click Apply and close the dialog box. Restart your system to make the change take effect.

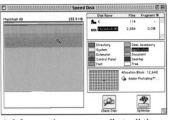

A defragmenting program collects all the small pieces of storage space that result when a disk is used and reused over time. Before defragmenting (top), the empty space (indicated by white) is in many small blocks. Afterwards, the space has been collected into a single large block, making it more efficient to store and retrieve new files.

open the 386 icon, and set Virtual Memory to a Permanent Swap file twice the size of your RAM.

On the Mac, from the apple menu at the far left of the menu bar, choose Control Panels, Memory, and turn on Virtual Memory. (Note that some graphics programs, like Adobe Photoshop, run better with Virtual Memory turned off; so if you're alternating between Photoshop and CorelDRAW, you may be making frequent trips to the Memory control panel.) If you have plenty of RAM in your system, you can assign more memory to Corel-DRAW. Working at the Desktop level, click the CorelDRAW icon once to select it; choose File, Get Info; and set the Preferred Size in the Memory Requirements to twice the Suggested Size.

- **Optimize your hard disk.** Use a utility set like ScanDisk and Disk Defragmenter, which come with Windows, or Norton Utilities' Speed Disk for the Mac to keep your hard disks operating as smoothly and as fast as possible.

- **Update your drivers.** Make sure you have the latest software drivers for all of the peripherals on your system. Most hardware manufacturers (developers of printers and video cards, in particular) provide free driver updates on their Web sites.

- **Cut down on "extras."** Dancing icons, system sounds, screen savers, wallpaper and the like all use valuable RAM and processor cycles. Screen savers also can kick on while CorelDRAW is performing a complicated task and really bog things down.

- **Adjust Undo levels.** For every step backward that Corel-DRAW's Undo command lets you take to recover from a mistake, a certain amount of RAM is occupied. You can set the Undo steps to the number you think you might actually need (say 7 to 10) by pressing Ctrl-J (⌘-J on the Mac) and finding Undo in the General section.

- **Back up your work.** If you use the File, Save As command to save a file periodically as you go along (for example, HOUSE1.CDR, HOUSE2.CDR) not only do you create a backup in case of system crash (CorelDRAW has been known to destroy the file on a crash), but you also store a valuable resource. If you make a mistake that can't be fixed with Undo, you can open the file you saved earlier and start from there. When you've completely finished a project, back up the files to CD-ROM or other off-system media, and then delete the work-in-progress files. On an unstable system it's a good idea to save to different physical drives if possible, and you may even want to make an off-site backup copy in case of real disaster.

CorelDRAW provides two ways to back up your files automatically: Auto-Backup and Make Backup On Save. Disable (or increase the time interval for) the Auto-Backup feature, or you run the risk of corrupting long file exports. Enabled, this feature

Simple Wireframe

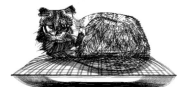

Wireframe

Draft

Normal

Enhanced

ARTWORK: MCLEAN

can lock up your system as it stops every 10 minutes to save a big file! If your system is really unstable, you may want to keep the Make Backup On Save feature enabled. Otherwise, disable this feature, too, use smart file management, and save time and disk space. You can find the backup settings in version 5 or later by pressing Ctrl/⌘-J and choosing the Advanced section (the Workspace, Save page in CorelDRAW 8).

- **Turn on Interruptible Refresh.** Unless you're willing to wait for your artwork to be completely redrawn before you're allowed to proceed, press Ctrl/⌘-J and turn on this function (it's called Interruptible Display in version 3) in the Display section.

- **Clean up virtual memory.** If you run out of scratch pad disk space for virtual memory it could be because CorelDRAW has created many temporary (TMP) files on the hard drive. These files aren't deleted until you shut down the program (File, Exit; *File, Quit on the Mac*), so if you've been working awhile, it's a good idea to clear everything up by saving your files, quitting the program, and then restarting it.

CHANGING YOUR VIEW

As you work, you'll want to change your view, and CorelDRAW has many to choose from! For starters, you can choose to work in a full-color mode (Normal) or the faster outline-only mode (Wireframe).

- Objects in **Wireframe** mode don't display outline or fill attributes — only the basic shapes. Wireframe mode is fast, but it's difficult to determine which objects are on top of others.

- **Normal** shows the outline and fill attributes for each shape, so it's easier to see how your artwork really looks.

In versions 7 and 8, there are three additional views: Simple Wireframe, Draft, and Enhanced.

- **Simple Wireframe** is even faster than Wireframe because it limits its view to "primary" elements, and doesn't display such "secondary" items as blend groups or extrusions (don't panic, the elements are there, just not displayed in this mode).

- **Draft** mode uses low-res versions of the Normal display to speed things up, but it's designed for speed, and it doesn't look good.

- **Enhanced** mode is just the opposite of Draft, using a very slow, but "super-sampling" algorithm to produce a very smooth and precise on-screen representation of your art. It only works in 16-bit and 24-bit color. Unless you have a really fast system, Enhanced mode means "please wait for the pretty picture"!

In any View mode you can use the Zoom and Panning tools to change your view.

In CorelDRAW 6, 7, and 8 you can save useful views so you can recall them to work on the same spot. Choose View Manager from the View or Tools menu. Pressing the "+" button in the View Manager saves the current view. To recall a view, you can either select it in the View Manager list and choose Switch To View from the pop-out menu, or just double-click on the page number or percentage.

ZOOMING AROUND

When you're zoomed in and you want to move to a different part of your artwork, sometimes it's quicker to zoom out and zoom in again than to drag with the Panning tool, because zooming out gives you an overall view so you can see where you want to go next.

BRING BACK THE FLYOUT!

If you're used to working with the Zoom Tool flyout from earlier versions, and you're having trouble changing your old habits, you can adjust CorelDRAW 7 or 8 to operate the same way: Right-click on the Zoom tool in the Toolbox, choose Properties, and turn on Use Traditional Zoom Tool Flyout.

In CorelDRAW 6, 7, or 8 you can also solve the problem by choosing View, Toolbars, Zoom, which opens a toolbar (shown below) that keeps the standard Zoom tools available all the time.

- **In CorelDRAW 7 or 8 to zoom in**, click on the Zoom In tool (the magnifying glass) in the Toolbox, then hold down the mouse button as you drag around the area you want to zoom to, or just click on the spot that you want to magnify. **To zoom out,** with the Zoom In tool selected, click on the Zoom Out button on the Property bar.

- **Earlier versions** work a little differently: **To zoom in,** choose the Zoom In tool (the "+" magnifier in the Toolbox) and click a spot or drag around the area you wish to enlarge. **To zoom back out,** just click on the Zoom Out tool (the "–" magnifier from the Zoom tool flyout).

- **To show objects at actual size,** click the "1:1" button in the flyout or Property bar.

These keyboard shortcuts work for zooming, though not all of them are available in all versions:

- Choose the Zoom In tool **F2**
- Zoom to the previous view, or zoom out by a factor of 2 **F3**
- Zoom to show the selected objects **Shift+F2**
- Zoom to show all objects **F4**
- Zoom to show the entire page **Shift+F4**

Holding down the mouse button and dragging with the Panning tool — the tool that looks like a hand — lets you move the page around to view different areas of your design.

ORGANIZATION AND PRECISION

CorelDRAW has powerful scaling and sizing tools, in addition to several management schemes to keep your design from becoming a hard-to-work-with jumbled array of stacked shapes.

- As you create objects in CorelDRAW, **the newest objects are the farthest forward** — you can think of them as being at

In all versions of CorelDRAW objects are "stacked" in the order they were created, with the most recent ones in front. If you select an object with the Pick tool, you can select the next object back by pressing the Tab key. If you press the Tab key repeatedly, you can work through all the objects on the page.

In CorelDRAW 8 there's a more efficient way to select an object that's hidden behind other objects: Choose the Pick tool, place the cursor over the area where the hidden object is, click to select the object on top and then **Alt-click** (*Option-click on the Mac*). The next item behind will be selected. Keep Alt/*Option*-clicking until you reach the object you want. The difference between this and the Tab method is that with the Alt/*Option* key, only the objects directly under the cursor will be selected, not objects located elsewhere in the workspace.

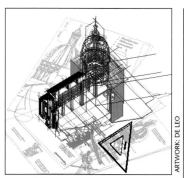

ARTWORK: DE LEO

The Duomo *illustration, shown in the "Gallery" at the end of this chapter, was organized in layers so parts of the artwork could be locked or made invisible, while the artist worked on other parts. The colors assigned to the layers don't affect the actual colors of the objects — only the way they look in Wireframe mode.*

LOCKING INDIVIDUAL OBJECTS

CorelDRAW 8 provides Object Locking so that even without using Layers you can lock any object to prevent it from being moved or modified accidentally. Just select the object and choose Arrange, Lock Object.

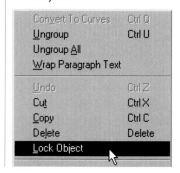

the top of the stack. However, the Arrange menu of all versions includes options for ordering elements in front of or behind one another, as well as sending an object to the very back or very front of the stack.

- You can also organize your work on different virtual **Layers.** From the Layout or Tools menu or by pressing Ctrl/⌘-F3, you can open the Layers list (in CorelDRAW 3, 4, and 5 it's in the Arrange menu, or use Ctrl-F1). Here you can define new Layers, move objects from one layer to another, and hide or lock layers so the objects on them can't be seen or disturbed, to make working on your design much easier.

- Along the top and left side of the CorelDRAW workspace you'll find **Rulers.** The position of the cursor is shown as dotted tick marks on each ruler. The Ruler settings default to Inches, but can be changed to nearly any unit of measurement, including Kilometers! So if a real-world 1 inch = 1 inch (1:1) scale doesn't meet your needs, you can change the Drawing scale. Changing the scale is a nice feature when you're designing dimensioned objects, because you can see and use the actual dimensions of the pieces without changing the paper size. "Working Large" in Chapter 2 tells how to make drawings to scale.

- The **Status bar,** a toolbar that provides information about the currently selected object(s), can be set up to show color, dimensions, location, and other properties. It also shows the Width and Height measurements as you draw the object, so you can size it as you draw. But if you need more accuracy in dimensioning an object than your hand-eye co-ordination can manage, you can key in the exact size by choosing the Scale or Size roll-up from the Transform or Arrange, Transform menu.

IMPORT ERRORS

If you are trying to import a bitmap into CorelDRAW and you get an error message with a file type that you know is supported, try opening it in Photoshop or PHOTO-PAINT first. Earlier versions of CorelDRAW don't support TIFF or Targa files with alpha channels, but will import them just fine if you remove the extra channels in Photoshop or PHOTO-PAINT and then save the stripped-down TIFF or Targa.

- The **Grid** option places a dotted blue reference grid on the desktop. You can use this feature to "eyeball" your layouts with more precision, or enable the Snap To Grid function, which aligns objects to the grid. There's more about using the Grid for drawing in "Using Guides and Grid" on page 26.

- **Guides** are nonprinting dotted lines that you can use to help line things up. To create a Guide, simply drag one from a Ruler onto the page area. You can then manually align objects using the guidelines, or enable the Layout, Snap To Guidelines option,

In CorelDRAW 8 the Guides can be rotated (as shown here), multi-selected, deleted, or nudged, just like other objects.

which will automatically pull selected objects to the Guides as you move the objects close.

FILE FORMATS

CorelDRAW uses its own CDR format to save and load files, in addition to the CMX Corel Presentation Exchange format to share graphic files among the other Corel graphics programs. CorelDRAW can also import a wide variety of file formats and can export from CorelDRAW in formats such as Encapsulated PostScript (EPS), TIFF, and (in CorelDRAW 8 for Windows) Adobe Portable Document File (PDF), that can be shared with other applications, with various degrees of success in different versions. In any version of Corel-DRAW, the File, Import and File, Export commands open dialog boxes that list all the file types the program can accommodate.

CAUTIONS FOR CORELDRAW

With all its creative strengths, CorelDRAW has also manifested some weaknesses over the years. Three of the most troublesome have to do with output: color surprises, when the color that prints doesn't look like the color on the screen (this is addressed in Chapter 3); occasional anomalies that crop up in shapes, fills, and outlines; and producing files that other graphics programs can't interact with successfully.

Avoiding Output Trouble

Chances are, your CorelDRAW projects are destined to move from your desktop into the real world, either as on-screen displays presented via the World Wide Web (see Chapter 7) or as ink printed on paper. With the ability to blend, combine, extrude, and variously distort shapes, to mask some objects inside others, and then to stack Lenses on top of the whole concoction, and with lots of files made by previous versions kicking around, it's not too difficult to produce files that are troublesome to print or output to the film used to make printing plates, or even to save in a format that other graphics programs can successfully interpret. Here are some tips for creating files so they won't choke your desktop printer or a high-resolution imagesetting machine.

- Stacking special-effects **Lenses** on top of each other is asking for trouble.

- In general, the fewer **hidden elements** there are in a CorelDRAW file, the more smoothly the printing or imagesetting is likely to go. Parts of complex elements that contribute nothing to the final image because they're hidden behind other objects should be trimmed away whenever practical. The Trim command (described in Chapter 4) can be used in versions 5 and later. In earlier versions, you'll need to balance the reduction in output angst against the time it will take to do the trimming. (To trim away part of an object in CorelDRAW 3 or 4, you can use the methods described in "Node-Editing" on page 27.)

- Large collections of **grouped objects** can create problems. This can be true especially of type that has been converted to curves, and most especially if the font wasn't built very well by its designer. For safety, after converting to curves, you can Ungroup and Break Apart the characters and their counters (the holes in the middle of "A's" and "O's," for instance) and then select and recombine the pieces until things look right again.

- If the Outline that you applied to your shapes was done with a **Nib shape** with sharp corners, little "horns" may develop in the outlines when you send the file for output. To prevent this, you can change the Nib shape to round.

- In CorelDRAW 7 and 8, you can **eliminate "missing font" problems** by using TrueDoc font-embedding technology. This feature saves any fonts that are used in your file right along with the image information, so you can transport the file to another system and be sure that any and all fonts that you used are available when the file is opened on someone else's desktop. This feature comes in handy when you send a file to a service bureau for output, since the output service may not have the same fonts installed on their imagesetting equipment. To ensure that your fonts travel along with your file, choose File, Save As and simply check the Embed Fonts Using TrueDoc option in the Save Drawing dialog.

Getting Help

If your colorful CorelDRAW art will be printed by the four-color process used for most books and magazines, or as a spot-color job with a special set of premixed inks, it will need to be converted to PostScript files and color-separated. But unless you're a prepress expert, skilled in preparing Postscript files and color separations, let someone else do that part. It *will* have to be done, but you probably don't have to do it.

Your best bet will usually be to produce the cleanest files you can from CorelDRAW (in .cdr, TIFF, or EPS format), and then turn them over to a competent imagesetting service bureau whose operators can produce the film separations that the printer will need to make the printing plates that will go onto the press. Your primary job in all this will be to *communicate*:

- **Find out from the printer what kind of film output is needed.** Should the film be made so it reads correctly when the emulsion side is up or when it's down? Should the film be positive or negative? What halftone line screen will be used for printing the job (133 and 150 lines per inch are two of the most commonly used line screens for color printing.) Communicate

Fonts embedded with the Embed Fonts Using TrueDoc option will be available only to ensure proper output of that particular file; they will not be installed on the output machine. In fact, if you forget to enable the TrueDoc option when you save this file again, you'll lose the embedded fonts.

PESSIMISTIC ABOUT FONTS

We've found that often when we open a CorelDRAW file, the program will warn us that we're missing at least one font that's required for the artwork. If the fonts listed in the Font Matching Results dialog box aren't handy, just click Temporary (so the file won't be permanently changed before you know if it's OK) and then click OK. CorelDRAW seems to keep track of fonts long after they've been eliminated from the file or converted to curves, so there's a good chance the file will look just the way it should when it opens. If not, close the file and set about searching for the missing font or a similar one you can substitute when you're prompted by the Font Matching Results dialog box the next time you open the file.

In producing this book for direct-to-plate printing, we learned quite a bit about how to get reliable output from all versions of CorelDRAW files, exported and placed in a page layout program. You can read about it in Appendix C.

all that information to the person who will be doing the final file preparation and film output. Don't necessarily expect that you'll need to talk to each party only once. Keep going back to these folks and asking questions until you all have the answers you need.

Today many print shops have their own in-house imagesetting services, sometimes to output film, sometimes to output your files directly to printing plates, and sometimes to go directly to press, without film or plates. Having the imagesetting and printing done in the same place can make communication easier, and it can also cut down on finger-pointing if something in the job goes a little bit wrong.

- **Provide a print** that shows the printer and the imagesetting service bureau what the page should look like. Often a black-and-white laser print will suffice. (If you're doing work for a client other than yourself, get your client to sign off on the print before you have the film output.)

- Once the film is produced, have the imagesetting service make a **contract proof,** such as a Matchprint, from the film. This kind of proof shows how the job should look when it's printed using that batch of film. If the proof looks the way you want the printed piece to look (this is another good place to get the client's OK), pass the film and proof to the printer. With the film and proof in hand, the printer will be able to make a contract with you to produce printed pages that will very closely match the proof.

- If your job will be output **direct-to-plate** or **direct-to-press,** there will be no film from which to make a contract proof. In this case the printer may provide a print from a low-resolution color printer for you to look at, or a proof like a Kodak Approval print, designed to more accurately predict what the printed piece will look like. If you can, get the printer to show you an example of a similar, previously printed job and the proof that was provided for the printer to match. *WOW!*

The illusion of depth and substance on a flat surface is often a matter of soft, subtle shading, a technique that **John Corkery** mastered in his portrait of 1940s movie star legend *Hedy Lamarr*, which won the grand prize in Corel's international design contest. Corkery's first order of business was to find and secure the rights to the photograph he wanted to work from.

When the legal work was finished, Corkery could begin his portrait. He scanned the image and imported the scan into CorelDRAW (File, Import), assigning it

to its own locked layer. ▶ *Placing a reference photograph on its own layer lets you lock it to prevent it from being moved accidentally, and also allows you to turn its visibility on and off to monitor the progress of your illustration.*

Using the Freehand tool, Corkery first drew out the main shapes, which he filled with gray tones chosen from the Grayscale Mode in the Uniform Fill dialog box (Shift-F11) to match the tones in the original photograph. More and more shapes were added, as well as many blend groups (constructed much like those in Cecil Rice's

Shakespeare portrait later in this "Gallery") to create the depth and shading found in the photo. PowerLines were employed to draw the hair, and although CorelDRAW 7 and 8 do not have this tool anymore, similar results can be obtained using a pressure-sensitive tablet and stylus with the Natural Pen tool. (PowerLines are discussed in "PowerLines for Posters" in Chapter 4.)

The jewelry is constructed of bead and link shapes, each topped with numerous round, teardrop, or crescent shapes with Radial Fountain fills to make the sparkles.

Marin Darmonkow and **Neil Ellis** are known for the off-the-wall graphic imagery in their "adverteasing" campaigns. In *Winner* the team combined different artistic elements, such as hand-drawn objects, clip art (the motorcycle, for instance), and bitmap images. Because CorelDRAW-created elements are separate objects, the two artists could divide up the work by breaking the design into parts that each one could work on individually. Then they used the File, Import command to combine all the pieces into a single composite image in the final steps, reorienting or resizing elements where necessary.

To support the quirky character of their image and because of the limitations involved in scaling, moving, and rotating CorelDRAW's Pattern fills, the design team "hand-patterned" some of their artwork: They created interesting shapes with the Freehand tool and duplicated them to make "pattern" elements. For instance, the starfish used for the tricyclist's shirt is made up of five copies of the same arm,

which were colored pink and grouped. The group was then duplicated many times and scattered to fill the shirt. The not-quite-perfect repetition of the pattern elements hints at wrinkles and draping of the fabric.

The shapes that make up the woman's coat were filled with one of CorelDRAW's Mineral Speckled Texture Fills, recolored to fit the color scheme of the artwork.

Elements like the faces and limbs were created using methods like those in "Modelling with Blends" in Chapter 3. The striped poles were created from a single shape filled with a custom blue Fountain fill with overlaid yellow Fountain-filled objects to make the bands. (The introduction to Chapter 3 discusses Fountain fills, Texture Fills, and Patterns. Other parts of Chapter 3 provide step-by-step instructions for using them, along with pages of printed samples.)

After finishing much of the work in CorelDRAW, Darmonkow and Ellis exported their *Winner* image as a bitmap

for further manipulation in PhotoPAINT to produce the subtler effects, such as in the painted sky and the speed-blurred motorcyclist.

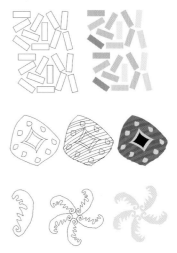

Cyber Goddess by **Sharon George** was the winning entry in the 1998 California Computer Expo Art Contest. She began with a pencil drawing, which she scanned as a template for developing the image in Corel PHOTO-PAINT 8.

She wanted to create the impression of highly polished metal, with light reflected by the individual pieces of jewelry. So she started by "roughing in" the metal shapes, using the Fill tool to color all the parts of the headdress the same color (orange), repeating the process for the left earring (green), and for the other earring and the baubles of the necklace, "pouring" paint into the spaces created by the pencil lines. She then used the Magic Wand tool to Shift-select colored spaces, adding more

areas by holding down the Shift key as she used the Magic Wand and using the Mask Brush tool with or without the Ctrl key to add to or subtract from the selection, refining the shapes. As each unit — headdress or earring, for instance — was complete, she applied the Eye Candy Chrome plug-in filter, controlling the direction of the light and type of gradation.

She applied "base" colors to the skin, lips, eyes, and red jewels. Then she saved the file as an RGB TIFF and opened it in MetaCreations' Painter to add details to the face and jewels. Although PHOTO-PAINT has an Airbrush tool, George prefers the feel and results she gets with Painter's airbrush applying paint at a low opacity with a very fine brush tip.

The circuit board in the background was created by scanning in a real circuit board, selecting parts of it, and stretching, rearranging, and recoloring the parts. She used the Rectangle Mask tool to select part of the circuit board to build the frame for the image.

To surround the Cyber Goddess with numbers, she set a string of 1's and 0's with the Text tool, filled it with blue, and applied the Object Transparency tool from left to right. She duplicated the type many times as separate objects; changed the color of some of the copies to purple using Image, Adjust, Replace Color; and applied the Object Transparency tool from right to left.

To "paint" *Shakespeare* in Corel-DRAW, **Cecil Rice** used a photo of a painting for reference and drew the portrait with his graphics tablet. The subtle shading that sculpts the features of the face, hands, and other elements of the portrait depends on blended shapes with Fountain fills made from the colors of a custom palette. To give himself a wider range of skin colors to choose from, Rice used the Blend feature, creating many subtle tones.

To mold the shapes of the hands and face, Rice used a technique like that described in "Modelling with Blends" in Chapter 3, in each case blending between a shape and an enlarged and recolored duplicate shape behind it, using many steps in the blend so that the color change was gradual rather than banded. He colored many of these pairs of objects with Fountain fills made from his custom palette. Blending from one Fountain-filled shape to another in this way added to the subtlety of the modelling created by the blends.

The feather was made by layering individual blends of fine curving lines over layered Fountain-filled shapes. Unlike the shape blends of the face and hands, the line blends in the feather used a small number of steps over a large enough distance so that each separate step of the blend was visible as a curving line.

The buttons were created by blending "petal" shapes in a 360° rotation around a center point, as described on page 31. The gold details in the coat were made with custom Fountain fills, like those described in "14K Type" in Chapter 6.

As the image became more and more complex, Rice made use of layers. Locking some layers and making them invisible, he could turn off groups of elements to speed up the screen refresh and to keep from accidentally selecting or nudging parts of the portrait.

When he tried to have the illustration produced as film separations, Rice ran into trouble due to the large number of blends and other complex effects. To solve his output problems, he finally had the image output to a film recorder as a high-resolution transparency, and separations were then made from a drum scan of this film. This method is popular for getting very complex files to press from earlier versions of the program, in which print

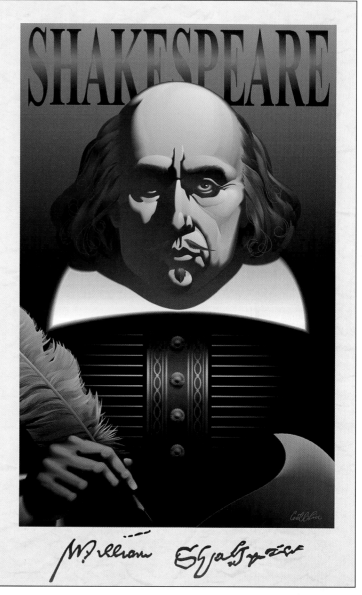

and export functions are not as robust as in the latest versions. ▶ *Exporting a file from CorelDRAW 7 or 8 as a CMYK TIFF at 300 dpi at final printed size (File, Export) avoids potential compatibility problems with page layout programs (like PageMaker, QuarkXPress, and FrameMaker), image-editing programs like Photoshop, and color-separation software, since these kinds of programs almost universally accept TIFF files. (Earlier versions of CorelDRAW also export TIFFs, but not necessarily good ones.)*

To create the extremely detailed *Duomo (Inner Cathedral)* illustration, **Antonio De Leo** began by surveying the church in person. Using his own measurements along with original documents produced by 17th-Century architect Giovanni Antonio De Rossi and procured from the Vatican, De Leo redrew "blueprints" of the structure by hand. These were used as reference for drawing the cutaway version of the church in CorelDRAW, and were also scanned, converted to CorelDRAW objects using CorelTRACE, and incorporated into the illustration as additional background elements.

To help manage the many complex elements, De Leo isolated areas to their own specific layers. He also set up a complex array of Guidelines to keep angles consistent and accurate. He duplicated elements when possible, such as the pillars. Lens effects were used to create the shadows and the translucent look of the plastic triangle. (Lens effects are described in Chapter 4.) In addition to applying a Lens, he exaggerated the distortion in the plastic triangle by moving the lines by hand with the Shape tool.

Stacking Lens effects on top of a complex object captured with CorelTRACE (as De Leo did in the shadow areas of the San Rocco

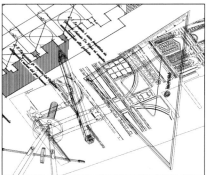

illustration) can result in mathematical complexity destined to confound even a powerful imagesetting device. Ultimately De Leo used a film recorder to produce a transparency of the image, which was then color-separated for printing.

Jolanta Romanowska uses a variety of techniques to color her artwork. In her landscapes Romanowska draws the large sky, land, and water shapes first, using many smaller shapes for shading, giving each a solid-color fill. (These techniques are described in "Creating a Hand-Drawn Look" in Chapter 2.) In *Night's Street* (above) Radial-filled ellipses create glows behind the white lamps, and large light shapes behind darker tree shapes create the appearance of highlighted

edges. In the buildings, areas of the underlying large shapes show through in between the smaller shapes to make lines. In *Lake* (top) layered shapes create the backlit clouds and the ripples, shadows, and highlights on the water.

For her illustrations of plants and animals, such as the *flowers* shown here, Romanowska uses color gradients set from the Fountain Fill dialog (F11) rather than solid-color fills, to achieve delicate color and soft shading.

Whether she uses solid colors or Fountain fills, Romanowska rarely uses outlines, preferring to create a sense of line by layering no-outline objects. ▶ *CorelDRAW artwork that doesn't rely on line weights for effects can be scaled up or down without worrying about whether the artist specified that the outlines should change weight when the image is resized. If you want line thicknesses to scale, choose Scale With Image in the Outline Pen dialog box (F12) when the drawing is made.*

RADIO BULGARIA   РАДИО БОЛГАРИЯ   RADIO BULGARIEN   راديو "بلغاريا"

РАДИО **БЪЛГАРИЯ**

BULGARISTAN RADYOSU   РАДИО-БУГАРСКА   Βουλγαρικὴ Ραδιοφωνία

Theodore Ushev derives inspiration from turn-of-the-century Russian constructionists for his contemporary designs, such as the *Radio Bulgaria* postcard, shown above. Starting with a freehand sketch, he first used basic shapes to map out the design in CorelDRAW. For example, the wavy curves started as straight lines, and then the Shape tool was used to add nodes, to turn the lines into zigzags, and to smooth the zigzags into curves (this technique and others used in this poster are described in "PowerLines for Posters" in Chapter 4). Ushev used PowerLines to transform simple lines into stylized varying-width shapes, such as the drumstick outlines. (With the PowerLines feature gone from the versions 7 and 8 of Corel-DRAW, artists may want to keep an older copy of the program active, or turn to third-party software such as MetaCreations' *Expression* to create such stylized line-based shapes.)

Ushev made heavy use of the Trim and Intersection tools to sub-divide his primary objects into smaller units, which were then given different fill colors to emphasize the areas of intersection, enhancing the geometric style of the design. The Blend roll-up (from the Effects menu) was used to blend a light- and a dark-colored object to create each of the subtle shading groups that suggest depth and dimension. ▶*The Interactive Drop Shadow tool in CorelDRAW 8 provides an easy way to create realistic, transparent shadow effects.*

Involved with the post–Iron Curtain re-emergence of the art community in his native Bulgaria, Ushev designed the *New Bulgarian*

NEW BULGARIAN ART

Art logo (above) for posters and additional printed materials to promote gallery showings and other art happenings. He used a modular design approach, creating individual pieces and then stacking them together to form a whole. The logo captures both traditional Soviet-inspired work imagery and contemporary design elements such as the computer screen. Just as the symbol suggests, Ushev worked with both old and new design tools to create the logo, combining scanned ink drawings with completely computer-generated elements.

DRAWING

"DRAWING" IN CORELDRAW means *defining* the shapes, or objects, you need in your artwork. ("Coloring" is the process of assigning outline and fill characteristics to the shapes you've drawn, and it's the subject of Chapter 3.)

As you use the program's various tools to draw and modify shapes, CorelDRAW translates your actions into a set of mathematical equations and coordinates. The artwork is stored as "shape math" rather than pixel-by-pixel color data as for bitmapped graphics such as photos or digital "paintings." As a result, CorelDRAW objects can be easily and successfully scaled (the program just multiplies the equation), or reshaped (some numbers are changed), or piled on top of one another (the "stacking order" of the equations is changed) without losing their integrity as shapes. "Math Versus Dots" on page 33 shows the benefits of the object-oriented approach.

DRAWING BASICS

Here are some definitions of drawing terms to help you understand the descriptions of drawing techniques presented in this chapter and throughout the book:

- A **path** is a shape, open-ended or closed, flat or curved. A path is defined by the *nodes* it passes through and the *control handles* that determine how the shape is curved between the nodes. In the on-screen Status line, CorelDRAW refers to a path as a "Curve."

- A **node** is an "anchor" point through which a path travels, and where it can change direction. These nodes are placed by CorelDRAW's drawing tools.

- A **line** or **curve** is the part of the path between nodes.

- A **control handle** is a "lever" attached to a node. This lever determines the direction of the curve as it comes into or goes out of the node. The length and direction of the control handles can be established when a node is made, or they can be changed later by **node-editing**, described on page 27. Dragging the **control point,** or "knob," on the end of a control handle changes the length or direction of the handle, which in turn reshapes the curve.

- A **subpath** is one of two or more parts of a path; subpaths can be produced by combining (Arrange, Combine) two or more paths into a single path or by splitting a path.

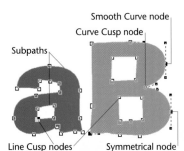

Smooth Curve node
Curve Cusp node
Subpaths
Line Cusp nodes
Symmetrical node

A Line Cusp connects two straight lines. A Curve Cusp is the connector to use between a straight line and a curve, or at a sharp point between two curves. The outer shape of a letter and its inner shapes, or counters — the "holes" in the letters "a" and "B," for instance — are subpaths of the combined path that is the entire letter.

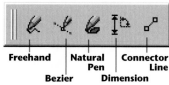

| Freehand | | Natural Pen | | Connector Line |
Freehand · Natural Pen · Connector Line
Bezier · Dimension

CorelDRAW 8's path-drawing tools

Dragging with the Freehand tool is the easiest way to draw complex, natural shapes.

ROMANOWSKA

UNDERSTANDING NODES AND CONTROL HANDLES

Nodes mark the spots that a path *must* go through. Control handles apply torsion to the path to determine how it curves between nodes. The *direction* of a control handle determines the general direction of the curve it controls. And the *length* of the handle determines the steepness of the curve — the longer the handle, the steeper the curve. The drawing tools — Freehand and Bezier — are used to place nodes.

There are four different types of nodes:

- A **Line Cusp** has no control handles, and the lines coming into the node or going out of it are straight.

- A **Curve Cusp** can have one or two control handles. A one-handled Curve Cusp node has a straight line on one side and a curve, which the handle controls, on the other side. For a two-handled Cusp, with curves on both sides of the node, the handles can be operated completely independently, so you can change one curve without changing the other.

- A **Symmetrical** node's control handles have to line up on a straight line through the node, and they must also be the same length. The result is that the "bend" of the curve — both the direction and steepness — coming into the node is symmetrical to the bend going out.

- A **Smooth Curve** node also has two control handles that line up in a straight line passing through the node. The *length* of the two handles can be controlled independently. The result is that the steepness of the two curves connected by a Smooth node can be different.

THE PATH-DRAWING TOOLS

The Freehand and Bezier tools provide the most "hands-on" ways to make paths in CorelDRAW. No matter how you lay your paths down, keep in mind that you can always go back later and reshape them, as described in "Node-Editing" on page 27.

The most natural way to draw is with the **Freehand tool, dragging** it around just as you would a pencil. Used as a pencil, the Freehand tool is **ideal for drawing natural shapes with detailed outlines.**

The Freehand tool can also be used to draw perfectly **straight lines: Click** to start a line segment, **click** at another point to stop it. After the second point, the tool is free to start a new path, not connected to the first. To make a series of *connected* line segments,

FEW OR MANY

The **slower** you drag, the **more nodes** the **Freehand tool** places to make the path.

Drawn fast

Drawn slowly

The Freehand tool is ideal for making a series of detached straight lines, like the marks dividing the hull in this developing starship. (The finished ship can be seen in "Taking Advantage of Symmetry" on page 44.)

KING

GRANEY

Single-clicking from point to point with the Bezier tool makes it easy to draw a series of connected straight lines like the shapes in this detail from an illustration of a skateboarder.

The Bezier tool is good for drawing smooth, mechanical curves like those of this detail from a border.

MOGENSEN

The Natural Pen tool, found in versions 7 and 8, can be used with a pressure-sensitive tablet and stylus to make freeform, "organic" shapes, with outlines (like the blue anemone) or without (like the layered strokes of the sun). Many artists find it easier to start each stroke at its narrow end, increasing pressure to widen the shape.

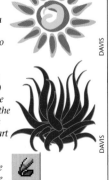

DAVIS

DAVIS

you can click to start and then double-click at each stop-start point from then on until you single-click at the last point. But it's usually more efficient to draw connected lines with the Bezier tool.

The **Bezier tool** can make Line Cusps, Curve Cusps, or Symmetrical nodes. **Single-click** from point to point to make a series of Line Cusps defining **straight segments.** To **curve** the line, instead of just clicking and moving on, **drag** as you place the node; this establishes the length and direction of the control handles of a Symmetrical node. To make a Cusp for a sharp change in direction, **double-click** to make the node.

In CorelDRAW 7 and 8 the **Natural Pen tool** is a way of drawing closed paths that look like the strokes of a marker or brush. The strokes can be plain (the same width along the whole curve) or fancy (changing in width to form a wedge or a teardrop, for instance), or changing with the pressure applied to the pressure-sensitive stylus of a drawing tablet. In CorelDRAW 4, 5, and 6 the PowerLine characteristic (assigned through the Effects menu) uses a different method to get much the same result as the Natural Pen does in versions 7 and 8. (The PowerLine provides even more drawing power than the Natural Pen, but it has a reputation for causing output problems, which may be why it was discontinued. Learn more about the PowerLine and Natural Pen in "PowerLines and Pieces for Posters in Chapter 4.)

CorelDRAW 4, 5, 6, 7, and 8 provide **Dimension** tools for drawing special-purpose labels that show measurements; the later versions work better and provide more options. Click with the Dimension tool at one extreme of the distance you want to measure, click at the other extreme, and then click once more to set the "depth" of the bracket and to show where you want the number label to appear. Measurements are based on the current Scale setting (for more about Scale, see "Working Large" on page 38).

The **Connector Line**, available in versions 6, 7, and 8, links two objects with a line that rebuilds itself if either of the objects is moved. To use it, turn on Snap To Objects in the Layout menu. Then click first on a snap point of one object and then on a snap point of the other. Now if you move either object, the line will stretch and reorient itself to keep the two connected.

USING GUIDES AND GRID

If you display the **rulers** (from the View menu) and drag inward from either one, CorelDRAW makes "magnetic" **guidelines.** Choose Show Guides and Snap To Guideline (from somewhere in the Display or Layout menu, depending on the version) to view them and make them "attract" nodes as you place them with the path-drawing tools. (In versions 6, 7, and 8, the guidelines also attract the control handles that shape the curves.)

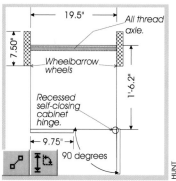

Red Connector Lines tie labels to the elements they name; Dimensions show measurements.

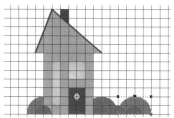

With Snap To Grid turned on, clicking from point to point with the Bezier tool drew the straight lines. Scallops were drawn by double-clicking to make Cusps at the bottom and dragging to make Symmetrical nodes at the top, snapping the control handles to the grid. In version 8 you can Show Grid As Lines, as shown here (Tools, Options, Document; on the Mac it's Layout, Document Layout, Grids And Guidelines).

The Node Edit roll-up in Corel-DRAW 6, 7, and 8 (top) and its pre-cursor in versions 3, 4, and 5 (below), houses the buttons required to change the properties of nodes and curves. The buttons used most often are at the top.

Add Node
Delete Node
Join Two Nodes
Break into Two Nodes
Extend To **Close**
Convert Curve **To Line**
Convert Line **To Curve**
Make Node into **Cusp**
Make **Smooth**
Make **Symmetrical**
Auto-Reduce Nodes
Extract **Subpath**
Stretch/Scale Nodes
Rotate/Skew Nodes
Align Nodes

CorelDRAW's **grid** — a system of dots, regularly spaced horizontally and vertically — can also be made visible (Show Grid) and magnetic (Snap To Grid). The grid can help with drawing several uniform objects, drawing from the same center point, or drawing precise, repeatable curves for regular shapes like zigzagged or scalloped edges.

NODE-EDITING

It's fairly rare, even among Corel-DRAW experts, that a path is drawn exactly right on the first try. But once you've drawn a path, it's easy to make changes. When you've finished drawing — or even while you're in the midst of drawing if you don't mind interrupting the process — you can use the **Shape** tool, alone or with the Node Edit roll-up, to make changes. In fact, in some cases as you'll see later in the book, it makes sense to do a quick-and-dirty job of placing points and then go back and tune up the curves.

Drag with the Shape tool on a curve to change its shape. Or drag a node to move it. Or instead of moving the node itself, drag on the tip of a control handle "lever" to reshape the curve.

In CorelDRAW 8, double-clicking the Shape tool in the Toolbox opens the **Node Edit roll-up**, with its buttons for making changes to paths. (In versions 3, 4, 5, 6, and 7 you can open the Node Edit roll-up by double-clicking anywhere on a path rather than on the Toolbox.) Or use the Ctrl-F10 keyboard shortcut (⌘-F10 on the Mac); it works in CorelDRAW 5, 6, 7, and 8.

To change a node's type so you can modify the shape of the incoming and outgoing curves, click the node with the Shape tool to select it, or Shift-click or

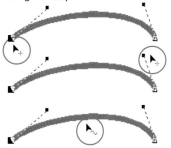

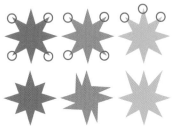

Alternate nodes of the top green shape were Shift-selected, the Stretch And Scale button in CorelDRAW 8's Node Edit roll-up was clicked, and a corner handle of the resulting highlight box was Shift-dragged inward to make the bottom green shape (Option-drag in Mac v.8). *The same four nodes of the top purple shape were treated with the Rotate and Skew button to get the shape in the bottom row. The top three nodes of the brown shape were treated with the Align button to get the bottom shape.*

Though a Polygon (left) looks flat-sided, and a Polygon As Star (center) is drawn with points, there's no ultimate difference between these shapes, since both have mid-side nodes that can be adjusted with the Shape tool. But the difference between a Polygon As Star and a Star (right) is real — **a Star is a compound object,** *which means it has a "hole" in the middle.*

6•7•8

In CorelDRAW 6, 7, or 8 right-click on a tool in the Toolbox (*Control-click on the Mac*) and choose Properties to open a dialog box for setting tool options. (In version 8 double-clicking the tool also opens the dialog box for many of the tools.)

drag-select to get more than one node at once. Then press any button on the Node Edit roll-up that isn't dimmed. **To change a curve's type,** click the curve with the Shape tool to select it, and you can then click an active button in the roll-up.

The illustration on the previous page identifies the buttons. The functions of the **Add, Delete, Convert,** and **Make Node** buttons are fairly obvious from their names. Here are some tips for using the others:

- The **Join** button turns two nodes into one, moving them together if necessary. In order to be joined, the two nodes have to be selected with the Shape tool, and in order to both be selected with the Shape tool, they have to be on the same path. So **to join nodes from two paths,** you first have to select the paths with the Pick tool and **Arrange, Combine** to make them subpaths of the same path. Then the nodes can be Shift- or drag-selected and joined.

- The **Break** button turns one node into two endpoint nodes, exactly on top of each other. They can then be moved apart with the Shape tool.

- **Extend Curve To Close** (in CorelDRAW 6, 7, and 8) works like Join, except that for nodes that are not together, it adds a straight segment between them, rather than moving the nodes toward each other.

- **Auto-Reduce Curve** (in versions 4, 5, 6, 7, and 8) is designed to eliminate any "extra" nodes that add complexity to the path without really affecting the shape of the curve.

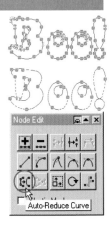

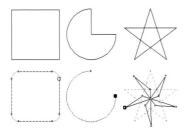

A shape made with the Rectangle, Ellipse, or Polygon/Star changes when the Shape tool drags one of its nodes: The corners of a rectangle round out (left). Dragging on the inside of an ellipse creates a "pizza" shape (top center); dragging around the outside creates an open arc. For a Polygon or Star, dragging "winds" it into a new shape.

In CorelDRAW 7 and 8 the Spiral tool can draw either Logarithmic spirals, whose width increases with each turn like a chambered nautilus shell, or Symmetrical spirals, with all turns the same width, like a mosquito coil. (Only the Symmetrical option is available in version 6.)

SALVIN-WRIGHT

To make this fish for smoked salmon packaging, the body segment just behind the head was drawn and grouped, it was duplicated three times (by pressing "+" on the numeric keypad), and each copy was moved and then scaled down by dragging inward on a corner handle of its highlight box.

SHAPE SHIFTERS

In CorelDRAW 8 the Rectangle, Ellipse, and Polygon tools are "smart." Each one "knows" when its cursor is over a highlight box handle for a shape it has drawn — the tool temporarily becomes the Pick tool so you can move, scale, skew, or rotate. Also, when the cursor is over a node, it turns into the Shape tool temporarily, so you can round the rectangle, turn the ellipse into a "pizza" shape or arc, or wind the polygon.

- **Extract** (in versions 6, 7, and 8) does essentially the same thing to a path as the Arrange, Break Apart command does: It separates subpaths into separate paths. But the Extract button lets you break out only the subpath(s) you select, rather than all of them.
- **Stretch, Scale, Rotate, Mirror** and **Skew** (found in various combinations in versions 4 and later) allow you to make the same transformations you could make with the Pick tool, but you can limit the changes to selected segments of a path.
- **Align** (in versions 4 and later) lets you line up selected nodes horizontally or vertically.

Additional possibilities for node-editing can be found in the Knife and Eraser tools in CorelDRAW 6, 7, and 8. Clicking a curve or node once with the **Knife** does the same thing as the Break button in the Node Edit roll-up, but clicking at a second point breaks the shape into two pieces, drawing matching straight lines to close the two parts.

Dragging the **Eraser** removes part of a path or cuts a swath through a shape, adding matching hand-drawn paths to close the newly generated objects. The Eraser tends to make a lot of Cusp points, which can make it fairly hard to edit the curves it creates.

STARTING WITH A SHAPE

Every version of CorelDRAW has tools for drawing rectangles and ellipses by holding down the left mouse button and dragging. Once one of these standard shapes, or *primitives,* is drawn, it can be scaled, skewed, or rotated with the Pick tool. It can also be modified symmetrically with the Shape tool as shown at the left. Or it can be reshaped in more detail by first converting it from a geometric object to curves (Arrange, Convert To Curves) that can be node-edited. With either the **Rectangle** or the **Ellipse**, holding down the Shift key (⌘ *in Mac v.6, the Option key in v.8*) draws the objects from the center outward, while the Ctrl key (*Shift in Mac v.6, ⌘ in v.8*) constrains the rectangle to a square or the ellipse to a circle.

In CorelDRAW 6, 7, and 8 more primitives exist, in the form of the **Polygon** tool. This tool can produce a shape with 3 to 500 straight sides. Or it can make "star" shapes by taking advantage of a node in the middle of each side, where the side is hinged so the figure can have pointed "arms." Moving any node (including midpoints) inward or outward with the Shape tool moves all the corresponding nodes (points or midpoints) the same amount. Double-clicking the Polygon in the Toolbox

COVERING THE PAGE

In CorelDRAW 8 double-clicking the Rectangle tool in the Toolbox draws a rectangle that exactly fits the page.

QUICK COPY

To copy a selected object (or objects) directly on top of itself, switch to the Pick tool and press the "+" key on the numeric keypad. On a system without a numeric keypad, you can choose Edit, Copy and then Edit, Paste.

Starting with a circle made with the Ellipse tool, the shape was turned into a section by using the Shape tool to drag its node around inside the circle. The section was converted to curves, the Shape tool was also used to stretch the square corner, and the center of rotation was repositioned by double-clicking with the Pick tool and then dragging the center. Then the Rotation roll-up was used to rotate a duplicate 45°, and this was repeated six more times. A small circle was added in the center, a larger one behind, and a square behind that.

CorelDRAW 8's Interactive Blend tool

For this greeting card, small 8-pointed stars were blended along the bottom and sides in 7 and 3 Steps respectively. In the top row 3-Step blends were made between the corner stars and an enlarged star in the center. The middle star in the bottom row was replaced with a dove, made by converting the star to curves and node-editing, and the dove and large star were blended in 3 Steps. This blend was separated and ungrouped, and each of the intermediate shapes was blended to a star in the top row in 1, 3, 5, or 7 Steps. The rest of the small stars were made by blending stars in the bottom row with stars on the sides.

opens a dialog where you can set the tool to operate as the **Star**.

Two other specialized drawing tools are the **Spiral** and the **Grid.** These are housed on the Polygon tool's fly-out palette.

TRANSFORMING

Instead of working node by node or line by line as described earlier in "Node Editing," you can also make transformations to an object as a whole. The simplest transformations you can make are done with the **Pick tool**: **moving** (by selecting and dragging the shape itself), **scaling** (by dragging on the handles of the highlight box of a selected object; dragging a corner handle scales proportionally); **flipping** (by dragging a top or side handle across the object); or **skewing** or **rotating** (done by clicking a second time on an object already selected with the Pick tool and then dragging a handle).

The commands in the **Transform** "family" provide a way to make some of the same kinds of changes you can accomplish by eye with the Pick tool, but with mathematical precision. **Position** and **Size** let you specify exactly where and what dimensions you want an object to be. **Rotate, Scale, Mirror,** and **Skew** let you give precise instructions for these functions. All these roll-ups also offer you the chance to duplicate your object and apply your instructions to the copy instead of the original. Used with the **Edit, Repeat** command (Ctrl-R; ⌘-R), the Transform roll-ups can automate object production, as in "Repeating Yourself" on page 62. More elaborate transformations can be made with the Arrange and Effects menus, covered in Chapter 4.

BLENDING

CorelDRAW's powerful Effects, Blend command (Ctrl-B; ⌘-Shift-B in Mac v.6) can be a great drawing tool. In CorelDRAW 7 and 8 its functions are also built into the Interactive Blend tool.

- Starting with **two identical objects** used as blend control objects — open or closed paths, groups, or combined objects — it can place as many copies as you want between the two.

- Starting with **two different objects**, it can manufacture the intermediate "evolving" shapes.

- It can **rotate** the blend objects it creates around a central point.

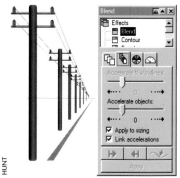

Using the Accelerate Objects setting produced a row of poles that seem to recede into the distance.

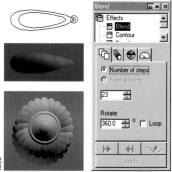

A "medallion" like Shakespeare's button (see page 20) can be made with a blend that's carried out over a 360° rotation: Two shapes can be grouped to make a "petal," the group can be duplicated on top of itself (using the "+" key on the keypad), and the two groups drag-selected and blended (Effects, Blend; or use Ctrl-B; ⌘-Shift-B in Mac v.6). The last step is to "tuck" one edge of the last "petal" under the first petal — a bit tricky because of the way object stacking works in CorelDRAW. The process is described in the "Tucking the Last Petal" tip in "Repeating Yourself" on page 62.

SHORTCUT TO THE PICK

You can instantly toggle from whatever tool you're using — except the Text tool — by pressing the spacebar; press again to toggle back. (Of course, if you press the spacebar when you're using the Text tool, you'll get — you guessed it — a space. Instead, use Ctrl-spacebar (⌘-spacebar on the Mac).

- It can **align** them along a path.
- In CorelDRAW 7 and 8 it can space them evenly or **bunch** or **spread** them apart at one end.

CorelDRAW's blends are "live," which means that when you move, recolor, or reshape a blend control object, the intermediate shapes respond and change accordingly. You'll find examples of using blends for drawing throughout the book.

USING SYMBOLS

Many useful shapes, from simple to fairly complex, can be found in the Symbols roll-up. In CorelDRAW 3 or 4, select the Symbol tool, housed on the Text tool's fly-out, and click on your workspace to open the roll-up. In later versions, use Ctrl-F11 (⌘-F11 on the Mac) to open the roll-up. You can pick from several libraries and then browse the symbols, using the "elevator" scroll button to move through the entire collection. Drag the symbol you want onto your workspace.

MODIFYING CLIP ART

All versions of CorelDRAW come with hundreds of pieces of **clip art.** Even if you can't find exactly the right piece, it may be

QUICK PATTERNS

The Tile option makes a repeating pattern when you drag a symbol onto your page from the Symbols roll-up. The copies can be modified individually, but changing the original also changes all the others. Here the original symbol was rotated with the Pick tool and then colored by clicking in the on-screen palette. One of the copies was also scaled, recolored, and duplicated to make a drop shadow.

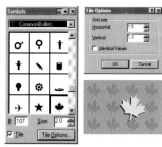

Before printing a Symbols-generated pattern or exporting it as an EPS file, choose Arrange, Convert To Curves and Arrange, Separate for trouble-free output.

This logo was developed using two clip-art files marketed by Dynamic Graphics. The sun from one and the palm tree from the other were flopped, scaled, and otherwise modified to make the design. Type was added, and then all the elements were selected and the Arrange, Combine command created the "positive-and-negative" look.

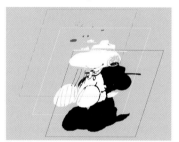

KING

Using CorelTRACE in its default Outline mode as in this detail from the Yearn to Learn *cover, shown in the "Gallery" at the end of this chapter, produces a stack of black-and white-filled shapes. (The top layer of black shapes is shown here in pink.)*

Mona Lisa was traced in CorelTRACE's Mosaic mode, 5000 Diamonds option. The result was imported into CorelDRAW over the recolored original, and some of the diamonds were removed.

CLIP ART CHAOS

Though clip art can be a great resource, there are some pitfalls to watch out for. If the original artist used heavy line weights and didn't turn on Scale With Image in the Outline Pen dialog box (F12), resizing the image can make it look strange. For instance when this butterfly (**clipart****insects****flying****pbutter.cmx**, found on CD-ROM #3 from CorelDRAW 7) is scaled down in CorelDRAW (below, left), it no longer looks right, and you'd have to spend lots of time editing the individual pieces, since there's no way to scale all the line weights at once.

A better solution in most cases is to make any modifications you want at the original size, and then export the result in Illustrator EPS format (File, Export), place it into the CorelDRAW file where you want to use it (File, Import), and scale it down with the Pick tool (right). You'll see a better representation of the art on-screen if you use a high-resolution Image Header setting, but even with a low-res header, it will print fine.

Better yet, if you export the clip art as an Encapsulated PostScript file with *no header*, then import it as PostScript Interpreted, you will still have vector art that you can manipulate, but with the lines updated to scale with the image, so you can successfully scale up or down.

worthwhile to modify something that's almost what you want rather than drawing it from scratch. Use the printed clip art catalogs that come with CorelDRAW to find a piece you can use and to find out where it's stored on the clip art CD-ROM. Once you've opened the clip art file (using File, Open or File, Import), you can use the Pick tool to scale, skew, or rotate it and the Shape tool and Node Edit roll-up to reshape the curves as described in "Node-Editing" on page 27.

TRACING

Another way to draw in CorelDRAW is to bring in a bitmap (File, Import) and use it as a guide for drawing, either by hand or automatically. By hand, you can use the Freehand and Bezier tools as described in "The Path-Drawing Tools" on page 25. Or use the **Freehand tool in Autotrace mode**, as described in the "Tracing on the Fly" tip on page 60.

Much more efficient than tracing by hand, and both more efficient and more accurate than using the Freehand tool in Autotrace mode, is using the **CorelTRACE** program that comes with every version of CorelDRAW. (It's called Corel OCR-TRACE in versions 6, 7, and 8, since it adds optical character recognition software for reading scanned text.) The tracing algorithms have changed a bit from one version to the next, and new modes and variations for

An ink drawing was scanned (top) and traced using the Map option of Corel-TRACE's Centerline mode to make single-weight outlines.

THREINEN-PENDARVIS

PHOTO: COREL

A scanned color photo (top) was traced in CorelTRACE's Outline (Low Detail) mode, which simplifies before tracing, for a posterized look (bottom).

tracing have been added, but tracing works basically the same in all versions: With CorelTRACE up and running, open a bitmap file and choose a tracing method. The program goes to work, automatically generating artwork that can then be opened in CorelDRAW (File, Open) or imported into an already open file (File, Import). Most people use CorelTRACE's default Outline mode, which produces shapes that can then be node-edited and colored in CorelDRAW. But other modes offer interesting possibilities as well. In addition to the artwork on these two pages, "Updating a Logo" on page 59 and the "Gallery" section at the end of the chapter show more examples of how CorelTRACE can be used. *WOW*

MATH VERSUS DOTS

Artwork that you create with CorelDRAW's drawing tools, or with CorelTRACE, is made up of objects — shapes described in mathematical terms. This object-based art can be enlarged without degrading the image or increasing the file size. This is one important difference between object-based and pixel-based artwork such as scanned photos, graphics downloaded from the World Wide Web, or CorelDRAW artwork that has been converted to a bitmap. Bitmaps don't stand up well to enlargement. That's because a bitmap suitable for use at a small size doesn't have enough information stored in its pixels to keep the image smooth and detailed if you stretch it. In contrast, object-based artwork can rebuild itself to any size you specify, based on the mathematical information stored in its objects.

MOGENSEN

The Cattail Cove *illustration above was drawn in CorelDRAW. The artwork is resolution-independent. That is, when the bird is enlarged, there is no degradation of the precise detail that the artist built into it.*

When the CorelDRAW artwork was exported as a TIFF file at 300 dpi at the size shown at the left, a bitmap was produced. When the bitmapped bird is enlarged, the pixels predominate and the image quality is lost. To maintain the original quality, a new TIFF would have to be exported at the size and resolution needed for each enlargement. This characteristic of bitmaps is also true of scans that are imported into a CorelDRAW file and of bitmaps generated from objects with the Convert To Bitmap command in CorelDRAW 7 and 8.

Creating a Hand-Drawn Look

Overview *Draw shapes with flat fills and no outlines; draw details at a larger size outside the "painting," group and reduce them, and drag them into place.*

3•4•5•6•7•8

All these versions have the drawing and fill tools needed for "painting" in this style.

1a

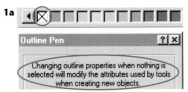

With nothing selected, right-clicking the X lets you set No Outline as the default.

1b

Romanowska's painting began with large shapes to define the sky, clouds, street, and sidewalks. More patches of color were added for the main mid-ground and foreground shapes.

2a

Shading objects were added. And to make "lines," narrow freehand shapes were drawn at the "seams" between lighter-colored objects.

2b

Details were drawn at a larger size, grouped, scaled, and assembled in place.

JOLANTA ROMANOWSKA

THE "LINES" OF JOLANTA ROMANOWSKA'S *Town* painting aren't lines at all, but narrow, no-outline filled shapes drawn freehand.

1 Working back-to-front. To draw shapes without outlines, set the default for the Outline tool to No Outline by clicking with the Pick tool on a blank area of your page (or in CorelDRAW 5 and later versions press the Esc key) and then right-clicking the X in the on-screen color palette (*Control-click on the Mac*) or choosing the X in the Fill tool's flyout. Working in Normal Preview mode (Shift-F9 toggles between Wireframe and Preview), "sketch" the large background shapes by dragging with the Freehand tool, ending on the point where you began. To fill each shape with color as you finish drawing it, click on a color swatch or use the Uniform Fill dialog box (Shift-F11) (see the start of Chapter 3 for tips on setting up a custom palette). With the background shapes in place, add more color-filled objects to make the major mid-ground and foreground shapes.

CLOSING SHAPES

If a path won't accept a fill, it's probably open. To close it so you can fill it, in CorelDRAW 7 or 8 you can press the Auto-Close button on the Property bar. In other versions, open the Node-Edit roll-up by double-clicking a node on the path; then drag-select the start and end nodes and click the Join button.

2 Adding details. Add shadows by drawing shapes and filling them with darker shades. Romanowska often just added black to the CMYK color mix used for the main shape. In the Uniform Fill dialog box, you can watch your new color develop as you drag the slider that controls the black (K) component. To make "lines," draw narrow shapes that cover the "seams" between blocks of color.

To build small details, you can see your work better if you work at a larger size outside the painting. Then drag-select each "vignette" with the Pick tool, group it (Ctrl-G; ⌘-G), drag it into place, and scale it by dragging on a corner handle of the highlight box. With no outlines, such details can be scaled without changing their look. *WOW!*

Converting a Logo

Overview *Import a scanned graphic to its own layer to make a template for tracing; color it and lock it in place; trace the parts of the graphic; add type; delete the bitmap.*

3•4•5•6•7•8

All versions have the Layers function, the Bezier tool, and the Outline Pen styles needed for this conversion.

1a

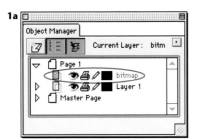

Setting up an extra layer to import a scan as a tracing template in CorelDRAW 8

1b

The scanned logo, saved as a black-and-white bitmap (TIFF) file and imported

---

COLORING IMPORTED BITMAPS

All versions of CorelDRAW allow you to add color to an imported black-and-white bitmap. To color the white background (it's actually transparent in versions 3, 4, and 5), click on the bitmap with the Pick tool and click a color square in the on-screen palette or use the Uniform Fill dialog box (Shift-F11). To color the black part, right-click (*Control-click on the Mac*) a color square or use the Outline Pen dialog box (F12).

USING THE FLEXIBLE LINE ATTRIBUTES of the Outline Pen tool, designer John Sparks was able to transform a hand-drawn logo into a computerized one. The relatively small file size, flexibility, and resolution-independent nature of a vector drawing would make it possible for the Yono photography studio to scale the artwork for a label (as shown here) and for other uses.

1 Making a "template." The original Yono logo, a small ink drawing, was scanned as a black-and-white bitmap.

To make a template for tracing as Sparks did, make a black-and-white (1-bit) scan of your artwork. Then open a new CorelDRAW file (File, New), open the Layers list (either the Object Manager or the Layers Manager or roll-up from the Layout or Arrange menu, depending on which version; *in Mac v.8 choose Window, Palettes, Object Manager*). Start a new layer by choosing from the pop-out menu, name the layer if you like ("bitmap," for example). In the Layers list make sure the new layer is active: in CorelDRAW 8 you can click the little rectangular icon; in version 3, 4, 5, or 8 click your new layer's name; in 6 or 7 click in the column to the left of the name. Now from the File menu, Import your reference bitmap. It will come in on the active layer.

With the imported bitmap selected, right-click (*Control-click on the Mac*) a color square from the on-screen palette, choosing a color that will contrast with the lines you'll be drawing. Sparks colored his scan orange and enlarged it (to enlarge a selected object, use the Pick tool to drag outward on a corner handle of the highlight box).

IMPORTING IMAGES

Although CorelDRAW will import many different file types, in versions 3, 4, and 5 it's a good idea to get into the habit of setting the List Files Of Type in the Import dialog box to the *specific file type* you want to import. If you leave the setting on All Files instead, some file types will be imported correctly, but you'll get an error message when trying to import other perfectly importable files that will come in with no trouble if you specify the file type.

You'll also get an error message if you try to import a color bitmap that contains extra channels or masks. This time the message is for real — you'll need to save a copy without the other channels before CorelDRAW will import it.

1c

Sparks enlarged the imported bitmap to about 4 x 6 inches so it would be easier to trace, and turned it orange to contrast with the black lines he would draw.

1d

The "bitmap" layer was locked and dragged below the drawing layer (Layer 1).

2a

To trace the essential shapes from the logo, Sparks used a 2-point black line with a square nib shape at a 45° angle, set to scale with the drawing. He used no fill so he could see what he was doing as he worked.

Now you can lock the "bitmap" layer so you don't accidentally move it during the drawing process: In CorelDRAW 6, 7, or 8 click in the pencil column of the Layers list to dim the icon (in version 3, 4, or 5 double-click the layer's name to get to Lock; rather than being "live" as they are in versions 6 and 7, the pencil and other icons in version 5 are just indicators). Finally, move the layer down beneath your drawing layer: Drag its name down below Layer 1 (the layer you'll draw on) in the Layers list.

2 Tracing the artwork. To get ready to trace your imported bitmap, set up the line and fill characteristics you want for your tracing: Press F12 for the Outline Pen dialog box or Shift-F11 for Uniform Fill.

With your Fill and Outline characteristics set, work with the Bezier tool in either Wireframe or Preview mode (toggle with Shift-F9). When you need to draw objects that are primarily straight lines with occasional curves, the Bezier tool is ideal. Using your bitmap as a guide, you can click from point to point to make straight lines. To make a curve point, instead of simply clicking, hold the mouse button down and drag a little to bring control points out of the node. The length and direction of the handles determine the shape of the curve (see "Drawing Basics" on page 24 and "The Path-Drawing Tools" on page 25 for tips on drawing with the Bezier tool). If you can't get the curve shaped exactly the way you want it, you can go on with your tracing anyway and come back later to do some reshaping (see below). To complete your closed shape, put your last node on top of the first.

If you need to do some node-editing to reshape a curve, open the Node Edit roll-up (in version 8 you can double-click the Shape tool in the Toolbox; in earlier versions double-click a node or curve). To simplify your curve, you may want to eliminate a node in the middle of a curved segment. Simply select it, and then click on the Node Edit roll-up's Delete or "–" button, or press the Delete key; in CorelDRAW 8 there's an even simpler way — just double-click the node. You can change the curve by dragging the control points, or by dragging on a node or line segment until the curve matches the reference bitmap beneath it. (For more about editing curves, refer to "Node Editing" on page 27.

Sparks traced all the shapes he would need. Thinking ahead, he realized that he had to draw only one "o" (since the two "o's" were exactly alike) and that the "Y" and "n" shared some components.

3 Making sprocket holes. The "holes" at the edges of the film in the Yono logo are not holes at all, but dotted lines in the background color (white in this case), drawn over the black-filled shapes. To start a series of dotted lines, open the Outline Pen dialog box (F12). Sparks used a white line with a square nib shape at 0°, and a dotted line style, chosen by clicking the down arrow at the

2b

When the essential shapes had been outlined, Sparks selected them all and changed the fills to black by clicking on the black color square in the on-screen palette. To change the outline to white, he right-clicked on the white square (Control-click on the Mac).

3

To add sprocket holes Sparks chose Outline Pen settings that would produce square dots the same size as the spaces between them.

4

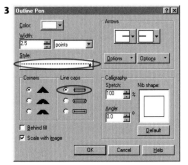

The "o" was duplicated to make the second "o," and parts of the "Y" were duplicated, flipped, and rotated to make the "n."

5

P H O T O   B Y

Futura Medium Condensed type was set spaced out to match the original logo. To set off the type, Sparks drew two 3-point lines by clicking with the Freehand tool.

right end of the Style box and then clicking on a choice. You can scroll through the list to reveal more dot and dash Style options.

Sparks's final step before clicking OK to define the line style was to turn on the Scale With Image option. This would keep the sprocket holes at a size proportional to the artwork. Enable this option if you plan to enlarge or reduce your artwork for a variety of applications, such as business cards, letterhead, and so on.

Sparks used the Bezier tool to draw the dotted lines, switching back and forth between the Bezier and the Pick tool to terminate one line and start another.

4 Finishing the logo mark. At this point, Sparks duplicated the shapes he needed to complete the word "Yono" (select the object and press "+" on the numeric keypad) and moved them into position with the Pick tool, again using the bitmap as a reference. For the swash on the "n" he flipped both pieces he had copied from the descender of the "Y" (to flip a selected object, use the Pick tool to Ctrl-drag [*Shift-drag in Mac v.6; ⌘-drag in v.8*] a side handle of the highlight box across to the other side) and then rotated the pieces into place by clicking again with the Pick tool and dragging a corner handle.

5 Setting type. Sparks set the type with the Artistic Text tool (F8). After opening the dialog box for formatting type (Ctrl-T; *⌘-T on the Mac*) so he could choose a font and size, he clicked on OK, then clicked on the screen and typed "PHOTO BY." To add space between the letters, he used the Shape tool to drag the right arrow marker; to increase the space between the two words, he Ctrl-dragged the same marker (*⌘-drag on the Mac*). (For more about setting and modifying type, see "Type Basics" in Chapter 6.)

Sparks drew straight lines above and below the type by holding down the Ctrl key to constrain the lines to horizontal (*Shift in Mac v.6, ⌘ in v.8*) and clicking from point to point with the Freehand tool.

Jettisoning excess baggage. The last step in the conversion process is to remove the bitmap. From the Layers list, select the "bitmap" layer and unlock it (by clicking to turn on the pencil or by deselecting the Lock function). Then choose Delete from the pop-out menu. *(WOW)*

Working Large

Overview *Establish a drawing scale for a large-format drawing; use the Freehand tool to draw basic shapes; color them; output the design at actual size using the tiling and scaling Print options.*

3•4•5•6•7•8

Drawing, coloring, scaling, and tiling are available in all these versions of CorelDRAW. However, the large page size available in versions 6 and later makes it easier to design and print a large drawing.

1a

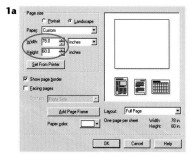

For this stained glass window, a page size of 60 x 78 inches (5 x 6.5 feet) would accommodate the three panels and their borders with a little room to spare on the sides.

1b

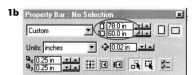

In CorelDRAW 7 or 8 there's another way to size a page: With nothing selected, key the dimensions into the Property bar (opened from the View menu).

1c

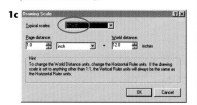

By setting a scale, you can work on a normal-size page but enter and read real-world dimensions.

GERALD TOOKE

FOR EACH STAINED GLASS WINDOW HE DESIGNS, Gerald Tooke prints both a small color version to use in choosing glass colors, and a full-size black-and-white "cartoon," or blueprint, for cutting the glass. Printing of the full-size design is done by *tiling* — CorelDRAW breaks the document into pages the printer can produce and uses as many sheets of paper as it takes to print the entire file.

1 Setting the scale. Strategies for getting large output from Corel-DRAW vary according to what version you're using. In version 6 or later you can define large pages, up to 1800 x 1800 inches, so you can work on large projects at actual size, which means you can enter real-world dimensions in any of the Transform roll-ups, read real-world dimensions from the Status bar, and be ready to print tiled output at full size. Set the page size by choosing Page Setup (either by double-clicking on the drop shadow that shows at the right and bottom edges of CorelDRAW's default page or by choosing Page Setup from the Layout menu in CorelDRAW 4 or later, or the File menu in version 3; *on the Mac it's Layout, Document Layout*). Set the page size close to the size of the artwork you plan to draw.

Alternatively, instead of working at actual size, you can establish a scale for the drawing. This might be especially useful if you're designing something very small rather than really large. For instance, for a graphic for a watch face, you may want the advantages of designing with the real-world dimensions even though you want to make larger prints so you can see the detail as the design develops. In CorelDRAW 6 or later you can set a scale by choosing the Layout, Grid & Ruler Setup dialog box, and clicking the Edit Scale button. From here, open the Typical Scales options and choose one that's appropriate.

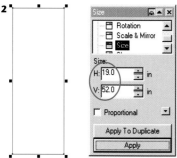

Tooke used the Size roll-up to define the panel size precisely.

Tooke referred to his rough sketches of panel designs as he drew a shape for each piece of glass.

Because slab glass is much thicker and harder to cut than thinner stained glass, Tooke kept the shapes relatively simple, using the Freehand tool to mix freeform curves and straight lines in the same object.

The finished design before coloring

5

In CorelDRAW 5, page size is limited to 30 x 30 inches, so you'll want to use scaling to work on a large project so that as you draw, you can enter real-world dimensions and read them in the Status bar and Rulers. To set the scale, choose Layout, Grid & Scale Setup; in the dialog box choose Use Drawing Scale and choose from the Typical Scales list.

3•4

CorelDRAW 3 and 4 have a limited page size (30 x 30 inches) and no scaling option, so you have to keep the scale in your head. For a large project like this, set up your page so that 1 inch represents 1 foot. That way, the *numbers* displayed in the Rulers and the Status bar will be correct, and all you have to do is mentally convert the *units,* changing "inches" to "feet." For example, for this project, page size could be set to 6.5 x 5 inches, to represent 6.5 feet (78 inches) x 5 feet (60 inches). It isn't an ideal solution, since the Status bar displays fractions as decimals, and most of us aren't used to thinking in terms of tenths of a foot. But it's workable.

2 Setting the limits. With the Rectangle tool Tooke drew a box the size of the finished window. The three 19-inch panels would fit into a 60 x 73-inch space, including 4-inch borders on the edges and between the panels. He dragged the rectangle tool until the Status bar showed dimensions close to the desired Width and Height. It's possible, but painstaking, to draw a dimensioned object by hand in CorelDRAW, reading the Height and Width in the Status line and adjusting until the object is exactly the right size. But instead Tooke used the Size roll-up (from the Transform or Arrange, Transform menu), a method that makes it easier to be accurate in CorelDRAW 4 and later versions. To specify Size dimensions, key in the exact Horizontal and Vertical measurements and click Apply. Tooke used the same method to draw and size each of the three panels.

3 Drawing shapes. Tooke filled the large rectangle with black by clicking the black square in the on-screen palette. Then, using a rough pencil sketch for reference, he worked in Wireframe mode for speed (press Shift-F9 to toggle between Wireframe and Normal Preview modes). First he set the default fill to white and the default outline to None, this way: With the Pick tool click on an empty area to ensure that nothing is selected, and then click on the white color square in the on-screen palette to set the default fill; right-click on the X in the palette to make No Outline the new default setting. Without outlines, Tooke's designs aren't dependent upon line widths, so they can be scaled without concern about whether the outlines will scale with the image.

Tooke drew with the Freehand tool to shape each piece of glass. To draw a curved line, simply drag with the Freehand tool; to add a straight segment, release the mouse button momentarily and then click to start the straight piece, move the cursor to where you want the end point of the straight segment, and click again. To continue

4

Coloring the shapes

5

Dashed lines in the Print Preview window show all the pieces of paper needed for printing. Tiling starts at the top left corner of the drawing (not the page) and works across and down. Laser printers can't print to the edge of the paper, so tiled prints need to be trimmed before being pasted together.

Another of Tooke's slab glass windows

In this design for a lighted stained glass panel, Tooke used Fountain fills (F11) to simulate the lighted panes.

from that point with a freeform curve, just hold down the mouse button and continue to drag.

4 Coloring. Once Tooke finished drawing the shapes for the windows in Wireframe mode, he saved the file and then saved a separate copy to work out the color scheme (File, Save As, using a new name), changing to Normal Preview (Shift-F9). Using the Pick tool, he Shift-selected several shapes that he wanted to be the same color and then clicked a color square from the on-screen palette to color them all at once, then Shift-selected another set, and so on. Since he was only approximating the colors of glass he would have available, he used the default CorelDRAW palette rather than taking the time to make custom-mixed colors.

5 Printing. Tooke printed his colorized file on a desktop color printer using letter-size paper. To reduce any design to fit the paper in the printer, choose File, Print (Ctrl-P; ⌘-P *on the Mac*) and choose Options, Fit To Page (*on the Mac it's the Corel Print Options button*).

Then Tooke went back to the uncolored version of the file. To print the cartoon at full size, he pressed Ctrl/⌘-P and clicked the Options (*Corel Print Options*) button in the Print dialog box, then selected Print Tiled Pages (in CorelDRAW 3 choose Tile from the Print dialog box). After a file is set up for tiling, you can see how the document will be printed by turning on the Preview image. Look for the Preview button in the Print dialog box in CorelDRAW 7 or 8; in other versions (except 3, which has no print preview) select Preview Image in the Print Options box.

Cutting the glass. Tooke used his color print for guidance in choosing his glass colors. Then he used the full-size black-and-white print to measure and mark the slab glass for cutting. He tapped the glass with a mallet against a chisel set into a tree stump, chipping away until each piece closely matched its corresponding shape in the image. The pieces were laid out according to the full-size diagram in a big box, and resin was poured around them to form the window. *WOW*

3•4•5

When your page size is limited, as in CorelDRAW 3, 4, and 5, you can use the Scale option to get oversized prints. First determine the size of your artwork by drawing a box over the image area and noting the Height displayed in the Status bar. Then figure out how big you want your image to print. Divide the height of the print you want by the Height of the box you drew, and multiply the result by 100. This will give you the percentage to enter for Scale. In our example, the print height is 60 inches. Because the file was set up using a 1-inch-equals-1-foot scale, the Height of the drawing is 5 inches. Since

$$60 \div 5 \times 100 = 1200\%,$$

you would enter 1200 for the Scale value: In version 4 or 5, choose File, Print, Options and enter a percentage, with Maintain Aspect Ratio selected; in version 3, choose File, Print, Scale and enter the percentage.

Masking To Make a Logo

Overview *Draw the picture that you want to mask inside the type; set the type; draw a background shape; combine type and background to let the picture show through.*

3•4•5•6•7•8

All these versions of CorelDRAW have the Combine command necessary for masking, so that objects with holes can be layered to make it look like type is filled with an image. An alternative approach in version 4 or later would be to use the PowerClip.

THE BRIGHT CALIFORNIA FRUIT-CRATE LABELS of the start of the 20th century inspired the style of Joe King's award-winning *Men from Earth* logo. Modern in design, yet with the bright look of those vintage labels, this logo for a comic book series and action figures combines an old style with new appeal.

1 Starting with the background. Using a hand-drawn sketch as a reference, King drew a background rectangle by dragging with the Rectangle tool, and filled it with a yellow-to-white Radial Fountain fill. To give an object a Radial fill, select it and press F11 to open the Fountain Fill dialog box and choose Radial for the Type. For the "To" color, choose the central color of the radiating fountain, either from the palette that's presented or by clicking the More button. Then click on "From" and choose the outside color.

Next King imported a clip-art earth. (You can find world maps on the CorelDRAW clip art CD-ROM). He filled the ocean shape with a blue-to-white Radial fill and the land shape with a brown-to-green Radial fill; a duplicate of the land shape (made by selecting with the Pick tool and pressing "+" on the numeric keypad) was given a light blue fill (press Shift-F11 to open the Uniform Fill dialog box and choose a color) and a light blue outline (press F12 to open the Outline Pen dialog box and assign an outline color and thickness). Then it was sandwiched in between the other land shape and the ocean. (To move an element backward or forward in the "stacking order" of objects, select it with the Pick tool and send it Back One or Forward One (from the Arrange [Order] menu).

King reshaped the round ocean so it would be the same width as his yellow background. To reshape one object to fit another, use the Shape tool to drag nodes or curves; you can also use the buttons of

1

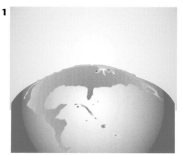

The logo started with a yellow-filled rectangle, partly overlaid with a modified clip art map.

A straight path was turned into a curve and reshaped to make an arc.

Clicking from point to point made half the rays.

Copying and flipping made the other half.

The two "half-suns" were joined to each other and then to a three-sided path to make the sky.

GOING TOO FAR

When you use the Pick tool to Ctrl-drag (*Shift-drag in Mac v.6, ⌘-drag in v.8*) a side handle of the highlight box across to the other side, the object flips, retaining its original size and proportions — as long as you stop soon enough! But if you drag too far, the flipped shape will be stretched to twice the width (or height). In that case, use Edit, Undo and start over.

the Node Edit roll-up (double-click the Shape tool in the Toolbox in version 8; double-click a node in versions 3 through 7).

2 Making the sunburst. To get the effect of the sun at the horizon, King created a piece of blue sky with its bottom edge cut away to look like the sun's rays, which he put on top of the yellow-filled background. To do that he first drew a curve to use as a guide for the bottom of the rays: He clicked at two points with the Freehand tool to make a straight line. Then, using the Shape tool, he selected both nodes of the line and clicked the To Curve button in the Node Edit roll-up. Now he could drag the center of the line up with the Shape tool to make the arc he wanted.

With the new curve and the yellow-filled rectangle to serve as guides for the inner and outer limits of the sunburst, King drew the rays. You can create a series of straight, connected segments by clicking on a starting point with the Bezier tool, then clicking at the next point, the next point, and so on. King continued making spikes until he had drawn half of the sunburst shape. Then he selected the new spiky shape with the Pick tool, duplicated it ("+"), and flipped the copy horizontally by holding down the Ctrl key (*the Shift key in Mac v.6, ⌘ key in v.8*), and dragging the left side handle of the highlight box to the right.

Next, King joined the two halves of the sunburst together. Since the Join command works only on nodes that are in the same path, to make the two paths into one, you have to Shift-select the two elements; then use Arrange, Combine. Drag-select the overlapping end nodes with the Shape tool and click the Join button in the Node Edit roll-up (in CorelDRAW 8 you could also use the Property bar).

The sunburst shape was then joined with a path drawn in the shape of the top of the background rectangle, and the new shape was given a blue outline and a blue-to-white radial fill. On top of the sunny sky, it made a striking sunburst.

3 Setting and filling type. King's next task was to make a mask that would put the sky, earth, and sun inside the "EARTH" type. This was a relatively simple process. First, he clicked with the Artistic Text tool and typed the word "EARTH." (For more about setting type, see Chapter 6.) Then he used the Pick tool to drag the type over the other elements, and stretched it to fit by dragging on the handles of its highlight box.

With the lettering finished, King began constructing the mask that would let the sunny sky show through the type. First he used the rectangle tool to draw a no-fill box around the text, large enough to completely obscure the earth and sky. He Shift-selected the box and the text and combined the two (Arrange, Combine). When you combine two overlapping objects, you create a mask — one shape cuts a hole in the other, and anything beneath the mask will show through the cutout. Clicking on the on-screen color

3a

After setting type and stretching it over the earth-and-sky artwork (left), King added a masking rectangle.

3b

Type and rectangle were combined to make "windows" of the letters.

4

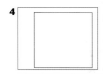

A second mask was made to hide the orange edges of the rectangle and to provide space on the left for more type.

5a

For the orbit an ellipse was drawn, stroked, skewed, and positioned over the mask.

5b

The ellipse was broken apart to make it look like it passes both in front of and behind the "EARTH" type.

palette, he gave the combined shape a black fill; he used the Outline Pen dialog box (F12) to assign an orange outline.

4 Making a second mask. Because the logo had to merge seamlessly with the black background in the comic book covers and the packaging design, King wanted to preserve the orange outline around the type but not around the black rectangle. Since the type "window" and the rectangle were now one combined shape, however, any outline he assigned to the type would also apply to the box. So he built another mask, with black fill and stroke, to cover the edge of the rectangle: He drew a black-filled rectangle that extended beyond the existing orange-stroked one, selected it with the Pick tool and duplicated it in place ("+"), sized the copy down by dragging inward on the handles of the highlight box, Shift-selected the outer rectangle, and used Arrange, Combine.

5 Adding the orbiting spaceman. To finish the logo, an orbiting astronaut was added. Because the type was now a mask, King couldn't actually place anything in front of the black but behind the letters, so he would have to break the elliptical path into pieces to make the far side of the orbit appear to be in back. First he drew the ring by dragging the Ellipse tool and assigning it an outline. Then he used the Pick tool to move it over the "EARTH" type, to scale it (by dragging a highlight box handle), and to slant it (by clicking on the selected Ellipse a second time with the Pick tool and dragging a corner handle of the highlight box to rotate it). Then the Ellipse was converted to curves (Arrange, Convert To Curves) so its nodes could be edited with the Shape tool. Taking away part of the outline of an object is a two-step process — first making the break points and then separating the pieces. Here's one way to do it: Double-click on the point where you want to break the curve, open the Node Edit roll-up, and click the Break button. Repeat this process until you have all the breaks you need; you now have a number of subpaths, all still combined in a single path. Then select the entire object (by drag-selecting or Shift-selecting with the Pick tool) and Break Apart (Ctrl-K; ⌘-K), so each line segment becomes a separate path and the ones you don't want can be deleted (select with the Pick tool and press Delete).

The space man was hand-drawn, scanned, and converted with CorelTRACE to produce a CorelDRAW graphic. (For tips on tracing, see "Updating a Logo," later in this chapter.)

Adding more type. The letters of "MEN" (in the Keypunch font that comes with CorelDRAW) were set as three separate text blocks so each could be placed in front of or behind the orbit. "FROM" was set and moved into place also. The type blocks were Shift-selected and assigned a solid white fill (click on the white square in the on-screen palette). The tag line "Heroes of the High Frontier!" was set in Futura Bold Condensed Italic, with a red outline and gold fill.

Taking Advantage of Symmetry

Overview *Draw basic shapes; then duplicate, transform, and fill them to add detail and dimension.*

3•4•5•6•7•8

Joe King built his packaging design largely by modifying Corel-DRAW's standard shapes and then "mirroring" the results.

1

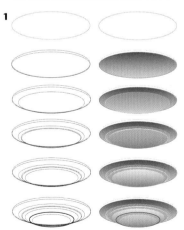

King stacked eight ellipses, most of them resized from the original, squashed, and Fountain-filled. When he added one that extended below the bottom of the first shape, the hull began to look three-dimensional.

WHEN JOE KING TOOK ON THE JOB of designing packaging for the Star Trek action figures, the project at hand had personal appeal. Building on his knowledge of the topic and a bold style from previous projects, he began the *Starship Enterprise*, shown above. He set out to bring the ship to life, taking advantage of CorelDRAW's ability to duplicate, flip, flop, stretch, skew, and otherwise distort a few shapes into many variations.

1 Shaping the saucer. The main hull of the spacecraft is basically a stack of ellipses, all generated from a single original. King drew the first white disk by dragging with the Ellipse tool, giving the oval shape a gray outline (press F12 to open the Outline Pen dialog box). This was then duplicated in place (by pressing the spacebar to select it with the Pick tool and pressing the "+" key on the numeric keypad) and squashed vertically by grabbing the top center handle of the highlight box with the Pick tool and dragging downward. This second ellipse was given a Linear Fountain fill from a tint of cyan to black (press F11 to open the Fountain Fill dialog box). This ellipse was in turn duplicated, and this time the copy was resized overall (not just vertically squashed) by dragging inward on a corner handle.

By drawing, resizing, and squashing ellipses, filling them with light-to-dark gradients to mimic the play of light, and nudging some of the shapes downward by varying amounts, you can model a smooth, aerodynamic shape. (For tips on drawing ellipses, see "Starting with a Shape" on page 29; for Fountain fills, see Chapter 3, "Coloring.")

2 Segmenting the hull. King clicked with the Freehand tool to draw short radiating lines to divide the right half of the hull into segments. The lines were drag-selected with the Pick tool and grouped together (Ctrl-G; ⌘-*G on the Mac*). This group was duplicated ("+") and flipped horizontally by holding down the Ctrl key (*the Shift key in Mac v.6;* ⌘ *key in v.8*) and using the Pick tool to drag the right side handle to the left, across the group of lines. To segment the bottom of the hull, these two mirrored groups were Shift-selected and duplicated and the copy was scaled down to fit the bottom ellipse.

2

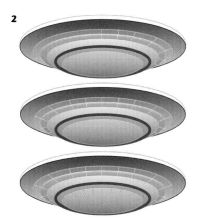

The two rings of marks that divide the hull into sections began as a series of two-node lines on the right side of the ship, which were given an outline in 10% black.

3a

King made windows from Uniform-filled rectangles, double-clicking with the Pick tool and dragging a side arrow to skew, or a corner arrow to rotate.

3b

Skewing and then flipping a copy vertically made the windows look as if they were wrapped around the edge of the hull.

4

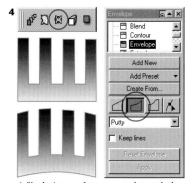

A Single Arc envelope was used to arch the hatch shape. An envelope can be applied with version 8's Interactive Envelope tool (top left) or with the Envelope roll-up.

3 Adding windows. King drew a window with the Rectangle tool. Duplicates of the window, sometimes in groups of two or three, were skewed, rotated, or flipped to fit around the edge of the hull. To rotate or skew an object, double-click on it with the Pick tool to change the handles of the highlight box to arrows. Dragging the corner arrows will rotate the object, while dragging the others will skew in the direction you drag.

The rotating and skewing were repeated until all of the windows for one side of the hull were finished. Then the windows were grouped and duplicated, and the copies were flipped for the other side.

4 Making hatches. Double-clicking from point to point with the Freehand tool with the Ctrl key (*the Shift key in Mac v.6; ⌘ key in v.8*) to keep lines horizontal and vertical, King drew the first of the four-pronged hatches, gave it a black-to-white Linear Fountain fill, and made duplicates. This shape was large enough so it had to be modified beyond a simple skew and rotation in order to fit the curves at the ends of the elliptical hull. So King tweaked it with an Envelope.

To put an arc in an object, select the object, then choose Envelope from the Effects menu, or in CorelDRAW 8 choose the Envelope from the Interactive tools fly-out in the Toolbox. Depress the Single Arc button (it's the second one; in version 8 it appears in the Property bar when the tool is selected); in Corel-DRAW 4, 5, 6, 7, or 8 click the Add New button. Then, using the Shape tool (which appears automatically), hold down the Ctrl key (*Shift in Mac v.6; ⌘ in v.8*) and grab the top center handle and drag upward. This also moves the bottom handle and creates an arched envelope; in version 4, 5, 6, or 7 click Apply. (See Chapter 4 for more about envelopes.)

The hatches from the right side were Shift-selected and copied, and the copy set was flipped horizontally to the left side. All five objects were grouped and duplicated, and the copies were reduced for the lower hull. To make the hatches on the far side of the ship, these were copied again, flipped vertically, rearranged, and resized.

5

A Single Arc envelope was applied to curve the type.

6a

Holding down the Shift key (⌘ key in Mac v.6) while dragging a corner of the Straight Line envelope causes equal stretching on the opposite side.

6b

Deleting the top center node and dragging upward made the arch. The shape was filled with a black-to-cyan gradient.

6c

The primary shape was duplicated and reshaped to make the side walls. Fountain fills in the side walls and differential coloring of the windows added dramatic lighting.

7a

Two ellipses were used as guides for drawing the engine pod. The small ellipse was then deleted.

7b

The large ellipse was given a light-to-dark Fountain fill, so that it became a beveled rim when a smaller red-filled copy was added.

5 Adding the insignia. The final detail on the saucer hull was the Star Fleet designation: NCC-1701-D. King set the type with the Artistic Text tool (choose the tool; choose Text, Character; and set the type specifications; click on your drawing where you want the text to start; and type). He converted the type to curves (Arrange, Convert To Curves), and again used the Single Arc Envelope to make it fit the hull.

6 Building the body. Next came the supporting strut between the saucer and the main body of the ship. This was drawn as a rectangle, then converted to curves (Arrange, Convert To Curves). From here, a Straight Line envelope was applied to the shape, so that the top two nodes could be pulled apart. To apply the Straight Line envelope, choose the Envelope tool or function (see step 4), depress the Straight Line button (it's the first button); in version 4, 5, 6, 7, or 8 click Add New. Then hold down the Shift key (⌘ *key in Mac v.6*) and drag the top right handle outward; this will move the top left handle in the opposite direction, making a symmetrical distortion. In version 4, 5, 6, or 7 click Apply when the envelope has the shape you want the rectangle to become.

To create a rounded top, King first took the object out of its envelope (Arrange, Convert To Curves). Then using the Shape tool, he selected the top center handle and deleted it (in CorelDRAW 8 you can double-click it to delete it; in other versions click on it and press the Delete key), and then dragged from the center of the top line upward to create the desired curve.

King duplicated the shield shape he had just made ("+"), and deleted all but three nodes — the top right corner, the bottom right corner, and the bottom center. Then this object was reshaped with the Shape tool by dragging the individual Bezier curve control points, and assigned a light gray outline (F12) and a Linear Fountain fill (F11). The resulting shape was then duplicated, and the duplicate was flipped horizontally and filled with a blue Fountain fill.

Rectangles — duplicated ("+"), grouped (Ctrl-G; ⌘-*G*), and rotated with the Pick tool — became a wall of windows. The group was duplicated and flipped to become the other matching set.

7 Assembling the engines. Next on King's "mission" was the engine assembly. To begin building the right engine, he drew the forward opening with the Ellipse tool. This shape was copied, downsized, and moved to represent the far end of the tube. Using the two ellipses as guides for drawing, King crafted a four-sided polygon with the Bezier tool. He manipulated control points and lines with the Shape tool to reshape the "far" end of the polygon to match the small ellipse. This elongated shape was then placed behind the original ellipse, and the smaller ellipse, no longer needed, was deleted. A copy of the original ellipse, filled with red and shrunk, finished the tube.

The leading edge of a "wing" to support the engine started out as a shape with four nodes, drawn with the Bezier tool. The Shape tool transformed it into a "lazy s." Then two more shapes were created in

Three overlapping shapes became a "wing" to support the engine. The top and bottom surfaces didn't have to fit perfectly, since the edge object hid them.

7c

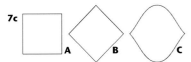

To shape the large central engine, a square (A) was rotated 45° and converted to curves (B), and its top and bottom points were smoothed (C). This shape was then squashed.

7d

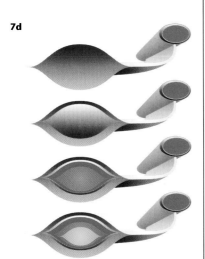

Layered, Fountain-filled shell shapes created the structure and glow of the engine.

8

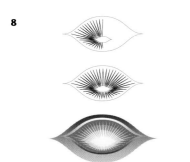

Zigzagging between guide shapes with the Bezier tool, mirroring, and joining created the starburst shape for the engine flare.

the same way, to represent the top and bottom surfaces of the wing. When you build a drawing of overlapping shapes, you need to perfect only the edges that will be seen. Just remember to select the appropriate object and bring it to the front (Arrange [Order], To Front), hiding any "rough edges" behind it.

The center engine housing is a "turtle-shell" shape. To make a shape like this, start by drawing a perfect square, holding down the Ctrl key (*Shift key in Mac v.6; ⌘ in v.8*) while dragging with the Rectangle tool. Then rotate the square 45° with the Pick tool and Ctrl key (*Shift or ⌘*) to constrain the rotation. Next convert the square to curves (Arrange, Convert To Curves) and then reshape it: In CorelDRAW 8 double-click the Shape tool in the Toolbox to open the Node Edit roll-up (in other versions use the Shape tool to double-click a node); drag- or Shift-select all the nodes and click the To Curve button in the Node Edit roll-up; then select just the top and bottom nodes and click the Smooth button. Squash this shape with the Pick tool to get the shell shape you want. King duplicated and downsized this shape four times, each time giving it a different fill, to build the center engine.

8 Firing up. To "turn on" the engines, King created a many-pointed star shape. Using two of the turtle-shell shapes as guides, he drew the starburst by hand, clicking from point to point with the Bezier tool, first on the inside guide shape and then on the outside one, then on the inside again, then on the outside, proceeding around the ellipse. When he had finished half of the starburst's rays, he duplicated the shape and flipped the copy to finish it off. To turn the starburst into a closed shape so he could fill it, he selected the two pieces and combined them (Arrange, Combine) and then joined the ends: Select each of the two pairs of end nodes (by drag-selecting them with the Shape tool, for instance) and then click the Join button in the Node Edit roll-up (or the Property bar in version 7 or 8) to make the two points one.

Next King gave the starburst a Radial white-to-yellow Fountain fill (F11 to open the Fountain Fill dialog box) and a white outline (F12 to open the Outline Pen box). To fire up the right outer engine, this shape was duplicated and reduced, and the inner nodes were offset down and to the left to suggest perspective (see the finished ship on page 44). To offset some of the nodes of a shape, Shift-select them with the Shape tool and drag to move only those nodes; the unselected nodes stay in position.

With the right engine finished, it was grouped, duplicated, and flipped to create the left engine pod. Skewing and resizing text for the left engine mount finished the Enterprise.

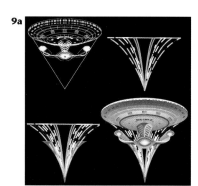

9a

King began by drawing a triangle (top left), bowed its sides by moving node handles with the Shape tool (top right). He duplicated and resized the shape several times, each time with a different outline Style, Line Caps option, and Color.

9b

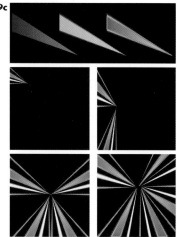

Blending pairs of hand-drawn shapes created a blast (top). Then a blend from the outside color of the blast to black created a fade (left).

9c

Layering three fountain-filled triangles formed a sparkling ray. Other rays were added to fill one quadrant, which was duplicated and rotated 90°. This half was mirrored, another copy of the original group was added, and individual rays were modified.

9 Completing the package design. "Warp speed" shapes, built from a triangle and assigned line styles through the Outline Pen dialog box (F12), were added for a "traveling through space and time" effect. In CorelDRAW 6 or 7, draw a triangle by double-clicking the Polygon tool in the toolbar, setting the Number Of Points to 3 in the dialog box, and dragging. Make it editable (Arrange, Convert To Curves) and use a Single Arc Envelope (see step 4) to "warp" it.

The blast in the center of the package design, below the spaceship, started with an irregular shape drawn by hand with the mouse. Three duplicates of the shape were rotated and reduced. Then, to get the exploding effect, blends were created between pairs of these objects: You can select both objects with the Pick tool, open the Blend roll-up (from the Effects menu), set the number of Steps, click Apply, then click the Node Mapping button (it looks like an old-fashioned elevator dial), click Map Nodes, and then click on a highlighted node in each object; or in CorelDRAW 8 you can drag from one to the other with the Interactive Blend tool and set up the node mapping in the Property bar. Another blend, between two circles, was centered behind the new blast images.

For the space-rays that extend from the center to the edge of the package, a triangle drawn by clicking with the Bezier tool was twice duplicated and reduced, and each copy in the stack was given a Fountain fill to create a sparkling ray. This ray became the basis for a variety of colorful beams. To avoid a "cloned" look, the beams were individually changed.

Since this was packaging for action figures, King added "transporter pads": A white-filled base ellipse was duplicated, and the copy was given no fill and a dotted white outline. This was again duplicated, and the two copies were blended to create the "transporter beam" area. Vertical lines, dotted and white, were drawn on both sides, completing the "beam me up!" effect.

The stars on the black background started out as a few shapes, which were copied and individually placed and manipulated to make an entire starfield. To finish the design, the logo and type were added. When the package was printed and assembled, the action figure was held in place with a molded transparent cover that allowed the illustration to show through. *WOW!*

3•4•5

Here's a quick way to draw an isosceles triangle (a triangle with two sides equal) in CorelDRAW versions 3, 4, and 5, which don't have the Polygon tool: Ctrl-drag with the Rectangle tool to create a perfect square, rotate it 45°, and convert it to an editable path (Arrange, Convert To Curves); select the top node with the Shape tool and press Delete. To make the triangle taller or shorter, Ctrl-drag the bottom point up or down.

Designing a Folding Mask

Overview *Design the layout; print, cut, and fold a prototype to make sure it works; draw and color the design elements.*

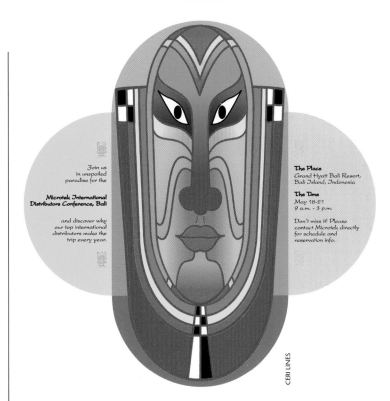

CERI LINES

3•4•5•6•7•8

All versions of CorelDRAW from 3 have the drawing, node-editing, and printing functions needed for this piece. The Intersection command in versions 5, 6, 7, and 8 (as well as the Intersection button on the Pick tool's Property bar in 8) makes it easier to make the internal shapes fit the mask edges precisely.

The back side of the invitation

The folded invitation with flaps interlocked

1a

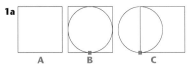

A   B   C

The invitation layout began with a circle formed inside a square and moved to one side.

OCCASIONALLY, THE JOB DESCRIPTION of "designer" or "graphic artist" expands to include "paper engineer." Charged with designing the invitation for Microtek's Bali Distributor Conference, Ceri Lines combined vibrant art with a simple, but intriguing folding scheme. Drawing inspiration from a Balinese clay mask hanging on his wall, Lines set a challenge for himself — to make the piece vibrantly colorful, but also unique and mysterious, to convey a truly inviting sense of excitement with a tropical flair.

Lines wanted to design the invitation so that when it was folded the flaps would create a stylized, eye-catching pattern that would hide the fact that the piece was also a mask. Only when the flaps were opened would the mask become recognizable. Using Corel-DRAW for design and layout, Lines was able to let his paper mystery unfold, with half-masks for the flaps (shown at the left) and two half-masks combined and modified to make the mask itself (above).

1 Designing the layout. Lines started by outlining the physical dimensions of the piece. He created a square invitation with four interwoven circular flaps. This piece would be printed on both sides on a large piece of card stock, then scored and die-cut, creating in essence a cardboard envelope. The flaps would interlace in a "Chinese box" style, each flap being half exposed, and half hidden. The clover-leaf shape is a little tricky to fold together, but it stays shut and it opens easily. This kind of design requires careful planning and precision die-cutting, so Lines made sure to work out the mechanical details with his printer beforehand.

There are many ways to make a square layout with round flaps with CorelDRAW. Here's one that leaves you with the four half-circle objects and one square object that Lines needed for his invitation: Draw the square the size you want by Ctrl-dragging (*Shift-drag in Mac v.6; ⌘-drag in v.8*) with the Rectangle tool. Then, starting at the lower right corner node of the square, Ctrl-drag (*Shift- or ⌘-drag*) with the Ellipse tool diagonally across the square until you have the biggest circle that fits inside the square. Toggle to the Pick tool (press the spacebar) and drag the circle to the left; after you start to drag, press and hold the Ctrl key (*the Shift key in Mac v.6; ⌘ key in v.8*) to keep the movement horizontal. When the right edge of the circle is even with the point where the circle's single (bottom center) node started out, stop dragging and release the mouse button; the circle's node should be on the bottom left corner of the square.

To turn the circle into a half-circle, convert the circle to editable curves (Arrange, Convert To Curves). Then select the Shape tool and open the Node Edit roll-up (double-click the Shape tool in the Toolbox in CorelDRAW 8, or in other versions double-click somewhere on the circle). Carefully Shift-select the circle's top and bottom nodes (without moving them) and click the Cusp button in the Node Edit roll-up. Then click on the circle's right node and press the roll-up's Delete (–) button to get rid of the node, or in CorelDRAW 8 you can simply double-click the node to delete it. You won't see a change until you turn the now nodeless right curve of the circle into a straight edge by clicking on it and then clicking the To Line button in the Node Edit roll-up. (If the edge of the half-circle and the edge of the square don't exactly coincide, drag sideways using the Pick tool with the Ctrl (*Shift or ⌘*) key to line them up.)

To shape the other side flap, select the half-circle with the Pick tool and duplicate it in place (press "+" on the numeric keypad). Flip the copy by Ctrl-dragging (*Shift- or ⌘-dragging*) the left side handle to the right, and then drag the copy to the right, using the Ctrl (*Shift or ⌘*) to constrain the movement, until it's in position. To make the top and bottom flaps, Shift-select the two half-circles, press "+," and click the copy again to get the rotation arrows. Drag a corner arrow around, using the Ctrl (*Shift or ⌘*) key to rotate the copy 90°.

1b

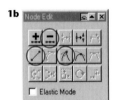

The Cusp (center), Delete (top), and To Line buttons of the Node Edit roll-up can be used to turn a circle into a half-circle.

1c

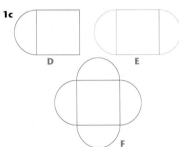

Designing a square invitation with half-circle flaps

2a

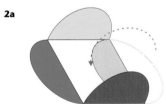

Lines made a half-size print of the invitation layout so he could check the folding.

2b

A ¼-inch bleed area (exaggerated here) would compensate for inaccuracies in printing and cutting.

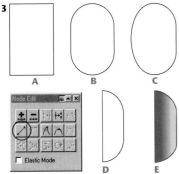

3

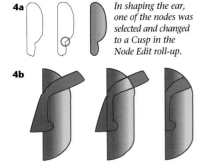

To shape half of the face, Lines altered a rectangle (A) with the Shape tool, rounding the corners (B), removing the points on the left side (C), converting the bulging curve to a line (D), and assigning a Fountain fill (E).

4a

In shaping the ear, one of the nodes was selected and changed to a Cusp in the Node Edit roll-up.

4b

The nose and other internal shapes that reach the edge of the mask can be trimmed with the Intersection command (as shown here) or by node editing.

4c

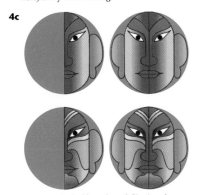

Copying the half-mask and flipping the copy allowed Lines to check the development of the face as he worked.

2 Making a model. When Lines was satisfied with his layout, he scaled it down so he could print it on his laser printer, cut it out, and fold it, to make a half-size mechanical model to test the design. Based on instructions from the printer, Lines designed his artwork with a ¼-inch bleed, extending the art beyond the live area of the mask into the part that would be trimmed away, to provide a greater margin for error in case a die shifted and cuts were slightly off the mark.

3 Drawing the mask. Once the mechanical limitations of the project were outlined and a template was drawn up, Lines could begin to draw the mask. For a design like this it's often easier to start with basic shapes, such as ellipses and rectangles, and modify them. Also, this design is symmetrical, so after one side of the face was built, it could be copied and flipped to create the other side.

For the main face shape, you can start with the Rectangle tool, drawing a rectangle as tall and wide as you want the face to be. Using the Shape tool, round the edges by dragging a corner node as far along the side as you want. Then convert the shape to editable curves (Arrange, Convert To Curves) so you'll be able to get rid of one half of the mask shape. (Working with a half-mask will make it easier to draw the symmetrical shapes of the face, since you can draw half of each shape and then duplicate all the shapes at once.)

To make a rounded rectangle into a half-mask shape, use the Shape tool to Shift-select the two nodes on the right arc and delete them (press the Delete key), leaving a bulge. Then with the Node Edit roll-up open, click on the bulging line to select it and click the To Line button to turn the bulge into a straight line.

Lines colored the half-mask shape with a Fountain fill — select the object, press F11, and choose To and From colors by clicking on the color chip to open the palette and then either choosing a color or clicking the More/Other button to specify a particular color composition. Lines used a horizontal (180°) Linear fill, applying a 25% Edge Pad (for more about using the Edge Pad, see page 78).

4 Designing the face. Drawing with the Bezier tool and other tools, and using the Shape tool for fine-tuning, Lines added the features of the face. By clicking from point to point, dragging slightly where you want control points for curve nodes, it's easy to build a shape quickly. Then you can fine-tune with the Shape tool, grabbing nodes and Bezier control points to smooth out and stylize the curves.

For the shapes on the sides of the mask, such as the cheeks and ears, Lines used near-horizontal (160°–180°) Fountain fills with the

4d

To finish the half-mask, a series of copying and shrinking steps made shapes that looked like a banded border behind the face.

4e

Lines were added to the ear, nose, and cheek to complete the half-mask

5a

The center of rotation for the half-mask was moved to the center of the square for the copy-rotating step.

5b

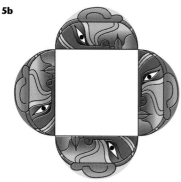

Half-masks arranged around the square

6a

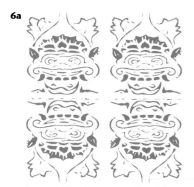

A scanned drawing was traced, and the result was filled, copied, and flipped to make a block of four.

25% Edge Pad. For the shapes in the center of the face, such as the nose and chin and the stripes at the top, he used vertical (90°) fills. An angled blue fill (40°) emphasized the angle of the eye.

Instead of painstakingly matching the edges of inside pieces like the nose and other facial features with the curve of the overall shape (the mask), it was easier to let the artwork overlap and then use Arrange, Intersect to cut away the overlap. In CorelDRAW 3 or 4, without Intersection, you can line up the edges with node editing. One way to do it is to form each inside piece by duplicating the overall shape in place ("+") and then reshaping the copy with the Shape tool, leaving the shared edge intact. (For more about the Intersection command, see Chapter 4.)

To see how the mask was progressing, Lines periodically drag-selected the developing half-mask with the Pick tool and grouped it (Ctrl-G, ⌘-G), copied it ("+"), and flipped the copy by Ctrl-dragging the left side handle to the right (*Shift-drag in Mac v.6; ⌘-drag in v.8*).

To make a multicolored border around the face, Lines duplicated a rounded half-rectangle and shrank it (use the Pick tool to drag on a side handle of the highlight box to make it narrower, and then Shift-drag on the top center handle to pull the top and bottom edges in toward the center to shorten the new shape).

5 Assembling the invitation. Lines duplicated the original half-circle mask three times and arranged the four faces around the square invitation. One way to make the three rotated copies is to use the Transform/Rotation roll-up opened via the Effects or Arrange menu in CorelDRAW 5, 6, 7, or 8 (the Rotate and Skew command from the Transform menu in version 3 or the Effects menu in version 4) to set up a copy-and-rotate move and then use Edit, Repeat (Ctrl-R, ⌘-R) to make more copies. Here's how: Double-click the original with the Pick tool to get the rotating handles. Drag the center of rotation to wherever you need it. For the invitation, the center of rotation was moved out of the mask and into the center of the square. When you've moved the center of rotation, choose the Rotate

function, enter a rotation angle of 90°, and click the Apply To Duplicate (or Leave Original) option. To repeat the process, press Ctrl-R (⌘-*R on the Mac*).

6 Designing the invitation block. Drawing with pen and ink, Lines created a face and a border element, both stylized from Balinese stone sculpture. He scanned these black-and-white drawings and used CorelTRACE in Outline mode (see "Updating a Logo" on page 59) to turn them into editable CorelDRAW shapes. The face

6b

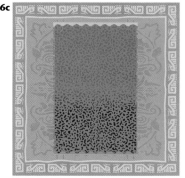

Other traced elements formed a border.

6c

Another background element was formed by coloring imported black-and-white bitmap art and placing it over a Fountain-filled rectangle.

6d

Three clip-art fishes (left) were adapted to fit the invitation's design. Lines eliminated details, used a brighter color palette, and set outlines to Scale With Image in the Outline Pen dialog box (F12) so the lines wouldn't look too thick when he reduced the fish.

was duplicated, flipped, and repeated to make a block of four, which was then grouped and sized to fit the square invitation.

To make a watery background for the fishes and other elements, Lines imported a black-and-white bitmap, assigned it a light blue color, and placed it over a Fountain-filled square. (For more about coloring bitmaps, see the description of coloring the curtains in "Modelling with Blends" in Chapter 3).

The fishes started as clip art. Lines browsed the extensive Fish subdirectory of the clip art that comes with CorelDRAW to find suitable ornaments. From the Totem subdirectory he imported three fishes, ungrouped each one (Ctrl-U; ⌘-U), and customized it. To recolor clip art, work in Preview mode, using the on-screen color palette or the Uniform Fill dialog box (Shift-F11) to specify colors.

7 Finishing the mask. To complete the mask side of the invitation, Lines copied and flipped his half-mask and made changes to give it a more sophisticated look and to adapt it to the space available. With the Pick tool he selected and removed the ears (press Delete). He added more rounded panels of color and a checkered black-and-white motif. Then he reshaped the entire mask by drag-selecting it with the Pick tool and adding an envelope — in CorelDRAW 8 you can choose the Interactive Envelope tool and click the Add New button in the Property bar; in other versions add a new envelope via the Effects menu; choose the Straight Line editing mode (the first button) and the Putty mapping mode (where it's available); drag the envelope's handles to reshape (Shift-drag to make the opposite handle move the same distance in the opposite direction; ⌘-*drag in Mac v.6*). For more about Envelope transformations, see Chapter 4. 〰️

6e

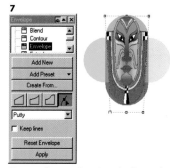

Lines added type, clip art, and other details.

7

Lines used an envelope to make the mask taller and wider at the top, emphasizing the eyes and strengthening the focus of the face.

Blending an Escape

Overview *Draw or import two blend control objects; blend; remove unwanted shapes; duplicate and blend each shape for a neon effect; blend shapes on a path.*

3•4•5•6•7•8

All these versions have the blending and mitering functions.

BRUCE BARYLA

1a

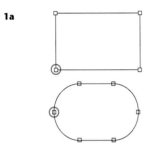

To make a shape like a link of chain, you can round the ends of a rectangle by selecting one of the corners with the Shape tool and dragging it to the middle of one side.

1b

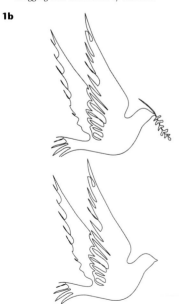

Baryla brought in a clip-art dove (top) and removed the olive branch so it wouldn't interfere with the blend.

IN SOME WAYS DESIGNING ON THE COMPUTER is really not that different from using traditional methods. Ideas are sketched out, reworked, and fine-tuned until the image on the screen matches the one in the mind's eye. In creating his poster for Amnesty International, Bruce Baryla experimented with CorelDRAW's Blend function to transform a simple link of chain into a dove, and to give his shapes a "neon" look.

1 Making the blend control objects. Use any of the drawing tools to form the two control objects, or start with ready-made objects. The clip art files that come with CorelDRAW include several doves. (For tips on drawing blend control objects, see "Troubleshooting Blends" in "Modelling with Blends" in Chapter 3.)

Baryla started by constructing a shape for one link of chain. Then he brought in the dove from a clip-art library. He pressed the "+" key on the numeric keypad to make a duplicate so he could stash the original safely on the pasteboard and use the copy as one of the control objects of the blend. The dove was a grouped object made up of bird and olive branch. He ungrouped it (Ctrl-U; ⌘-*U on the Mac*) and removed the branch so it wouldn't interfere with the blend.

2 Making the first experimental blend. Now try out your first blend. In version 7 or 8 you can choose the Interactive Blend tool to open its Property bar so you can set the number of Steps. In other versions, Shift-select your two control objects, open the Blend roll-up (from the Effects menu). Once the blend is set up, dragging from one object to the other with the Interactive Blend tool or clicking Apply in the roll-up produces the blend. After selecting the dove and the duplicate link, Baryla entered 4 Steps in the Blend roll-up to create four new objects in between his two control objects.

3 Refining the blend. If you didn't get the results you wanted at step 2, you can try generating more steps than you need and then choosing from the resulting shapes.

2

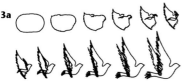

A four-step blend gave Baryla a total of six shapes, but not the six he wanted.

3a

A 10-step blend produced some intermediate shapes that were closer to what Baryla was looking for.

3b

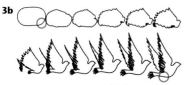

Node mapping a point in the lower right part of the link to another in the lower mid part of the dove and blending in 10 steps produced some good shapes.

4a

Baryla deleted all the steps he didn't want, leaving a six-step shape progression.

Since the blend that Corel-DRAW creates is dynamic, Baryla was able to increase the number of objects in the blend (by changing the number of Steps in the Blend roll-up). Then, to better control the blend, he used node mapping, experimenting with different start and end nodes until he was happy with the results.

To do node mapping, choose Map Nodes — the icon that looks like an old-fashioned elevator dial — in the Blend roll-up (in version 7 or 8 you can use the Property bar instead). Click the Map Nodes button and click on a node in one of the control objects. Then click on the matching node in the other control object. Finally, in versions that have an Apply button, click it.

4 Choosing from the intermediate shapes. With a blend that includes good-looking objects, but more than you need, you can now pick the intermediate objects you want to use in your design. But to be able to select and delete the others, you'll need to take the blend apart. With the blend selected, choose Arrange, Separate. This will break the blend into three pieces — the two control objects and the blend group. To remove objects from the blend group, use Ungroup (Ctrl-U; ⌘-*U*), Shift-click with the Pick tool to select the objects you want to remove, and press the Delete key.

Baryla eliminated all but four of the intermediate steps, leaving six steps in all. He Shift-selected the six parts along with the original link of chain from step 1, arranged them in a horizontal line (Arrange, Align [and Distribute]), and rotated the row about 25° to get the upward movement. (To rotate an object, click on it twice with the Pick tool, drag the center-of-rotation marker to the place you want it to pivot around, and then drag a corner rotation handle.)

5 Creating a neon glow. You can generate a neon effect like the one Baryla used for the elements of the link-to-dove transformation by layering lines, with the thinnest and brightest line on top and the thickest and darkest at the back. Start by selecting the object with the Pick tool and assigning a thickness and color with the Outline tool (F12) to make the backmost element. Then duplicate the still-selected object ("+") to make a copy exactly on top of the original. With this copy still selected, assign it a lighter color and thinner weight. Then drag-select both and blend, experimenting with line weights, colors, and number of steps until you get a smooth, glowing transition.

WHEN TO GIVE UP

Sometimes, even with node mapping, you can't blend a set of pleasing shapes. Instead of reblending for hours aiming for perfection, settle on a blend that's fairly good, separate and ungroup the blend, and node-edit the individual steps.

ON THE LEVEL

When you want to angle a blend, if you work horizontally at first, you can use the Align command (from the Arrange menu) to line up the objects before you tilt the array. In CorelDRAW 6, 7, or 8 you can even space the objects evenly using Arrange, Align [and Distribute].

4b

Baryla added another link of chain, aligned and grouped the shapes, moved the center of rotation to the left end of the group, and rotated the row. (He later replaced the dove with the original one carrying the branch.)

5

For every neon object the top blend control object was a 2.75-point copy, 8% black. For the first link the other blend control object was a 20-point stroke of 92% black, and a total of 12 line weights were used. The middle object shown here, starting with a 15-point back line at 69% black, required only 10 steps. For the dove, the blend started with a 12-point line at 54% black and consisted of 7 steps total. A low miter limit produced spikes.

6

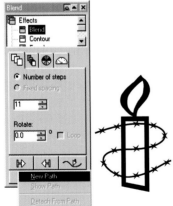

To spread the Symbol barbs along a path, Baryla chose New Path from the Blend On A Path menu from the Blend roll-up. Then he separated and ungrouped the blend and used the Pick tool to move the barbs.

Baryla started with the first link of chain; a blend of 12 steps produced a smooth, seamless glow. He used the same routine to make each of the other steps glow. But since he wanted the objects to lighten up as the chain became a dove, he decreased the line weight and lightened the color of the darkest line for each succeeding object. As the starting lines got thinner, he needed fewer steps for the neon transition. To get spikes to add the dynamic look of chain breaking and birds taking flight, Baryla set the miter limit (Ctrl J; ⌘-*J*) to 6° instead of the default 45° (see "Setting Miter Limits," below). He drew connecting bands between the first two pairs of links and gave the bands a neon glow like the other objects.

SETTING MITER LIMITS

The Miter Limit controls how pointed the sharp corners of objects will be — the lower the setting, the sharper the corners. To set the Miter Limit, first press Ctrl-J (⌘-*J* on the Mac); in version 7, you'll need to choose Display; in 8 choose Workspace, Edit. A single miter limit applies to all objects in open Corel-DRAW files. Since the miter limit doesn't travel with a file, export the file as an EPS to preserve the miter.

Miter limit 45° (default/maximum)　　Miter limit 5° (minimum)

6 Blending along a path. The barbs came from Symbols (in version 3 and 4, the Symbols tool is in the Text tool's fly-out palette; in version 5, 6, 7, or 8 press Ctrl-F11; ⌘-*F11*). After dragging a four-pointed star into his art file, Baryla duplicated it in place ("+"), moved the copy with the Pick tool, and blended in 11 steps. He applied the blend to a path to which he had assigned a thick-and-thin outline (F12). (For tips on making calligraphic lines, see the start of Chapter 3.)

To make a blend follow a path, create the blend and draw the path, then select the blend and choose New Path from the Blend roll-up (click the button with the curved line if there is one, or choose from the roll-up's pop-out menu). If you want to spread the blend along the whole path, choose Full Path; choose Rotate All to orient the objects to the curve; click the Apply button.

Baryla separated the blend, ungrouped the blend group, selected the path, and used node-editing to cut the wire so the parts that should go behind the candle could be deleted. In version 7 or 8 you can drag the Eraser tool (from the Shape tool fly-out) along a path to remove part of it.

Finishing the poster. The "Amnesty International" type was set on a path (for more about setting type on paths, see Chapter 6). Baryla added a background Fountain fill from black (80C, 60M, 100K) to blue (80C, 70M). To match the upward movement of the bird, the Fountain fill was set at a 45° angle. (For more about Fountain fills, see Chapter 3.) 🌟

Building Medallions

Overview *Scan and CorelTRACE the line art; in CorelDRAW ungroup and combine it; construct a frame; apply color; duplicate and offset to make a shadow.*

3•4•5•6•7•8

The Trim command in 5, 6, 7, and 8 makes it easier to build the frames.

1a

An Outline tracing was made in CorelTRACE.

1b

In CorelDRAW, ungrouping and combining let the background show through (right).

1c

A Deep Yellow fill was assigned.

2a

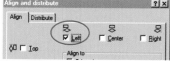

Aligning a guide to the left edge

AS ORNAMENTS for the *Yearn 2 Learn* packaging shown in the "Gallery" at the end of this chapter, Joe King turned scanned pen-and-ink drawings into colored outlines and added "frames," using a "geometric" approach that's useful for those instances when Corel-DRAW's built-in construction functions won't quite do the trick.

1 Converting and coloring the drawings. King traced the artwork in CorelTRACE's Outline mode, which produced stacked black- and white-filled shapes (procedures for using CorelTRACE this way can be found in "Updating a Logo" later in this chapter). He brought the artwork into CorelDRAW (File, Import). Imported CorelTRACE art comes in grouped; it must be ungrouped (Ctrl-U; *⌘-U on the Mac*) before it can be Combined (Arrange, Combine) to make the white parts transparent. After ungrouping and combining the art, King assigned it a Deep Yellow fill (click a color square from the on-screen palette) and no outline (right-click the X; *Control-click*).

2 Building the frame. King built a frame that at first glance seems to be a scalloped rectangle with a smaller duplicate inside it. But, as is often the case, a simple duplicate-and-scale procedure wouldn't produce the desired shape — a double frame with corners aligned and a relatively deeper scallop on the inside border. Here's a way to construct such a frame:

Drag with the Rectangle tool to make the outer rectangle. To duplicate it in place, choose the Pick tool (press the spacebar) and press "+" on the numeric keypad. Shift-drag (*⌘-drag in Mac v.6, Option-drag in v.8*) a corner handle inward to make a smaller version centered inside the first. Click with the Freehand tool to draw lines near all four sides of each rectangle; then use the Align And Distribute dialog (Ctrl-A; *⌘-Shift-A*) to move them exactly into position one by one. For instance, select a vertical guideline and then the outer rectangle, and choose Left from the top row of choices.

Use the Ellipse tool to draw a circle the right size to "bite" into the corners of the rectangles, and center-align it to the guidelines for the outer rectangle like this: Select the circle and then its vertical guide and in the Align dialog box choose Center from the top row. Then select the circle again and its horizontal guide and choose Center from the left column. This will center the circle on the corner of the rectangle. For each other corner, duplicate the circle ("+"), Ctrl-drag (*Shift or ⌘-drag*) the copy horizontally or vertically to the next corner, and align to the guide. Then repeat the whole process for the inner rectangle, using copies of the same original circle.

When you use the **Align** command, **select the stationary item last**. All other selected items will move to align with its position.

2b

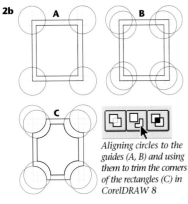

Aligning circles to the guides (A, B) and using them to trim the corners of the rectangles (C) in CorelDRAW 8

3

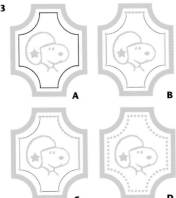

The outer frame was assigned a Deep Yellow line, and small circles were blended to make the inner frame.

4a

A border unit was made from blended circles and shapes drawn with the Bezier tool.

4b

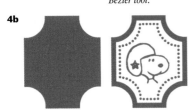

The entire border assemblage was duplicated and the copy was assigned a dark red fill (left), then the outer frames were selected and assigned no fill and a dark red outline (right). This shadow was then sent behind the yellow artwork.

With all the circles in position, in version 5, 6, 7, or 8 you can use the Trim command to cut away the corners. First combine the four circles for the outer rectangle by Shift-selecting them and choosing Arrange, Combine. Then use the combined object as the trimmer: In version 7 or 8, select the trimmer (the four circles), Shift-select the "trimmee" (the outer rectangle), choose the Pick tool, and click the Trim button in the Property bar. In version 5 or 6 choose Arrange, Trim to open the Trim roll-up. Select the trimmer, then click the Trim button and use the fat arrow cursor to click the trimmee; the corners will be scalloped. Then repeat the combining and trimming process to use the inner set of circles to trim the inner rectangle.

3 Coloring. After making four copies of the frame and dragging each Snoopy into its frame, King assigned a thick Deep Yellow outline to the outer frame (F12). For the inner frame he made a small Deep Yellow–filled, no-outline circle, duplicated it ("+") seven times, positioned these circles at the eight corner points of the frame, and blended, using each circle as the ending blend control object for one segment of the frame and the starting object for the next segment. To blend, select two blend control objects with the Pick tool, open the Blend roll-up (from the Effects menu), set the number of steps, click Apply, choose New Path (click the button with the curve or choose from the roll-up's pop-up palette), click the path segment to blend along, and click Apply.

4 Assembling. King dragged each medallion into position and added borders. To make a copy for the shadow wasn't simple, since the outer borders had outlines but no fills and all the other elements had fills but no outlines. Here's a way to do it: Drag-select all the elements with the Pick tool, group them (Ctrl-G; ⌘-G), and make a copy. Assign the copy a dark fill (King used the color of the background with 30% black added [Shift-F11]). Then drag the copy down and right. For each medallion Ctrl-click (⌘-click) the outer edge to select it alone from the group, and give it a dark outline (F12) and no fill (X). Send the shadow group behind the original (Arrange [Order], Back One). *WOW*

3•4

In versions of CorelDRAW without the Trim command, you can use the circle-and-rectangle construction as a guide for drawing the two scallop-cornered rectangles with the Freehand and Shape tools. For step-by-step directions, see Note 1 in Appendix A, "Workarounds."

ALL OR PART?

When you blend along a path, the default is to fit the blend to the **path *segment*** you click on. If you want to fit the blend to the entire path instead, set up the Blend roll-up or Property bar to use the **full path** instead.

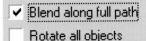

☑ Blend along full path
☐ Rotate all objects

Updating a Logo

Overview *Use CorelTRACE to convert scanned line art into shapes; color the shapes in CorelDRAW; place the scanned line art on top for crisp outlines.*

 The **Flanders.cdr** file is provided on the Wow! CD-ROM so you can examine it.

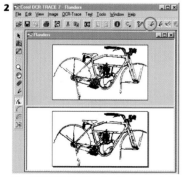

The first step was to produce and scan a clean ink drawing of the motorcycle body.

CorelTRACE's Outline function converted the line art into shapes.

AFTER 50 YEARS IN THE MOTORCYCLE accessory business, the Flanders company decided it was time to revamp the corporate image. To develop the symbol that would be the basis for the new Flanders identity scheme, Shane Hunt used CorelTRACE to convert scanned line art to a vector drawing and then overlaid the scan.

1 Building the bike. Working from a photo, Hunt produced an ink drawing he could scan and trace for the main components of the motorcycle. Since the wheels would be easier to construct with CorelDRAW's Ellipse tool than by hand, he left them out of the hand-drawn illustration. The drawing was scanned as 1-bit line art (that is, black-and-white, not grayscale) and saved as a TIFF.

2 Tracing the image. With a 1-bit TIFF you have several tracing options. Often it's easiest just to import the bitmap into a CorelDRAW file, turn its white areas transparent (they're already transparent by default in CorelDRAW 3, 4, and 5), and then use the Freehand or Bezier tool to draw shapes behind the line art to fill the image with color. Another possibility is to autotrace with the Freehand tool (see "Tracing on the Fly" on the next page). But for the motorcycle, since there were so many pieces involved, Hunt worked with CorelTRACE (called Corel OCR/TRACE in later versions).

Generally speaking, the cleaner and sharper the scan, the better the trace. Hunt scanned his black-and-white drawing at full size at 600 dpi, to give a good tracing and smooth lines for when he would add the line art to the CorelDRAW file (in step 7).

To create a vectorized version of your artwork in CorelTRACE, start the program and choose File, Open, then choose the bitmap you want to trace. Choose the Outline method from the OCR/TRACE (or Trace or Tracing Options) menu, or click the Outline button if your version has one. The program will create CorelDRAW-editable objects for the shapes in your design. Save the trace as a Corel Presentation Exchange (**.cmx**) file in CorelDRAW 6, 7, or 8 or as Encapsulated PostScript (**.eps**) in earlier versions.

3

When the tracing was imported into CorelDRAW, it came in as stacked, no-outline black- and white-filled objects.

4

The dark red gas tank shape (top) was duplicated, downsized, and filled with bright red. Then these two blend control objects were blended in 10 steps.

3 Importing the trace. In CorelDRAW open a file or make a new one; choose File, Import; in the Import dialog box change the Files Of Type setting to Corel Presentation Exchange 6/7 (CMX) in version 6, 7, or 8, or CorelTRACE (EPS) in version 3, 4, or 5; and select your file.

Your tracing will appear on the page as a group of objects. The first thing to do is ungroup it (Ctrl-U; ⌘-*U on the Mac*). Now you should have a large black-filled overall shape with white-filled detail shapes on top of it and possibly more black and then more white shapes, alternating in a stack arrangement. (If CorelTRACE has added one or more large "bounding box" shapes, get rid of them by selecting them with the Pick tool and pressing Delete.)

4 Coloring the shapes. Selecting each shape and assigning a color fill will bring the design to life. It's easier to work in Preview mode during this process rather than Wireframe, so you can see which shapes have been colored. (Shift-F9 toggles the view between Preview and Wireframe.) Use the Pick tool to Shift-select all the shapes that you want to be a particular color. Then click a color square in the on-screen palette or use the Uniform Fill dialog box (Shift-F11) to assign a color. (For more about making and assigning colors and palettes, see "Color Basics" starting on page 71 and "Assigning Colors" on page 75.) To add more dimension to some parts of the bike, Hunt used Radial Fountain fills (F11).

To add depth to the gas tank, he duplicated the shape (select a shape with the Pick tool and press "+" on the numeric keypad), and downsized the duplicate inside the original (Shift-drag inward on a corner handle; ⌘-*drag in Mac v.6, Option-drag in v.8*). (If this method doesn't produce the shape you want, in version 5 or later try Effects, Contour, choosing Inside, setting the Steps to 1, setting the appropriate Offset, and clicking Apply; then choose Arrange, Separate.) If necessary, adjust the smaller shape with the Shape tool by dragging individual nodes. The larger gas tank shape was colored dark red, and the front shape bright red. In CorelDRAW 7 or 8 the blend for rounding the edges can be made by dragging with the Interactive Blend tool from one blend control object to the other,

TRACING ON THE FLY

When working with a 1-bit bitmap (black-and-white) imported into CorelDRAW, you can use the Freehand tool to do limited autotracing. If you first select the bitmap with the Pick tool, then choose the Freehand tool, the cursor becomes the autotrace right-pointing crosshairs. When you click on the bitmap, CorelDRAW scans to the right of the cursor until it comes to a color break and works down and around, tracing the bitmap image.

You can control the tracing options to adjust the quality and accuracy of the line. Press Ctrl-J (⌘-*J* on the Mac) to get to the settings for Autotrace Tracking, Corner Threshold, and Straight Line Threshold values. (In CorelDRAW 6, 7, or 8 you can also right-click [*Control-click*] over the Freehand tool in the toolbox to open the Properties dialog box to make these entries.) For each setting, the lower the number, the more closely the tracing sticks to the lines of the bitmap, but also the more nodes there will be and the more complex the line.

With a 1-bit bitmap selected, the Freehand tool goes into autotrace mode, and clicking inside an enclosed area results in a shape (shown here in pink) that you can fill and outline.

5

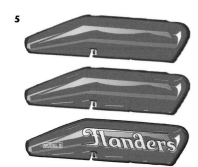

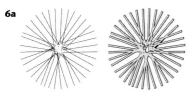

Highlight shapes drawn with the Freehand tool and Fountain-filled, gave the tank a shiny look (top), and adding white lines for gleams completed the highlighting. The logotype and other text were added.

6a

Each spoke was drawn with two clicks of the Freehand tool (left). Black and gray outlines, stacked up, gave form to the spokes.

6b

Stacked circles (left) were given Uniform, Radial, and even Conical fills (F11).

6c

Combining pairs of circles resulted in "donut" rings. The rings and spokes were repositioned slightly, and each gleam curve was drawn by duplicating a circle in place ("+"), giving it a white outline (F12), and dragging its node around the outside with the Shape tool to reduce it to an arc.

7

The bitmap layered over the drawing

setting the number of Steps in the Property bar. Hunt Shift-selected the two shapes and blended by opening the Blend roll-up (from the Effects menu), setting up a blend in 10 Steps, and clicking Apply.

5 Adding gleams and highlights. After all of the CorelTRACE-supplied shapes were colorized, Hunt used the Bezier tool to draw shapes to fill with lighter colors and Fountain fills to represent shiny reflections, and also drew light-colored lines to act as gleams. When you draw the gleams — or any other lines or shapes with outlines — turn on Scale With Image in the Outline Pen dialog box (F12) if you want to be able to resize the final art without adjusting line weight.

6 Making wheels. With a hand-drawn sketch for reference, Hunt drew the spokes in Wireframe mode. Then in Preview mode the lines were drag-selected with the Pick tool and assigned a 1.8-point black outline (F12). The set of lines was drag-selected with the Pick tool and duplicated ("+"), and the copy was given a 1-point gray outline.

To start the tire and rim, a circle was drawn with the Ellipse tool. Holding down the Ctrl and Shift keys (*Shift and ⌘ in Mac v.6, ⌘ and Option in v.8*) both constrains the shape and draws the circle outward from the starting point at the center of the spokes. With the Pick tool chosen, the initial circle was duplicated in place ("+") and downsized inside the original with the method described in step 4. This process was repeated to make several more circles. In Preview mode each circle was given an outline (set to Scale With Image) and a fill. Then the circles were Shift-selected in twos with the Pick tool and combined (Arrange, Combine) to make open rings. To give depth to the tire, some of the rings were nudged up slightly, and the spokes object was selected and moved in front of these (Arrange [Order], Bring To Front). White-outline, no-fill gleams with round end caps were added, and the parts of each wheel were grouped.

7 Aligning the bitmap. The scan that had been used for the Corel-TRACE was now laid on top of the color-filled shapes, to add the look of crisp, hand-drawn line work. To bring in the scan, choose File, Import and choose the original TIFF. In CorelDRAW 6, 7, or 8 click the X in the on-screen color palette to turn the white part of the TIFF transparent; in version 3, 4, or 5, it's transparent automatically.

Now work in Wireframe to match the bitmap to the CorelDRAW artwork. (For tips on viewing bitmaps, see "Bitmap Beauty" on page 36.) Use the Pick tool to move and scale the TIFF until the two kinds of artwork align. You can use the Nudge function, pressing the arrow keys to move the selected art in small steps. Preview the image (Shift-F9) to make sure everything is lined up correctly. Then choose Edit, Select All and group (Ctrl-G; ⌘-G) so nothing will get knocked out of line accidentally. *Now*

ADJUSTING THE NUDGE

To change the size of the steps for the Nudge, press Ctrl-J (⌘-J) to get to the dialog box where you can reset the Nudge distance.

Repeating Yourself

The potential for "medallions" — symmetrical, circular designs — is limitless when you use Corel-DRAW's Blend roll-up or the Rotate roll-up and the Repeat command. The four medallions on this page were created by repeating elements. In each case the element was selected with the Pick tool, and then clicked again with the Pick tool to display the center of rotation, which was dragged to where we wanted the center of the medallion to be. The shape was then turned with the Rotate roll-up with Apply To Duplicate selected, and then the operation was repeated around the circle (Ctrl-R; ⌘-R on the Mac).

A symbol from the Festive Symbols library was rotated at 45° and repeated. Shapes were Shift-selected and colored. The circle was made by Ctrl-Shift-dragging from the center (⌘-Shift-drag in Mac v.6, ⌘-Option drag in v.8).

An "f" was typed with the Text tool, converted to curves (Arrange, Convert to Curves), rotated at 60°, repeated, and combined (Arrange, Combine) to produce a lacy center. A red dot was added, rotated, and repeated.

*The **Flowr041** file from CorelDRAW's clip art collection was given a 51.43° duplication-and-rotation with the Rotate roll-up and repeated (Ctrl-R; ⌘-R on the Mac). Then a "v" from the Wood Ornaments typeface was added between two flowers, converted to curves (Arrange, Convert To Curves) and rotated at the same angle.*

A "stack" of three overlapping red circles was given a 45° rotation and repeated. Selecting all and choosing Arrange, Combine cut holes where the circles overlapped. A copy (+) was shrunk with the Pick tool, positioned between "arms," colored black, and rotated and repeated. Another copy of the medallion was added in the center. Small black circles were added, rotated, and repeated on top of the red arms. A green and a pink circle were added behind.

GETTING THE ANGLE RIGHT

To make medallions using the Rotate roll-up and the Repeat command (Ctrl-R; *⌘-R on the Mac*), you need to know the correct Angle Of Rotation setting to use for the number of "arms," or medallion sections, you want. The angle can be computed by dividing 360° by the total number of sections you want. Here are some example values:

Sections	Angle
3	120°
4	90°
5	72°
6	60°
7	51.43°
8	45°
9	40°
10	36°
11	32.72°
12	30°
13	27.69°

TUCKING THE LAST PETAL

When you make a "medallion" by blending or by repeating a rotation, if the "petals" overlap, you have some more work to do to get the last petal to look "tucked in" under the edge of the first. You can do this in versions 5 and later with the Trim command. It's a matter of selecting the "trimmer" first and then the "trimmee," and retaining Other Objects. The exact procedure varies a bit from one version of CorelDRAW to another; it's covered in more detail in "Cutting Holes" in Chapter 4. If your "petal" is a group, it will have to be ungrouped (Ctrl-U; *⌘-U on the Mac*) and dealt with as individual elements for trimming.

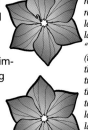

The petal was rotated and repeated, leaving the last petal "untucked" (top). Then this petal was trimmed with the first petal, to make the left edge of the last petal appear to be tucked behind.

Tom Graney specializes in creating clip-art libraries, and **Wheat Barn** was designed with that in mind. Graney usually starts with a pen-and-ink drawing, which he scans and turns into shapes using Corel-TRACE. He can then edit, simplify, and colorize this artwork in CorelDRAW to produce the stylized look he's after.

Because clip art is designed to be used at many different sizes, using varied outline weights is impractical, since the thick-and-thin, line-and-space effect can be distorted or lost when the artwork is scaled down. So Graney uses CorelTRACE's Outline method, which makes no-outline filled shapes, rather than the Centerline method, which draws lines, all the same thickness. With the Outline method, even the line work is traced as shapes, so the hand-drawn line quality is retained. Graney filled the "lines" with solid colors and the large shapes with Fountain fills.

A veteran clip-art creator, Graney is no stranger to shortcuts. The leaves in this image came from the "Plants" collection in the Symbol sets supplied with the CorelDRAW program. The grass symbol was flipped, duplicated, resized, and in some cases broken into individual leaves. All the leaves were then selected and welded together (Arrange, Weld in versions 4, 5, 6, 7, and 8) so they could be given a single Fountain fill.

The rows of grains in the wheat stalk were made by drawing one grain, duplicating it, blending to make one column, flipping and

mirroring the blend and adding smaller grains at the top. By grouping a stalk with the grain objects, Graney could warp the entire seed head with CorelDRAW's Envelope, using the Unconstrained mode for the greatest flexibility in changing the shape.

When he had finished moving and stretching the wheat, Graney ungrouped the objects and welded all the stalks together with some more leaves of grass to make one big object. This shape was then given a single Fountain fill, which contrasted with the wheat grains.

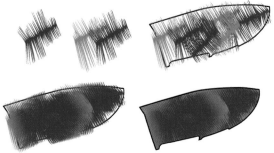

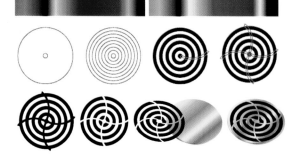

Reed Fisher was contracted by a bold entrepreneur to help realize a wild new *Supercomputer* design. It was Fisher's job to create a realistic representation of the gold-plated keyboard, the fine polished-wood finish, and the leather-padded palm rest.

First he scanned and imported a photo of a new ergonomically designed keyboard, which he could use as a tracing template to set up the correct angles for the illustration. Then he painstakingly traced the outline of the keyboard and every key and character with the Bezier tool. He started with large black-filled shapes that would show through between the light-colored key tops and slightly darker sides, to form the shadows and the edges of the keys. This method gave a slightly non-uniform, realistic look that simply outlining the keys wouldn't have achieved.

Using additional photos of gold-plated objects for reference, Fisher employed a variety of CorelDRAW fill techniques to simulate materials. Custom Linear Fountain fills in several color families add to the gold and brass sheen on the computer's edges and speaker grilles. For the wood, Fisher used a technique he learned from an article by Barry Meyer in *Corel* magazine (see "Showing Motion" in Chapter 5), which involves PowerClipping objects into a container. He started by drawing one "spiky" object, selected it with the Pick tool and duplicated it by pressing "+" on the numeric keypad. He filled the two objects with slightly different shades of

reddish brown, and used CorelDRAW's Blend to produce 8 intermediate Steps, making a feathery shape. He built two more similar blends, and by overlaying the three on a slightly darker background shape he achieved the warm, glowing look he wanted for the wood grain. Then he used the PowerClip (available in versions 5, 6, 7, and 8) to mask the blends into the background shape.

For the stitching on the leather, Fisher used a tan outline with a duplicate brown dashed line on top of it, about one-third the line weight of the original, drawn with round Corners, Line Caps, and Nib Shape, set in the Outline Pen dialog box (F12). Blends were made for the subtle highlights on the leather (a method is described in "Modelling with Blends" in Chapter 3) and the soft drop shadow under the computer (drop shadows are detailed in Chapter 6).

Making a speaker grille was an exercise in positive and negative space. It started as two concentric circles, which were Blended in 7 steps. The blend was separated and ungrouped, then combined and filled with black. A four-armed curved shape was then welded to this set of rings. The new shape was broken apart, the outer ring deleted, and the remaining parts combined. The result was set on top of a Fountain-filled circle with a Fountain-filled edge shape, and all shapes were squashed vertically. White highlights were added, and this grille was duplicated and downsized to make the smaller one.

"Good evening, Mrs. Ferguson. I need some milk."

"I didn't choose to be a pig. It just happened."

Paul Kantorek's whimsical cartoons appear in a variety of North American and European newspapers, including *The Globe and Mail, The National Enquirer,* and *Stern.* After hand-sketching an idea, Kantorek inks the drawings for easy scanning and tracing with CorelTRACE in Outline mode, which produces a stack of black and white shapes. He imports the trace into CorelDRAW, where he not only colorizes the white parts, but also draws backgrounds, props, and shadows with the Bezier tool, Freehand tool, and shape tools. In Wireframe mode you can see which elements were first drawn in ink and traced (the heavier-looking "double-line" shapes), and which were created within CorelDRAW (the "lighter-weight" single-line shapes).

In "**Good evening, Mrs. Ferguson**" he created the ink drawings as the separate pieces shown here, for more flexibility in assembling them in CorelDRAW.

Kantorek colors his characters to look almost luminous. For example, the Radial Fountain fills (F11) used for the dog and pig in "**I didn't choose to be a pig**" make the animals appear to be lit from within, with colors expanding from very light at the "heart" to darker pastels at the edges.

In areas where Kantorek's hand-drawn lines don't fully enclose a shape, CorelTRACE produces no white-filled object. So in "**Mice**," for example, where openings above the eyeball and on the arm prevented white shapes from being formed, Kantorek used the black line work as a guide for drawing color-filled, no-outline shapes, as shown below. By creating these shapes on top of the black line work, he can make sure the color-filled shapes overlap the black outline shapes, so that when he sends the colored

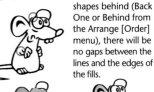

shapes behind (Back One or Behind from the Arrange [Order] menu), there will be no gaps between the lines and the edges of the fills.

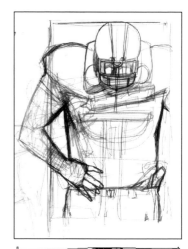

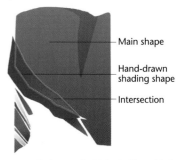

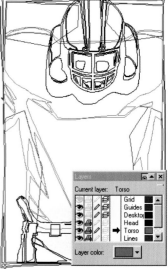

Main shape

Hand-drawn
shading shape

Intersection

Cecil Rice created this burly *Football Player on Scale* for an investment firm's annual report. Starting with a pencil sketch, he developed ink drawings of the player and scale, creating each piece individually to keep his options open. The drawings were scanned and further modified in Corel PHOTO-PAINT: Rice painted out sections of the artwork, dividing the football player into several files. Each of these separate files was then traced with CorelTRACE independently in Outline mode. The head and pelvis pieces were made separate from the torso, and also from the background pieces. (For tips on

using CorelTRACE, see "Updating a Logo" earlier in this chapter.)

When Rice imported each of the tracings into CorelDRAW, he created a new layer for it and assigned the layers different colors. That way it was easy to see in Wireframe mode which section of the illustration the overlapping shapes belonged to. By locking layers he could adjust proportions of one part of the football player — making the torso taller, for instance — without stretching the whole illustration.

The shapes were filled with Uniform and Fountain fills from a palette of custom colors chosen to be used throughout the report. To

suggest shadows and add depth, Rice added shading shapes. For each shaded area he drew an approximate shape, larger than he needed, and then used the Arrange, Intersection command to trim away excess so its edges exactly matched those of its main shape. The resulting piece was made a darker shade by adding more black in the Uniform Fill dialog box (Shift-F11).

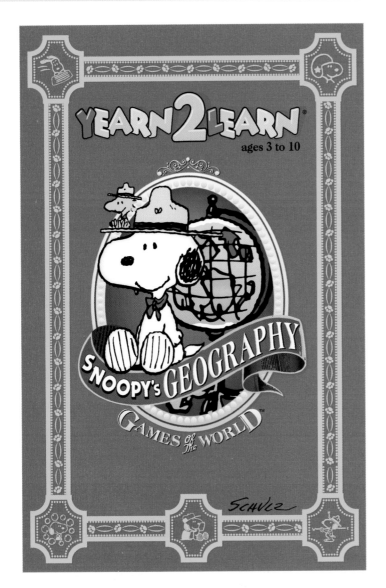

In his packaging design for the *Yearn 2 Learn* software featuring Charles Schulz's Snoopy character, **Joe King** started with pen-and-ink drawings supplied by the client. He scanned and traced the pieces in Outline mode in CorelTRACE and then imported them into CorelDRAW. (CorelTRACE tips are provided at the beginning of this chapter and in "Updating a Logo.) The tracing of the central Snoopy figure was ungrouped so the separate objects could be selected and colored individually with Outline Pen styles and Uniform or Fountain fills. A 200-step blend between a large dark red circle and a small red copy in its center added depth to the area behind the imported graphics.

The process of making the small Snoopy icons used as "medallions" on the border is described in "Building Medallions" earlier in this chapter.

The development of the "Yearn 2 Learn" title is shown above right. Duplicate color-filled letter shapes were layered over shapes with thick black outlines. Then highlights were added by drawing short, straight lines with rounded ends and corners, setting round Corners and Line Caps in the Outline Pen dialog box (F12). This rounded look matched the highlights to the soft-cornered look of the lettering. Grouping each letter shape, its black outline piece, and its highlights made it easy to overlap the letters.

A slightly skewed copy of the lettering, filled with a color made by adding 30% black to the background color, made a subtle shadow for added emphasis. King selected the shadow letters with the Pick tool, King clicked with the Pick again to get the rotation and skew handles on the highlight box, and dragged the top center handle to the right to move the tops of the objects while the bottoms stayed rooted in their original positions. He added a thicker outline to the shadow pieces in the same color as the fill.

C **ecil Rice** created an idealized "traditional building" for the cover of a suspense novel *The System.* He built the design in symmetrical halves, completing one whole side, then duplicating it and flipping the copy with the Scale & Mirror roll-up (Alt-F9 in all but v.3; *Option-F9 on the Mac).* ▶ *To make a mirrored copy, with your object selected and the Scale & Mirror roll-up open, click the Horizontal Mirror button, then Apply To Duplicate.*

Rice used blend groups and Fountain fills to emphasize the central light source, and to give each half of the building a unique

coloring. All blends and fills go from dark on the outside to a lighter center color.

To further enhance the sense of drama created with the central lighting, Rice exported the image from CorelDRAW (File, Export) as an RGB 300 dpi TIFF, and then altered the bitmap in Corel PHOTO-PAINT, Using the Artistic, Vignette feature. ▶ *In versions 7 and 8, you can convert the image to a bitmap and apply the vignette effect without leaving CorelDRAW: Select your objects, then convert them to a bitmap with the Convert To Bitmap option from the Bitmaps menu. Then, select the bitmap and choose Vignette from the Artistic effects fly-out,*

also from the Bitmaps menu. From the Vignette dialog (below) you can change things such as the Color and Shape of the effect. Click the Preview or eye button to see the effect, and click OK to apply it.

Doctor Doolittle At Home

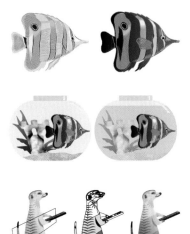

When **Stephen Arscott** created his whimsical _Dr. Doolittle poster_, he started out with a clear idea of what he wanted: a sense of drama and depth, with the television as a strong lighting source and characters assembled in front of it in profile. He found many of the animals for his TV viewing audience in the CorelDRAW clip-art library. He imported these files and ungrouped them or broke apart combined objects as necessary, and then recolored them.

Once the animals were copied and pasted into the large poster file, Arscott worked with their new colors to develop Fountain fills for the shading. Arscott couldn't find all of the animals he wanted as clip art, so he created many of them himself using the Freehand tool, Linear Fountain fills and blends, shading from dark on the left to bright colors on the right, consistent with

the single light source of the glowing television. He added life and depth with extra shapes for subtle shading.

Arscott also created some of the animals by sketching on paper first, then scanning and tracing the illustration with CorelTRACE in Centerline mode to make simple shapes. He imported these files into CorelDRAW, colored them, and added detail.

Arscott painstakingly recolored the fish, from the Fish clip-art library, and used a Transparency Lens on the fishbowl to give the colors a blue cast.

A little meercat with remote control parodies the lookout that's always on alert outside a meercat colony. The shaded areas on the meercat were created with the Intersect command (available in versions 5 and later) to create bands that could be given darker tones.

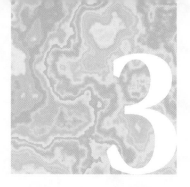

COLORING

Solid colors, Fountain fills, and blended shapes add dimension and lighting to this illustration. (See the illustrations on pages 79 and 81 for descriptions of the various fills used.)

DAVIS

Coloring objects can transform them from simple flat shapes into dimensional objects, even without the use of "color" per se. The Uniform and Fountain fills used in this product illustration help add dimension and surface characteristics even though the artist used only black, white, and shades of gray. (This illustration is described more fully in the Gallery at the end of Chapter 5.)

SHELASKY

BRIGHT OR SUBDUED, MONOTONE OR MULTIHUED, *color* is one of the most important qualities of an illustration or page design when it comes to evoking a response from the viewer. In CorelDRAW "coloring" means choosing from a wide variety of *outline* and *fill* options, and sometimes it means creating color change by *blending* from one color-filled shape to another or by *importing* a photographic image and using it to color an object.

An **outline** adds color, line width, and other characteristics to a path. Any path, closed or open, can have an outline. Techniques for applying outlines are described in the "Outlines" section later in this chapter and in examples presented throughout the book.

The **fill** is the coloring that's contained inside a closed path. It can be a solid (or Uniform) color, a multicolor gradient (or Fountain) or one of several kinds of patterns. You'll find information about specific techniques for applying fills in "Assigning Colors" on page 75 and in "Fills" on page 78, also in the description of James Avanzo's use of pattern fills in "Patterning" on page 96, and in many other examples presented in the book.

In CorelDRAW as in other object-oriented programs, because colors are *assigned to objects* as outlines and fills rather than painted one pixel at a time, it's easy to assign new characteristics. With one quick command you can change the color of an outline or fill, so you can experiment with new color ways to your heart's content as you develop a design or adapt artwork for several uses. And you can assign and tweak outline and fill characteristics *independently* of each other, which adds flexibility — you can modify one without changing the other.

Blending can be used for color transitions that are more complex than the geometric color gradients of Fountain fills. Coloring with blends can be seen in the trees in the illustration at the left and in "Modelling with Blends" and "Building a Shine" later in this chapter. In addition, by blending along a path, you can make "patterned outlines" as described in "Patterned Lines" on page 77 and "Repeating Yourself" on page 118.

CorelDRAW offers the opportunity to **import** photographs and other complex visual material in order to color shapes. One such technique was used in the *Men From Earth* logo described in "Masking To Make a Logo" in Chapter 2.

COLOR BASICS

Every version of CorelDRAW gives you several ways to make colors, to assemble them in palettes, and to choose colors from existing palettes. The color interface varies from version to version, and you'll need to get the particulars from the manual or on-screen Help for the version you use. But there are some basic ways of looking at color that should be helpful no matter what version you use.

Color Composition

CorelDRAW lets you mix color using several different *color models*. A color model is a system for formulating color from a set of basic components — either colored lights, colored inks, or the physical properties of light, like wave length (hue) and wave amplitude (brightness). (Don't worry if physics isn't your favorite pastime — CorelDRAW has put all those properties into relatively easy-to-use dialog boxes.)

The color models available in the various versions of CorelDRAW include RGB, CMY/CMYK, HLS/HSB, L*a*b, and YIQ, Grayscale, and Registration Color. Each color model has a *gamut*, or range of colors it can produce. The gamuts of the various color models overlap a great deal but not completely.

- In the **RGB model,** colors are made by mixing the three primary colors of light (red, green, and blue). When all three primaries are mixed together at full intensity (settings of 255), white light is produced. (*Primary colors* in a color model are the "basics" from which any other color in the model's gamut can be mixed.)

- The **CMY, CMYK,** and **CMYK255 models** represent colors as mixtures of three primary colors of ink (cyan, magenta, and yellow) used in the printing method most commonly used for

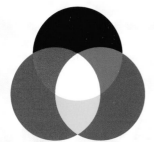

In the RGB color model, red, green, and blue light are combined at different intensities to make all the other colors. When all three primaries are mixed at full intensity, white light is produced.

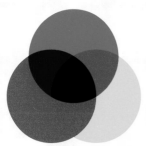

In process color printing, colors can be "mixed" on the page by overlaying cyan, yellow, and magenta inks. Black ink is usually added to the mix to make dark colors look crisper. These four colors are the basis for the CMYK color model.

If you're experienced with color mixing for print, or if you have a printed color reference, you can use the CMYK interface for specifying a color by entering ink percentages to get the specific mix you want.

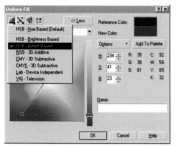

For many artists, specifying color by hue, saturation, and value is intuitive: In CorelDRAW 8's color interface, first choose HSB - Wheel-Based from the Color Viewer list. Choose a hue family by position on the color wheel (or a number from 0 to 360 degrees), then decide whether to decrease its purity (saturation) to make it more neutral, and finally make it lighter or darker. (Saturation and brightness can be chosen as percentages between 0 and 100.)

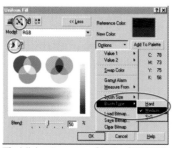

The Mixing Area, opened in CorelDRAW 8 by choosing Mixing Area from the Mixer button's pop-out menu, offers an eyedropper for sampling color. It also has brushes in three different sizes and "hardnesses" for applying the new color in a uniform thickness or in a "spray" like an airbrush. As the Blend setting is decreased, more of the color you're painting with (and less of the color you're painting over) is used to mix the color.

books, magazines, and other color printed materials. Black ink (referred to as "K" rather than "B" so you won't mistake it for blue) is added in the CMYK models as a more efficient way to darken colors — it takes less black ink to darken a color than if you had to add enough cyan, magenta, and yellow inks together to get a similar result. And anyway, the CMY mixture can actually produce a muddy dark brown rather than a crisp black. In the CMYK model, colors can be specified as 0 to 100 percent cover of the paper by each of the four colors of ink. In the CMY and CMYK255 models, used to mix colors for desktop three- and four-color printers respectively, settings from 0 to 255 can be specified.

(The gamuts of the RGB and CMYK color models are not the same. There are some colors that can be produced in the RGB model — they look brilliant on-screen — but that can't be reproduced in the CMYK model — when you try to print them they look really dull.)

- The **HLS** and **HSB models** are two methods of using the three fundamental properties of light — *hue, saturation,* and *value* to specify a color (value is also called lightness or brightness). On a practical level, without getting into physics, **hue** can be thought of as the section of the color wheel that a color comes from. We tend to use hue in naming colors and color families, such as "green," "red," or "purple." **Saturation** refers to whether a color is intense and vibrant (saturated) or gray and neutral (not saturated). **Value** is the lightness or darkness of a color, with white being the lightest and black the darkest.

- The **L*a*b** and **YIQ color models** use brightness (*L* or *Y*) and two color axes (*a* and *b* or *I* and *Q*) to specify color components. YIQ is a color model used for television. L*a*b is a color model whose gamut includes all the colors of both the RGB and CMYK color models.

- **Grayscale** is a model that includes only brightness variations. In effect, in the Grayscale model, saturation is always 0, so hue makes no difference. Grays can be specified from 0 (black) to 255 (white). Some artists start most of their illustrations in Grayscale in order to work out the lighting and tonality before adding color.

- The **Registration Color model** includes only one choice. You can assign CorelDRAW's Registration Color to make sure that specially designed objects known as registration marks can be precisely aligned when the printing plates are put on the press to print the job. When you use Registration Color, CorelDRAW automatically mixes a color that includes 100% of every ink that appears in the artwork, so when color separations are made, the mark appears on the printing plate for each ink color and the plates can be aligned by aligning the marks.

To create a graphic that's "color-coordinated" with a photo, save an 8-bit or a 24-bit photo in uncompressed .bmp format, then load it into the Mixing Area, and sample and save colors from it to make a custom palette.

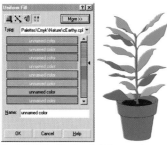

By default the Custom Palette area shows CorelDRAW's own Uniform Fills palette. But you can open a specially formulated thematic color scheme. The CMYK version of the Earthy palette from CorelDRAW 8's Palettes is shown here.

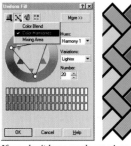

If you don't have much experience putting together color palettes, CorelDRAW 8's Color Harmonies interface can help you choose pleasing color schemes. Open it by choosing from the list of Mixers in the Uniform Fill or Outline Pen dialog box or other color interfaces.

CONVERTING TO CMYK

When you create a CorelDRAW file, you may mix your colors using RGB values, or pick from a fixed palette like the Pantone Matching System, and then find out later that you need to print in process inks — CMYK. Failing to convert from one color system to another can cause output problems. To get specific instructions for how to ensure that all the colors are converted to CMYK, consult the "Color" and "Printing" topics of the on-screen Help for your particular version of CorelDRAW.

Making Colors

In any of the CorelDRAW versions from 3 onward, you can get to the full range of the program's color-making options for Uniform fills (solid-colors) by pressing Shift-F11 to open the Uniform Fill dialog box. Likewise, you can press F12 to open the Outline Color dialog with all the options for making outlines. You can also get to these full-featured color-making interfaces by choosing More/Other(s) whenever a palette of colors is offered in any dialog box.

When it comes to specifying colors, one way is to use a scientific approach, numerically specifying the amount of each color component you want. For instance, for the RGB model, you can type any value between 0 and 255 for the amount of Red, Green, or Blue light you want in your color. Or in the CMYK model, type in the amount of each ink as a percentage, from 0 to 100.

If you'd rather work more intuitively, you can mix colors completely by eye — by clicking to choose a color or by using the expertise built into CorelDRAW's color interface to choose sets of colors that work well together, or even by sampling and "painting" to mix a color. This works especially well if you're designing something that will be seen on-screen. For print, it's better to use a printed reference (see "Getting the Color You Expect" on page 74).

Making Palettes

When you've made a color, you can save it by adding it to the current palette. Choose Add Color To Palette from the pop-out Palette list in the color interface where you've created the color — for instance, in the Uniform Fill dialog box (Shift-F11), the Outline

PALETTE CONSISTENCY

If you've made an illustration and you want to make others whose colors match those in the first one — like a series of graphs, for instance — you can use CorelDRAW 8's New Palette From Document (or New Palette From Selection) command from the Tools menu. With it you can capture, name, and save the palette. Then you can use the Palette Editor (also found under Tools) to Sort the colors into the order you like. Finally, to display your new color set as a palette, choose View, Color Palette, Load Palette, pick your named palette, and click the X in the upper right corner of the Palettes list to close it.

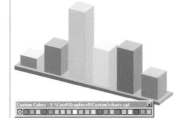

In CorelDRAW 8 you can bring up the Fixed palettes by clicking the icon that looks like a swatchbook.

As you drag a color from the on-screen palette in CorelDRAW 7 or 8, an interactive drag-and-drop cursor signals when you will change the outline (left), and when the fill (right), if you release the mouse button.

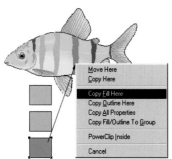

In CorelDRAW 7 or 8 you can copy an outline or fill simply by holding down the right mouse button (or the Control key on the Mac) as you drag and drop the item whose properties you want to copy (the blue-filled rectangle here) over the other object (the stripe on the fish).

QUICK CHANGE

In CorelDRAW 8 you can change the outline or fill color of a selected object just by double-clicking a swatch on the Status bar to open the Outline Pen dialog box or the appropriate Fill dialog.

Pen dialog box (F12), or the Color roll-up, available in some versions of CorelDRAW by choosing from the Fill tool fly-out. In the same place where you find the Add Color option, you'll also find choices for deleting colors from a palette. If you don't plan to use them all, deleting makes the palette smaller and thus easier to manage on-screen. And in some versions you can replace one of the palette colors with the one you've mixed.

The steps involved in creating a palette, adding colors, and saving the palette differ from version to version. For more information about saving colors and making palettes in the version you're using, check the on-screen Help topic "Color palettes."

Using Fixed Palettes

In addition to the palettes you can load, CorelDRAW provides a set of palettes whose colors are standardized and restricted to a particular system of specialized printing inks, such as the Pantone Matching System, Focoltone Colors, or TruMatch Colors. These palettes are helpful for two-color print jobs — for instance, if you want to print in greenish-blue and black and you don't want to pay for a four-color print job. They are also good for specifying exact, standard colors. For example, some companies specify a particular Pantone color for use whenever their logos will appear in print; you'll find an example on page 128.

Besides the custom ink palettes found in earlier versions, Corel-DRAW 8's fixed palettes also includes the Netscape Navigator color set. By choosing exclusively from this palette, you can be sure that the colors in artwork prepared for display on the Internet won't be changed by the Netscape browser when the art is downloaded to a web-site visitor's computer. (You'll find more about using Corel-DRAW to develop art for the web in Chapter 7.)

GETTING THE COLOR YOU EXPECT

Even with the latest versions of CorelDRAW — and all the other popular graphics programs, as well — the color you see on-screen is a little different from the color that you'll see when your artwork is printed. Various versions of CorelDRAW have different ways of helping you compensate for these differences. For instance, some versions try to show you on-screen the closest CMYK-printable color to the one you've chosen from a different color model. If you know the characteristics of your display monitor and of the printer or printing system you'll be using for output, CorelDRAW 8 can be set to display color on-screen that's closer to the color that will print. Nevertheless, regardless of which version of the program you use, the best way to get predictable color is to use a printed reference such as the *PostScript Process Color Guide,* for colors mixed as percentages of CMYK inks, published by Agfa Prepress Education Resources (800-395-7007; www.agfadirect.com) or the *Pantone Color Formula Guide* or *Pantone Solid To Process Guide* for using custom solid Pantone inks or for finding the closest achievable CMYK simulation of Pantone colors (888-726-8663; www.pantone.com).

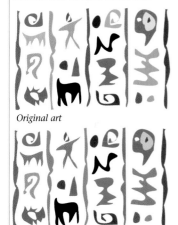
ASSIGNING COLORS

As in everything else you do in CorelDRAW, there are several ways to assign outline characteristics. These topics are covered in detail in the "Outlines" and "Fills" sections that follow, but here are three quick ways to assign colors:

- If you want to **assign a color from the current palette,** clicking (for a fill) or right-clicking (for an outline) on one of the color squares in the on-screen palette (may be the quickest and most accurate way to do it (*Control-click on the Mac*).

- If you want to **match the outline or fill** of an existing object, you can copy this property by selecting the object whose properties you want to change and then choosing Edit, Copy Properties [or Style] From. In version 7 or 8 you can just right-click the object you want to color. When the Copy Properties/Style dialog box appears, you can specify which properties you want to copy, then click OK, and use the thick arrow to click the object you want to copy from.

- In CorelDRAW 7 or 8 you can use the **Color Styles** feature to capture the colors in a specific file or section of a file by drag-selecting objects with the Pick tool and then choosing Layout, Color Styles and clicking on the Auto Create Color Styles button.

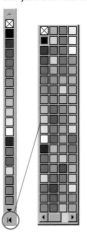

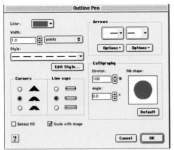

The Outline Pen dialog, opened by pressing F12, offers control of all aspects of an outline, including the ability to assign any line width you want.

When you click OK in the Automatically Create Color Styles dialog box, CorelDRAW will create an on-screen "palette" of **parent colors** (hues) and **child colors** (shades and tones of the parent hues). You can display swatches of the parent colors by clicking the "+" symbol next to the name of the file in the Styles roll-up, and you can display any child colors by clicking the "+" next to the name of a parent color.

The color swatches can be dragged-and-dropped, just like the colors in the on-screen palette. The colors can also be modified or added to the on-screen palette by right-clicking the swatch and choosing Edit Color or Add To Custom Palette from the pop-out menu. Or choose Create Shades to make a set of tints (intermediate tones between the color and white) of a selected parent or child color.

OUTLINES

The Outline Pen dialog box (F12) lets you control all of the outline characteristics of a selected path.

- To change the **line weight,** type in the width you want or use the up or down arrow next to the entry.

- To change the **color,** click the Color swatch to open the palette; click the color you want or click the Other/More button for additional color options.

- To make a **dashed line,** choose from the Style menu. In version 7 or 8 you can choose Edit Style to easily create your own dash pattern.

- To sharpen or round the **corners** of a path, use the Corners option. The first option results in pointy corners. If you use this option, you need to consider the Miter Limit setting (see "Blending an Escape" in Chapter 2).

- To change how the **ends of a line** will look, you can choose from three kinds of Line Caps or a variety of Arrows, both heads and "tails." You can design your own arrows by pressing the Options button for each end of the line. Line Caps show up better on thick lines than on thin ones. And of course, Line Caps and Arrows won't show up at all if assigned to a closed path — only an open one.

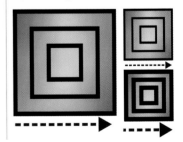

The Behind Fill option in the Outline Pen dialog (F12) hides the inside half of the line width, as if it were tucked behind the fill. This option can be useful for outlining type and other objects with narrow parts that would be distorted by a line that extended into the fill. Here are two versions of the same artwork, the bottom one outlined with Behind Fill enabled.

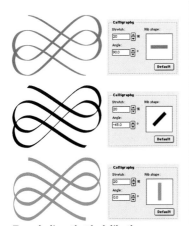

To make lines that look like they were drawn with a calligraphy pen, decrease the Stretch value and change the Angle in the Calligraphy section of Outline Pen dialog box.

- To give your lines the ribbon-like look of calligraphy, change the settings in the Calligraphy section.

Variable-Width Lines

Another way to build variability into line width, besides adjusting the Calligraphy settings in the Outline Pen dialog, is to use the Natural Pen tool in versions 7 and 8 or the Powerline (in versions 4, 5, and 6). Instead of actually drawing lines, these tools draw closed, fillable shapes that *look like* variable-width lines. The Natural Pen tool has four settings: to draw a Fixed-width line, to change line width in response to Pressure, or in response to stroke direction (Calligraphy mode), or to produce a Preset kind of shape. Both the Natural Pen and Powerlines, which can undergo more sophisticated editing than the shapes produced with the Natural Pen, are discussed in "Pieces and Power-Lines for Posters" in Chapter 4.

Layered or Blended Lines

By using CorelDRAW's basic Outline Pen characteristics on lines that are stacked on top of each other, or blended, you can achieve the look of roadmaps,

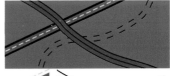

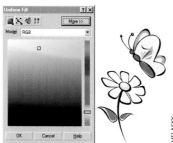

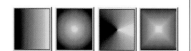

Clicking the on-screen color palette is a quick way to assign a Uniform Fill color to a selected object. You can then modify the chosen color from the Uniform Fill dialog (Shift-F11) by dragging the tiny square cursor. Moving the cursor up lightens the color and moving it left reduces the saturation, resulting in softer colors, as in this spot illustration.

There are four basic Types of Fountain fills. Left to right, they are Linear and Radial (found in all versions), Conical (found in versions 4 and later), and Square (found in versions 5 and later).

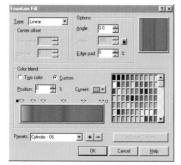

The four Types of Fountain fills are all available from the Fountain Fill dialog box (F11). They can be applied as simple Two-Color fills like the gold examples above or as Custom Fountain fills as shown here.

neon, patterned borders, and other complex line effects. Some examples are provided in the "Patterned Lines" tip on page 77 and in "Repeating Yourself" on page 118.

FILLS

If a path is closed, with ends that meet to make an enclosed shape, it can be given a fill as well as an outline. Closed shapes can be filled with flat color, gradients, textures, or patterns.

A **Uniform fill** colors an object with a single color. You can apply a Uniform fill by clicking on a color square in the on-screen palette or choosing or mixing a color in the Uniform fills dialog box (Shift-F11).

Fountain fills provide a way to fill shapes with smoothly changing colors. In the latest versions of the program a Fountain fill can be anything from a simple transition between Two Colors to a Custom multicolor transition, and the gradient can be shaped as any of four Types, chosen from the Fountain Fill dialog box: Linear, Radial, Conical, or Square (not all available in all versions).

CorelDRAW's Fountain Fill dialog box, especially in the latest versions, is worth exploring. Here are some of the ways you can modify a Fountain fill:

- For Linear, Conical, and Square fills you can set the Edge Pad to determine how much solid color there is before the color change starts to occur.

- For Two Color Fountain fills, you can move the Midpoint to affect how fast the color change happens once it starts.

- The maximum setting of 256 Steps ensures the smoothest color transitions.

- Changing the Angle setting rotates the gradient — counterclockwise for positive settings, clockwise for negative settings. (For Linear fills you can also change the angle by dragging in the preview square.

- For Radial, Conical, and Square fills you can offset the center of the Fountain fill by changing the Horizontal or Vertical setting or by dragging in the preview square.

- For Custom Fountain fills you can sometimes save time by choosing from the Presets list of fills. Either use an already

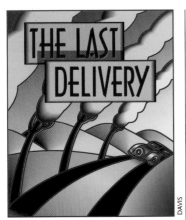

THE LAST DELIVERY

DAVIS

Two-Color and Custom Fountain fills serve well to render simple shapes and smooth surfaces. The hills in the background were colored with Conical fills, the center of the road and most of the parts of the car with Linear fills, the hill in the foreground with a Radial fill, and the boxes that hold the type with Square fills.

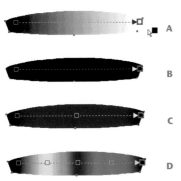

The Interactive Fill tool in CorelDRAW 7 and 8 makes it easy to create a multicolor Custom Fountain fill. Drag across the shape to start a Fountain fill (A). Then drag colors from the on-screen palette to change the starting or ending color (B), and drop colors between (C, D).

designed Fountain "as is," or modify it (as described below) by adding more colors or moving its existing control points. (To make it easier to choose a Preset, you can refer to the printed examples in the "Fountain Fill Presets" catalog on page 84.)

- To add a color to a Custom Fountain fill, double-click above the color bar to create a control point where you want the new color to be and then choose the color you want there.

- To change any color in a Custom Fountain, including the start or end color, click on its control point to select it and then choose a new color.

- To change the rate at which a color change happens, slide the control points for those two colors.

Texture fills are mathematically generated color bitmaps. The computations work on properties like color, light direction, and number of spots, all of which you can specify in the Texture Fill dialog box, opened by choosing the Texture icon on the Fill tool's fly-out in the Toolbox. You can experiment with Texture fills by unlocking and changing any of the parameters offered in the Texture fill dialog box. Just click a padlock icon to unlock it, make your changes, and click the Preview button to see the new result. If you lock all settings except Texture #, each time you change the number you'll see one of thousands of preset variations on that particular Texture's math.

Like CorelDRAW's other kinds of fills, a Texture fill maintains a link to its dialog box, so you can edit the color of a Texture-filled object by selecting it and choosing the Texture fill icon from the Fill tool's fly-out. When you've finished editing, click OK to complete the color change.

Texture fills are often ignored because people don't know how to get predictable, nonpixelated results in their printed output. But they're too good to ignore, even if the color is the only setting you

For most Fountain fills you'll want smooth color transitions. But on the rare occasion when you might want a fill consisting of sharply defined stripes, you can make it by using two color control points for each color band you want — one control point where the color band starts and one where it ends. The start point for each new color band will overlap the endpoint for the previous band.

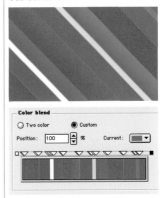

The Custom striped fill was constructed in the Color Blend section of the Fountain Fill dialog box (F11), and the fill was angled by dragging in the preview window of the Options section in the upper right corner of the box.

Texture fills can add surface texture and dimension. Here the Surfaces texture from the Styles library was recolored with light and dark color ways to suggest brick and stucco surfaces, in shadow and in direct light. A gridwork of solid lines was laid on top of large Texture-filled objects to create the look of stacked brick construction.

SPEEDY SPECIAL FILLS

In CorelDRAW 7 and 8, double-clicking the Fill tool in the toolbox opens the Special Fill roll-up, where you can choose a Fountain, Texture, or Pattern fill.

change in the Texture Fills dialog box. A printed record of what the default Texture fills look like is provided in "Texture Fills" on page 86, and "Good-Looking Texture Fills" (below) provides a short tutorial in getting the resolution right. The description of Rémi Forcier's "Steel" in the Gallery at the end of this chapter also gives pointers on resolution.

In CorelDRAW 8 Texture fills can be applied as repeating tiles. For tiling and other techniques for using Texture fills, check the tips in "Texture Fills" on page 86.

GOOD-LOOKING TEXTURE FILLS

Using a Texture fill involves making sure you have just enough bitmap color information (or resolution) for it to look good when it's printed, but no more. That's because if the resolution is too low, the artwork looks pixelated when it's printed — the individual square dots that make up the picture show up, so the texture or image doesn't look smooth and continuous. On the other hand, the higher the resolution, the bigger the file.

For Texture fills the printed resolution and file size are controlled with the Bitmap Resolution setting and the Maximum Tile Width setting, both in the Texture Fill Options dialog box, opened by choosing the Texture fill icon from the Fill tool's pop-out palette and then clicking the Options button:

- The Bitmap Resolution should be set at 1.5 to 2 times the halftone line screen at which the artwork will be printed; for Texture fills with soft color transitions, 1.5 will work fine; but if the fill has sharp color breaks, use 2. So, for instance, if the art will be printed at 150 lines per inch, the Bitmap Resolution should be set somewhere between 225 and 300 dpi.

- The Maximum Tile Width should be set to a number that's at least as big as the Bitmap Resolution times the length or the width, whichever is bigger, of the Texture-filled object when it's printed. So, for instance, an object whose bounding box is 4 x 5 inches, filled with a sharp-edged Texture and printed at 150 lines per inch, would require a setting of at least 300 x 5 = 1500. In the Maximum Tile Width list there's only one setting that's at least as big as 1500 — the 2049 setting — so you would choose that one. (Note that if the Bitmap Resolution is high enough and the object is big enough, it's easy to get a number bigger than 2049, in which case the texture fill can look fuzzy or pixelated when it's printed.)

CUSTOM TEXTURE FILLS

If you modify a Texture fill and want to save it so you can use it again, click the "+" button in the Texture Fills dialog box, choose a library to add it to from the Library Name list, or create your own new library name by typing it in the Library Name dialog box, and click OK. (You can't save back to the Styles library, which is write-protected. So to save a texture you've modified from this library, select another library to save to, or start a new one.)

You could also start a new library to make a smaller collection of CorelDRAW's standard Texture fills that you want to have handy. To save time and get a better look, you can refer to the "Texture Fills" section, starting on page 86, to pick the ones you want.

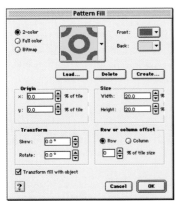

The Pattern dialog box presents 2-Color fills in black and white. But you can choose any two colors for the foreground (Front) and background (Back) colors.

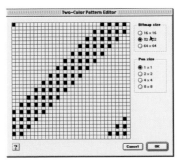

Some 2-Color patterns can be modified by choosing the pattern you want to start with, clicking the Create button, and changing the dot pattern that appears in the gridwork of the Two-Color Pattern Editor. In other cases the pattern doesn't appear in the grid when you click the Create button. If you want to edit one of these, you can use the grid to reconstruct it from scratch.

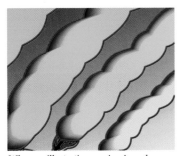

When an illustration requires irregular shapes with complex modeling, Corel-DRAW's Blend function is useful. Each of these trees (see the full illustration on page 79) was rounded by blending from a color-filled top shape to a darker, slightly offset larger copy behind it.

A **Pattern fill** repeats to fill the object you assign it to. Open the Pattern Fill dialog by choosing the checkerboard icon from the Fill tool's fly-out. Then use one of the 2-Color or Full Color patterns, or create your own, as described in "Patterning" on page 96.

PostScript fills, chosen from the Fill tool's fly-out in the Toolbox, are precisely repeating geometric patterns. In CorelDRAW 6 and later you can see what the patterns look like by clicking Preview Fill in the PostScript Texture dialog box that opens when you choose the tool. These specialized fills are designed for printing on PostScript-based output devices. They won't look right on-screen (except in the Enhanced preview in versions 7 and 8), and they won't print properly if a Corel-DRAW file is output to a non-PostScript-based desktop printer. Some artists have reported output trouble even on PostScript-based printers and imagesetters. However, if you export the file or selected objects in EPS format and then convert that file to a bitmap of appropriate resolution for your print job, PostScript is no longer required. A catalog of PostScript fills and tips about using them can be found on pages 93 and 94.

COLORING WITH BLENDS

Sometimes it takes more than a custom Fountain fill to get the color transition you want — for instance, if you want the color change to follow a curve, or to parallel one, or if you want to use lights and darks to model an asymmetrical three-dimensional surface. In those cases Blends can be helpful. "Sculpting with Blends" later in this chapter is one of several examples in the book of creating depth with color blends.

OTHER "FILL" METHODS

You can also color a shape by masking other shapes or lines, or even imported images, inside it. Import the bitmap (File, Import) or use CorelDRAW's tools to create the lines or filled objects that you want to mask. Then put this color source behind the object you want to fill, using the appropriate Arrange [Order] commands.

CorelDRAW's color bitmap fill options (Two Color and Full Color patterns, Texture Fills, and imported bitmaps) will add significantly to your file size, whereas a vector-based fill from a Full-Color **.pat** file or a PostScript fill will not.

As CorelDRAW became more sophisticated, it added the ability to scale or rotate Pattern fills along with the objects they fill. In versions that have the options, you'll find them in the Options or Tiling sections of the Pattern dialog. In versions where patterns don't scale or rotate with the object, you can try exporting the object (File, Export) as an Encapsulated PostScript (EPS) file with no header. Then import the new file (File, Import) with Files Of Type set to PostScript Interpreted. This should import a converted version of the pattern that can be manipulated in CorelDRAW.

If you blend between a dark-filled front shape and a shape behind it filled with the background color, the forward object seems to blend into the background. This method lets you control the color transition to affect the character of a shadow, by controlling the shape of the background-colored object.

A blend between a small "rich gray"-filled ellipse (20Y, 80K) and a larger white ellipse, all on a white background

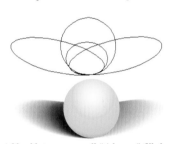

A blend between a small "rich gray"-filled ellipse and a shape made by combining (Arrange, Combine) a white-filled ellipse with a flipped duplicate of itself, all on a white background. The Weld command (Arrange, Weld) could have been used instead of Combine, to produce a different kind of fall-off from dark to light.

If you combine (Arrange, Combine) overlapping objects like the rectangle and type shown here, the result is a compound object with a "hole" in it that lets any objects or bitmaps behind it show through.

If you want to lighten or slightly tint a piece of flat-color CorelDRAW art but you aren't sure exactly how much of a change you want to make, a Blend can  be helpful. Shift- or drag-select all the objects in the art you want to change, group them (Ctrl-G; ⌘-G on the Mac), duplicate the group (Ctrl-D; ⌘-D), either color the copy all white to lighten (click the white square in the on-screen palette) or all one color (for tinting). Then move the copy so there's enough space for several more copies between it and the original. Shift-select the two groups and blend (Effects, Blend), using as many Steps as you want variations. Pick the one you like best. Then separate the parts of the blend (Arrange, Separate; click on the Blend group of intermediate steps and choose Arrange, Ungroup) so you can keep the variation you want and delete the rest. Or reblend between two steps to generate intermediate possibilities to choose from.

The bright red clip art at the top was grouped and duplicated, and the copy was filled with white. A 4-Step blend between the red and the white created the other variations shown.

Create a rectangle large enough to cover up the color source, move it just behind the object you want to fill, and combine the object and the rectangle (Arrange, Combine). The object will become a hole in the rectangle and the color source will show through. To preserve this "fill," group the combined object and the color source (Ctrl-G; ⌘-G).

TRANSPARENCY

Transparency is the quality that lets objects that would otherwise be hidden behind a filled object show through it. Transparency has been one of the most difficult problems to solve in object-oriented drawing programs, and CorelDRAW has been at the head of the pack in achieving it. Transparency appeared first as the Transparency Lens in version 5. In versions from 5 on, you can make an object transparent by selecting it and then choosing Effects, Lens, Transparency. Then in the Lens roll-up you can select a color and a percentage of Transparency, and then click Apply. (There's more about how Lenses work in Chapter 4, "Transforming.")

In version 7 or 8 the options for transparency have expanded. The Interactive Transparency tool, whose icon in the toolbox looks like a glass goblet, gives you the option of applying fills other than Uniform color and transparency. Selecting an object and then choosing the Interactive Transparency tool gives you the option to choose Uniform, Fountain, Pattern, or Texture from the pop-out list on the Property bar.

If you choose Fountain and drag the tool across the object, you'll apply a gradient from the current default From color

The Property bar for the Interactive Transparency tool In CorelDRAW 7 and 8 offers the chance to make Pattern and Texture fills partially transparent.

(specified in the Fountain Fill dialog box, F11) to whatever degree of transparency you set in the Property bar. As you drag you'll see an arrow that shows the starting and ending points of the transition from color to transparency, as well as the direction of the gradient. For Fountain transparency the Property bar also gives you the same choices as for Fountain fills — Linear, Radial, Conical, and Square. In version 8 a slider along the arrow between the starting color and transparency lets you control the rate of change from color to transparency.

If you choose Pattern or Texture in the Property bar, you can select from the Two Color patterns or the Textures libraries that become available in an icon or pop-out list on the Property bar. You can control the transparency of two colors independently with the sliders provided. The colors of a Pattern will be governed by the settings in the Pattern or Texture Fill dialog box; to change the Pattern colors or the Texture Fill colors, select the object, choose the Pattern or Texture icon from the Fill tool's pop-out in the Toolbox, choose new colors, click OK to close the box, then choose the Interactive Fill tool and adjust the sliders for the two colors in the Property bar. *WOW!*

BEYOND CORELDRAW

Although CorelDRAW offers a great deal of versatility in coloring artwork, it can't imitate the full range of natural media. For the flowing strokes of paint on canvas, artists turn to a painting or image-editing program like Adobe Photoshop, MetaCreations Painter, or Corel PHOTO-PAINT. Instructions for using these programs are beyond the scope of this book, but two images that show some of the effects that can be achieved with PHOTO-PAINT are included in the "Gallery" at the end of this chapter.

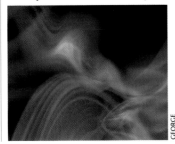

PROMPT PASTELS

If you're working in version 5 or later, here's an easier way to give your colors a pastel look than manipulating each color individually. Put a shape over the artwork; choose Effects, Lens, Transparency, choose white for the color, and adjust the Rate setting until the colors look right.

To preserve the black line work while softening the colors in the "squiggle" object in the logo below, Tom Graney duplicated the squiggle in place (select the object and press "+" on the numeric keypad), and turned the duplicate into a 50% white Transparency Lens. (The original "full-strength" squiggle is shown at the top. Both the original and the 50% transparent white copy are behind the shapes that make up the black line work.)

Another option is to use the Color Adjustment commands from the Effects menu. You can adjust the Brightness, Contrast, Intensity, and more to transform the color scheme of your object. The disadvantage of this method is that the colors are actually transformed, while with a Lens the original color information is retained, so if you delete the Lens the original color returns. Also the Color Adjustment options don't work on Pantone colors, such as those that Graney used in this butterfly example.

Fountain Fill Presets

The Presets list in the Fountain Fill dialog box of CorelDRAW 4, 5, 6, 7, and 8 provides a variety of prefab gradients. The Circular and Cylinder fills are in version 5 and later. Version 4 also has four color-to-gray gradients (not shown).

Circular–Blue 01

Circular–Blue 02

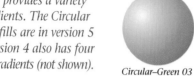

Circular–Green 01

Circular–Green 02

Circular–Green 03

Circular–Grey 01

Circular–Orange 01

Circular–Orange 02

Circular–Pink 01

Circular–Purple 01

Circular–Red 01

Circular–Red 02

Circular–Red 03

Cylinder–01

Cylinder–02

Cylinder–03

Cylinder–04

Cylinder–05

Cylinder–06

Cylinder–07

Cylinder–08

Cylinder–09

Cylinder–10

Cylinder–11

Cylinder–12

Cylinder–13

Cylinder–14

Cylinder–15

Cylinder–16

Cylinder–17

Cylinder–18

Cylinder–19

Cylinder–20

Cylinder–21

Cylinder–22

Cylinder–23

Cylinder–24

Cylinder–25

Cylinder–26

Cylinder–27

Cylinder–28

Cylinder–29

Cylinder–30

Cylinder–Blue 01

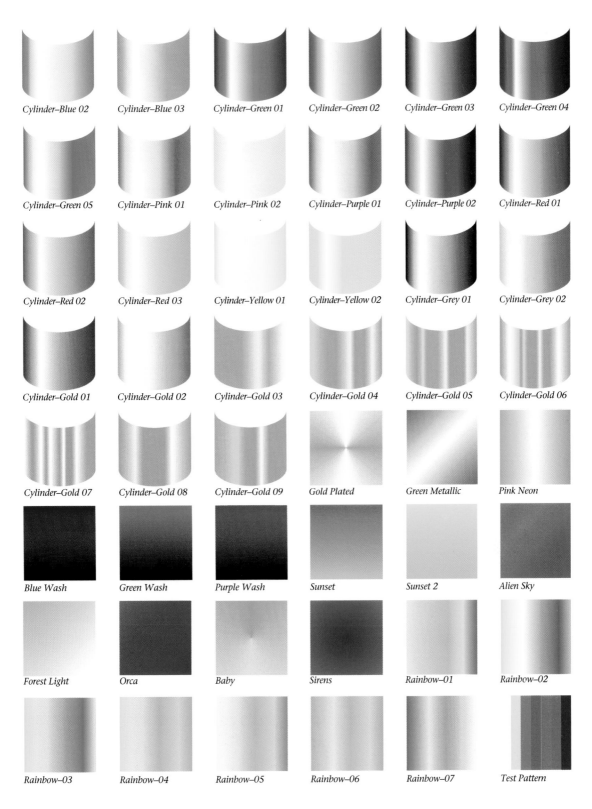

Cylinder–Blue 02 Cylinder–Blue 03 Cylinder–Green 01 Cylinder–Green 02 Cylinder–Green 03 Cylinder–Green 04

Cylinder–Green 05 Cylinder–Pink 01 Cylinder–Pink 02 Cylinder–Purple 01 Cylinder–Purple 02 Cylinder–Red 01

Cylinder–Red 02 Cylinder–Red 03 Cylinder–Yellow 01 Cylinder–Yellow 02 Cylinder–Grey 01 Cylinder–Grey 02

Cylinder–Gold 01 Cylinder–Gold 02 Cylinder–Gold 03 Cylinder–Gold 04 Cylinder–Gold 05 Cylinder–Gold 06

Cylinder–Gold 07 Cylinder–Gold 08 Cylinder–Gold 09 Gold Plated Green Metallic Pink Neon

Blue Wash Green Wash Purple Wash Sunset Sunset 2 Alien Sky

Forest Light Orca Baby Sirens Rainbow–01 Rainbow–02

Rainbow–03 Rainbow–04 Rainbow–05 Rainbow–06 Rainbow–07 Test Pattern

Texture Fills

Texture fills are available through the Fill tool's flyout menu in all versions since CorelDRAW 4. To help you choose a Texture fill to use "as is" or to customize, they are cataloged here. Shown on this page and the next two is the **Styles** library, which is found in CorelDRAW 4, 5, 6, 7, and 8.

Aerial photography

Biology1 2C(olor)

Biology1 3C(olor)

Biology1 5C(olor)

Biology2 2C(olor)

Biology2 3C(olor)

Biology2 5C(olor)

Blend corners

Blend edges

BubbleMania hrd 2C

BubbleMania hrd 3C

BubbleMania sft 2C

BubbleMania sft 3C

Cosmic clouds

Cosmic energy

Cosmic mineral

Cotton 2C(olor)

Cotton 3C(olor)

Cotton 5C(olor)

Drapes

Eclipse 2 colors

Fiber

Fiber embossed

Flames

Hypnotic1 2C(olor)

Hypnotic2 2C(olor)

Leather 2C(olor)

Leather 3C(olor)

Leather 5C(olor)

Mandel0

Mineral cldy 2 colors

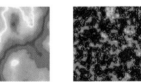
Mineral cldy 3 colors

Mineral cldy 5 colors

Mineral frctl 2 colors

Mineral frctl 3 colors

Mineral frctl 5 colors

Mineral spckld 2 colrs

Mineral spckld 3 colrs

Mineral spckld 5 colrs

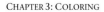
Mineral swirld 2 colrs

Mineral swirld 3 colrs

Mineral swirld 5 colrs

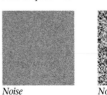
Noise

Noise blended

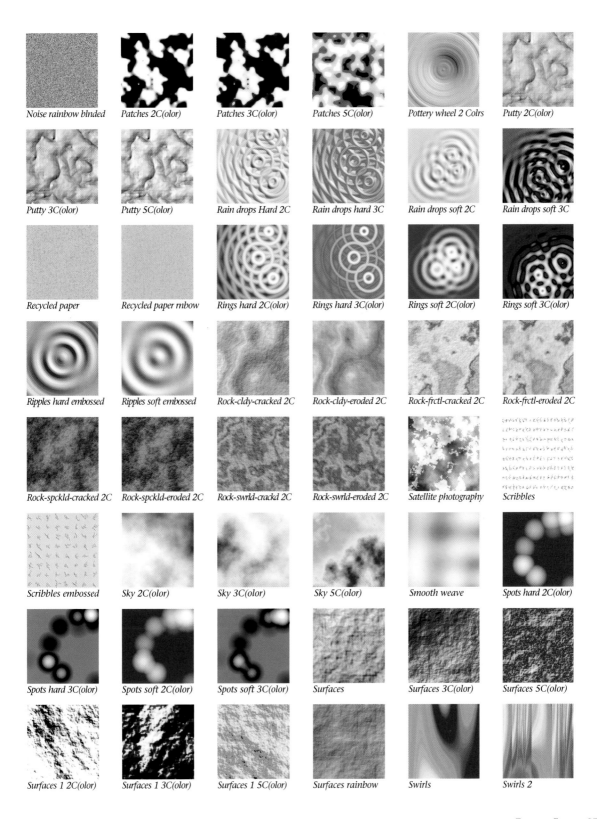

Noise rainbow blnded

Patches 2C(olor)

Patches 3C(olor)

Patches 5C(olor)

Pottery wheel 2 Colrs

Putty 2C(olor)

Putty 3C(olor)

Putty 5C(olor)

Rain drops Hard 2C

Rain drops hard 3C

Rain drops soft 2C

Rain drops soft 3C

Recycled paper

Recycled paper rnbow

Rings hard 2C(olor)

Rings hard 3C(olor)

Rings soft 2C(olor)

Rings soft 3C(olor)

Ripples hard embossed

Ripples soft embossed

Rock-cldy-cracked 2C

Rock-cldy-eroded 2C

Rock-frctl-cracked 2C

Rock-frctl-eroded 2C

Rock-spckld-cracked 2C

Rock-spckld-eroded 2C

Rock-swrld-crackd 2C

Rock-swrld-eroded 2C

Satellite photography

Scribbles

Scribbles embossed

Sky 2C(olor)

Sky 3C(olor)

Sky 5C(olor)

Smooth weave

Spots hard 2C(olor)

Spots hard 3C(olor)

Spots soft 2C(olor)

Spots soft 3C(olor)

Surfaces

Surfaces 3C(olor)

Surfaces 5C(olor)

Surfaces 1 2C(olor)

Surfaces 1 3C(olor)

Surfaces 1 5C(olor)

Surfaces rainbow

Swirls

Swirls 2

Swirls 2 horizontal

Texture blend horiz.

Texture blend vert.

Threads

Threads embossed

Threads rainbow

Vapor 2C(olor)

Vapor 3C(olor)

Vapor 5C(olor)

Water 2C(olor)

Water 3C(olor)

Water 5C(olor)

Water color

Water color2 2C

Water color2 3C

Water color2 5C

CREATING SEAMLESS PATTERNS

Although Texture fills are very versatile, they are not seamless tiles that automatically repeat to fill an entire object regardless of its size. Seamless tiles are useful for making backgrounds and for applying as surfaces on 3D models.

With a little work you can harness the pattern potential of Texture fills to create your own seamless tiles. First drag the Rectangle tool with the Ctrl key held down to make a perfect square (*in Mac v.6 use the Shift key; in v.8 use ⌘*). Choose Texture fill from the Fill tool flyout and right-click the X in the on-screen color palette so the square will have no outline (*Control-click on the Mac*). Export the square as a color bitmap (a TIFF or BMP file) with the File, Export command at the resolution of the bitmap file you want to use it in.

Open the file in an image-editing program such as Corel PHOTO-PAINT or Adobe Photoshop. Enlarge the canvas to double the width and height, with the original square in the lower left corner. Then duplicate the square, flip the copy horizontally, and drag it horizontally to abut the original. Now select the entire two-square rectangle, duplicate it, flip the copy vertically, and drag the copy upward to complete the large square.

If you now select this square and define it as a pattern, the tile will repeat without any obvious "seams," or disconnects, in the pattern. Depending on the nature of the texture, the resulting "repeat" may be obvious or nearly undetectable.

WHAT YOU SEE . . .

CorelDRAW's Texture fills are generated in RGB — they take up less RAM and less disk space that way. To make the on-screen color of Texture fills look more like the printed color will look, you can choose View, Color Correction, Accurate in version 5, 6, or 7; in version 8 choose Tools, Options, Global, Color Management, Calibrate Colors For Display to get a CMYK preview.

Or you can use a printed reference like these pages. The Texture swatches shown here were exported from CorelDRAW as TIFFs, placed in Adobe PageMaker pages, and then converted from RGB to CMYK with a program called Preprint (version 1.6).

Strictly speaking, these pages are accurate predictors of color for Texture fills only if the fills are exported, separated, and printed exactly the same way this book was produced. The safest way to predict printed color for your own project is to have your printer make you a contract color proof from your file — a proof that he or she can confidently say is an accurate predictor of the way the color will print.

*Shown on this page are the Texture fills from the **Samples** library, found in CorelDRAW 4, 5, 6, 7 and 8.*

Aerial clouds

Air brush

Alabaster

Banded malachite

Blocks

Clouds heavenly

Clouds midday

Clouds morning

Cloudy nebula

Curtains

Diamonds

Diorite

Gouache wash

Layered marble

Mineral cloudy 5C

Moon surface

Neon slice

Night spot

Ocean water

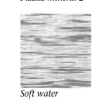
Pizzazz mineral

Pizzaz mineral 2

Purple haze

Quartz polished

Red brick

Ribbon candy

Seurat closeup

Soft water

Solar flares

Solar flares 2

Stucco

Swimming pool 1

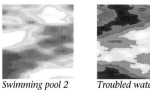
Swimming pool 2

Troubled water

Vegetation

Words of wisdom

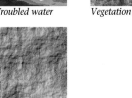
Yellow foil

ADD DEPTH WITH COLOR

Assigning lighter or darker colors to the same Texture fill creates the illusion of light and shadow to add depth to an object, as in the surfaces of this solid, drawn in two-point perspective as described at the beginning of Chapter 5. To arrive at the right colors, try changing the Brightness ± setting in the Texture Fill dialog box (+ values for lighter; – values for darker), Preview the new look, then click OK to apply it.

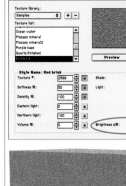

*The Texture Fills on this page are from the **Samples 5** library, found in CorelDRAW versions 5, 6, 7, and 8.*

Bacteria

Beads

Blocks, rainbow

Blue valley

Blur rainbow

Boil

Borealis mountain

Bubble land

Canyon

Coral forest

Cow hide

Crater

Curled donuts

Curved space

Flares 1

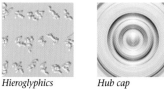
Flares 2

Fossile

Fungus

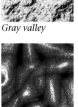
Glass blocks

Gray valley

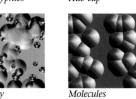
Hieroglyphics

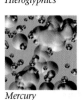
Hub cap

Impressionist

Ink spots

Lava

Liver

Mercury

Molecules

Night lights

Night sky

O's

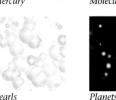
Paint drops

Pearls

Planets

Plant sketch 1

Plant sketch 2

Plastered wall

Purple brain

TEXTURES IN PHOTO-PAINT

CorelDRAW's Texture fill, essentially a bitmap feature, is also available in Corel PHOTO-PAINT. To make use of it there, double-click the Fill tool, choose the same Texture fill icon you would in CorelDRAW, and choose a Texture. To open the dialog box that lets you choose a different variation or customize the Texture, click the Edit button.

Red clay pottery

Spagetti

Turtle shell

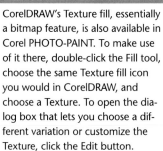
Weather report

Brake light

Circuit board

Cobwebs

Cotton balls

Cotton candy

Eclipse of the sun

Electric fence

Elephant skin

Epidermis

Evening ripple

Exhaust fumes

Gingham

Hall of flame

Islands in the stream

Lava river

Mitosis

Moonray

Nail pops

Oatmeal

Orbit

Shimmering silk

Stormy sky

Volcano

Waterfall

Wrapping paper

"BLEACHING," DARKENING, OR TINTING

To make type or a graphic show up on a Texture-filled background but still look "at home" in its surroundings, start with the background shape, choose the Texture fill icon from the Fill tool's fly-out menu, and fill the shape with a Texture, using the shade or color of you want for your type or graphic. It's important to choose a Texture that's relatively low in contrast and "fine-grained" when compared to your type or graphic. Duplicate the background shape in place (select it with the Pick tool and press "+" on the numeric keypad) and fill the new copy with the shade or color you want for the background. Add the shape or type on top. Select the type with the Pick tool and then Shift-select the duplicate background shape (the one just behind the type) and combine them (Arrange, Combine). This will knock the shape or type out of the duplicate, allowing the Texture in the original background shape to show through. The fill in the type will line up perfectly with the fill behind it. You can do the same kind of thing with a Uniform- or Pattern-filled shape or with an imported image.

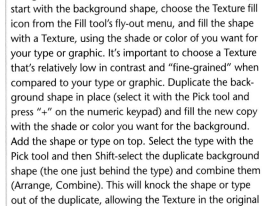

A square was filled with the Borealis Mountain Texture fill from the Samples 5 library, colored the way we wanted the graphic to appear (A); the square was duplicated in place, and the top copy was refilled with a darker version of the Texture fill, made by changing the Brightness setting in the Texture Fill dialog box to −40 (B). A graphic from the Zapf Dingbats Symbols library was added on top (C) and combined (Arrange, Combine) with the top square (D). To darken the graphic (E) rather than bleaching it, we reversed the stacking order of the squares at step B. For the look of stamped color (F), we selected the combined element from E with the Pick tool, then opened the Texture Fill dialog box and clicked the Preview button until we saw a texture we liked (#508).

*The Texture Fills on this page are from the **Samples 7** library, found in CorelDRAW versions 7 and 8.*

Above the earth

Algae

Autumn cloth

Aztec cave drawing

Chocolate raisins

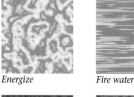
Concrete

Contour map

Copper

Dazzling delight

Drylands

Energize

Fire water

Fold of silk

Ivy on a wall

Lens flare

Mask

Midnight velvet

Moss

Neon spandex

Painted stucco

Pilot light

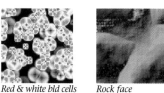
Plankton

Plaster medallion

Polar surface

Psychedelic cavern

Rainbow storm

Red & white bld cells

Rock face

Solar flare 3

Thousand lakes

Undiscvrd country

TRANSFORMING TEXTURE FILLS

By default in CorelDRAW 8 when you rotate a Texture-filled object, the fill is rotated along with it. (If you wanted to for some reason, you could keep the fill from being transformed — click the Tiling button in the Texture Fill dialog box and turning off the Transform Fill With Object feature.)

In earlier versions of the program, the Texture fill isn't rotated along with the object. To rotate the Texture, you can export the Texture-filled object as a bitmap, then import it again and rotate it.

In CorelDRAW 8 the Texture fill automatically rotates along with the object. In other versions it takes some doing.

Utah stone

Wool

*Shown on this page are the 25 Texture Fills from the **Samples 8** library, found in CorelDRAW 8.*

Blue lava

Cell

Cement

Chrome curtain

Colour storm

Dark cloud

Glacier

Green corosion

Horizon

Loam

Moon surface

Moss

Nebula

Neon lint

Noise

Plasma

Purple seal

Rainbow glow

Red globs

Scan wave

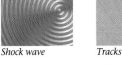

Shock wave

Tracks

Turbulence

Twine

Ultra violet

Weave

Wood grain

TILING TEXTURE FILLS

New to CorelDRAW 8 is a Tiling button in the Texture Fill dialog box. It allows the Textures to be used in a repeating fashion. The tiled Textures are not seamless — the repeat is quite obvious, producing a "wrapping paper" or "shower door" effect, for instance. (To turn Texture fills into seamless tiles, see the "Creating Seamless Textures" tip, at the end of the Styles library swatches.)

To make a Texture fill into a tiling pattern as shown below, click the Tiling button, and set the Width and Height you want for the tile. You can also set a Skew value to make the tiles "lean over" or a Rotate value to repeat the pattern diagonally rather than horizontally. And you can Offset the tiles so the rows or columns are shifted a bit (like brickwork, for instance), rather than being stacked directly above and beside each other. The default for the Origin (where the pattern starts) is 0, 0, which puts the upper left corner of the first pattern tile at the upper left corner of the bounding box of your object.

Note: CorelDRAW 8's ability to tile can cause problems if you open a file with a Texture-filled object created in an earlier version: A Texture that smoothly filled the object may now appear tiled. To fix it, select the object, then open the Texture Fill dialog box and set the Height and Width at the dimensions of a box that would just enclose the object.

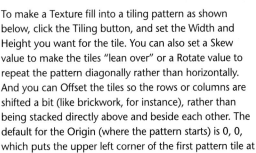

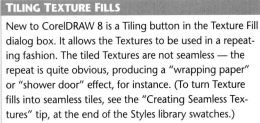

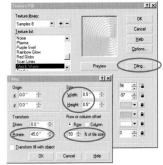

PostScript Pattern Fills

PostScript pattern fills are available through the Fill tool's flyout menu. The filled squares are shown at their original size. The PostScript patterns were applied in CorelDRAW 8 with their default settings.

We had no success exporting the pattern-filled squares as TIFFs directly from CorelDRAW 8. Instead we exported them in EPS format, then opened them in Photoshop 5 at 1200 dpi to avoid the softening that was caused by antialiasing when we tried a lower resolution (300 dpi).

Archimedes

Bars

Basketweave

Birds

Bricks

Bubbles

Carpet

CircleGrid

ColorBubbles

ColorCircles

ColorCrosshatching

ColorFishscale

ColorHatching

ColorLeaves

ColorReptiles

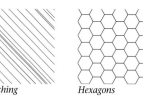
Construction

Cracks

Craters

CrossHatching

CrystalLattice

Denim

DNA

Fishscale

Grass

GreenGrass

GreenLeaves

Hatching

Hexagons

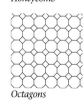
Honeycomb

Impact

Landscape

Leaves

Mesh

Motifs

Octagons

Patio

Rectangles

Reptiles

SpiderWeb

Spirals

Spokes

Squares

StainedGlass

StarOfDavid

Stars

StarShapes

StoneWall

Text

Tiles

TreeRings

Triangle

Waves

Some of the more "organic" PostScript pattern fills provide interesting and useful variations when you change their settings in the PostScript Pattern dialog box. Even the geometric PostScript pattern fills vary in interesting ways, with larger, smaller, or more or less densely packed shapes. In addition to making adjustments like the ones shown here, you can vary the contrast of many PostScript patterns by changing the Gray settings from black and white to shades of gray.

• The Horizontal and Vertical values in the Spokes pattern determine where the center of radiation is. You can also control the Number of spokes.

Number: 120;
Horizontal: 0;
Vertical: 0

Number: 120;
Horizontal: 50;
Vertical: 50

Number: 50,
Horizontal: 50;
Vertical: 50

• Using the same value for Maximum Distance and Minimum Distance in ColorCrosshatching produces a regularly spaced plaid. Changing the Angle to 90 or 180 produces horizontal or vertical stripes.

Max. Distance: 75;
Min. Distance: 0;
Angle: 45

Max./Min.
Distance: 75;
Angle: 45

Max./Min.
Distance: 75;
Angle: 90

• Decreasing the Separation setting in the SpiderWeb pattern makes more bands, closer together. Setting the Maximum Angle and Minimum Angle to the same value makes the segments of the web perfectly regular.

Separation: 300;
Max. Angle: 40;
Min. Angle: 10

Separation: 100;
Max. Angle: 40;
Min. Angle: 10

Separation: 100;
Max./Min. Angle: 40

• Increasing the Number of blades for the GreenGrass pattern makes a thicker lawn, and decreasing the Maximum blade size makes it shorter overall.

Number: 100,
Maximum Size: 35

Number: 300,
Maximum Size: 35

Number: 300,
Maximum Size: 10

• Changing the Number of letters in Text makes the characters (and the spaces between them) smaller. Reducing the Space setting packs the letters more densely.

Frequency: 4;
Spacing: 100

Frequency: 15;
Spacing: 100

Frequency: 15;
Spacing: 50

Patterning

Overview *Make a drawing; select elements; apply Two-Color or Full-Color pattern fills, either existing CorelDRAW patterns or ones that you modify or create yourself.*

3•4•5•6•7•8

All versions from CorelDRAW 3 have the ability to apply existing patterns and create new ones.

1a

A wireframe view shows the shapes that make up D'Avanzo's approximately 3-inch-square drawing.

1b

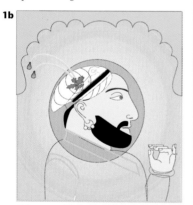

Color was added with outlines and both Uniform and Fountain fills.

1c

A blend, mapped to a curve, formed the hair at the neck (Effects, Blend, New Path).

JAMES D'AVANZO

PATTERN FILLS PROVIDE A QUICK WAY to distinguish between geographical features in a map or bars in a graph, or to embellish a drawing. They can add a high degree of detail for relatively little drawing effort. James D'Avanzo used five customized pattern fills in creating his mystic, Eastern-style *Mewar* image: two different color variations of a pattern from CorelDRAW's Two-Color pattern collection; a design from CorelDRAW's Full-Color pattern collection, edited to fit the color scheme of his drawing; and two different variations of a color pattern compiled from clip-art elements.

1 Making the drawing. D'Avanzo used the Rectangle, Ellipse, and Outline Pen tools to shape the elements of his drawing. He applied Uniform fills (Shift-F11) to some shapes, such as the hand, face, hat, eye, and parts of the earrings, and Fountain fills (F11) to other elements, such as the tips of the hat's plumes, the green background, the white of the eye, and parts of the earrings. (For tips on using the drawing tools, see Chapter 2, "Drawing," and for more about Uniform and Fountain fills, see the beginning of this chapter.)

He used the Blend roll-up from the Effects menu (Ctrl-B; ⌘-*Shift-B in Mac v.6*) to blend from shapes filled with the skin color to shapes filled with black for the hair, sideburn, mustache, and beard.

2 Applying a Two-Color pattern. The Two-Color Pattern fill allows you to modify existing patterns and create new ones based on black-and-white designs. Choosing the checkerboard button from the Fill tool's flyout menu opens up the Two-Color Pattern dialog box, where you can pick from a collection of two-color fills supplied with CorelDRAW, recolor them, or create new patterns.

2a

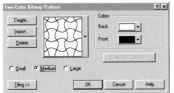

D'Avanzo opened one of CorelDRAW's Two-Color Pattern fills as a starting point for making a pattern fill for the hatband and cuffs.

2b

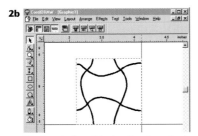

The lines in the original pattern turned out to be too fine to show up in a print when the tile size was reduced to the 0.11 x 0.11-inch Tiling dimensions D'Avanzo wanted to use for the hatband and cuffs. One way to make it more robust was to fill a 1-inch square with the pattern at Large size, trace the lines with the Bezier tool, assign a line width of 1.5 points (F12), delete the original pattern-filled square, and then use the Create Pattern command (from the Tools or Special menu) to define a Two-Color Pattern.

2c

The reconstructed pattern was assigned two shades of gold for the larger parts of the hatband and the cuff, and a different color scheme was assigned for the small part of the band.

3a

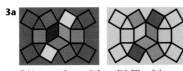

*D'Avanzo changed the solid fills of the shapes that made up the **staingls.pat** file. The square that had been used to define the original tile (outlined here) was retained when D'Avanzo saved his edited version.*

D'Avanzo modified a pattern from the Corel collection to fill the hatband and cuff. To choose a pattern, click on the preview box to open the palette of patterns. Use the scroll bars to move through the collection of black-and-white tiles. When you find something you like, double-clicking on it will make it the active pattern.

Although all of the patterns start off as black-and-white, after choosing a pattern you can assign any two colors: Simply click on the color buttons for the black and white parts and pick the new colors of your choice. D'Avanzo applied two shades of gold to the pattern used in the cuff and two parts of the hatband, then selected the other part of the hatband and changed the colors in the Two-Color Pattern dialog box to apply a different version of the pattern.

In the Tile Size section of the dialog box (click the Tiling button to open this section), you have precise control of the height and width of the pattern tile.

Generally, you'll want the pattern to be automatically scaled in proportion if you resize the drawing, so check the Transform Fill With Object box in CorelDRAW 8 (Scale Pattern With Object in other versions). When you've finished setting all the color and tiling parameters, click OK.

> **3•4**
>
> CorelDRAW 3 and 4 don't have a Scale Pattern With Object option. If you need to reduce or enlarge your drawing, you can refill pattern-filled objects after resizing, scaling the pattern to fit using Tile Size in the Two-Color Pattern or Full-Color Pattern dialog box.

3 Editing a color pattern.

CorelDRAW ships with many full-color pattern files that you can use "as is" or customize to your own tastes. To modify a pattern (**.pat**) file, first open it by choosing File, Open; change the Type Of File to Pattern File; and choose from the list of Corel-supplied patterns (called Vector Fills in some versions) in the **custom** directory (the **draw** directory in version 3).

To make a pattern fill for the braid on the jacket, D'Avanzo opened the **staingls.pat** file (*Stained Glass on the Mac*) and modified it: To recolor the pattern so it was more appropriate for his design, he selected components of the design by Shift-clicking with the Pick tool, and changed the fill by clicking the on-screen color palette or opening the Uniform or Fountain Fill dialog box (Shift-F11 or F11) for more choices.

After making your changes, save the file under a different name, such as **staingl2.pat** in this case, so that the original file remains intact (File, Save As). This new pattern file can be loaded from the Full-Color Pattern dialog box by using the Load command. If you save your pattern in the same directory with CorelDRAW's native patterns, the new version will also appear in the Full-Color Pattern palette, opened by clicking the preview.

3b

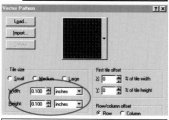

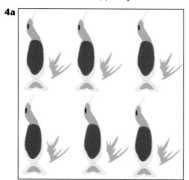

D'Avanzo applied the edited pattern by using the Full-Color Pattern function, choosing the icon next to the Two-Color icon on the Fill tool's fly-out palette.

4a

D'Avanzo started with a clip-art bird and modified it to get the primary elements to use for his pattern. To make the pattern tile, he copied and pasted the bird several times, To keep the design from being too mechanical, he positioned the birds in a slightly irregular grouping,

4b

D'Avanzo used Create Pattern to select the square of birds and save it as a .pat file.

MAKING YOUR OWN PATTERN DIRECTORY

By default, when you save a vector pattern you've edited, the Save As command will put it in the same directory or folder as the original — the one that includes CorelDRAW's native patterns if that's where you started from. But if you don't want to have to sort through so many pattern names to find your own designs, you can designate a different directory or folder in the Save Drawing dialog box, or create a new one.

4 Creating your own Vector pattern. If you don't find a .pat file that you like "as is" or with editing as described in step 3, you can make your own by using Create Pattern. First, hold down the Ctrl key (*Shift key in Mac v.6, ⌘ in v.8*) and draw a square with the Rectangle tool. This will define the boundary of your pattern tile. Then draw your pattern in the square. (You can let pattern elements extend to or even beyond the edges of the square if you like, but you may have to make adjustments to the tile to make the pattern repeat seamlessly.)

To turn your tile into a pattern, delete your bounding square and choose Create Pattern from the Tools menu (in CorelDRAW 6, 7, or 8) or the Special menu (in version 3, 4, or 5). Select the Full-Color option (the Vector option in version 6), and then click OK. The cursor will now become a set of full-screen crosshairs. Ctrl-drag (*⌘-drag in Mac v.8*) to select your tile. Click OK and save your .pat file as in step 3.

D'Avanzo used Create Pattern to develop his bird pattern. First he opened a clip-art image of a bird and modified it. His completed bird was a vertical element, but he didn't want a large amount of background space between birds, and he didn't want the elements to be stretched wider to fit the square tile that's the basis for CorelDRAW patterns. So he copied the bird (Ctrl-C; ⌘-C) and pasted it several times (Ctrl-V; ⌘-V) into a square, two-row-by-three-column arrangement that he could use as the basis for a pattern. He captured the square pattern tile with the Create Pattern command. Then he used this pattern and another variation of it with the bounding square filled with gold, to fill parts of the jacket to finish the file.

STARTING WITH A SQUARE

The CorelDRAW manual says you can drag the Create Pattern crosshairs to make a rectangular pattern tile of any aspect ratio you want — tall and thin or short and wide. The pattern element will stretch to fit a square, but then you can use the Tile Size controls in the Tiling section of the Two-Color Pattern, Vector Pattern, or Full Color Bitmap Pattern dialog box to bring the pattern elements back into the proper proportions. This process is tedious at best, and if you do this to a bitmap pattern, it produces artifacts that can result in an ugly tile. To avoid these problems, design your tile as a square to begin with: Either use guidelines (dragged in from the rulers) to set up a measured square tile, or draw a square that you can use as a guide, and then hold down the Ctrl key (⌘ key in Mac v.8) to constrain the Create Pattern crosshairs to a square selection.

Painting with Objects

Overview *Import a scan of a photo for reference; draw no-outline shapes with the Freehand tool; fill and blend the shapes to emphasize highlights and shadows.*

3•4•5•6•7•8

All versions support importing a bitmap, Freehand drawing, and blending.

1

The imported bitmap served as a guide for drawing with the Freehand tool. Here the shapes are shown in Wireframe view.

2

Using the original painting as a guide, Levin assigned a Uniform color fill to each shape as it was drawn.

3

Many of the leaves and flowers in the scarf were blended from objects with different numbers of nodes, creating a silky look.

DALIA LEVIN

INTRIGUED BY THE IDEA OF CREATING an electronic version of her large-format *Ethiopian Woman*, Dalia Levin set out to make digital dabs of paint to replace the brush strokes of the original acrylic painting.

1 Importing a bitmap. Open a new CorelDRAW file (File, New) and bring in a scanned photo (File, Import). Use the Layer Manager, Layers roll-up, or Object Manager (from the Layout, Arrange, or Window menu) to create a new layer. Lock the layer (by turning off its pencil icon or turning on its lock) to prevent it from being nudged accidentally.

2 Drawing dabs of color. Use the Freehand or Bezier tool to trace around shadow and highlight areas to create a series of overlapping objects. Rather than relying on the screen for color accuracy, Levin used a Trumatch color book, where she found the colors she wanted and noted their CMYK percentages. Then she keyed the percentages into the Uniform Fill dialog box (Shift-F11). She also enabled the Color Correction option. (Color Correction, to make the color of the on-screen display look more like the printed color will look, can be selected from the View menu in CorelDRAW 5, 6, or 7. In version 8 choose Tools, Options, Global, Color Management, Calibrate Colors For Display.)

3 Blending colors. Now you can soften the "too smooth" look of your shapes by creating smaller objects on top of the primary shapes and blending them together using the Blend roll-up (Ctrl-B; ⌘-*Shift-B in Mac v.6*) with enough steps for smooth color transitions. When the two blend control objects have different numbers of nodes, the resulting blends can produce random, twisting color changes. On the other hand, if you want a smooth color gradient, you can make one of the blend control objects a downsized duplicate of the first, ensuring the same number of nodes: Select the first object with the Pick tool and press the "+" key on the numeric keypad; then drag inward on a corner handle of the highlight box to shrink the duplicate.

Lighting a Planet

Overview *Draw a circle; set up a lighting scheme with a Radial Fountain fill; add surface features with more Radial fills; adjust the fills to match the planet's lighting.*

3•4•5•6•7•8

In all these versions of CorelDRAW you can draw circles and assign Radial Fountain fills. The Interactive Fill tool in versions 7 and 8 makes it easier to adjust the fills.

1

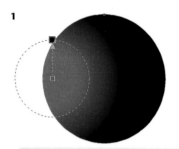

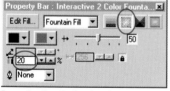

In version 7 or 8, choosing the Interactive Fill tool and clicking the Radial button in the Property bar gives you the controls you need for a Radial Fountain fill. To offset the center, move the central color swatch on the circle diagram that appears on the object.

2a

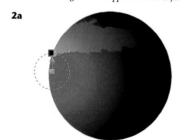

The Radial Fountain fill of a surface shape can be centered at or near the center of the background circle's Radial fill, as shown here for the top "sea" shape.

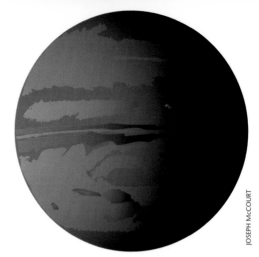

JOSEPH McCOURT

TO MAKE HIS RED PLANET look like a sphere with a strong light shining on it from the left, Joseph McCourt made a montage of CorelDRAW shapes, each with its own Radial Fountain fill, oriented to match the overall lighting scheme. The planet is from the *IMAX Poster* shown in the "Gallery" at the end of Chapter 6.

1 Drawing the planet and establishing the lighting. To build a planet, you can start from scratch or use a template, as McCourt did. Starting with a not particularly good scanned photo of Mars, he increased its contrast in Adobe Photoshop to differentiate the reds. He imported the TIFF into CorelDRAW (File, Import), locked it on a layer of its own so it wouldn't be knocked out of place accidentally, and used it as a reference for drawing. (For tips on importing a bitmap on a locked layer, see step 1 of "Converting a Logo" in Chapter 2.)

The planet starts with a circle: Hold down the Ctrl key (*Shift in Mac v.6,* ⌘ *in v.8*) as you drag with the Ellipse tool to make a perfect circle. From the Fountain Fill dialog box (opened by pressing F11) choose the From (outside) and To (central) colors, and choose Radial for the Type. In CorelDRAW 7 or 8, you could use the Property bar to set up the Radial fill (choose the Interactive Fill tool to open the Property bar); the From color is on the left, and the To color on the right.

Once you get a look at the filled shape, you may want to experiment with changes to the Radial Fountain. In version 7 or 8 you can

---

3•4•5•6

In version 3, 4, 5 (shown here), or 6, with no Interactive Fill tool, set up a Radial fill in the Fountain Fill dialog box (F11). Offset the center of the fill by entering numbers for Horizontal and Vertical, or by dragging in the preview window. Set the Edge Pad and Midpoint by entering numbers. If you need to make changes to a fill later, select the object you want to change and open this dialog box again.

You can use a trial-and-error process of changing (with the help of the preview box), pressing OK, checking the result, and changing again if necessary.

2b

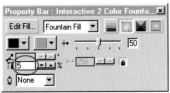

A second large shape was added, with the center of its fill near that of the other sea and the background circle. The Edge Pads for the seas were set at 5%, so these shapes don't fade to black as fast as the larger circle, making them look somewhat reflective.

3

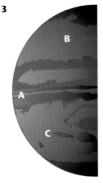

Slightly curved shapes near the equator helped round the planet (A). A bright streak looks shiny (B), and brightly lit "mountains" cast shadows (C).

use the Interactive Fill tool: Select the object and then choose the tool. A circle diagram will appear, with a swatch of the To color in the center and a swatch of the From color at its edge. By dragging the To swatch, you can change the offset of the center of the fill. Dragging the From swatch changes the Edge Pad; and in version 8, there's a bar for adjusting the midpoint. McCourt set the Edge Pad for the circle at 20%.

2 Adding surface features. McCourt traced the bitmap template with the Freehand tool to make the two large "seas" above and below the planet's equator. He assigned them Radial Fountain fills (you can use any of the methods described in step 1). To unify the lighting, you can use the Interactive Fill tool (in version 7 or 8) to drag the center of the radiating color for each surface feature object to a point near the spot used as the center of the highlight in the large background circle.

To try different shades of color as McCourt did, choose a color from the on-screen palette and drag it onto the drawing until the arrow pointer (not the color swatch, but the pointer) is on the Interactive Fill swatch whose color you want to change. McCourt used a lighter and duller red for the central color of the fill for his seas and black for the outer color. (If you want to change to a color that isn't in the palette, use the Edit button on the Property bar or press F11 to open the Fountain Fill dialog box so you can mix a color. Or in version 8 put the pointer over a color in the palette and press and hold the mouse button to open a block of related color swatches you can choose from.)

3 Adding details. When the large features are in place, add smaller details. Curving a shape, especially a long, thin horizontal object, adds to the illusion of the planet's roundness. Departing from the overall lighting scheme by using bright colors in a relatively dark area makes a feature look shiny or gleaming. To add surface relief, layer Fountain-filled shapes over darker shadow objects. *WOW!*

INTERACTIVE FILL BEHAVIOR — BEYOND THE EDGES

With the Interactive Fill tool, available in CorelDRAW 7 (shown here) and in 8, you can create or edit a Linear Fountain fill so the color gradient begins and ends outside the filled object. The part of the gradient beyond the edges of the object doesn't show, and the edited object now seems to be filled with only part of the gradient. But with a Radial Fountain fill, it's different:

• You can control the position of the center of the color gradient, moving its swatch outside the object if you like.

• You can change the Edge Pad by moving the outer swatch.

• But when you've spread the colors to the point where the outside color is at the outer edge of the object, further spreading doesn't change anything, even in a multicolor gradient. (Version 8, however, has swatches for the intermediate colors, which can be moved to change the gradient.)

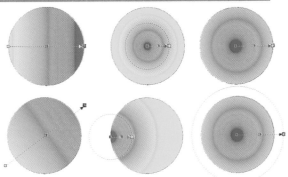

Before (top) and after editing a Linear Fountain fill

Before (top) and after moving the center of a Radial Fountain fill

Dragging the outside color can change the edge pad to 0 (top), but dragging farther has no effect.

Corralling Fountain Fills

Overview *Blend thin to thick lines for a neon look; combine tick marks with objects to control the build of Fountain fills.*

3•4•5•6•7•8

All these versions of CorelDRAW can create Blends, combine objects, and fill combined objects with Fountain fills.

The complete package layout

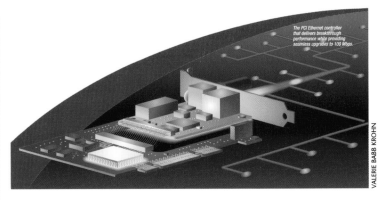

VALERIE KROHN HAS BUILT A FAVORITE PALETTE using only cyan, magenta, and yellow. She prefers to use mainly bright colors, mixing most hues from two out of three of these primaries, and adding the third color if she wants to darken a color or make it more neutral, less intense. The palette came in handy for this six-color packaging design for one of the Compaq family of products. With the job headed for a six-color press, Krohn used cyan, magenta, yellow, "Compaq red" (Pantone Matching System 200 CV) for the corporate logo, and a Pantone blue for type, and still had one color reserved for the varnish that would complete the package printing.

1 Drawing the shapes. Krohn's goal was a stylized but accurate image of the product she was illustrating. A stripped-down version of the engineering drawing was created in the 3D orientation she wanted and was supplied to her as an AutoCad DXF file. She imported the file (File, Import) to use it as a guide, locking it on its own layer (see step 1 of "Converting a Logo" in Chapter 2 for tips on importing and locking a template). When the DXF file was imported, it came in as separated line segments rather than fillable objects, so although it looked right, it wasn't useful as a basis for her drawing. Using the imported template as a guide and the real controller board for reference, Krohn clicked from point to point with the Bezier tool, constructing four-sided closed objects. Trying to draw abutted objects with shared lines can lead to tiny gaps at the edges. And since edges lie exactly on top of each other, it can also make objects more difficult to select in Wireframe mode, where you have to click on a line rather than a fill to make the selection.

2 Creating connectivity. To suggest a network, Krohn blended lines: She started with blue lines about 4.5 points thick. (To specify color, line weight, and other characteristics for a series of lines you want to draw, with no object selected press F12, choosing Graphic, to open the Outline Pen dialog box, then set the line characteristics and click OK; these traits will be applied to every object you draw until, with nothing selected, you press F12 again and redefine them.)

Using the Freehand tool, Krohn created a series of separate line segments connecting to a central triangular core. She gave the triangle

Valerie Krohn drew the illustration for the Compaq Netflex-3/P Controller board using an AutoCad file as a template. For edges that would show when the shapes were filled, she drew accurately, following the template precisely. But she built overlaps for edges that would be hidden by other surfaces. This made it easier to grab the lines in Wireframe mode.

2a

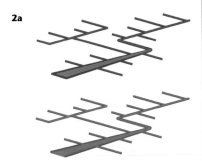

A group with a thick blue outline and a duplicate with a light green hairline (top) were blended in 20 steps to produce rounded tubes.

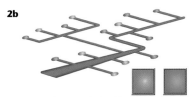

Shapes drawn with the Ellipse tool and given one of two Radial Fountain fills (F11) made round lights at the ends of the circuit branches.

3a

Filling the smaller object with the same color gradient as the background object wouldn't create the look needed for making a glow that fades onto the circuit board.

3b

In order for the smaller object (outlined here in black) to get the same Fountain fill progression as the larger background object, "tick marks" were combined with it to create an object with the same overall dimensions as the larger one.

3c

The combined object was duplicated and broken apart (Ctrl-K; ⌘-K on the Mac). Then the main piece was selected with the Pick tool, scaled down by Shift-dragging (⌘-drag in Mac v.6, Option-drag in v.8) inward on a corner handle, filled with yellow, and recombined with the tick marks (Shift-select the tick marks and choose Arrange, Combine). A 20-step blend created a yellow glow that fades into the background.

In another package design Krohn matched up multicolor Fountain fills. Starting with the Alien Sky Fountain fill preset, she added colors to make a custom fill by double-clicking new points along the color bar and choosing colors.

shape the same color for both its outline and its fill (press Shift-F11 to open the Uniform Fill dialog box). Using the Pick tool (press the spacebar to toggle to the Pick), she drag-selected all the lines and the triangle and grouped them (Ctrl-G; ⌘-G *on the Mac*) so she could duplicate them all in place by pressing the "+" key on the numeric keypad. She made the outline of the duplicate group very thin (about 0.22 points) and assigned it a light green color for both outline (F12) and fill (Shift-F11). Working in Preview mode with the green lines still selected, she was able to Shift-select the thick-outlined group and Blend (from the Effects menu).

3 Matching up Fountain fills. Krohn wanted to give the microchip on the controller board a glow that blended seamlessly into the Fountain-filled background shape. To do this she would fill a shape the size of the chip with a glow color and blend it to a slightly larger version underneath that was filled with part of the background Fountain. The trick would be to figure out a way to give the bottom-of-the-glow object exactly the right range of the more extensive Fountain fill of the background shape underneath it. CorelDRAW calculates Fountain fills from the physical dimensions of an object, with one end color of the fill at one extreme of the object and the other end color at the other extreme. So if you assign the same fill to a large object and to a small object on top of it, the entire fountain will appear in each object, looking more compressed in the small one and more stretched in the larger.

To get the two gradients to match, Krohn had to make the bottom-of-the-glow object seem to CorelDRAW to be as big as the larger background piece. She gave both the bottom-of-the-glow and the background object no outline (right-click the X in the on-screen palette; *Control-click on the Mac*) and the same Fountain fill (F11 opens the Fountain Fill dialog box; for tips on setting up a Fountain fill, see step 2 of "Shimmering Color" on page 104). Then she drew small "tick marks" (very short lines made with the Freehand tool) at the horizontal and vertical extremes of the large background object. Shift-selecting these along with the bottom-of-the-glow object, she combined them (Arrange, Combine). Then she copied the fill from the larger background object (choose Edit, Copy Properties From and click on the background object). The bottom-of-the-glow object became invisible against the larger one, since their colors matched exactly.

Next, to make the glow, Krohn duplicated the combined shape-and-tick-marks in place ("+"). She broke the copy apart (Ctrl-K; ⌘-*K*), scaled the shape down, gave it a yellow fill (Shift-F11), Shift-selected the tick marks, and recombined. Then she Shift-selected the bottom-of-the-glow and blended. Because the shapes had no outline, the tick marks didn't show up. (Krohn has found, however, that remnants of the tick marks sometimes appear when the file is printed, so she covers the marks with no-outline shapes filled with the color behind them, or with white if they fall on an empty part of the page.) 🖱

Shimmering Color

Overview *Create a gradient fill for the background rectangle; on top of the background, draw overall shapes for your iridescent elements; fill the shapes with multicolor gradients with highlight bands; create the iridescent elements themselves from gradient-filled bands with spaces in between; add several sets of thin colored lines on top of the bands, with spaces between the lines to allow all underlying colors to show.*

4•5•6•7•8

Version 3 has no way to make a multicolor gradient, so this iridescent effect isn't practical.

Purcell started with a pencil sketch.

CHRIS PURCELL

EACH PIECE OF CHRIS PURCELL'S AWARD-WINNING ARTWORK for the Compaq product line is unique but also ties in with the entire family of products (see the "Gallery" section at the end of this chapter). For the SmartStart server program, Purcell envisioned a "tower of power," representing the massive storage capacity of a *file server*, the computer on a local area network that holds most of the data. For this art, Purcell wanted to create an iridescent stack of disks, like the spinning platters in a giant hard drive.

1 Sketching the concept. In computer design, sketching your ideas on paper often makes for more efficient computer work and more professional results. To get the iridescent look he wanted for the towers, Purcell would set up an interaction between underlying left-to-right multicolor gradients and several overlying sets of rings that would contribute their own color and also let the underlying gradients show through.

2 Making the background. Create a background for your illustration. Purcell made a large rectangle by dragging with the Rectangle tool and then built and applied a Custom Linear Fountain

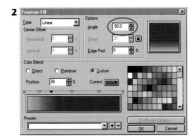

2

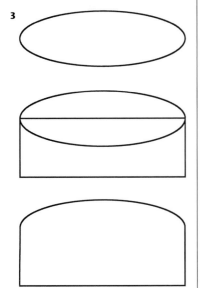

A background rectangle was given a Custom Fountain fill. The default Angle setting (90°) spreads the color changes over a vertical gradient, with the left-end color from the gradient bar at the bottom of the filled shape.

3

The basic tower shape (shortened here), can be built by welding together an ellipse and an overlapping rectangle.

fill. To make the fill, start by opening the Fountain Fill dialog box (F11). Clicking Custom opens a preview strip that lets you add and change colors and control the rate at which each color changes to the next (in version 4 click Options and then Custom). To add another color to the Fountain, double-click above the point in the preview strip to add a marker where you want the color to appear. When a marker is selected (it appears black), you can choose a new color for that spot in the band. To control how gradually a color blends with the ones before and after it in the gradient, drag its marker to a new position along the strip.

3 Building the basic shapes. Now draw the overall shape for your iridescent object. To make a cylindrical shape like the one Purcell used for his center tower, use the Ellipse tool to draw the shape of the top of the cylinder. Use the Rectangle tool to form the body of the cylinder by drawing a rectangle whose top edge runs through the middle of the ellipse. Use the Pick tool to drag-select (or Shift-select) the ellipse and rectangle, and then weld them together; this can be done by drag-selecting the objects with the Pick tool and choosing Arrange, Weld (in versions 6 and later you'll also need to click the Weld To button and then click on one of the objects). Make a duplicate of the shape (pressing the spacebar changes any tool to the Pick tool and pressing the "+" key on the numeric keypad duplicates the Pick-selected object in place). Drag the duplicate onto the pasteboard so you can use it later in the development of the iridescence.

To make smaller cylinders, like those Purcell used for the side towers, duplicate the cylinder shape and reduce its dimensions to about 80% by dragging a corner handle inward. To make a flat edge that will fit against the large central cylinder, draw a rectangle to trim away the right or left side of the structure; this can be done with the Arrange, Trim command in version 5 or later (in version 5 first select the "trimmer" with the Pick tool, then the "trimmee," and then choose Arrange, Trim; in versions 6 and later, choose the "trimmer," then the command, then click the Trim button, then choose the "trimmee.") CorelDRAW 4 has no Trim command; for the workaround, see Note 4 in Appendix A.

To make a flipped copy for the other small cylinder, duplicate the shape in place (Pick, "+"), and then hold down the Ctrl key as you drag one of the side handles across the shape to the other side (*in Mac v.6 use the Shift key; in v.8 use ⌘*).

4 Making the left-to-right color gradients. An important component of the iridescent look is the side-to-side color banding that shows between the rings. Purcell set up a custom color fill for each of the three cylinders. The front cylinder shows brighter tones, while the back ones are darker and less saturated, to contribute to the illusion that they are farther away than the center tower. To fill

4a

The central tower shape was filled with a custom gradient that included a highlight band near the left edge.

4b

Two additional 0° gradients were made to fill the side towers.

your shape with a color gradient, select it, press F11, and set up another custom gradient, as you did at step 2.

5 Adding rainbow rings. The next step was to build the stacks of rings that would give volume to the towers. To make the edge of the top disk in the stack, Purcell started with a copy of the ellipse-and-rectangle shape he had stored on the pasteboard. He copied this new shape in place ("+" from the numeric keypad), dragged the copy downward a little, and trimmed it (Arrange, Trim in version 5 or later; see Note 2 in Appendix A for a workaround for version 4).

With the Pick tool Purcell selected the arc band produced by this trimming and positioned it at the top of tower, leaving the ellipse on the pasteboard. Next he used the Rectangle tool to make a closed, straight bar the same thickness as the thickest part of the arc shape, and the same length. He positioned this band where he wanted the bottom of the tower.

KEEPING COPIES ALIGNED

To make sure a duplicate object ends up directly above or below the original when you drag the duplicate up or down with the Pick tool, hold down the Ctrl key as you drag (*in Mac v.6 use the Shift key; in v.8 use the ⌘ key*).

He Shift-selected both the top and bottom bands and filled them with a custom Fountain fill. Then he opened the Blend rollup (Ctrl-B; ⌘-*Shift-B in Mac v.6; Effects, Blend in v.8*) and applied a 26-step blend. The result was a stack of rainbow rings with small spaces in between that would allow the vertical color bands from step 4 to show through. Blending between an arc at the top and a straight bar at the bottom contributed to the perspective illusion of looking up at the tower, since the ellipses created by the blend get rounder as they go up the stack, as if the viewer were at the level of the bar at the bottom, looking up at the structure.

6 Adding more sets of rings. The next step was to add several sets of very thin rings that would add more color but allow both the Fountain-filled bands and the vertical color bands to show through. Using the large ellipse-and-rectangle shape stored on the pasteboard, Purcell cut off the top part by clicking with the Knife tool (use the Node Edit roll-up in versions before 6; click with the Shape tool where you want the break and then click the broken chain button to cut the curve at that point). He used the Node Edit functions to create a single arc.

He positioned that arc at the top and a straight line at the bottom, selected both, and assigned them a color and a hairline thickness in the Outline Pen dialog box. (With the objects selected, press F12 to open the Outline Pen box, enter a value for the Width, and click the Color button and then the More/Others bar to choose a color; turn on Scale With Image so the thickness of the rings will be scaled if you resize the artwork. Next Purcell made a 26-step blend, just as he had done for the arcs (in step 5).

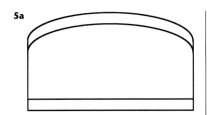

5a

The Trim command can be used to produce an arc band.

5b

Purcell's arc band was filled with a 14-color Custom rainbow gradient.

5c

Blending the arc and a straight band produced a stack of rainbow rings.

6

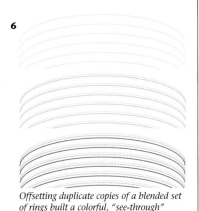

Offsetting duplicate copies of a blended set of rings built a colorful, "see-through" overlay for the towers.

To make more copies of the stack of rings, you can use the Place Duplicates And Clones command (accessed with Ctrl-J; ⌘-*J*); set Horizontal at 0 and Vertical at the spacing you want between rings, so the Edit, Duplicate command (Ctrl-D) will put a copy of the stack of hairline rings (Edit, Duplicate) slightly below the original (in version 7 or 8 you'll need to choose Workspace, Edit, Duplicate Placement after pressing Ctrl/⌘-J). Purcell assigned his ring-stack copy a new color (you can use the Outline Pen dialog box by pressing F12). This process of duplicating and recoloring was repeated another seven times, for a total of nine offset stacks of thin rings, completing the illusion of iridescence in the large tower. A similar process was applied to build stacks of 34 partial rings for the two side towers.

7 Capping the towers. To make the cone for the top of the central tower, Purcell drew a triangle (a quick way to draw an isosceles triangle can be found at step 9 on "Taking Advantage of Symmetry" in Chapter 2). He filled it with a Custom Conical Fountain fill, modified to make the spread of the color to fit the cone. (To color a cone in version 4, which lacks a Conical Fountain fill, you can use the method described for the *Halloween poster* on page 127.)

The cones on the side towers started out as duplicates of the top cone, sized down with the Pick tool. A fourth node was added to each one with the Shape tool, and the nodes were repositioned so it would look like the small cones were partially hidden behind the central tower.

8 Adding shadows. Purcell first drew a basic shape for the shadow cast onto the central tower by the custom-made "clip art" disk he would add in the foreground. He made a mirror copy of the shadow shape by pressing "+" on the keypad and using the Pick tool to Ctrl-drag the left side handle across the shape to the right (*Shift-drag in Mac v.6; ⌘-drag in v.8*). He moved the shapes into place on the central tower, Shift-selected both shapes and chose Arrange, Combine to make them into a single shape that he could fill with a dark version of the gradient for the central tower. (In CorelDRAW 7 or 8, you can select one or more objects and use Effects, Color Adjustment, Hue-Saturation-Lightness to adjust all the colors at once rather than darkening individual Uniform fills (Shift-F11) or the colors of a Fountain fill (F11).

Next Purcell wanted to put copies of the ring sets into the shadow shape; to do that, you need to make each set of rings into single object: A pink set of rings is duplicated, separated

7a

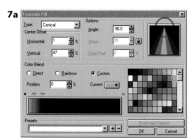

Purcell's Custom Fountain fill for the large cone went from light pink to red to black fairly quickly. The center offset was dragged to the top of the Fountain Fill dialog's preview box.

7b

Once the large cone was finished (left), it was duplicated, resized, and reshaped to make the small ones. Reshaping moved the Conical fill off center, so the offset was readjusted in the preview box.

SINGLE-HUE INTERSECTIONS

When you perform an Intersection, the new object retains the Outline and Fill of the *last* item selected. So be sure to *select your objects in the right order.*

8

Each combined ring object (shown only partially here, left) was overlaid on the combined shadows shape and trimmed with the Intersection command. Then the original set of rings was selected and deleted (right).

9

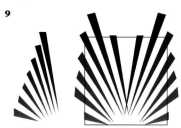

A blend between two gradient-filled triangles produced intermediate rays (left). These were stretched (right) so they could be trimmed to fit the background.

(Arrange, Separate), ungrouped (Arrange, Ungroup), and then combined (Arrange, Combine).

To put a series of shapes (like the sets of rings) into a background shape (like the shadow) in CorelDRAW 5 or later, use the Pick tool to select first the background shape, then a foreground shapes; then choose Arrange, Intersection to create a new object that fits inside the background shape. (In CorelDRAW 4, which lacks the Intersection command, use the Shape tool to adjust the shapes of the pieces.)

The first intersection set of rings was recolored darker and less saturated. Repeating this procedure with six more sets of rings in turn produced the illusion of shadows on the tower. Shadows for the side towers were similarly made. (Since Arrange, Combine assigns the same color to all the components of the combined object, the sets of rings had to be combined and added to the shadow one set at a time.)

9 Adding spotlights. To make the illustration more exciting, Purcell added one more element to the background — an array of spotlights like you might see at a Hollywood film opening. He selected the background shape and moved it to the front temporarily (Arrange [Order], To Front) so he could work with it. He drew a first, nearly vertical spotlight as a triangle using the Freehand tool. Then he duplicated it ("+" on the numeric keypad), resized, rotated, and moved the copy to the lower left (you can use the Pick tool, dragging a corner handle to resize, then clicking again and dragging a corner to rotate, then dragging inside the object itself to move it).

He filled each triangle with a Fountain fill, the bottom one darker. Then he used a 5-Step blend to create the beams in-between. The blend didn't produce exactly the shapes he wanted, so he separated the blend group from the two original control objects (Arrange, Separate), and then stretched the group. Next he ungrouped the rays (Arrange, Ungroup) and moved each one into place with the Pick tool. The spotlight group was drag-selected with the Pick tool, duplicated ("+"), and the duplicate was horizontally flipped, like the side cylinder in step 3.

One at a time, Purcell trimmed the rays to fit inside the background, as he had done with the sets of rings in step 8. Then the spotlight beams were selected and grouped (Arrange, Group), and the group was sent behind the towers (Arrange [Order], To Back). Then the background shape was sent behind the spotlights (Arrange [Order], To Back).

Finishing the package front. In the foreground Purcell added a disk from his own handmade "clip art" collection. Then he drag-selected all parts of the illustration with the Pick tool, copied it to the clipboard (Edit, Copy), opened the layout file for the package front, and pasted (Edit, Paste). He set the type and added a border rectangle in the Pantone red (200 CV) specified for the logotype for all Compaq-brand products. *WOW*

Building a Shine

Overview *Import a scanned photograph; trace it with the Freehand tool; add color and blend groups to give depth and shine to the surfaces.*

3•4•5•6•7•8

All versions allow you to import a bitmap for tracing and to color and blend. CorelDRAW 7 and 8 are the only versions with the Interactive Transparency tool for making the windshield. But there are workarounds for versions 4, 5, and 6, and even for 3, though for version 3 the process involves a lot of node-editing.

REED FISHER

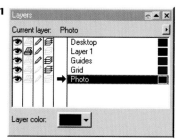

Importing a bitmap into its own layer and locking the layer (by clicking to dim the pencil icon) was the first step in manually tracing the scanned photo.

Fisher traced the imported photo using a contrasting Outline color.

REED FISHER STARTED WITH A PHOTOGRAPH for reference when he re-created this 1966 Shelby Cobra. Digitizing the image with a hand-held scanner and importing it into CorelDRAW gave him a template for tracing. Then, using the original color photo as a template, he matched the car's paint scheme. From there artistic license kicked in as Fisher colored and blended shapes to make the drawing even crisper and more visually interesting than the photo.

1 Making a template. The original photo was scanned as a gray-scale TIFF, and imported and locked onto its own layer. To import a scan, open a new CorelDRAW file (File, New), open the Layers roll-up, Layer Manager, or Object Manager from the Layout, Arrange, or Window menu. Choose New from the fly-out menu, and name the layer if you like. To make it the active layer, in the Layers list, click the layer's name (in version 3, 4, 5, or 8) or click in the column to the left of the name (in 6 or 7). Now from the File menu, import your reference scan (File, Import); it will automatically come in on the active layer. Lock the layer so the reference photo is deselected and can't be accidentally moved: In version 6 or later, click on the pencil icon to dim it; in 3, 4, or 5 choose Edit from the Layers palette's pop-out menu and click Locked. Finally, move the scan layer down beneath your drawing layer: Drag its name below Layer 1 (the layer you will draw on) in the Layers list.

2 Tracing the artwork. Fisher first drew the large shapes and then worked down to the smaller details. Although the car would eventually be red, he set the Outline color to bright yellow so it would stand out against the gray reference photo. (To set the Outline color, right-click on a contrasting color in the on-screen palette; *Control-click on the Mac.*) Also, Fisher worked in Normal/ Preview mode (press Shift-F9 to toggle between Wireframe and

3

The cobblestones and shadow were loosely drawn, stylized for the illustration.

4

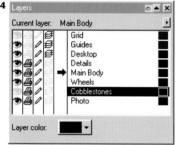

Using layers to hide some sections of the design while he worked on others helped Fisher to cut down screen refresh time and speed up his drawing.

5a

Large shapes (shown here in blue) were paired with small shapes (shown in pink) as the blend control objects that would be used to make the color transitions in the hood, fenders, door, and trunk of the car.

GETTING PREDICTABLE COLOR

On-screen colors sometimes look quite different from their printed equivalents. So if you want to be sure how a color will print, look at an accurate color chart. See "Getting the Color You Expect" on page 74 for some examples of printed charts.

Normal/Preview). In CorelDRAW 7 and 8 bitmaps are shown in high resolution in the Normal and Enhanced modes (from the View menu); for a high-res view in version 5 or 6, choose View, Bitmaps, High Resolution; in 3 or 4, you need to choose Display, Show Bitmaps to see the imported bitmap at all.

Fisher traced the main body shape of the car first, using the Bezier tool, and continued tracing until all the main elements were outlined. You can modify your objects with the Shape tool and the Node Edit roll-up, opened by double-clicking on the Shape tool in the Toolbox in versions 7 and 8, or by double-clicking on a curve with the Shape tool in other versions.

To make the illustration convincing and photorealistic, Fisher paid attention to detail. Where he could, he saved time by duplicating. For instance, he drew one headlight and copied it (by selecting it with the Pick tool and pressing "+" on the numeric keypad), moved the copy (by dragging with the Pick tool), and downsized it (by dragging inward on a corner handle of the highlight box). He did the same for the bumpers and for the seats.

3 Tracing the cobblestones. Next Fisher made the cobblestone road. It wouldn't be the focus of the illustration, so he stylized and simplified it. First he created another new layer. Next, with the scanned photo as a rough guide and his yellow outline color, he drew a large shape to make a shadow under the car and to provide "mortar" between the stones. Then he wielded the Freehand tool like a pencil to quickly draw the shape of each stone. He Shift-selected stones and gave them gray fills by clicking grays from the on-screen palette, and assigned no outline by right-clicking the palette's X (*on the Mac, Control-click*). The background shape was filled with the black at the beginning of the on-screen palette (100K) and also assigned no outline.

4 Hiding parts. To speed up the next part of the process, Fisher made the Cobblestones layer invisible as he worked, so CorelDRAW wouldn't have to redraw the stones as he zoomed and scrolled around to colorize the car.

5 Colorizing. Moving on to coloring and shading, Fisher first deleted his reference scan by selecting it in the Layers list, unlocking it (to unlock, click on the pencil icon in version 6 or later; or in version 3, 4, or 5 choose Edit from the pop-out palette and disable Locked). He then selected the bitmap and pressed Delete.

He matched the color of the Cobra paint using a Pantone Matching System swatch book. After choosing Pantone 160 CV as the best match, he used the Uniform Fill dialog box (Shift-F11) to assign the color. In CorelDRAW 7 or 8 it works this way: In the Uniform Fill dialog box's group of four buttons, click the button for Fixed Palettes. For the Type, choose Pantone Matching System. In

5b

The shapes were filled with the CMYK equivalent of Pantone 160 CV and with light and dark variations of this color.

6

Blending rounded the car's surfaces and created the highlights and shadows of polished paint.

7b

Sky
Horizon
Street

The curves of the chrome wheel and headlight rim reflect more detail than the polished paint on the body of the car. Small "coloring" shapes were given horizon, sky, and street fills.

7b

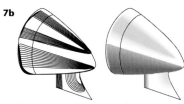

The housing of the mirror reflects the car color.

the Name or Search field, type in the color number; Fisher typed "160." Because he planned to print the finished drawing with four-color process inks rather than with custom Pantone inks, Fisher converted the Pantone color to its CMYK equivalent. To do this in CorelDRAW 7 or 8, click the Models button (the first in the group of four), and choose CMYK for the Model.

6 Adding shine with blends. Fisher now added shapes to give depth and shine to the image. If you look at a photo of any vehicle, you'll notice how the light and dark reflections of the sky and landscape respond to the roundness of its curves. In the case of the car, the darker surrounding landscape results in full, rich colors in the lower half of the car, while the lighter sky mixes with the body color to create the highlight tones.

Working in Wireframe mode with the photo on his desk for reference, Fisher drew shapes with the Bezier tool, this time without his scanned guide. For each lighted surface he drew the large gleam area, filled it with a light red made by moving the selectors in the CMYK color square in the Uniform Fill dialog box, and then drew a smaller shape on top, filled with the Pantone color.

Once he had colored one small shape, he could color others by Shift-selecting them and choosing Edit, Copy Properties From, and clicking the arrow on a shape with the fill he wanted. When the large and small shapes were colored, he Shift-selected them pair by pair, and for each pair, opened the Blend menu (Effects, Blend), set the Steps to 20, and pressed Apply. (The number of steps you need will increase as the space the blend will cover gets bigger and as the amount of difference between the starting and ending colors increases.)

3•4•5•6

Choosing a Pantone color and converting it to its CMYK equivalent is different in different versions of CorelDRAW. You always start by pressing Shift-F11 to open the Uniform Fill dialog box.

3

Choose Spot rather than Process, and for the Model, choose Names. Pick the Pantone color by name. Then switch from Spot to Process and choose CMYK for the Model.

4

For the Show setting, choose Pantone Spot Colors and turn on Show Color Names. Choose the Pantone color by name. Then change the Show setting to CMYK Color Model.

5

For the Show setting, choose Pantone Spot Colors. Then in the Search For field, type in the number of the color (for instance, "160" for Pantone 160 CV). Change the Show setting to CMYK 255 Color Model.

6

For the Show setting, choose Pantone Spot Colors. Then in the Search field, type in the name of the color. Choose Color Models and pick the CMYK Model.

8

To create the look of a glass windshield, fill the shape with white (center) and then use the Interactive Transparency tool with a Linear (shown) or Radial transparency gradient to reduce the white fill to transparent glass with a glare.

FLATTENING FILES

When you've finished a design, it's a good idea to make a copy of the file (File, Save As) and in this copy move all artwork to a single layer. That way you'll have one file that's organized logically and efficiently with layers in case you need to re-work it, and another file for trouble-free imagesetting, which can be a problem with multilayer files.

To put everything on one layer, first open the Layers list (choose Layout, Objects Manager in Windows v.8; press Ctrl-F3 in version 4, 5, 6, or 7; Ctrl-1 in version 3; ⌘-F3 in Mac v.6; Window, Palettes, Object Manager in v.8), and make sure all your layers are unlocked — with pencils turned on in 6, 7, or 8 or with Locked unchecked in 3, 4, or 5 (choose Edit for the Layers list's pop-out menu). Also, make sure you're set up to select from all layers (enable Edit Across Layers in the pop-out menu in 6, 7, or 8; in 3, 4, or 5 enable MultiLayer). From CorelDRAW's main Edit menu choose Select All. Then in the Layers list choose Move To from the pop-out menu, and click on the name of one layer.

7 Creating reflections. Reflections in chrome show more detail than polished painted surfaces. For this reason the convex chrome rims of the headlights of Fisher's car were colored with Uniform fills (Shift-F11) to show the gray of the street and tan for the horizon, and a Radial Fountain fill (F11) for the sky. For the concave wheels, the bottom half reflects the sky, and the top reflects the street. The mirror reflects the sky on top and the red of the car below.

8 Simulating glass. The windshield in the illustration looks like a transparent sheet of glass with reflected light from the sky changing the colors behind it. To accomplish a transparent windshield effect like this in CorelDRAW 7 or 8, use the Pick tool to select the shape you want to make transparent (in this case the shape of the glass in the windshield) and fill it with white (click the white square in the on-screen palette). Then click on the Interactive Transparency tool (this will automatically open its Property bar) and drag from above and outside the corner where you want the reflection to be strongest (in this case the upper right corner) to below and outside the corner where you want the glass to be most transparent (in this case the lower left). This will produce a gradually fading transparency, which will look like glass with a strong highlight. By starting and ending the fade beyond the limits of the shape, you ensure that the glass is never fully transparent or fully opaque, making the effect more subtle.

A Radial gradient can be used to simulate a bright sun instead of more diffuse daylight. If you change the type of gradient by clicking the Radial button on the Property bar, you'll need to click the Edit button to reverse the To/From colors for the fade to work correctly.

Preparing for output. To cut down on the likelihood of output glitches, you can reduce your file to a single layer, as described in "Flattening Files" (left). *WOW!*

3•4•5•6

To make a transparent-looking windshield without the Interactive Transparency tool, you can draw and color shapes to represent the objects seen through the windshield, as well as the reflections. In version 6, draw a glare shape; choose Arrange, Intersection; select Target Object and deselect Other Object(s); click the target (the windshield shape in this case) with the fat arrow. In version 5, select both objects (the glare and the windshield in this case) before choosing Arrange, Intersection; after the intersection shape is made, delete the extra objects.

In version 3 or 4, with no Intersection command, the curves have to be reshaped with the Shape tool, as described in "Node Editing" at the beginning of Chapter 2. Lighten the intersections by lowering the CMYK percentages in the Uniform Fill dialog box.

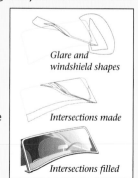

Glare and windshield shapes

Intersections made

Intersections filled

Modelling with Blends

Overview *Import a photo; trace primary shapes with the Bezier tool; draw highlight shapes; color shapes with Radial Fountain fills; blend between filled shapes; use a blend to make a lace pattern; export and reimport the lace; color it; place it over a Fountain-filled shape.*

3•4•5•6•7•8

The importing, tracing, and blending that shaped the figure of the boy in *Late Afternoon* can be done in CorelDRAW 3 and all later versions, as can the exporting and reimporting that makes the curtain (shown below at its original scale) look soft. The Texture fills

used for the chair and table aren't available in version 3, so these would have to be created in another way — for instance, by making a Two-Color or Full-Color pattern.

1

Original photo, scanned, saved as a TIFF, and imported

IN HIS CORELDRAW "PAINTING" *Late Afternoon* Wil Dawson wanted to capture the mood and the strong lighting of the moment on the digital canvas. He made expert use of blends to sculpt the figure of the boy, he modified Texture fills to make woodgrain, and he wielded the blending, exporting, and importing functions like a set of fine brushes to paint the soft, transparent curtains.

1 Importing the photo for tracing. Dawson began by scanning a black-and-white photo and importing it into CorelDRAW as a bitmap so he could use it as a tracing template to draw the figure of the boy. To import a scan, choose File, Import. So that the bitmap can exist on its own layer and you won't accidentally move it, you can first lock the bitmap layer and then make a new layer for the drawing: Using the Object Manager in CorelDRAW 8 (the Layer[s] Manager or Layers roll-up, from the Layout or Arrange menu in earlier versions), lock the layer (in versions 5 and earlier, double-click on the "Layer 1" name to open a dialog box that lets you choose Locked and then click OK; in version 6 or later you can lock the layer more easily, by simply clicking in the Lock column of the Layers list to turn on a lock icon or turn off the pencil icon). Now choose New from the Layers list's flyout menu; the new layer (Layer 2) will be created directly above Layer 1.

2 Tracing by hand. Dawson traced the main shapes for the image. Using the Bezier tool, draw lines over your bitmap guide. (For tips on drawing in Bezier mode and adjusting curves, see "Drawing Basics" and "Node Editing" at the beginning of Chapter 2.) Dawson first outlined all the large shapes in the figure, leaving the detail and shading attributes for later.

3 Setting up for blending. Dawson used Radial Fountain fills and blends together to add depth to his objects. This technique allows much more sophisticated "sculpting" than a Fountain fill or blend alone. For each shape that he wanted to model, he would

2

Large shapes traced in a bright color to contrast with the grayscale scan

3a

Highlight shapes (shown here in black) for the arms, legs, and face were made by duplicating and reshaping the original large shapes (shown in magenta).

3b

Dawson organized his drawing in layers. A different color wireframe for each layer made it easier to distinguish the parts, and locking and invisibility made it easier to work on one part without disturbing another.

3c

The Radial Fountain fills for the arm's large shapes (top) and highlight shapes

---

shade the shape he had drawn with a dark Radial fill, then blend this object to an object with a lighter Radial fill. The in-between objects not only changed shape but also changed colors as one Radial fill palette transformed to the other to create a smooth color transition.

To use Dawson's method of "sculpting," first duplicate the original shape (select it with the Pick tool and press the "+" key in the numeric keypad). Then downsize it by dragging inward on one or more of the handles of the highlight box, move it into place, and do any node-editing needed to finish this as the second control object for your blend.

When you think you have a satisfactory shape for the second blend control object, open the Fountain Fill dialog box (F11), and set up the fill. Change the fill Type to Radial, pick your colors for the gradient (the "From" color becomes the outside, and the "To" color becomes the center), and offset the center of the fill if necessary (by dragging the center spot in the Preview window or typing in numbers for the Horizontal and Vertical values under Center Offset). Then click OK. Dawson's "From" color for the highlight shapes on the arm was a tan, and the "To" color was a light cream. The center of the radial fill was offset to the top left, so the lighting on the boy would seem to come from the window he planned to add.

Next select and fill your other blend control object the same way, using different colors for the fill. Dawson gave his large shapes a Radial fountain fill also, but with colors from a much darker palette.

4 Making the blends. A CorelDRAW blend will create interim steps for both Outline and Fill attributes, but in modelling a smooth shape, the objects to be blended should have no outline. To get rid of the outline, Shift-select all the shapes you want to change and right-click (*Control-click on the Mac*) the X in the color palette. Now select both shapes, and open the Blend roll-up from the Effects menu. The number of steps you'll need depends on how much the colors change from one control object to the other and on how big a distance the blend has to cover. The greater the color change and the bigger the distance, the more steps you need.

5 Blending along a path. The knitted neckband of the boy's shirt is a group of two blends, one for each side. First, for the bottom of the neckband, Dawson drew a rib with the Rectangle tool, filled it with a red-to-blue Linear Fountain fill (F11), and skewed it: To skew an object, click it once or twice with the Pick tool to

3d

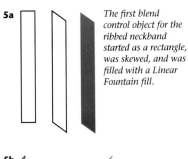

Filling the shapes in the arm (the forefinger was given its own Radial fill)

4

The default setting of 20 Steps was more than enough for these subtle blends.

5a

The first blend control object for the ribbed neckband started as a rectangle, was skewed, and was filled with a Linear Fountain fill.

5b

The rib unit was duplicated to make three more blend control objects, and these were rotated and dragged into position.

change the highlight box handles to the rotate/skew arrows and then grab a side arrow and drag.

For each side of the neckband Dawson's skewed rectangle was duplicated ("+"), and the copy was moved to the top of the neckband, downsized (drag inward on a corner arrow) and rotated (click again with the Pick tool and drag a corner handle). Dawson then used the Bezier tool to draw a path that the blend would follow.

To draw a path to guide a modelling blend, you'll want the line to have no outline attributes that will show up on the final, but you'll need to be able to see it as you work. To accomplish this, you can draw the line with no outline and then work in Wireframe mode (Shift-F9) to make it visible.

Viewing both your path and the blend control objects, select both of the blend control objects, activate the Blend roll-up, set the number of Steps (Dawson used 40 for the left side of the collar), and click Apply. Now to assign the blend to the path, click on the Blend To Path button (an arrow on a wavy line), then New Path, then click on the blend control path you drew, and click Apply. Dawson repeated the process for the other side of the neckband.

6 Adding detail. The process of drawing shapes and making blends was repeated to create most of the color work in the

---

TROUBLESHOOTING BLENDS

Here are some perplexing things that can go wrong with blends. Once you figure out what the problem might be, they're easy to fix.

- If you see pronounced bands of color in your artwork — that is, you can see a stutter-step of transitions — try increasing the number of steps in your blend.

- If you try a blend and it has plenty of steps but it still looks choppy, check to see if your blend control objects have outlines. If so, Shift-select the two objects, remove the outlines by right-clicking (*Control-clicking on the Mac*) on the X in the color palette, and the blend will be remade without outlines.

- If you set up a blend from a small object to a larger one in Wireframe mode but then you don't see the desired result in Normal/Preview, it may be that your smaller shape is actually behind the larger one, instead of in front of it — so the blend is happening but it's completely hidden! Undo the blend (Edit, Undo), then select the large shape and send it behind the smaller one with Arrange [Order], Back One.

Too few steps (6)   *Number of steps increased to 20*

Blended with outlines   *Outlines removed*

A blend with the smaller control object in back   *With the smaller control object moved to the front*

5c

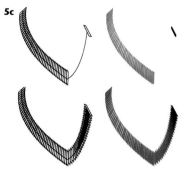

A 40-step blend for the left side and a 23-step blend for the right, each along a no-outline curved path, finished the neckband.

6a

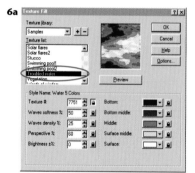

To make a woodgrain texture, Dawson chose the Troubled Water Texture fill.

6b

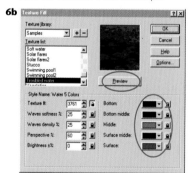

Clicking the Preview button brought up variations of the Texture. Dawson chose one and changed its colors.

6c

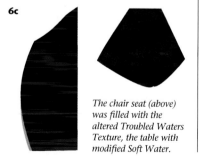

The chair seat (above) was filled with the altered Troubled Waters Texture, the table with modified Soft Water.

Afternoon image. Additional smaller shapes were also drawn and Fountain-filled to add more detail, shadows, and highlights.

The wood effects in the chair and the table are recolored Texture fills. To fill a shape with a Texture, select the shape, and open the Texture Fill dialog box by clicking its icon in the Fill tool's fly-out menu; choose from the Texture Library list and then from the Texture list. For the chair Dawson selected Troubled Water from the Samples library, shown in "Texture Fills" on page 89. Then he changed the colors from the default blue palette to shades of brown. Click on Preview after you change the colors or other options to create the new color texture. If you click on Preview again, another variant of that Texture will build. You can keep clicking and modifying until you see a version of the Texture that you like.

7 Making lace. To get a soft look for the curtains at the window, Dawson started by drawing crisp, lace panels in CorelDRAW. He used blending first to make a lace medallion and then again to repeat the medallion to build a fabric panel. To start the lace he Ctrl-dragged the Ellipse tool to draw a circular ring the approximate size of the lace medallion he wanted (*Shift-drag in Mac v.6, ⌘-drag in v.8*). He assigned this ring no outline or fill (click and right-click [*Control-click*] on the X in the on-screen palette). The he drew a smaller circle and assigned it a 0.6-point black outline (F12). This shape was duplicated (Ctrl-D; ⌘-*D on the Mac*), and both copy and original were Shift-selected. In the Blend roll-up (Ctrl-B; ⌘-*Shift-B*), 10 Steps were set, the Blend-To-A-Path button was pressed, and New Path was chosen. Dawson clicked the New Path arrow on the large circle, and clicked to turn on Full Path in the Blend roll-up, to space the small circles around the entire large circle. When he clicked Apply the small circles were evenly spaced but not touching, so he Shift-selected the two original

> **3**
>
> In CorelDRAW 3, which doesn't have Texture fills, you can make woodgrain or other texture by importing a scanned photo or a texture painted in Corel PHOTO-PAINT or another image editor and saved in Bitmap (**.bmp**) format. Then choose Special, Create Pattern, Full Color, Ctrl-drag to select a square area of the imported image, and name the pattern file. Your new pattern will be available through the Full-Color Pattern icon from the Fill tool's fly-out menu. (You'll find more about creating and using patterns in the "Patterning" section on page 96.)

SAVE THAT TEXTURE!

Texture fill (available in CorelDRAW 4 and later versions) is very flexible. You can change the colors and other properties of your fill any time in the life of your CorelDRAW file. However, if you ever save the file in CorelDRAW 3 format, the Texture fill will be permanently converted to a Full-Color pattern, which doesn't allow you to change the colors or other pattern attributes easily. So if you need to convert your file to version 3 format but you want to keep the fill "live," be sure to also save a copy in a later version.

7a

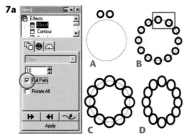

Two small circles were blended around a larger no-outline ring. Circle size was adjusted and the ring of circles was squeezed to make an oval medallion.

7b

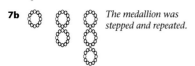

The medallion was stepped and repeated.

7c

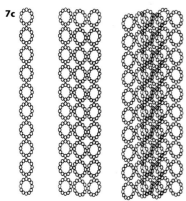

A panel of lace was built by copying the medallion, moving the copy, and using the Edit, Repeat command to step-and-repeat it. The panel was duplicated several times, some of the copies were skewed, and the strips were arranged to form a drape.

8

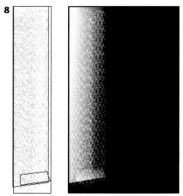

The curtain was exported as a Black And White TIFF at 150 dpi, reimported, assigned a cream outline color, and placed over two Fountain-filled panels.

blend control objects with the Pick tool, and dragged a corner handle of the highlight box until the circles touched all around the ring. The medallion was drag-selected with the Pick tool and reshaped by dragging a side handle inward.

A step-and-repeat method was used to copy the medallion several times to make a vertical strip of curtain material. You could also use a blend; if necessary, adjust the spacing between elements after blending by selecting one of the two control objects and moving it up or down with the Pick tool.

When Dawson's strip of curtain lace contained enough medallions, it was drag-selected and duplicated (Ctrl-D; ⌘-D) several times, some of the copies were skewed (click again with the Pick tool and drag a side arrow), and the strips were arranged to form a drape of material.

8 Exporting and importing. To get a soft look for the fabric, he drag-selected the curtain, exported a copy as a bitmap, and then imported it back into the image: Choose File, Export; name your bitmap, choose TIFF Bitmap from the file Type list, and click to turn on the Selected Only option; then click OK. From the Bitmap Export dialog box, set Colors to Black And White, set Size to 1 To 1, and set Resolution to no higher than 150 dpi. Click OK. The low-resolution bitmap would give the curtain a somewhat textured and softer look. (In CorelDRAW 7 or 8, you can shortcut the export/import process by using Bitmaps, Convert To Bitmap instead.)

While all of the objects you've just exported are still selected in your main file, it's a good idea to save them to disk, separately from the file. This will give you a copy in case you want to create the bitmap again with a different resolution — for a different look, or for reuse in another image. From the File menu, select Save As; give the new file a name of its own, and choose the Selected Only option, then click OK. With a copy safely filed you can now delete these objects from your main image.

Working in your image file, select File, Import, and then choose your new black-and-white bitmap file. With the newly imported bitmap selected, Dawson chose a creamy color for the Outline, which colorized the black parts of the bitmap. With no fill color assigned, the white parts of the bitmap (the holes in the lace) remained transparent. *WOW!*

Repeating Yourself

Overview *Several sophisticated effects can be created simply by repeating a line or a shape and then assigning it new outline and fill characteristics. Here are three ways to simulate neon against a black "sky," a method for making "patterned" lines for borders, a quick way to add a thick outline around artwork, and a way to make a "banner" of flowing lines.*

One way to achieve a neon effect is by blending a thin-outlined white path in a bright color with a thicker-outlined brightly colored copy directly behind it. Draw the curve, or set type, for the neon, and duplicate it in place (with the Pick tool active, press "+" on the numeric keypad). Assign the top copy a thin outline in white (F12); we used a 0.5-point outline here. Then press the Tab key to select the curve behind, and assign it a thick outline in a bright neon color (we used 4 points). Shift-click on the top curve again to select it also; choose Effects, Blend; set the number of steps (we used the default 20), and click Apply if necessary.

To make the neon really glow, make a duplicate of the white line (click on the white line with the Pick tool and press "+" on the numeric keypad), assign it the same width as the brightly colored bottom line of the neon, and send it to the back (Arrange [Order], To back), behind the neon. Then duplicate this line again, again send it to the back, and assign it a black outline (assuming your background is black) and a width about 1.5 to 2 times the width of the white copy. Now select the neon and nudge it out of the way with the arrow keys so you can select the white copy; click to select the black copy underneath as well. Then blend (Effects, Blend); we used 20 Steps.

To change the brightness of the neon, try increasing or decreasing the width of the white or black outline slightly.

To create the effect of neon light behind a solid object, start with a shape that looks thick enough to be cut out of sheet material (here we used a thicker version of the musical note). Give the shape a black fill and a very heavy black outline (F12); we used 12 points. Then duplicate it in place (with the Pick tool active, press "+" on the numeric keypad) and change the outline of the top copy to white or a light color, and greatly reduce the outline width (F12); we used 0.5 point. Then drag-select the two with the Pick tool, open the Blend roll-up (Effects, Blend), set the number of Steps (we used 20), and click Apply if necessary. You can make the glow spread farther by increasing the width of the shape with the black outline. You can brighten the light by lightening the color of the outline of the top shape or increasing the width of the outline used for the white- or color-outlined shape.

The effect is slightly different if you use a rich black for the background — that is, a black that includes the neon color (a 60% tint of yellow in this case) as well as 100K.

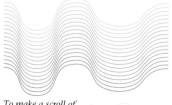

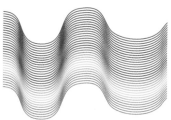

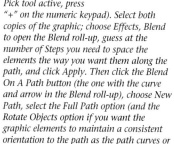

One way to stylize a series of illustrations is to use the Outline Pen to create matching thick borders around them. You can't just start with your artwork, select all, and assign a thick outline, though. That would change the weight of the internal outlines also. Here's how you can thicken the outside borders only: Drag-select all parts of the artwork with the Pick tool, group it (Ctrl/⌘-G), duplicate it in place (press "+" on the numeric keypad), assign an outline twice the width you want for your border (F12). This will thicken all the lines. But when you send the duplicate to the back (Arrange [Order], To Back), only a thick outer border will show.

To make a "patterned" outline, you can repeat a graphic element along a path: Draw the path. Make the graphic; if it's made up of several objects, select them all (drag around them with the Pick tool) and group them (Ctrl/⌘-G). Duplicate the graphic (with the Pick tool active, press "+" on the numeric keypad). Select both copies of the graphic; choose Effects, Blend to open the Blend roll-up, guess at the number of Steps you need to space the elements the way you want them along the path, and click Apply. Then click the Blend On A Path button (the one with the curve and arrow in the Blend roll-up), choose New Path, select the Full Path option (and the Rotate Objects option if you want the graphic elements to maintain a consistent orientation to the path as the path curves or turns the corner), click on the path, and click Apply if necessary.

To make a scroll of waving parallel lines, draw the top curve, assign it a color and width (F12), duplicate it, (with the Pick tool active, press "+" on the numeric keypad), and drag the copy directly down to make the bottom curve. Change the color of this line if you like. Then Shift-select the top curve and blend the two (Effects, Blend) with as many Steps as you want intermediate lines.

You can change the way the sheet of lines flows by modifying one or both blend control curves with the Shape tool, moving individual nodes to new positions.

To make a multicolored sheet, assign your beginning and ending colors to your two curves, blend using as many steps as you want color changes, and then separate the blend elements (Arrange, Separate) and ungroup the intermediate steps (Ctrl/⌘-G). Now select and recolor each of the separated and ungrouped curves, and use these curves as the blend control objects for more blends, made as follows: Select the top curve and the one below it (the second curve) and blend between them, using as many steps as you want. Then use the second curve again, as well as the third one, to make the next blend. Continue blending between pairs of curves until the multicolored "fabric" is complete.

LEONARDO'S DELI & CAFE

To make this *logo for Leonardo's Deli & Cafe*, **Tom Graney** started by automatically tracing a pen-and-ink drawing with CorelTRACE in Outline Trace mode. The result of the trace is shown above (top). It consists of stacked black-and white-filled objects.

Graney imported the tracing into CorelDRAW (File, Import). To lighten the overall effect, reducing the black and thinning the heavy black "lines" (actually

the closed, filled shapes produced by CorelTRACE), Graney selected all the stacked objects — both black and white — and used the Outline Pen dialog box (F12) to assign them a thick white outline, shown here against a contrasting background. The white outlines reduced the amount of black in the image, by extending into the black shapes.

▶ *When you assign an outline in CorelDRAW, half the width of the line*

extends outward from the path and half extends inward, covering part of the fill, unless you enable the Behind Fill option so the inside half of the line is hidden behind the fill.

Adding the outlines to lighten the image made the artwork dependent on the width of the white lines. So Graney designated his outlines to Scale With Image so he could successfully enlarge or reduce the logo.

All the shapes in *Skateboarder* by **Tom Graney** are composed of straight-line segments with Uniform color fills. To turn the scanned photo of the skater into a stylized illustration, Graney first simplified the photo by posterizing it in Corel PHOTO-PAINT (to posterize, look for the Posterize command in PHOTO-PAINT's Effects menu or one of the Effects submenus; *in version 6 on the Mac use Corel Artisan, choosing Image, Effects, Posterize*). He imported the posterized image into CorelDRAW (File, Import) and traced by hand to make a drawing. Clicking from point to point with the Bezier tool made the angular shapes.

Graney's drawing consisted of a large black-filled shape with color shapes on top of it. For the most part, Graney filled the shapes with Pantone custom ink colors, selected from a printed reference and chosen in the Uniform Fill dialog box (Shift-F11). But the flesh tones and some of the blue-purples were mixed as process colors.

▶ *In versions of CorelDRAW that will produce PostScript color separations, in order to print a spot-color illustration with four-color process instead of custom inks, you can choose the Convert Spot Colors To CMYK option in the Separations section of the Print Options dialog box (opened by choosing File, Print, Options [or Corel Print Options], Separations or File, Print, Separations) to convert all of the Pantone colors to their process equivalents. Keep in mind that the converted colors won't exactly match a printed reference for the custom inks.*

Reed Fisher's illustration of his friend Dave Peter's *1921 T-Bucket*, a street-rod version of the Ford Model T, was developed from a photograph. Fisher built the image in essentially the same way as the Cobra car in "Building a Shine" earlier in this chapter, scanning in the photograph and using it as a guide to redraw the image. Separate layers were used for the car and the shadow pieces, so the car can be displayed with or without a background.

The glass effect in the windshield was easy to create with a Lens. The windshield shape was given a white fill, and then made 85% Transparent using the Lens feature. This muted the objects behind it, resulting in a realistic glass look. (Lenses are discussed in Chapter 4.)

For the firewall reflections, Fisher used thinner lines and slightly duller (less saturated) colors than for the hardware itself. For instance, he changed the wires from a bright yellow

fill (100Y) to thinner shapes with a duller color (7C,4M,66Y,4K) in the reflection. He also used blends in the reflection to soften some of the sharp color breaks.

To create this landscape of *Lake Louise*, nestled in the Canadian Rockies, **Valerie Babb Krohn** started by rendering the impressive scene with paper and pencil, using a photo for reference. She then converted her drawings to simple shapes using the CenterLine mode in CorelTRACE. When Krohn opened the trace objects in CorelDRAW she found that they were overly complex, so she deleted nodes. ▶ *In versions 5 and later the Auto-Reduce option in the Node Edit roll-up can be used to remove extra nodes (in versions 7 and 8 the Property Bar for the Shape tool also has an Auto-Reduce button).*

Working from back to front, Krohn blocked in each section piece by piece. Once a section was finished, it was given its own layer, locked, and made invisible to speed up screen refresh.

The trees on the hills resulted from blending along a path, from a small jaggy-edged shape to a larger, slightly modified duplicate in front of it. Using green-to-lime Linear Fountain fills resulted in the look of rolling hills. Krohn created the conical shapes of the first row of trees by blending between a shape made up of narrower, shorter, darker spikes and a shape made of wider, taller, lighter ones behind it.

The individual pine trees are variations on a single design. Each tier was created by blending from a blue shape to a yellow-to-green Fountain-filled shape behind it. The far-away versions of the tree were given less color variation and more neutral colors than the the foreground pine, to suggest distance.

The flowers started as basic shapes that were duplicated and recolored to populate the garden. The tulips, for instance, are a repeating assemblages of leaf, stem and flower shapes. And star shapes were Welded to stems, duplicated, flip-flopped and stretched to become stalks of leaves.

A clever use of blended, wavy dotted lines makes up the yellow dandelions in the grass. Krohn changed the line from solid to a dot pattern with the Style option in the Outline Pen dialog box.

Thin wavy lines blended to slightly thicker ones make the water sparkle, but the trick here is that Krohn changed the Nib Shape from square to a horizontal cigar shape. This was done by changing the Calligraphy options in the Outline Pen Dialog box (F12), setting the Stretch to 10% and the Angle to 90°, and also selecting the Round Corners option.

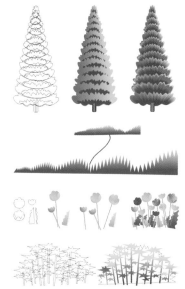

The clouds are simple shapes, filled with a white-to-blue Fountain fill, which subtly contrasts with a light-blue-to-powder-blue Fountain fill in the sky.

Valerie Babb Krohn

Valerie Babb Krohn takes an impressionistic approach to lighting, capturing the nuances of the moment in her images. For the scenes she used for *The Artist's Assistants* for the front of her business card (top) and for *Morning Tea*, used for a promotional flyer (right), the lighting was changing with the moving sun, so drawing the scenes directly into the computer would have been impossible. Instead she captured the scene with photos and then scanned and imported them into CorelDRAW as separate layers that could .

Although the photos for the promotional flyer were taken at the same time of day, the lighting, angles and vanishing points were not the same for the two pictures. So Krohn first mapped out the

design using guidelines to work out a scheme for aligning all the pieces into a new, uniform configuration.

For straight-lined shapes like the outline of the dog, Krohn clicked from point to point with the Bezier tool. Rounded elements, like the edges of the couch and the scallops of the lamp shade were drawn by dragging with the Bezier tool and then blending from light forward shapes to larger, darker shapes behind.

The edges of many of the highlights and cast shadows in the images are sharply delineated, though some were softened by using Fountain fills. When a shadow or highlight fell over an object, Krohn darkened or lightened the intersection shape. But when a shadow fell over another

shadow, as with the coffee cup on the table, she made the darker shadow predominate, as it does in the real world. By creating blends between the highlight and shadow shapes that made up the dog and cat, she achieved the soft look of fur.

Krohn used a rich, bright palette, mixing cyan, magenta, and yellow to achieve darker tones, rather than adding black. The scanned photos provided shape and contrast cues, but Krohn preferred her own coloring interpretation to the harsh darker colors in the photos. ▶ *For predictable printed color, monitor the CMYK values in the Uniform Fill dialog box (Shift-F11; click the More button if necessary to expand the dialog box to reveal the CMYK values), and always compare your colors to a printed reference.*

Samples, Clouds, Midday

Styles, Minerals, Speckled 2 Colors

Styles, Sky 5 Colors

Styles, Sky 5 Colors

R émi Forcier modified the color ways of Texture fills, chosen from the Texture Libraries available from the pop-out palette for CorelDRAW's Fill tool, to create unique patterns for this wall-sized *Steel* image used in a trade-show booth. For the large-output format Forcier wanted a bold, art-deco feel. He changed the color and other settings for the Texture fills to customize the textures for his drawing, picking tones consistent with the turn-of-the-century look he was after. To change colors, in the Texture Fill dialog box he simply clicked on a color chip to open the palette, and then clicked on the color of his choice.

For convenient transfer to the service bureau, Forcier needed a relatively small file. To transfer the file, he left the Texture fills at their default setting of 120 dpi Bit-map Resolution and 257 pixels Maximum Tile Width. Then his service bureau printed directly from CorelDRAW to a large-format color printer, first resetting the Bitmap Resolution and increasing Maximum Tile Width in the Texture Options dialog box (opened by clicking Options in the Texture Fill dialog box) to avoid pixelation in the Texture fills. ▶ *In general, a CorelDRAW vector drawing can be enlarged or reduced without changing the file size or degrading the quality of the artwork. However, Texture fill information is stored as a bitmap when you save your CorelDRAW file. If you increase the Maximum Tile Width value in the Texture Options dialog, your file will be dramatically bigger when you save it, as more information has to be stored in the bitmap. To avoid this file enlargement when saving files with Texture fills, Windows versions 7 and 8 offer compression options; for the best savings on file size, click the Advanced button in the Save Drawing dialog box, and then enable the Rebuild Textures When Opening The File option. This saves the Texture fills as mathematical information and generates the bitmaps anew when the file is opened.*

To put *Egyptians* together, **Barry Monaco** gathered pieces from CorelDRAW's clip-art CD-ROM. ▶ *All versions of CorelDRAW come with thousands of clip-art images, to use whole or for parts. Some versions shipped with the files in Corel Presentation Exchange (.cmx) format, while others provide the art as CorelDRAW (.cdr) files. No matter what the extension is, you can open or import the images the same way.*

The seated figures were developed from the *symb382* file. Monaco broke apart the symbol (Arrange, Break Apart), which allowed him to select and recolor each shape.

The eyes are from a cartoon of Arsenio Hall (*arsenni*), which Monaco imported (File, Import), ungrouped (Ctrl/⌘-U), and selected and deleted all but the pieces that made up a single eye. He used the Pick tool to rotate the eye to a different angle, positioned it in the face of one of the Egyptians, and then copied the eye (press "+" on the numeric keypad). He flipped the copy by

Ctrl-dragging a side handle across to the other side (Shift-drag in Mac v.6, ⌘-drag in v.8), and positioned it in the face of the other figure.

The border (*bord29*) was rotated 90° (hold down the Ctrl key while dragging a corner handle with the Pick tool to constrain the angle of rotation; use the Shift key in Mac v.6, the ⌘ key in v.8), and the torches (*torch2*) were broken apart and colored. The lighting established by a peach-to-tan Radial fill in the background rectangle is enhanced by a walnut-to-white Radial fill in the ball above the trefoil. ▶ *You can offset the center of a Radial fill in the Fountain Fill dialog (F11) or with the Interactive Fill tool in later versions: From the Fountain Fill dialog, you can either key in new Horizontal and Vertical values for the Center offset, or simply drag the center-point in the preview window to a new position. In version 7 or 8 the Interactive Fill tool lets you manipulate a Fountain fill, adjusting it "live" until it looks the way you want. In version 8 you can even change the edge-pad setting by dragging the middle slider back and forth.*

Lance Ravella created this *Oracle* icon to identify the "Ask the Oracle" column in the *Internet Insider,* a specialty newsletter. Because the site is a take-off on the ancient Greek Oracle at Delphi, Ravella used the Parthenon for inspiration.

Composed of basic geometric shapes, the building gets its depth from creative shading. A slightly different Fountain fill was applied to each object, to create a more realistic play of light than if all columns (which are duplicates of the same objects) had the same fills. The shafts, bases, and capitals all have Linear fills, each with a unique angle. ▶ *You can change the angle of a Linear Fountain fill by keying in a new Angle value in the Fountain Fill dialog (F11), by dragging in the Fountain Fill dialog preview window, or by using the Interactive Fill tool in versions 7 or 8.*

The entablature is filled with the Diamond texture fill from the Samples library, available from the Fill tool fly-out. The eye is a collection of lines drawn with the Freehand tool within a gray circle, sitting at the center of the Radial-filled triangular pediment. The steps were created by blending rectangles filled with Linear Fountains and outlined in medium gray.

KEEP YOUR EYES ON THE KIDS.

DRIVE WITH CARE OCTOBER 31st.

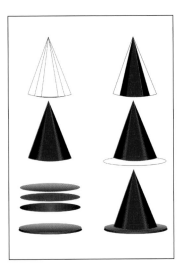

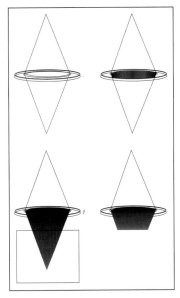

Watching kids playing near a street around Halloween time, **Kent Looft** noted how much the traffic cones looked like witches' hats. By blending simple shapes to create roundness and using Fountain fills to create reflections, he developed this *Halloween poster.* The hat started with a triangle created like that shown in step 9 of Taking Advantage of Symmetry in Chapter 2. He used the Shape tool and Node Edit roll-up to convert the base of the shape to a curve. To get the shapes he needed for blending to round the cone shape, he duplicated the rounded triangle in place twice (by pressing "+" on the numeric keyboard), each time sizing the copy down with the Pick tool with the Shift key held down to keep the shape centered within the larger shape (use the ⌘ key in Mac v.6; the Option key in v.8). Then he made necessary adjustments to the curved bases with the Shape tool. He filled the smallest triangle with blue and the other two with black. A blend from the blue one to the next larger one, as shown at the right, would produce a color gradation that would blend seamlessly into the large black shape, and would produce better rounding than if he had simply blended from the small shape to the large without using an intermediate size. He made a 20-Step blend (Effects, Blend).

The hat brim was created by stacking Fountain-filled discs drawn with the Ellipse tool. To create the reflection on the brim of the hat and on the implied street surface, Looft first made a flipped duplicate of the largest component shape of the cone (duplicate the shape in place with the "+" key, then select the new copy with the Pick tool, and with the Ctrl key held down, drag downward on the top center control handle to flip [*use the Shift key in Mac v.6; the ⌘ key in v.8*]. The next step is to Ctrl-drag the flipped copy upward (*Shift-drag in Mac v.6; ⌘-drag in v.8*) to move it straight up so that the rounded bases overlap). Using the Intersect command (Effects, Intersect) on the lower triangle (shown in blue) and the top ellipse of the brim, he created the reflection on the brim.

Drawing a rectangle over the lower triangle and then using the Trim command, he cut away the overlapping area, resulting in the reflection that falls on the street. For the background rectangle and the reflection, Looft used Linear Fountain fills, both ending in the same color. This made the reflection appear to blend into the surface the cone was sitting on.

Looft duplicated the hat shape twice to make the two traffic cones. Since the blend was still live, he could simply change the colors of the triangles to produce the new color scheme he wanted. ▶ *When you blend between a color-filled shape and a black-filled one, you can avoid having the blend look "gray" if you use a rich black — that is, one defined as 100K plus the components of the color you're using.*

To complete the poster, Looft added rectangles with type, a large round moon, and a bat assembled from several copies of a "boomerang" shape drawn with the Freehand tool. The boomerang shape used for the bat was also used to produce wrinkles in the hat. To form a wrinkle, the shape was duplicated in place and sized down. The larger object was filled with blue and the smaller with black, and the two were blended.

I n his award-winning *package designs for the Compaq product line*, shown here and in "Shimmering Color" earlier in the chapter, **Chris Purcell** uses bold, often highly saturated, complementary colors — that is, many pairs of colors that are opposite each other on the color wheel. Although the colors he chooses for the Compaq packaging range over a broad spectrum, Purcell has omitted most of the yellow-green section of the color wheel. This restriction, as well as the intense complements and the use of "Compaq red" (Pantone 200CV) for the logotype, helps unify all the package designs. In addition, Purcell uses strong geometric shapes and repeats the use of his own custom-made "clip art," such as the disk, coloring it to match the individual package designs.

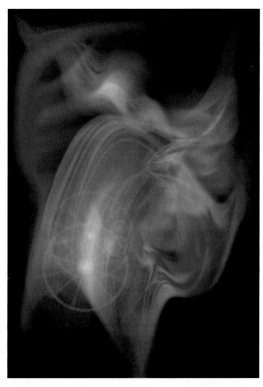

To get the semitransparent, flowing color mixtures that she wanted for *Smoke* (top) and *Gold Thing*, two images she created for display online, **Sharon George** had to go beyond the capabilities of CorelDRAW. She called upon the versatility of Corel PHOTO-PAINT 8 and a pressure-sensitive tablet and stylus. (You can see these and others of her paintings in all their RGB glory at **www.gorgeousgeorge.com**).

She started each image as a new PHOTO-PAINT file with black Paper. For each brush stroke that she wanted to add, she used the Objects docker to add a new Object (by clicking the New Object button, the rightmost in the group of four at the bottom of the docker). She chose the Paint tool and then picked a brush from the pop-out Nib palette on the Property bar, chose a Paint color (double-click the Paint block to open the color palette), and made a dab or stroke on the new Object. She added paint in separate Object layers and experimented with the Object Transparency Brush tool (it's nested with the other Transparency tools) and with the Effect tool (second in the Paint tool nest; double-click it to open the Tool Settings palette) with various Smear settings to draw out streaks and swirls of color.

For *Smoke*, George made extensive use of the Transparency Brush and the Mesh Warp (from Effects, 3D Effects). She also used the Object, Transform commands to distort objects, playing around until she had the gossamer shapes she liked. Finally she applied two lens flares (Effects, Render, Lens Flare, 35mm Prime).

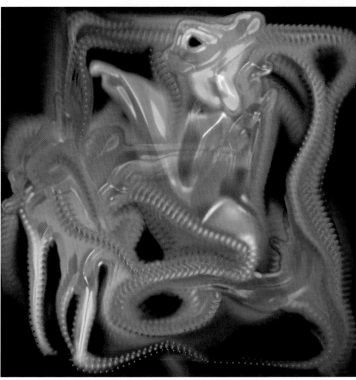

To make each of the "tentacles" for *Gold Thing* she added an Object and painted a small freeform blob or squiggle stroke on it. She used the Glass filter from Alien Skin's Eye Candy to give depth and shine to the strokes (you could also use PHOTO-PAINT's own Glass filter (from Effects, 3D Effects). To get the segmented look of the appendages for this 600-pixel-wide image, she set the Effect tool for Motion Blur and used a hard-edged 30–50-pixel Nib to create the "stuttered" repetition to make up the tentacle. If the result looked too "hard," she went back over it with a softer brush, still using the Motion Blur. ▶ *If the spacing of the repetitions created with the Motion Blur is too tight or too loose, you can undo and then change it by increasing or decreasing the Spacing in the Dab Attributes section of the Tool Settings dialog box (click the tab with the dashed line icon to open to Dab Attributes).*

TRANSFORMING

AFTER YOU'VE CREATED AND COLORED AN OBJECT, CorelDRAW has dozens of ways to transform it. You can duplicate, stretch, rotate, and otherwise tweak your pieces to your heart's content. And if you're still not happy with the results, you can simply transform again. Unlike the bitmap art generated in a paint program, CorelDRAW objects remain infinitely malleable. You can even get back the original by using Clear Transformations from the Effects, Arrange, or Transform menu.

There are many ways to perform CorelDRAW's transformations — with the Pick tool, menu commands, dialog boxes, roll-ups, and keyboard shortcuts, or with the Property bar in the most recent versions. (Changes made by moving individual nodes with the Shape tool are discussed as part of the object-drawing process in "Node-Editing" on page 27 in Chapter 2, and changes to color are the subject of "Assigning Colors" on page 75 in Chapter 3.)

BASIC TRANSFORMATIONS

If you want to **move, duplicate, stretch** or **shrink, rotate,** or **skew** a selected object or objects:

- You can do it **interactively** with the **Pick tool**. Click an object (or Shift-click several objects) with the Pick tool once to get the bounding box handles for sizing and moving, click again to toggle to the rotation and skewing apparatus, click again to toggle back, and so on. If you've read Chapters 1 through 3, you've seen many examples of this way of transforming — dragging an object to move it, or dragging a handle to change size or angle.

CorelDRAW's transformations can be important in illustrating organic subjects as well as in creating geometric and dimensional effects. (You can read about Robert McCoy's Autumn Farm illustration in the "Gallery" at the end of this chapter; learn how we generated the gears on page 138.)

- When precision is more important than hands-on manipulation, you can use a **dialog box,** a **roll-up,** or the **Property bar** to enter **precise numbers** for placement, scale factors, or angles. Open the dialog boxes via commands in the **Transform** menu or the Transform submenu under Arrange or Effects, depending on the version. The Property bar's transformations (in versions 7 and 8) become available when the Pick tool is chosen.

MCCOY

COPYING AND CLONING

There's more than one way to duplicate an object in CorelDRAW, and the method you choose will depend partly on what's most convenient and partly on what you want to do with the copy once you've made it.

To copy an object (or objects) exactly in place, you can select it with the Pick tool and then:

- Choose **Edit, Copy** and then Edit, Paste (or use the keyboard shortcuts for your version of the program).
- Or, if your keyboard has a numeric keypad, **press the "+" key**.

To make a copy that's offset by a standard amount, use the **Duplicate command** (Ctrl/⌘-D). You can set the horizontal and vertical offsets by pressing Ctrl/⌘-J and resetting the horizontal and vertical offsets (in version 8 you'll find the settings under Workspace, Edit).

To make a copy that's moved, rotated, scaled, or skewed by an amount you specify:

- Use the appropriate **Transform roll-up** (or dialog box) to make the change and then press the **Apply To Duplicate** (or Leave Original) button in the roll-up
- If you're working with a two-button mouse, you can also do it with the Pick tool and the **right mouse button**: Start the transformation, click the right mouse button to make a duplicate, and finish the transformation.

CorelDRAW's **Clone** function, available from version 4 on, provides the ability **to make copies with a "memory."** Copies made by selecting an object (or objects) with the Pick tool and choosing Edit, Clone will maintain their relationship to the original. There are certain rules that govern cloning:

- **You can make more than one clone** of a "master" (original) object. Just select the master and choose Edit, Clone again.
- But **you can't clone a clone.** If you select a clone object, the Clone command will be dimmed in the Edit menu.
- If you **alter the master, any clones will change** as well.
- However, if you **change a clone, it won't change the master or the other clones.**
- And once you **change some aspect of a clone, any future changes to the master won't affect that aspect of that clone.** So, for instance, if you have a green-filled clone system and you change the fill of one of the clones to brown and then change the fill of the original to gold, the one clone will stay brown and the others will change to gold.

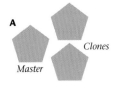

A

B

Master

Clones

Changing the shape of the master

C

Changing the fill of one clone

D

Changing the outline and fill of the master

A "master" shape was cloned twice by selecting it and choosing Edit, Clone once and then repeating this process (A). Changing the shape of the master changed both of the clones (B). Changing the fill color of one of the clones affected neither the master nor the other clone (C). When the master's fill and outline were changed, the clone whose fill had already been changed maintained its own independent fill, but its outline changed; the other clone, which hadn't undergone any independent changes, reflected both the fill and outline changes of the master (D).

Of the four editing modes offered in the Envelope roll-up, Unconstrained mode gives you the most flexibility in changing the shape of the envelope. You can move any node in any direction, and you can add and subtract nodes.

Once an envelope has been applied to an object, it can be reshaped by repositioning its handles or choosing a preset. (In some versions you have to click the Apply button to implement the changes.) You can also use the Create From button (in some versions it looks like an eyedropper or suction bulb) to copy an envelope from another enveloped object or to make an envelope from any single-path closed object.

CHANGING SHAPES

Besides making complex changes to a path node-by-node or curve-by-curve with the Shape tool as describe in "Node-Editing" in Chapter 2, you can make overall shape changes using the Envelope command or the Add Perspective command (both in versions 3 and later), and some of the Lens commands (in versions 5 and later), as well as the Interactive Perspective tool and the Interactive Distortion tool (both in version 8).

USING ENVELOPES

When it comes to warping an illustration, shaping a paragraph of text, or any other task that involves stretching or squashing a CorelDRAW object (or objects) with claylike flexibility, it's time to check out the Envelope commands, found in the Effects menu (In CorelDRAW 4 and later versions, these commands are gathered in the Envelope roll-up.)

The Envelope is an enclosure you can apply to any object or group (except a bitmap) to make it easier to remold that object's shape. Without an envelope, the process of editing a drawing to fit a particular form might involve lots of repositioning of individual curve segments, nodes, and control points. Likewise, reshaping text could mean introducing a custom indent or line break to almost every line. But with an envelope, the reshaping is done automatically, or with a few easy manipulations of the envelope's handles.

How an Envelope Works

When you select a CorelDRAW element whose shape you want to change and then choose Add Envelope, a dashed rectangular outline appears around the object. You can start with this default envelope or copy an envelope from an already enveloped shape (with Effects, Copy, Envelope From). In versions 4 and later you can also choose from a library of preset shapes (press the Add Preset button in the Envelope roll-up and choose one). Or press the Create From button to use the shape of any single-path object (not a combined object or group) as an envelope.

Editing Envelopes

Once you have assigned your initial envelope, you can reshape it by dragging its handles with the Shape tool until you're happy with the result. In CorelDRAW 3 the object responds immediately to any change you make in the envelope shape, but in versions 4 and later you have to click the Apply button in the roll-up in order to apply the envelope edits to the object.

The default rectangular envelope has eight handles, one at each of its four corners and one in the middle of each side. Other envelopes have as many handles as necessary to regulate their shape. As soon as you add an envelope, the Shape tool is automatically

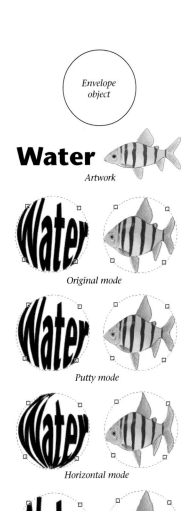

Envelope object

Water

Artwork

Original mode

Putty mode

Horizontal mode

Vertical mode

The mapping modes of the Envelope command and the Interactive Envelope tool give you four different options for fitting elements to the envelope you apply. Here the fish and type were each assigned the default envelope in CorelDRAW 8 (Envelope, Add New) and then a circle object (top) was chosen as the envelope shape using the Create From button. Changing the mapping mode and clicking the Apply button produced the results shown.

selected so you can go to work adjusting the envelope.

Besides choosing the envelope shape, you can also pick an *editing mode* (from the four little pictures in the roll-up) and a *mapping mode* (from the drop-down list). The four **editing modes** determine how the segments of the envelope between handles will behave. You're not restricted to one editing mode per envelope. You can use one mode to edit a particular part of the envelope, then click another editing mode button to change modes and edit some more.

- The **Straight Line mode** maintains the segments between envelope handles as straight lines. It's the mode to use to get a Perspective-like effect but with more control handles and greater flexibility.

- The **Single Arc mode** forms a single convex or concave curve between any two envelope handles when you move one of them. With the Shift key, Single Arc mode can be used to "blow up" an object as if it were on a balloon if you drag outward on handles, or to pinch a shape inward, as if it were constricted by a corset, if you drag handles inward.

- The **Two Curves mode** makes a wave-shaped curve between handles.

- In **Unconstrained mode** each control handle comes equipped with Bezier control points, and the envelope behaves like a fully node-editable object. So you can regulate the shape of the envelope by moving the nodes, tweaking the control points, adding or deleting nodes, even drag- or Shift-selecting several nodes at once so you can change them together.

In the Straight, Line, Single Arc, and Two Curves editing modes, a handle can be moved only horizontally (side handles) or vertically (top and bottom handles) or

INTERACTIVE ENVELOPING

CorelDRAW 8 allows you to distort your objects in "real time" using the Interactive Envelope tool (found on the Interactive Blend tool fly-out). This tool works like the Envelope command, only the changes take place the second you drag and release an envelope node, giving you instant feedback. Instead of using the Envelope roll-up, you access the options from the Property bar. Most of the functions you'll need are there, but to copy an envelope from another object, you'll need the eyedropper tool from the roll-up, or choose Effects, Copy, Envelope From.

BREAKING THE ENVELOPE

As long as an envelope is "live," the Shape tool will work only on the envelope, not on the nodes of the object inside it. If you want to edit the nodes of the object, you have to "freeze" the envelope by selecting it and choosing Arrange, Convert To Curves.

Here are some samples of the Interactive Distortion tool applied to Stone Sans Bold type, the typeface used for the figure numbers in this book. Shown here are very mild applications, except the second Twister (bottom, in case you can't read it).

Lenses are controlled through the Lens roll-up from the Effects menu. In CorelDRAW 6 and later Windows versions the Lens roll-up is nested inside the Effects roll-up group. You can leave it there, or drag its icon out of the scrolling list so that it stands on its own, as it does in Mac versions.

both (corner handles). Also in these three modes holding down Ctrl/⌘ or Shift while moving an envelope handle has the following effects:

- **Ctrl/⌘ moves the opposing handle in the same direction.** For instance, dragging left on a side handle moves the other side handle left also. (*In Mac v.6 use the Shift key.*)
- **Shift moves the opposing handle in the opposite direction.** So moving the top middle handle up also moves the bottom middle handle down. (*In Mac v.6 use the ⌘ key.*)
- **Ctrl/⌘ and Shift together cause all four corners or sides to move in concert.** For example, moving one of the corner handles inward moves all of them inward.

In the **Unconstrained mode,** any handle can move in any direction. There's no built-in restriction on the direction of motion, and Ctrl/⌘ and Shift act like they do when you use the Freehand tool: Use Ctrl to constrain movement of a node to horizontal, vertical, or the Constrain Angle set in Preferences (Ctrl/⌘-*J*). Shift-click to select an additional node or to deselect one of several selected nodes.

The **mapping modes** let you determine what factors are most important in fitting the contents into the envelope:

- The **Original mode** stretches the object to fit the basic form of the envelope.
- In **Putty mode** the contents are also stretched to fit the basic shape of the envelope, but this mode causes less distortion to the objects than the Original mode.
- **Horizontal mode** stretches the contents to fit the basic shape of the envelope but then compresses the contents horizontally to force them to fit the envelope's outline; Horizontal mode makes tall distortions.
- **Vertical mode** does the opposite, stretching the contents to fit the basic shape and then compressing the contents vertically to fill the envelope's shape; Vertical envelopes tend to make wide distortions.

THE INTERACTIVE DISTORTION TOOL

CorelDRAW 8's Interactive Distortion tool is like a wild and crazy envelope on steroids. It's a little hard to think of many practical applications for it, but you can have lots of fun with it when your brain needs a break. If you choose it from the toolbox, then set its parameters in the Property bar, and drag it across a selected object, it provides one of four kinds of distortion: **Zipper** (a kind of zigzag effect); **Twister** (perhaps the most useful, it can introduce a gentle ripple at a low setting or a whirlwind if you enter a number higher than 1 for the number of revolutions, or if you wind it up tightly); **Push** (an effect like poking into a not-too-full balloon at a number

The Viewpoint feature of the Lens function in CorelDRAW 7 and 8 can be especially useful with a Magnify lens. The circle was drawn and positioned in a convenient spot. Then Effects, Lens, Magnify was chosen and the Viewpoint was activated. Clicking the Edit button caused the crosshairs to appear, and they were dragged to the spot we wanted to magnify. Adding a matching pointer completed the graphic.

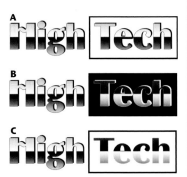

Type was assigned a Custom Fountain fill, and a duplicate, sent behind, was given a black fill to make a shadow (A). The Rectangle tool was used to make a shape for a lens; then choosing Effects, Lens, Invert reversed the tonality of the word "Tech" and the white page behind it (B). When the Remove Face option was activated in the Lens roll-up, the inversion applied only to the objects under the lens (the type in this case), not to the blank page behind (C).

of points), and **Pull** (like expanding a balloon that has adhesions). (Push and Pull are part of the same mode of the tool; you get the Push effect if you drag inward on the selected element and the Pull effect if you drag outward.) You can center each of the four effects anywhere you want to on the selected elements.

PERSPECTIVE

The Perspective command from the Effects menu and the Interactive Perspective tool in version 8 are useful for creating a three-dimensional look. Their use is covered in Chapter 5.

LENSES

A CorelDRAW *lens* is an object that changes the way the objects behind it look. Making a lens is a two-step process — first you make the object that will serve as the lens, and second, you assign it a Lens property from the Lens roll-up in the Effects menu. Then you can move the lens around, changing the look of anything underneath it, like holding a piece of colored acetate or a magnifying glass in front of your design.

Several of CorelDRAW's effects let you make a change to your artwork and then remove it later if you wish. But the Lens effect is the only one that lets you freely move the effect around your document, changing whatever artwork is underneath it and giving the art back its original look when the lens moves on. That feature makes it a great design tool.

The way a lens changes the look of artwork isn't random — it's consistent and predictable. A given lens will produce the same results each time you use it. For example, the Invert lens will always turn black to white, pink to green, yellow to blue, and so on. After working with lenses for a while, you'll be able to predict the results of applying lenses to different kinds of artwork. Use the examples in "Lens Demo" on page 140 to get an idea what will happen when you apply a particular lens.

Making and applying lenses. You can assign a lens attribute to any closed path — to artistic text or to any object, simple or combined (but not grouped). To turn any shape into a lens, select the shape and open the Lens roll-up (Effects, Lens). Then scroll through the Lens options, pick the effect you want, and Apply it to the object. Some Lens effects are variable, which makes them even more valuable as design tools. For instance, you can set the opacity and color of the Transparency Lens or the type of color gradient in the Custom Color Map.

Preventing Lens woes. Although lenses are easy to make and apply, they are processor-intensive and present a computing challenge when you output them. And the more lenses you use, the greater the processing complexity.

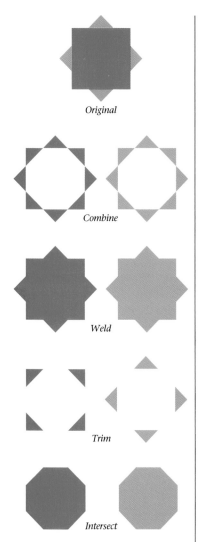

Original

Combine

Weld

Trim

Intersect

These illustrations show what happens when the two overlapping figures at the top of the column are treated with each of four commands from the Arrange menu: Combine, Weld, Trim, and Intersect. There are two figures for each treatment, because the color of the result depends on which object is selected last (see the "Combining Order" tip on page 138) or designated with the pointer provided by the roll-up.

One way to cut complexity and processing time is to export your file in a bitmap format like TIFF (.tif) or Windows Bitmap (.bmp) at the resolution you need for printing. When you export a color bitmap version of your file, your system no longer needs to calculate the Lens effects every time you preview, print or save, which really can speed things up.

New Lens features. Lens effects have been around since version 5, but CorelDRAW 6 added the Frozen and Viewpoint features, and the Remove Face option appeared in version 7. The **Frozen** feature does exactly what it implies: It freezes your Lens effect. Normally, a lens just changes the way things look, calculating everything "live" on the fly. But when you activate the Frozen feature, CorelDRAW freezes the effect and creates new objects that are no longer a lens and the artwork underneath it, but a group of new shapes that permanently reproduce the Lens effect. This is a nice feature, as these objects are then pieces that you can manipulate and that don't require intense processing when you print. (As long as you don't ungroup the lens group, you can "unfreeze" later, if you want to experiment with the lens some more: Select the lens group with the Pick tool and in the Lens roll-up deselect the Frozen option and click Apply.

Try it out: Create an object, and fill it with a Texture fill. Add Text on top of the filled object, and apply the Transparency Lens effect to this text. Move the text around and watch the effect move with it. Now click on Frozen and then Apply. CorelDRAW will create a new text object and fill it with the modified Texture fill. Now the lens is "dead", and replaced with new objects that mimic the lens effect, without the need for complicated calculations. By doing the processing before you print, the Frozen feature takes some of the complexity out of managing files that include Lens effects.

The **Viewpoint** lets you "capture" a copy of what's behind your lens at the moment and move the captured material around your image. With your lens shape selected, click on the Viewpoint box in the Lens roll-up and click the Edit button that appears. Crosshairs will show the current viewpoint. To capture the current view, press the Apply button. Now you can move your lens, with its captured copy of what it "saw" when you pressed the button, anywhere you like. It provides tremendous flexibility to try elements in different positions quickly and easily.

Viewpoint also has another trick up its sleeve. Instead of capturing what's beneath it, it can be made to look at and copy any other part of your file: After you click in the checkbox to activate the Viewpoint, and you press the Edit button, drag the crosshairs anywhere on the page to change the view, and then press Apply. Again, you have a copy of the view you chose, and you can move it around your page. This can be especially useful with the Magnify lens.

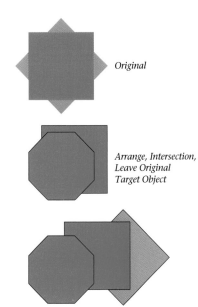

Original

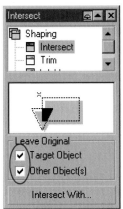

Arrange, Intersection, Leave Original Target Object

Arrange, Intersection, Leave Original Target Object, Leave Original Other Object(s)

The Trim and Intersection commands give you the option of retaining the Target Object unchanged as well as the trimmed or intersection shape. You can also opt to keep any Other Objects involved in the interaction. Above, the blue object was trimmed, with the orange one acting as the trimmer (black lines have been added so you can see the resulting shapes clearly). The dialog box shows the settings that produced the bottom figure.

The Remove Face option is available in versions 7 and 8, only for lenses that change the color of the objects beneath them. It lets you show the lens only where it overlaps other objects — not where it falls over blank space. You can set up this option by clicking the Remove Face check box when you create the lens. Or add the option later by selecting the lens with the Pick tool, clicking the check box, and clicking Apply.

POWERLINES

PowerLines, available in CorelDRAW versions 4 through 6, provide shape-editing possibilities that are in between the node-by-node approach of the Shape tool and the overall approach of the Envelope and Interactive Distortion. See "Pieces and Powerlines for Posters" on page 148 for coverage of PowerLines.

OBJECT INTERACTION

CorelDRAW provides a variety of commands for using one shape to change another: Combine, Weld, Trim, and Intersection. It's often much easier to use one of these commands to change an object's shape than to redraw it manually. Like most things in CorelDRAW, the shape-interaction commands get "smarter" and more numerous in later versions of the program.

In all versions of CorelDRAW from 3 onward you can find the **Combine** command.

- Using the Arrange, Combine feature you can use one object to **punch a hole** in another. For instance, you can transform two stacked circles into a "doughnut."

- You can also use the Combine command on objects that *don't* overlap. The objects then become **subpaths of a single path**. And since a path can have only one outline and one fill, all the subpaths will match, taking their characteristics from the last object selected before they were combined (see the "Combining Order" tip on page 138).

- Use the **Arrange, Break Apart** command **to release combined subpaths**, turning them back into individual objects. But the released elements won't have any "memory" of their previous outlines and fills, so they will all retain the characteristics they had as a combined path. (To restore their original characteristics, you would have to work backwards using Edit, Undo.)

The **Arrange, Weld** function introduced in version 4 can **join together any number of overlapping objects** into one new shape. Unlike Combine, Weld doesn't make holes — it simply lumps things together.

The **Arrange, Trim** command in versions 5 and later can be used **to cut away the part where one object overlaps another.**

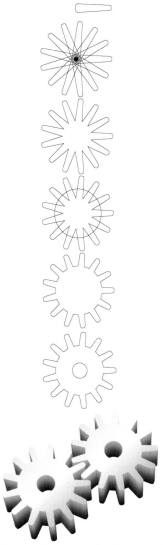

(You'll find more about the Trim command in "Cutting Holes" on page 152.)

Finally, the **Arrange, Intersection** (or Intersect) command in versions 5 and later is what you need **to create a new object where two selected objects overlap.**

The roll-ups for Weld, Trim, and Intersection in some versions give you the option of keeping or discarding the original shapes and any extra pieces that are generated in these operations — for instance, the separate pieces that are welded together or the part that's being trimmed away.

The **PowerClip,** found in versions 5 and later, makes it possible to mask a number of objects inside another object. The routine is simply to select the objects you want to mask, then choose PowerClip from the Effects menu, and click on the object you want to use for the mask. "Showing Motion" on page 158 and the *Autumn Farm* image in the "Gallery" provide two very different examples of how the PowerClip can be put to use.

COMBINING ORDER

When you combine several objects with the Arrange, Combine command, the combined form takes on the outline and fill characteristics of the last object selected. So select your "characterizer" object last. If you select several objects by dragging across them with the Pick tool or by choosing Edit, Select All, the line and fill characteristics will come from your backmost object — often that's the first one you drew. If you want the combination to take on the characteristics of one of the other objects, set it up ahead of time: Select the object whose characteristics you want and select Arrange [Order], To Back. Then choose Arrange, Combine.

In versions 3, 4, and 5 of Corel-DRAW the same sort of order of operations applies for the other combining commands — Weld and Intersection. Later versions have Weld and Intersection roll-ups with a button you click before designating the object that will determine the outline and fill properties of the welded object or the intersection piece.

The gears above were made with a series of transformations. The Rotate roll-up was used to rotate a copy of the original shape 27.7° around the center of rotation, which had been moved to one end of the shape; then the Repeat command (Ctrl-R; ⌘-R on the Mac) was used 11 times to generate more "arms." The rotated shapes were selected and welded together (Arrange, Weld), and the new shape was then welded to a circle (Arrange, Weld). The result was combined with a small circle in the center. This gear shape was duplicated, the two gears were combined (Arrange, Combine), and the result was given a Fountain fill and extruded to give it thickness (Effects, Extrude). The extrusion was separated from the original (Arrange, Separate) before the file was exported as an EPS file.

GENERATING NEW SHAPES — CONTOUR, EXTRUDE, AND BLEND

Resident in the Effects menu are three commands that generate new shapes based on a starting object. The Contour command traces the shape of a closed object at a specified distance inside or outside the existing path. By selecting an object and choosing Contour, you can add a single contour or a series of evenly spaced ones. "Bevelling a Logo" in Chapter 5 and "Contouring for Colorful Type" in Chapter 6 have details on how to use Contour.

The Extrude function also adds shapes based on the existing shape, but instead of building larger or smaller copies, it builds "side walls" to give the shape a 3D look. You can build an extrusion larger or smaller than the existing shape, you can set the depth of the 3D effect, and you can rotate the extruded form. Extrusion

MOGENSEN

CorelDRAW's full range of transformations are useful in creating special effects for type, like the ones shown here. You'll find these examples explained in Chapter 6.

was used to make the 3D type in "Shaping and Framing Type" in Chapter 6.

"Blending" on page 30 provides an introduction to the use of the Blend command, one of the most versatile functions in Corel-DRAW. And you'll find descriptions of using the Blend in every chapter in this book. Blending can be used to generate intermediate shapes to show a transition, as in "Blending an Escape" on page 54, or to try out different colorways, as in the "Color-Testing with Blends" tip on page 82. With it you can evenly space a given number of copies of an object across a certain distance or along a path or around all or part of a circle. Learn how to use it to add dimensionality in "Modelling with Blends" and "Building a Shine" in Chapter 2 and in "Puffed-Up, Popped-Out Type" in Chapter 6. It can be used to repeat an object along a path, or to "grow" organic, solid-looking shapes, even to document that growth as an animation, as described in "3D Animation with Blends" in Chapter 5.

Once you've made a blend from two initial blend control objects, you can keep it "live" and editable — it will reblend to reflect the changes you make to either of its two blend control objects. When you're sure you have the blend you want, you can "freeze" it by choosing Arrange, Separate. At that point it splits into three parts — the two original control objects and the blend group of intermediate steps. Then you can use Arrange, Ungroup to free the parts of the blend group so you can change them individually.

BITMAP EFFECTS

New to CorelDRAW 7 and 8 is the ability to convert object-oriented artwork into a bitmap right in the program. In previous versions, you can export the image to create a bitmap (File, Export), but then you need to use a bitmap-editing program (such as Adobe Photoshop or Corel PHOTO-PAINT) if you want to change it before bringing it back into CorelDRAW (File, Import) to integrate it into your drawing. Not only do CorelDRAW 7 and 8 let you create a bitmap within the program (by selecting the artwork you want to convert and using the new Bitmaps, Convert To Bitmap command), but you can also manipulate it with the filters supplied with the program or with any other Photoshop-compatible plug-in filter. See "Bitmap Effects" on page 142 for examples.

If you need more bitmap-editing capabilities than the filters can provide, in CorelDRAW 8 you can seamlessly move into PHOTO-PAINT, do your editing there, and then seamlessly move back into CorelDRAW. Once you've converted your selected artwork to a bitmap, you can use the Bitmaps, Edit Bitmap command to get to PHOTO-PAINT. When you've finished your work there, just click the X in the upper right corner to close the file, and click Yes when you're asked whether you want to save the editing changes in your CorelDRAW file. *WOW!*

Lens Demo

CorelDRAW 5 has eight special effects engines available in the Lens roll-up. Versions 6, 7 and 8 have more, for a total of 11. On these two pages is an alphabetical catalog of Lens effects, with variations that show what happens when you change their settings, hinting at the special effects potential of Lenses.

For any Lens effect you want to use, first make an object, then choose the Lens roll-up from the Effects menu and pick one of the effects from the list. Adjust its settings if you like, and click Apply. Move the Lens object around to affect different parts of your artwork.

The original CorelDRAW artwork for this demo, before Lens effects were applied, is in the top left corner, labelled "No Lens Effect (None)." It was designed with object (or vector) art on the left and an imported bitmap on the right. It has black, white, and all the primary colors of the RGB and CMYK color models, and it includes Uniform and Fountain fills, as well as outlines. To change the look with a lens, a same-size square was drawn on top of this one and the Lens effect was assigned to that square.

* The filters marked with an asterisk are included with versions 6, 7, and 8 only.

No Lens Effect (None)

Brighten: 50%

Color Add: 50% Cyan

Color Add: 50% White

Color Limit: 50% Cyan

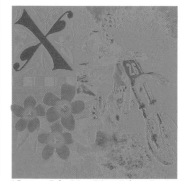
*Custom Color Map: Direct Palette C to M

*Custom Color Map: Forward Rainbow C to M

*Custom Color Map: Reverse Rainbow C to M

Heat Map: 0% Palette Rotation

Heat Map: 35% Palette Rotation

Heat Map: 75% Palette Rotation

Invert

Magnify: 2.0x

FISH EYE AND BITMAPS

The Fish Eye Lens in CorelDRAW 8 shows an improvement over the one found in versions 6 and 7: It works not only on objects but also on bitmaps.

Tinted Grayscale: 100 M

Transparency: 50% black (default)

Fish Eye: 100% (v.8)

Transparency: 50% White

*Wireframe: Outline Black, Fill Pale Yellow

Fish Eye: 100% (v.6 & 7)

Bitmap Effects

Overview *CorelDRAW 7 introduced the ability to manipulate bitmap images within CorelDRAW itself. In versions 7 and 8 you can import a bitmap, or use the Convert To Bitmap feature from the Bitmaps menu to convert your CorelDRAW objects into pixel-based elements. Shown on the next four pages are examples of the filter effects you can apply by choosing from the list at the bottom of the Bitmaps menu. Some of the filters have many potential settings, to produce a wide array of effects. The treatments shown here are the default settings unless otherwise indicated.*

* The filters marked with an asterisk were provided with version 7 but not with version 8.

Original, converted to bitmap

2D Effects: Edge Detect

2D Effects: Offset

2D Effects: Pixelate

2D Effects: Swirl

2D Effects: Wet Paint

3D Effects: 3D Rotate, 30°

3D Effects: Emboss, Depth 5

3D Effects: Page Curl

3D Effects: Perspective

3D Effects: Pinch Punch

3D Effects: Map To Object, Sphere 30%

Artistic: Glass Block

Artistic: Impressionist

Artistic: Vignette

Blur: Gaussian

Blur: Motion, Speed 20

Blur: Smooth

Color Transform: Psychedelic

Color Transform: Solarize

Noise: Add Noise

Noise: Remove Noise (after "Add Noise")

Sharpness: Sharpen

Sharpness: Unsharp Mask, Radius 6

Plug-Ins: Digimarc, Embed Watermark

Plug-Ins: Fancy, Alchemy

*Plug-Ins: Fancy, Glass, Leaded

Plug-Ins: Fancy, Julia Set Explorer, Rip In Time

Plug-Ins: Fancy, Terrazzo, Pinwheel

*Plug-Ins: Fancy, The Boss

Plug-Ins: HSoft, SQUIZZ, Brush

*Plug-Ins: Intellihance, Intellihance RGB

*Plug-Ins: KPT Gradient Designer, Frames, Soft Edge Yellow Frame

Plug-Ins: KPT MetaToys, Lens f/x, Twirl

Plug-Ins: KPT Texture Explorer, Bing, Screen

Plug-Ins: KPT Video Feedback

Plug-Ins: PhotoLab, CSI GradTone, Mauve

Plug-Ins: PhotoLab, CSI HueSlider, Green Glow

Plug-Ins: PhotoLab, CSI Levels, Extreme Contrast

Plug-Ins: PhotoLab, CSI MonoChrome

Plug-Ins: PhotoLab, CSI Negative

Plug-Ins: PhotoLab, CSI Noise 25

Plug-Ins: PhotoLab, CSI PhotoFilter, After Tea

Plug-Ins: PhotoLab, CSI Pseudocolor

Using a Shape as an Envelope

Overview *Create a grid of lines; pick a shape for the envelope; use the shape to distort the grid and to hide any parts of the grid that project outside the shape.*

*The **Envelope.cdr** file is provided on the Wow! CD-ROM so you can examine it.*

4•5•6•7•8

CorelDRAW versions 4 and later allow you to create an envelope from an existing shape. Version 4 doesn't have the PowerClip, but you may be able to use node-editing to get the result you want.

1

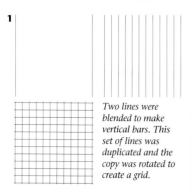

Two lines were blended to make vertical bars. This set of lines was duplicated and the copy was rotated to create a grid.

2

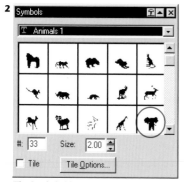

The Symbols libraries contain many useful shapes.

THE CREATE FROM FEATURE on the Envelope roll-up lets you use virtually any closed shape — the elephant in this case — as a morphing tool to apply custom "warping" to an object — in this case a grid of lines. Then PowerClipping the warped element into the shape provides a container that hides any "loose ends" that stick out beyond the shape.

1 Creating the grid of lines. The grid starts with a straight, vertical line: Choose the Freehand tool, click to make one end point, then hold down the Ctrl key to constrain the line to vertical and click again where you want the other end point (*in Mac v.6 use the Shift key, the ⌘ key in v.8*). Duplicate this line (press "+" on the numeric keypad), then drag the duplicate to the right, again holding down the constrain key to limit motion to horizontal. Now Shift-select both lines and choose Effects, Blend. Change the number of Steps to 10, then click Apply. With the blend group still selected, choose Arrange, Transform, Rotation. Change the Angle to 90° and click on Apply To Duplicate. This will complete the grid of lines by duplicating the original and rotating this copy. Drag-select all the lines and group them together (Ctrl-G; ⌘-G on the Mac) so you can apply an envelope later on. Assign a line weight and color (F12).

2 Choosing a shape for the envelope. The next step is to choose the shape you want your object (in this case the grid) to conform to. We used the elephant silhouette from the Animals 1 Symbols shape library supplied with CorelDRAW. To use one of the symbol shapes, start by opening the Symbols roll-up (in Corel-DRAW 5 and higher press Ctrl-F11 (⌘-*F11 on the Mac*); in version 4 choose the Symbols tool — it's the star that pops out when you press and hold the Text tool in the Toolbox. Choose a library and then a symbol, and drag the symbol onto your page. The libraries are

A WEALTH OF SYMBOLS

If your Symbols roll-up lists only a few libraries, you can run the CorelDRAW Setup program, do a Custom installation, and add just the Symbols libraries.

You can't create an envelope from a shape that's combined from two or more subpaths. You can tell that a shape that has been combined from subpaths if the Break Apart command is available in the Arrange menu when the shape is selected. Also, any shape with a "hole" in it is made up of at least two subpaths.

Using the Create From button and Putty mode to force the grid into an elephant-shaped envelope.

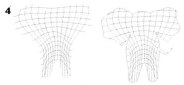

Before (left) and after PowerClipping the grid of lines into the elephant to hide the parts that would otherwise extend outside the container's borders

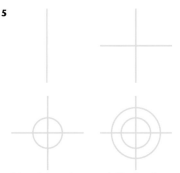

A target element was created by drawing a vertical line with the Freehand tool, duplicating it and rotating the copy, then drawing circles from the center outward.

arranged in alphabetical order; you can scroll through them with the scroll bar or the arrow keys. Scroll through a library of symbols to find the one you want, and drag it onto your page. You will use this shape for both the envelope and the PowerClip.

3 Modifying with an envelope. Select your object with the Pick tool; we selected the grid group. Then open the Envelope roll-up (Effects, Envelope). Click on the Create From button (it looks like an eyedropper in some versions), then click the resulting arrow on the shape you choose for the envelope; we clicked on the elephant. This will create an envelope around the grid in the shape of the elephant symbol. Check to make sure that the Envelope mapping mode (how CorelDRAW fits the object to the envelope) is set to Putty. This setting produces less exaggerated distortions than the Original mode (see page 134 for an explanation of the mapping modes). Click the Apply button to warp the grid into the envelope shape.

4 Fine-tuning the fit. Select your enveloping shape — the elephant here — with the Pick tool and drag it over the shape you just warped — our grid — centering it by eye. There may still be parts of the lines that project outside the outline of the envelope shape. In versions 5 and later you can use the PowerClip to solve that problem: We selected the warped grid, and chose Effects, PowerClip, Place Inside Container. Then we clicked on the elephant shape to constrain the grid inside. This hides the parts of the grid of lines that projected outside the shape.

5 Finishing up. At this point you can assign a final color and line weight (F12) to the shape you added in step 4. To finish the design, a target was created and given a yellow outline color. Type was set in place and converted to curves to avoid font problems (Arrange, Convert To Curves). The background is simply a rectangle, filled with a two-color, Radial Fountain fill from black to blue.

In CorelDRAW 6 and later you can make a grid with the Graph Paper tool (it shares a space with the Spiral in the Toolbox). But if you warp it in an envelope, it behaves like the collection of rectangles that it is (right) rather than like a set of crisscrossing lines.

The Keep Lines checkbox in the Envelope roll-up lets you specify that straight lines in your enveloped object should remain straight.

4

If you're using CorelDRAW 4, which doesn't have the PowerClip, you can either skip step 4 and go on to step 5, or freeze the envelope (Arrange, Convert To Curves) and then use the Shape tool to node-edit the enveloped object until all of it fits inside the envelope shape.

Pieces and PowerLines for Posters

Overview *Sketch out your design, drawing basic shapes and straight lines; to refine shapes, add nodes midway between existing nodes, convert lines to curves, and smooth them out; change the lines to chiseled design elements; make new objects from overlapping shapes.*

5•6•**7**•**8**

PowerLines (shown in color below) were introduced in Corel-DRAW 4, but dropped after version 6. The Natural Pen tool in versions 7 and 8 can produce similar results with a graphics tablet, but the shapes it produces are not the versatile objects that PowerLines were. (If you have CorelDRAW 5, you may want to save it in order to use PowerLines.)

The absence of PowerLines in CorelDRAW 3 can be overcome with a workaround. But versions 3 and 4 also lack the Trim and Intersect features, which are critical for subdividing objects for this style of illustration.

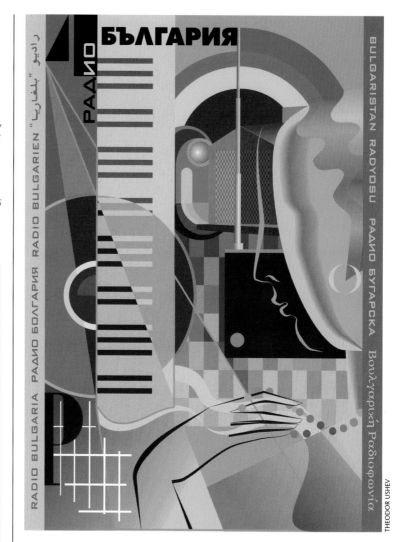

THEODOR USHEV

INFLUENCED BY RUSSIAN CONSTRUCTIVISM of the early 20th century, Theodor Ushev created this bold *People & Lifestyle* poster for Radio Bulgaria. He started with basic shapes, then subdivided those using CorelDRAW's Intersect and Trim functions, and finally colored each piece. To get smooth curves, he used the technique of clicking from point to point with the Bezier tool to make straight lines and then converting them to curves and smoothing and stylizing curves with the Shape tool. Variable-width "lines" were created as PowerLines.

1 Drawing circles. Using the Ellipse tool, Ushev held down the Ctrl key (*the Shift key in Mac v.6; ⌘ in Mac v.8*) to draw a perfect circle, toggled back to the Pick tool (spacebar), duplicated the circle (pressing "+" on the numeric keypad), and downsized the duplicate by holding down the Shift key (*the ⌘ key in Mac v.6; the Option key in v.8*) while dragging a corner sizing handle inward. This method

1

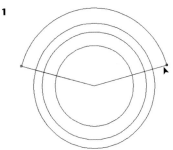

Using the Shape tool on an ellipse lets you create either open arcs or closed "pizza slices." Dragging the node around on the inside of the ellipse creates the closed shape.

2

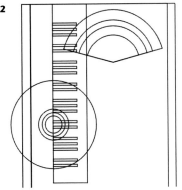

To get even spacing for the black piano keys, two rectangles were given a 25-step blend. To get the right spacing between the keys, one of the blend control objects could be dragged up or down. Then the blend was separated and ungrouped so that some of the keys could be deleted.

3

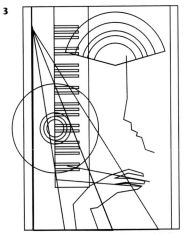

After the main shapes were drawn with the Rectangle and Ellipse tools, straight lines were drawn to quickly map out what would later become curved shapes.

creates a smaller circle within the original, with the same center point. Ushev repeated this duplicate-and-downsize process to create a series of concentric circles.

The same process was used to make circles at the top of the poster. Then the Shape tool was used to reduce them to partial circles.

2 Drawing rectangles. Ushev first drew rectangles to define the boundaries of the poster, the keyboard shape, and the individual keys. To get the even spacing for the keys, he used the Blend function in the following way: First, draw a single key shape with the Rectangle tool (this will be the top key), then switch to the Pick tool (tap the spacebar), and duplicate the rectangle ("+"). To keep the copy aligned with the original, hold down the Ctrl key (*Shift key in Mac v.6, ⌘ in v.8*) as you move the duplicate down to become the bottom key. Shift-select both the original rectangle and the copy, then choose Blend (from the Effects menu), change the Steps to 25, then click Apply. While the blend is still "live," you can adjust the spacing between the keys by dragging one of the blend control objects straight up or down. When the spacing is right, choose Separate from the Arrange menu, and then ungroup (Ctrl-U; ⌘-U). Now Ushev deleted a few rectangles to get the right spacing for the black piano keys, and then drag-selected the remaining keys and combined them (Ctrl-L; ⌘-L) into a single object, so that the Intersect and Trim commands (coming up in step 4) would work on it.

3 Drawing triangles and curved shapes. Ushev used the Bezier tool to quickly map out other design elements, such as the "broadcast triangles," hands, and face. To quickly draw a triangle, choose the Bezier tool from the toolbar, click on a starting point, then move to the next point and click again, then move to the next point and click again, and finally, place the cursor on top of the original point and click. For the hands and face Ushev clicked from point to point with the Bezier tool to make straight lines that he would later shape into curves as described in step 4 and then turn into PowerLines as described in step 5.

4 Smoothing curves. For each curve Ushev started with a path made up of straight lines (see step 3) and used the Node Edit function of the Shape tool to create smooth, sweeping curves with the following method: With the Shape tool, Shift-select both end nodes of a straight line. Then from the Property bar in version 7 or 8 or the Node Edit roll-up (Ctrl-F10, ⌘-F10), click on the "+" button to add a node midway between the selected nodes. Clicking the "+" button again will add two more nodes, again equally spaced between the currently selected nodes, for a total of five nodes. Click on nothing to deselect all the nodes, then select the second node, and Shift-select the fourth node. Now drag these two selected nodes away from the line to create a saw-toothed line. Drag- or Shift-select all the nodes, and click the To Curve button. This will change the

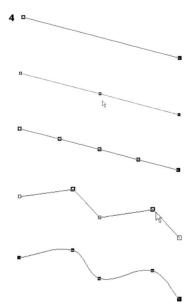

4

To make smooth curves, equidistant nodes can be added between the endpoints of a line. Then Shift-selecting every other node and dragging results in a jagged line. Selecting all the nodes and clicking the To Curve button, then the Symmetrical button results in perfect, sweeping waves.

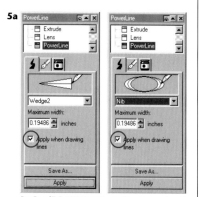

5a

In CorelDRAW 5 or 6 any line (even closed objects such as circles or text) can have PowerLine attributes — you can apply them to an existing line or set them up in advance and apply them as you draw, as shown here. If you open a file that contains PowerLines in a later version that doesn't support them (7 or 8), they are automatically converted to static objects.

lines to curves, though you won't see the change until you click on the Symmetrical button, which constrains the angle between the control points for each node to 180° and makes both control handles equal in length, resulting in the same curvature on both sides of the node. Then the curves can be adjusted by repositioning the nodes with the Shape tool.

5 Adding PowerLines. To his smooth paths Ushev added PowerLine attributes, which allow varying and stylized contours (PowerLines are available in versions 5 and 6; see workarounds on the facing page for other versions). With a path selected, open the PowerLine roll-up from the Effects menu (Ctrl-F8, ⌘-*Shift-P*), choose Wedge2, then click Apply to place the chisel point at the starting point of the line and the wide point (where the pencil appears in the PowerLine icon) at the end. Ushev used many different PowerLines, such as Wedge2 in the hands, Wedge3 in the face, and Nib for the earring shape.

6 Intersecting and trimming. Ushev divided up his main shapes into subdivisions according to where they overlapped one another. For instance, to be able to color the area where the keyboard and large circle intersect, Ushev created a new shape using the Intersect command. With the circle selected, he chose Arrange, Intersect to open the Intersect roll-up (version 6, 7, or 8), then enabled the Leave Original options, since these shapes would be needed for future intersections and trims; finally he clicked on the Intersect With button and clicked on the rectangle. (In version 5, after choosing Intersect, you can simply click on the rectangle shape to create the new intersection object.) The intersection resulted in a new closed shape that Ushev could fill with color by clicking a color swatch in the on-screen color palette, or opening the Uniform fill dialog (Shift-F11) for more color options. Ushev used the Intersect function to create many shapes, and also to fit all of the shapes inside of the bounding box.

The Trim command is essentially the opposite of Intersect. Ushev used Trim to chop away pieces of objects, like this: Select the "trimmer" rectangle shape and choose Arrange, Trim. In version 6, 7, or 8, this opens the roll-up; click the Trim button, then click on the "trimmee" circle shape to complete the function of trimming away the area in the circle that's overlapped by the rectangle. In 5, without a roll-up, simply selecting the rectangle, then choosing Arrange, Trim and then clicking on the circle shape does the job. (Reversing the order of selection would dramatically change the results, cutting the rectangle in two instead of the circle.)

5b

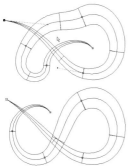

PowerLines remain "live" until you choose Arrange, Separate. This means you can reshape the line as shown above, or change the type of PowerLine at any time, even choosing None to get rid of the effect.

6a

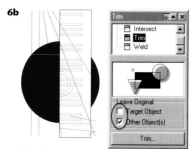

Ushev created a new object that he could fill with its own color by using Intersect on the overlapping circle and rectangle shapes. CorelDRAW 6, 7, and 8 use a roll-up to add more functions to the Intersect command.

6b

The Trim command cuts away the area occupied by both objects. Ushev used it to cut the circle into two new shapes.

Ushev used the resulting shapes from the initial Intersect and Trim steps for more intersection and trimming. For example, once he had made the piece where the circle intersects the keyboard, he trimmed away the area occupied by one of the triangle beams. With the Trim accomplished, he was then able to create the two-tone piano keys by making the intersections of the rectangular keys with the new trimmed shape. *WOW*

7•8

With practice and a steady hand, you can use the Natural Pen tool to get results similar to those of the PowerLine in versions 5 and 6, although they will be only as smooth and symmetrical as you can draw them "live." For best results, use a graphics tablet with a physical guide (a plastic French curve works well) to steady the stylus as you draw.

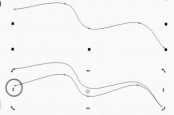

The Natural Pen has four modes of operation, chosen with the buttons at the left end of its Property bar:

• Fixed Width makes a shape at the width you set.

• In Pressure mode the shape will respond to pressing harder or softer as you move your stylus, making the line thicker or thinner. If you don't have a graphics tablet, you can simulate pressure by pressing the up or down arrow key as you draw.

• Calligraphic mode varies the width as you draw, according to the maximum width and angle you set.

• Clicking the Preset button and choosing from the pop-out list of styles (similar to those of the PowerLine) will transform your line after you finish drawing it.

3•4 . . . 7•8

In all versions of CorelDRAW, you can get results similar to a PowerLine on an open path by combining two copies of the same path. Draw your parent path using the process described in steps 3 and 4 to get smooth curves. Then duplicate the path (click the path with the Pick tool and press "+" on the numeric keypad), and click on the duplicate to reveal the skew handles. Drag down on the skew handle opposite the end where you want the "chisel point." This will move one end of the path, but the other end will stay in place. Drag- or Shift-select both paths, and combine them (Arrange, Combine). With the Freehand tool click on one of the nodes at the open end and then click the other node. With the Shape tool, drag-select the two overlapping nodes on the pointy end and click the Join button in the Node Edit roll-up (or Property bar). The shape is now closed. You can fill it with any color, or modify the curves with the Shape tool.

Cutting
Holes

Overview *Set and arrange type;*
duplicate it on another layer; apply
the Combine and Trim commands
to cut away overlapping areas in
both layers, keeping all parts
aligned; copy the finished cut-outs
and fill the copy with gray to
make a drop shadow.

TOM GRANEY

5•6•7•8

To do this kind of cut-out work in
versions 3 and 4, which lack the
Trim command, you could use
Combine to make a single-color
"WhaT'S" cut-out shape; then
make the shadow (step 7), export
the artwork (letters and shadow)
as a TIFF at the size and resolution
you need for printing, and use the
Paint Bucket tool in Corel PHOTO-
PAINT or Adobe Photoshop to
color the shapes.

1

Graney set the letters of "WhaT's" and
then arranged them to overlap in a lively
design: "W," Bauhaus Heavy; "h," Trade
Gothic Bold Condensed; "a," Amazone;
"T," a Bodoni display face; "s," LoType
Medium Condensed. The development of
the three letters shown here will be followed
in steps 3 through 6.

2

Graney set the word "up" in Bodoni Poster
Compressed, changed it to an object
(Arrange, Convert To Curves), and then
used the Pick tool to narrow it (by dragging
in on a side handle of the highlight box)
and to rotate it (by clicking it again and
dragging around on a corner handle). He
then combined it with the blue arrow.

WHEN IT COMES TO PUNCHING HOLES, CorelDRAW's Combine command does an excellent job. Tom Graney used it to create the
knock-out for the "up" piece of this lively artwork for a clip-art
library. But for the word "WhaT's" he wanted to control the color
of each individual letter. Since the Combine command assigns the
same fill and stroke to all the solid parts of a combined object, he
used the Trim command for "WhaT's" in order to give himself
more flexibility.

1 Setting type. Graney started by choosing a variety of different
typefaces and styles, setting each letter as a separate type block so it
could be individually sized and rotated into position. For each letter or block of type you want to set, choose the Artistic Text tool
from the toolbox (or press F8), click it where you want to put your
type, and then choose Text, Character (Ctrl-T; ⌘-T *on the Mac*) to open
the Character Attributes dialog box to choose a font, size, and style.
Click OK to close the box and type your letter. Give each letter a
solid fill and no outline. (For tips on filling, see "Fills" on page 78.)

Graney drew a triangle for the apostrophe. (In CorelDRAW 6, 7,
or 8 you can make a triangle with the Polygon tool.)

2 Combining. For the word "up" Graney wanted a simple knock-
out effect, with the letters acting as a "cookie cutter" to punch
holes in the blue arrow. (One way to make an arrow is to turn on
Show Grid and Snap To Grid via the Layout menu, and then use
the Bezier tool to click from grid-point to grid-point.) Once the
arrow is built, your can tilt it (as Graney did) by turning off Snap To

CONTROLLING THE COLOR OF THE COMBINATION

Selection order is important when performing a Combine. The outline and fill
attributes of the new combined shape will either come from the last object
selected, or, if you drag-select several objects, from the backmost of the
objects. When you drag-select, though, it may be difficult to predict which
outline and fill will be chosen for the new shape, since you may not be able to
tell where some objects fall in the stacking order. To make sure you get the
outline and fill you want, you can select all the objects by dragging, and then
simply hold down the Shift key, click the desired object to deselect it, and then
with the Shift key still down, click it again to reselect it. This **Shift-double-click**
maneuver makes this object the last one selected and thus ensures that it's the
one that contributes its outline and fill to the combined object.

3a

The large letters show how the type was overlapped; the small letters at the upper right have been moved apart to show the current shape of each letter.

3b

A duplicate set of letters was hidden and locked on Layer 2. Here the red icon indicates the currently active layer.

4

On Layer 1 the "W" was used to trim the left side of the "h," and then the "a" was used to trim the right side. (Not shown, the "T" was trimmed with the "a" and "s.")

5

On Layer 2, now visible and unlocked, the "h" and "T" were used to trim the "W," "a," and "s."

AUTO-CONVERSION

When you use the Combine, Intersection, Trim, or Weld command on type, there's no need to use Convert To Curves first. The conversion is made automatically. Of course, once the type is converted, it can no longer be edited as text.

Grid, choosing the Pick tool, clicking on the object to show the rotation handles, and dragging a corner handle to make the rotation.)

With the Pick tool Graney selected the word "up," moved it into position on the arrow, Shift-selected the arrow, and chose Arrange, Combine to punch the holes.

3 Setting up for trimming. The Trim command takes two shapes and "trims" away the overlapping area. Based on the order of selection, one shape acts as the "trimmer," or cookie cutter, and the other has a part cut away, or "trimmed." For artwork like Graney's "WhaT's," where the desired effect involves trimming the shared part away from *both* objects, the trimming operation has to be done twice, first with one piece acting as the cookie cutter and the other as the "dough," then again with the roles reversed.

To perform the two trimming operations you'll need two copies of your overlapping objects. And to keep from knocking the parts of one set out of alignment as you work on the other set, you can store them on separate layers. Open the Layers list. (You'll find it as the Layers Manager or roll-up or the Object Manager in the Layout or Tools menu, depending on which version of the program you use.) Create a New Layer (Layer 2) by choosing from the flyout menu. Then Shift-select your objects with the Pick tool, choose Copy To from the flyout menu, and click on the Layer 2 name in the Layers list. Click in the eye column in front of the Layer 2 name to make the objects on this layer invisible. (In CorelDRAW 6, 7, or 8 this can be done directly in the Layers list. In version 5, it's done in the Edit Layers dialog box, opened by double-clicking the layer name in the list.) Click in Layer 2's pencil column in version 6, 7, or 8 (or the lock column in version 5) to dim the pencil (or bring up a lock) so the layer will be protected from change. You'll still see your artwork on Layer 1, and that's what you'll work with in step 4.

4 Making the first set of trims. With the top layer locked and hidden, activate the bottom layer (by clicking to put the heavy arrow or icon to the left of it in the Layers list in version 6, 7, or 8 or by selecting its name in version 5) and trim the even letters — the second, fourth, sixth, and so on — using the odd letters as the trimmers, as described next. (In step 5 you'll reverse the roles, using the even letters to trim the odd ones in Layer 2.)

Graney first used the "W" to trim the "h": In version 6, 7, or 8 select your first trimmer, then choose Arrange, Trim. With Leave Original Other Objects checked, click Trim at the bottom of the roll-up, and use the heavy Trim arrow to click on the object you want trimmed.

5

In CorelDRAW 5 both objects must be selected *before* you choose the Trim command, and the order of selection is all-important. The first object you select becomes the trimmer, and the second is trimmed.

6a

When both layers were unlocked and made visible, no cut-outs were evident.

6b

Removing the whole letters from each layer, leaving only the trimmed ones, revealed the cut-outs.

7

The letters were selected, grouped and duplicated, and the copy was filled with gray to make a shadow.

EFFICIENCY — AT A PRICE

You might be tempted to use a simpler way to create the cut-out shapes of a design like "WhaT'S up": Without making a copy of the array and without locking a layer, you could select the first pair of letters or objects and perform an Intersection (Arrange, Intersection) to make a new object in the shape of the overlap; then duplicate the new intersection shape so you have two of them. Next select one of the original objects and one of the intersection pieces and choose Arrange, Combine. Finally combine the second object and the other intersection piece. You would now have both letters with cut-outs, right in place. The problem is that for some reason Intersection followed by Combine can leave a residual outline around the edges of the cut-away areas.

Next Graney used the "a" to trim the other leg of the "h," selecting the "a," choosing Trim, clicking the Trim button, and clicking the "h." Repeat the trimming process for every second element in your assemblage of overlapping objects, choosing trimmer-trimmed pairs.

5 Making the second set of trims. To make the complementary set of trims, you'll need to hide the pieces you've been working on and make the other set visible: In the Layers list, turn off the eye and pencil icons for Layer 1, making it invisible and locking it, and turn on the eye and pencil for Layer 2, making it visible and unlocked.

With Layer 2 active, repeat the process of selecting and trimming objects, this time using the even objects (second, fourth, and so on) to trim the odd ones (first, third, and so on). Graney used the "h" to trim the "W" and "a," and used the "T" to trim the "a" and "s."

6 Throwing away the extras. Now it was time for Graney to get rid of the whole letters, keeping only the ones with cut-outs. To remove the trimmers, leaving only the trimmed objects, start on Layer 2, since it's visible and unlocked. Shift-select any whole objects (in this case the "h" and "T") with the Pick tool and press the Delete key. Then make Layer 1 active, visible, and unlocked, and remove all the whole letters from this layer too (the "W," "a," and "s"). What remains will be an entire set of trimmed letters, exactly in place.

7 Making the shadow. To pop the artwork off the page and to make it clear that the white areas are holes, not just white patches, Graney grouped all the shapes (Ctrl-G; ⌘-G) and duplicated the group in place by pressing the "+" key in the numeric keypad. This duplicate was given a 12% Black fill and was sent to the back (Arrange [Order], To Back). To create the illusion of depth, the shadow shape was shifted down and to the left by selecting and dragging it with the Pick tool.

Variations. Here's another treatment for overlapping letters. Instead of holes, you end up with different colors in the overlaps. Use the Pick tool to Shift-select a pair of objects. Choose Arrange, Intersection to create a new object in the area where the two overlap. Then choose the next pair of objects, and choose Arrange, Intersect again. When you've made intersections for all the overlaps, you can select each intersection shape with the Pick tool and fill it. *WOW*

Intersections colored to simulate transparent overlays: The original letters were filled with 100C, 100M, and 100Y; intersections are filled with 100C/100M and with 100M/100Y.

Intersections colored for a "random" look

Blasting Holes

Overview *Use the Rectangle tool to draw a sign, rounding the corners with the Shape tool; rotate the sign; add type or a graphic; create a see-through bullet-hole effect using the PowerClip function; trim Fountain-filled rings to make metal edges.*

5•6•7•8

All versions after 4 support the PowerClip feature and the Trim function.

Use the Rectangle tool to draw the squares for the sign. Use the Shape tool to round the pointy edges of the square into a street-sign shape.

The Windows Character Map utility allows you to select "special" hidden characters available within a font. Hold the cursor over a character to enlarge it (such as the copyright symbol above) and click to select it. Once you copy the character, you can paste it into CorelDRAW as an Artistic text element and change the typeface, size, and color. (On the Mac use Key Caps.)

GARY PRIESTER

WORKING WITH MARY CARTER on her book project, *Electronic Highway Robbery,* Gary Priester envisioned the cover art in a flash and turned to CorelDRAW with its PowerClip function to realize his concept: a highway sign riddled with bullet holes. One of the challenging aspects of the project was to get the bullet holes to penetrate both the black symbol and the yellow sign background. Another was giving the metal sign a little dimensionality.

1 Making the sign. The basic shape of the sign starts with a perfect square drawn with the Rectangle tool. Holding down the Ctrl key while dragging creates a perfect square (*use the Shift key in Mac v.6, the ⌘ key in v.8*). The corners can be rounded with the Shape tool, by dragging one of the corner nodes slightly.

To get the black line that parallels the edge, duplicate this rounded rectangle by pressing the "+" key on the numeric keypad. Assign it a black outline by right-clicking the black swatch in the on-screen palette (*Control-clicking on the Mac*) and no fill by clicking the X in the palette. Then downsize it by dragging a corner handle inward with the Pick tool, holding down the Shift key (*the ⌘ key in Mac v.6, the Option key in v.8*) during the scaling process to scale down from all sides simultaneously, resulting in a smaller copy centered inside the original. Shift-select both pieces. Rotate 45° by

2b

Rotate the squares 45° to make the sign, and align the special copyright character in the center using Align and Distribute.

3

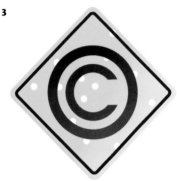

Circles were drawn with the Ellipse tool to represent bullet holes. To punch them through the sign, Priester selected the circles and the yellow sign shape and combined them.

4a

To put the holes through the other sign elements, Priester used the PowerClip feature from the Effects menu. This trick works to put holes through imported bitmaps as well as native CorelDRAW elements.

clicking again on the selected objects to activate the skew and rotate arrows, holding down the Ctrl key (*Shift in Mac v.6, ⌘ in v.8*) to rotate in 15° increments until you reach the desired 45°.

2 Adding a special character. Inside the sign Priester wanted to use the copyright symbol (©). This character does not appear on the computer keyboard, but it's a part of the character set for most fonts. To find this and other "hidden" characters, you can use the Windows Charmap (Character Map) utility to see all of the characters available (*Key Caps, in all versions of the Mac System, does the same thing; or simply press Option-G to get ©*). With the Character Map open, find your desired character, and select and copy it. (*In Key Caps hold down the Shift key, then the Option key, and then the Shift-Option combination in turn to view the characters until you see the one you want, and click it*). You can now Close the application. In CorelDRAW, select the Artistic Text tool, click on your desktop, then Paste the character into place (Ctrl-V; ⌘-V). This will create a text object, which you can then manipulate like any other text object, including changing the font.

> **ADDING THE CHARACTER MAP**
>
> The Character Map program is in the Accessories folder in all versions of Windows. To add it to your Windows 95–based system, double-click on My Computer, then Control Panels, then Add/Remove Programs; then click on the Windows Setup tab, double-click on Accessories, and click the box next to "Character Map" to enable it. Place the Windows 95 CD-ROM in your CD-ROM drive, then click both OK buttons, and the Character Map utility will be installed on your system.

To center the symbol inside the sign, click the copyright symbol, then Shift-click on the sign pieces, and open the Align and Distribute dialog (from the Align menu), select the horizontal and vertical center align buttons, and click Apply.

Priester filled both the sign background shape and the copyright symbol with angled Fountain fills (F11), using lighter, more neutral shades on the lower right to match the photo he would use for the background.

3 "Shooting" holes in the sign. Priester used the Ellipse tool to draw a perfect circle to punch holes through the sign. To create a perfect circle, hold down the Ctrl key (*Shift in v.6, ⌘ in v.8*) while dragging with the Ellipse tool. Priester duplicated the circle several times (press "+"), and scattered the copies around the sign to represent holes. He Shift-selected all of the circles and also the sign background and combined them (Arrange, Combine). Now the holes allowed anything behind the sign to show through the holes, but at this point the holes appeared to be behind, not through, the copyright symbol and the black border. Priester's next step was to remedy that situation.

4 PowerClipping the sign. He selected the copyright character and the black border piece. From the Effects menu, he chose

4b

With the copyright symbol and border clipped inside the "holey" yellow sign shape with the PowerClip feature, the open holes went all the way through the sign to allow anything behind it to show through.

5

A circle was given a Custom Conical Fountain fill (left) and combined with a smaller circle to create highlight effects for a bullet-hole ring object.

6

To make the bullet holes more jagged, Priester used a 12-pointed star (left) to Trim the ring shape.

7

A signpost and bolt head were drawn and filled with sunset colors. Circles combined with a Texture-filled rectangle made holes in the center of the signpost. (The Texture was Mineral. Cloudy 5 Colors from the Styles library, with colors set to grays.) Other Texture-filled rectangles and colored lines completed the post.

PowerClip, Place Inside Container, and clicked the arrow on the bullet-riddled sign shape. The copyright symbol and border were now masked within the "holey" shape, and the bullet holes seemed to "punch" through it.

5 Adding dimension to the holes. Next Priester added metal edges to the holes to give the sign substance. Using a process like the one for the squares in step 1, he drew two concentric circles — one slightly larger and one smaller than the holes — and combined them to form a ring (Arrange, Combine). He used a Fountain fill (F11), changing the Type to Conical, and the Color Blend setting to Custom. Clicking on the left node on the preview ribbon, he clicked the Twilight Blue chip on the palette, then clicked on the right node and chose Pale Yellow. Double-clicking on a point between the two nodes, he created a new color point and clicked on 70% Black. He changed the Angle to –137° so the lighting would match that in the sign and the background photo and clicked OK.

6 Making jagged edges. To add more realism to the bullet holes, Priester changed the smooth ring shape to jagged edges. In versions 6, 7 and 8, the Polygon tool lets you easily generate a star shape that can be used to Trim away parts of the ring. Right-click (*Control-click on the Mac)* the Polygon tool to open the Properties dialog and choose the Polygon As A Star option. Priester changed the Number of points to 12. He clicked on OK to close the menu, and then dragged the Polygon tool while holding down the Shift and Control keys (⌘-*Shift in Mac v.6,* ⌘-*Option in v.8)* to draw a perfect star over the ring shape. (To make the star shape more or less pointy or to change the angle of the points, drag on an inside node with the Shape tool.) Then, with the star still selected, he opened the Trim dialog from the Arrange menu, deselected the Leave Original options, clicked the Trim button, and then selected the ring shape. This trimmed away the star from the ring, leaving a ragged edge. The trimmed shape was duplicated ("+") and the copies were dragged over the holes.

7 Finishing touches. Priester imported an image from the Corel Sunsets stock photo CD-ROM and placed it behind the sign. The book title was typed across the top. He also made a metal signpost and a bolt head and its shadow from simple shapes, and added light yellow highlight edges to the right side of the sign. 🔊

Showing Motion

Overview *Make a blend from a white, circular highlight on the speeding object to a teardrop "speed trail" shape; for each background shape the speeding object passes over, duplicate and recolor the blend and mask it inside the shape.*

5•6•7•8

The PowerClip, a necessary tool for making this speed blur, doesn't exist in CorelDRAW 3 or 4.

 *The **pinball.cdr** file is provided on the Wow! CD-ROM so you can examine it.*

1a

After storing a no-fill, no-outline pinball shape on the clipboard, Meyer used a steel blue (20C, 70K) to fill another copy of the shape (left); then he made a highlight (center), and moved it off-center to the left.

1b

Converting the larger circle to a curve and dragging a side node formed a teardrop shape.

2

Meyer rotated the teardrop and small circle into position (left) and then blended to create the basic blur element.

A MOTION BLUR MAKES AN OBJECT look like it's speeding past, leaving a fading trail in the eye's memory. In his *Pinball* illustration Barry Meyer started with a blend that created a blurred highlight for his speeding ball. Then he altered its color for each part of the background it passed over. It was CorelDRAW's PowerClip function, which allows you to mask objects inside another object, that made the illusion possible. In fact, the blurring and soft lighting effects throughout the image were all done using PowerClips. The entire piece from which the detail above is taken is shown in the "Gallery" at the end of this chapter.

Here's a look at how to make a speeding object. First you'll draw the ball itself. Then you'll shape the speed blur by duplicating the object twice and modifying one copy to become the highlight and the other copy to become the outer edge of the visible blur. Blend to make the blur, and then PowerClip a recolored copy of the blur into every object the speeding ball passes over.

1 Creating control curves for the speed blur. First draw the speeding object itself. To draw a ball like Meyer's, hold down the Ctrl key (*Shift key in Mac v.6;* ⌘ *key in v.8*) and drag the Ellipse tool to draw a circle. Give it a solid fill (press Shift-F11 to open the Uniform Fill dialog box, and then specify a color) and to make the ball photorealistic, give it no outline (right-click the X swatch in the on-screen palette; *Control-click on the Mac*). Store a copy of the circle in the clipboard (Edit, Copy). This stored copy will become the pinball itself (in step 3), while the original circle will be modified to help make the blur.

3

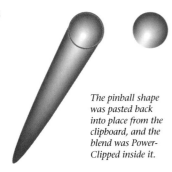

The pinball shape was pasted back into place from the clipboard, and the blend was Power-Clipped inside it.

MEGA-NUDGES (3, 4, 5, 6, 7, 8)

CorelDRAW lets you set a numerical value for Nudge, the distance an object will move if you select it and then press one of the arrow keys on the keyboard. Press Ctrl-J; ⌘-*J on the Mac* (in version 8 you'll then choose Workspace, Edit). In CorelDRAW 7 or 8 you also have a SuperNudge setting, so you can have a small Nudge for moving objects just slightly and a large SuperNudge for mega-nudging with a Ctrl-/⌘- or Shift-arrow key combination.

If you set the Nudge (or Super-Nudge) distance relatively high — at 1 inch or more, say — your nudges will be dramatic, which can be very useful for storing a copy of your art out of the way and then bringing it back into its original position later: Just select the object and nudge it up, down, left, or right with an arrow key or key combination. When you need to move it back into position, select it again and press the opposite arrow or combination, the same number of times as you did originally. For many projects, mega-nudging art-work into and out of position can be more efficient than tying up the clipboard or working with layers, locking and unlocking and making things visible and invisible.

To make the highlight, duplicate the circle (select it with the Pick tool and press "+" on the numeric keypad). Shrink the dupli-cate circle by dragging inward on a corner handle; then use the Pick tool to drag this highlight circle into position. Meyer shrank his highlight circle to about 15% of the diameter of the original and moved it to the left. Give the highlight a white fill (click the white swatch).

Now click the large circle with the Pick tool to select it. The next step will be to turn it into the teardrop shape that will define the outer edge of the blur: Convert it from an Ellipse to an object with nodes you can edit (Arrange, Convert To Curves). Use the Shape tool to node-edit this copy by dragging one of the side control nodes outward. Meyer moved the left node farther left. Then rotate your still-selected shapes to the angle you want.

2 Making the blend. This step makes the basic blend that will then be PowerClipped into the ball and the various background shapes it traverses. But before blending you'll reorient the speed blur so it follows the angle of motion you want: With the Pick tool Shift-select the teardrop shape and the small white circle, and then click it again to bring up the rotation handles; drag one of the cor-ner handles to angle the blur shape.

With the small circle and the teardrop shape still selected, open the Blend roll-up (Effects, Blend) and set up a blend with no rota-tion and enough steps to make a smooth, unbanded color transi-tion, then click Apply. Meyer used a 40-step blend for his blur, which would extend over about 3 inches.

3 Masking the blurred highlight inside the speeding object. Before you carry out your first PowerClip to mask the blur inside the shape of your speeding ball, make a copy of the blur so you'll have it when you need it later: Duplicate it by pressing the "+" key. Then make sure the Nudge setting (or SuperNudge in CorelDRAW 7 or 8) is large (see "Mega-Nudges" at the left) and nudge the duplicate blend out of the way with an arrow tool (or Ctrl-/⌘- or Shift-arrow for SuperNudge).

One more thing before you PowerClip: You need to make sure the PowerClip options are set up right. Press Ctrl-J (⌘-*J on the Mac*), working in the Workspace, Edit section in version 8, and uncheck the Automatically Center New PowerClip Contents option (in CorelDRAW 5 it's Auto-Center Place Inside).

Now paste the circle you stored in the clipboard back in step 1

TURNING OFF CENTERING

By default CorelDRAW automati-cally centers a selected object when you PowerClip it inside another object. But for an application like a speed blur, you won't want the blur shape to shift to the center when you mask it inside the shapes it passes over. So you'll need to be sure the centering option is turned off in the Special, Preferences or Tools, Options dialog box.

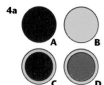

4a

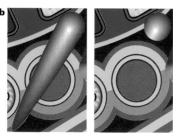

Meyer's pinball elements are stacked no-outline, Uniform-filled concentric circles, so the blur can be seamlessly PowerClipped into each element.

4b

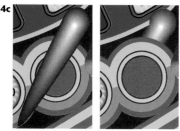

PowerClipping the blend into the pinball shape

4c

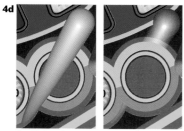

Recoloring the blend and PowerClipping it into the background

4d

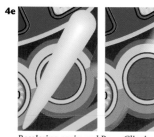

Recoloring the blend and PowerClipping it into the outer red shape

4e

Recoloring again and PowerClipping into the first yellow ring

(Ctrl-V; ⌘-*V on the Mac*) and move it into position. To mask the blur inside the pinball shape, click the Pick tool on the original blend group, and choose Effects, PowerClip, Place Inside Container. Your pointer will change to a big arrow. Click on your object, in this case the circular pinball shape. The blend group will be clipped inside the circle.

4 Making the highlight trail. For every element that your speeding object passes over, you'll need to duplicate the blend that you've nudged to the side, change the duplicate's color to match the shape you want to mask it into, nudge the duplicate back into the blur's original place, and PowerClip it into that shape. Because all the blends will have the white highlight, you need only select the teardrop-shaped control curve in the blend group and change its fill color to that of the element it's passing over. For example, the dark gray background in Meyer's pinball illustration required the blend to go from dark gray to white.

To start the masking process, first make a copy of the blend ("+"). Then click the teardrop control object with the Pick tool and assign it a fill to match the backmost object it passes over (you can match the fill by choosing Edit, Copy Attributes From, and clicking on object you want to match); the blend will recolor itself.

With the new blend selected, nudge it back into place, choose Effects, PowerClip, Place Inside Container and click the back-most shape.

Repeat the duplicating, recoloring, nudging, and masking for each shape that your speeding object passes over. **Note:** Before you PowerClip the blur into each succeeding element, be sure to duplicate the blend group each time, so that you still have a copy available for the next PowerClip. Meyer PowerClipped a recolored blur into each element of his background, including the "B" and "O" of the word "BONUS," which had been converted to curves (see the opening illustration).

Adding a shadow. To improve the illusion of an object flying above the surface, you can add a shadow. To make the ball's shadow, Meyer added a circle with the Ellipse tool, a little larger than his original pinball. Then he duplicated, recolored, and PowerClipped it inside the appropriate shapes (see the opening illustration). *WOW!*

QUICK MOVES: POWERCLIP

Need to move an item to the middle of the stacking order in your illustration? You could select the item and move it back a step at a time (Arrange [Order], Back One) until it was in the right place. But there's a quicker way using the PowerClip: Select the item you want to move and choose Effects, PowerClip, Place Inside Container; then click the big arrow on the object that you want *just behind* your item; this masks your item inside that object. Now choose Effects, PowerClip, Extract Contents; the item will be released and will end up just in front of the object you temporarily clipped it into.

Besides using a speed blur, here are some other ways of graphically communicating motion:

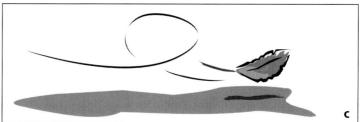

- For a complex object speeding over a solid-color background, you can sometimes use a blend from all or parts of your final graphic (in front) to a smaller (more distant) copy in which all fills and outlines are in the background color (A). Before you blend, group all the parts of the background-color object together (Arrange, Group), and also group the parts of the original graphic. Apply a blend to make the speed blur; try out the Accelerate options in the Blend roll-up, which allow you to control the speed of the color change and the distance between steps over the course of the blend.

 Here we grouped and blended all but the large brown shape that made the limbs and "outlines." We then added the original illustration on top of the blend and drew three brown-filled "speed streaks."

- In CorelDRAW 7 or 8 another option is to turn the objects into a bitmap (Bitmaps, Convert To Bitmap) and apply a motion blur (Bitmaps, Blur, Motion). You can then add the original unblurred graphic on top (B).

- Show complex motion — with bounces or loops, for instance — by including the path of the motion in your drawing (C).

- "Speed streaks" can be created by using the Shape tool and Add Node button of the Node Edit roll-up to add nodes to the outline of a shape in groups of three, then selecting the center node of each threesome and dragging in the direction opposite the motion you want to show (D).

- For back-and-forth motion like jumping, shaking, or wagging, add "jitter" marks, small shapes at the edges of your graphic (E).

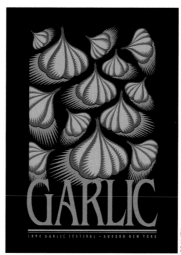
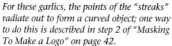

For these garlics, the points of the "streaks" radiate out to form a curved object; one way to do this is described in step 2 of "Masking To Make a Logo" on page 42.

"Jitter" marks, drawn with the Bezier tool, were used here to make the soccer ball dance and the sun sparkle.

Antonio De Leo's *Duomo: Inner Cathedral* is a detailed study of the interior of the cathedral in Tuscany, Italy, based on black-and-white photographs. In developing this complex image, De Leo made good use of shortcuts. For example, the star tiles in the dome were duplicated from a single master ("+" on the numeric keypad) to make a column of five. The five were selected and grouped (Ctrl-G; ⌘-G on the Mac) so that Add Perspective (from the Effects menu) could be used to distort and twist them into position for the dome. De Leo also used the Envelope (from the Effects menu) to tweak the tiles into the desired perspective. Some of the columns of tiles were made by duplicating this group, others by blending between two copies of the group. Blends were separated (Arrange, Separate), then ungrouped (Ctrl-U, ⌘-U), so they could be manipulated further. ▶ *To recolor objects for lighting effects, in CorelDRAW 6 and later versions you can use the Color Adjustment option from the Effects menu. Selecting each object in turn and changing the Brightness-Contrast-Intensity values can make an object seem shaded or highlighted.*

To manage the huge volume of data in this project, De Leo decided to develop each section in a separate file. Once he had the main shapes worked out in the primary file, he assigned each

section its own color-coded layer. (For more about assigning layers, see "Cutting Holes" earlier in this chapter.) Then he selected each section in turn, chose File, Save As and Selected Only, and saved the file, giving the new file the appropriate Layer name, as shown in the list below.

The smaller files reduced the time spent working on each section, as there was less information for the computer to deal with at one time. When the sections had been completed and the files saved, they were brought back into the appropriate Layers of the master file by activating a layer, choosing File, Import, and choosing the

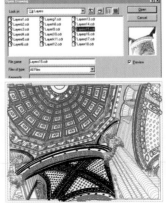

appropriate section file. The final result is shown in Wireframe view below; each section appears in the color assigned to its layer. ▶ *In versions before 8, CorelDRAW's File, Import command puts the imported .cdr file in the same position on the page that it was saved in. In CorelDRAW 8 (which gives you a cursor for determining the import size and location) you can open each file and use Edit, Copy and Edit, Paste to drop it into the position in the master file.*

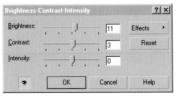

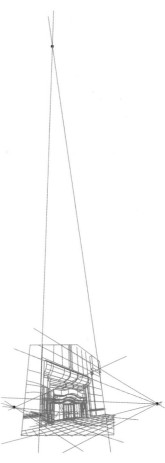

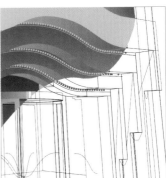

When **David Brickley** was commissioned to draw this *Entrance* image as a print demonstration for a CalComp electrostatic plotter, he created the perspective effect by hand. Working from reference photos, Brickley first mapped out the page, clicking with CorelDRAW's Freehand tool to draw grid lines trailing to three hand-placed vanishing points, as shown at the right, all three of which were beyond the edges of the drawing page. He drew a sweeping curve to divide the page into filled objects and simple lines. Then he drew each of the shapes he needed for the floor and the building by clicking or dragging with the Bezier tool, making separate objects for the color-filled and "wireframe" sides of the curve and manipulating nodes with the Shape tool to line up perfectly to the grid and to the corresponding points on the other side of the curve. To complete the illusion of a 3D wireframe, or x-ray view, on the left side of the drawing,

Brickley drew the hidden details inside the building.

▶ *The Lens effect in CorelDRAW 5 and later offers a Wireframe feature that can generate a line-art look from a color drawing, as shown at the right. For this to work, though, you have to be sure to draw the filled shapes that you'll need for the 3D cutaway, so the hidden lines are there to be revealed by the Wireframe Lens. Then draw a shape over the area you want to turn into a wireframe, and open the Lens roll-up (from the Effects menu). Select the Wireframe option, and click Apply. Note that you have no control over the width of the line using the Wireframe Lens, because it displays and prints all lines beneath the lens at the default hairline width, which won't scale with the image. But if you freeze the Lens before printing (by clicking the Freeze button in the Lens roll-up, or by exporting the file as a TIFF or EPS), the wireframe lines will be able to be scaled along with the drawing.*

n assembling *Autumn Farm*, **Robert McCoy** made use of several of CorelDRAW's Transform commands. The leaves and trunk of the tree were drag-selected and duplicated in place (press "+" on the numeric keypad). The parts of the duplicate (still selected) were then fused (Arrange, Weld) to make a single shape for the shadow. This shape was flipped and skewed with the Pick tool and further warped by applying and editing an envelope (Effects, Envelope). The shape was assigned a Fountain fill (F11) to fade the shadow. Finally, the shadow shape was cropped within the frame of the illustration using Effects, PowerClip.

Barry Meyer's *Pinball* was the cover illustration for an issue of *Corel* magazine dealing with motion effects. Meyer, author with J. Scott Hamlin of *CorelDRAW Design Workshop* (Sybex), used PowerClips of blends, shadow-toned objects, and Fountain-filled shapes to achieve the look of motion blurs for the speeding ball and the flipping levers and to make the shadows and gleams of reflected light.

Although the process of PowerClipping each blend or shadow or highlight object into many shapes is time-consuming and work-intensive, the result is crisp and convincing. In the mostly wireframe view at the right, the colored areas show where the PowerClips are. The PowerClipping techniques and the blending methods for the speeding ball are described in "Showing Motion" earlier in this chapter.

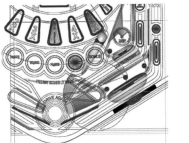

Each of the heads of the screws was made by blending between a large gray circle and a small white one, offset down and to the left, to create a round-looking object whose highlighting matched the rest of the image. The slots in the screw heads are Fountain-filled and Uniform-filled rectangles with a shorter trapezoid shape on top.

 The **pinball.cdr** *file is provided on the Wow! CD-ROM so you can examine it.*

ADDING DIMENSION

For this illustration, CorelDRAW's Blend command was used to round the planet, its Add Perspective command was applied to flatten the planet's rings, and the Extrude command was used to create the Voyager spacecraft.

The Blend command, used with Custom Fountain fills to create highlights, can produce some convincing three-dimensional structures, such as the blood vessels in this anatomical illustration.

ALTHOUGH CORELDRAW ISN'T A TRUE 3D DESIGN PACKAGE, you can easily create the illusion of depth by following a few simple rules that artists have been using for years. If you are working in Corel-DRAW 6, 7, or 8 (Windows), you can also turn to CorelDREAM 3D, a program packaged with these versions that automates the processes of modelling 3D forms from 2D paths, as explained in "A Brief Introduction to CorelDREAM 3D" on page 169, lighting a scene of assembled models, and "photographing" the scene. But even if you have CorelDREAM available, there will be times when it makes more sense to use readily available CorelDRAW techniques to achieve a dimensional look as described in "Making Things Look Solid" (below) and "Creating Distance" (on page 167).

MAKING THINGS LOOK SOLID

Highlights and shadows can play an important role in making a flat, two-dimensional shape look like it has the substance of a three-dimensional object. You can create a three-dimensional look by imagining a light source and then coloring surfaces that face the light with lighter and brighter colors, and by drawing them with relatively more detail. You can also cause your foreground objects to cast shadows. On the other hand, you can make surfaces that face away from the light, or that sit in the shadow of another object, darker and less detailed. Two of the tools that CorelDRAW offers to accomplish this kind of coloring are the Blend (either the command or the interactive tool), and the interactive drop shadow in version 8.

The Effects, Blend command (or the Interactive Blend tool in version 7 or 8) can be used to round a shape in three dimensions, as described in several of the techniques presented in Chapters 2 and 3 — for instance, "Modelling with Blends" on page 113 and "Building a Shine" on page 109 — and in "Modelling Space" in this chapter on page 175. The technique involves blending from one color-filled shape to a darker one to create the illusion of a curved surface receding into shadow. Blends can even be used to "grow" some very convincing three-dimensional structures, as shown in "Animating with Blends" on page 188.

An object can also be "solidified" by making it cast a shadow. This can be done in any version of CorelDRAW by making a dark

A shadow falling behind and to the right indicates a light source in front and to the left of the subject. The Interactive Transparency tool (in versions 7 and 8) can be applied to fade a shadow. In other versions you can fill the shadow object with an angled Linear Fountain fill from the darkest shadow tone to the background color.

With CorelDRAW 8's Interactive Drop Shadow tool you can create a bitmap drop shadow for either a drawn element or a bitmap. The shadow remains "live," so it changes if you change the shape or position of the shadowed element. You can also change the shadow's direction (by dragging the black control point), opacity (by moving the slider), or color (by dragging a color from the on-screen palette onto the black control square). Other characteristics can be changed in the Property bar.

Simply reducing contrast can make objects appear more distant, creating atmospheric perspective.

Overlapping objects (left) or reducing size and spacing (right) can create the illusion of depth or distance through visual perspective.

duplicate of the object (select the object with the Pick tool and press "+" on the numeric keypad), sending the copy behind the object (Arrange [Order], Back One), and then moving it slightly (for a drop shadow) or skewing it for a cast shadow (click it once or twice with the Pick tool to bring up the skewing handles and drag the top handle sideways; you'll probably also want to click again and "squash" the shadow to about half the height of the original, or less). This kind of shadow will have a sharp outline. To soften the shadow, making it look like the light source is less direct or more diffuse, you can blend the shadow shape to another one behind it with a fill and thick outline in the background color, so the shadow fades at the edges, as described in step 4 of "Adding Character to Your Characters" on page 200. Here are some simple rules for shadows:

- An object's shadow falls in the direction opposite where the light source is.

- In general, the brighter and more focused the light that casts the shadow, the darker the shadow will be and the sharper its outline.

- For a shadow cast by an object that's standing up, the shadow is attached to the object at its base, with the other end projecting away from the light source. A longer shadow indicates a light source that's closer to the horizon, a shorter shadow a light source that's higher overhead.

- For the drop shadow of an object floating above the page, the denser the shadow is and the sharper its outline, the closer the object appears to be to the page. A drop shadow offset to the side of its object indicates a lower light source, off to the side, than if the drop shadow is directly beneath its object; this is illustrated in the "Light and Shadow" tip on page 184.

- More than one drop shadow or cast shadow indicates more than one light source (see the "Shaping Shadows" tip on page 82).

CREATING DISTANCE: PERSPECTIVE

Three more techniques that artists use to create the illusion of distance in artwork are *atmospheric* (or *aerial*) *perspective*, *visual perspective*, and *linear perspective*. **Atmospheric perspective** imitates the effect of atmospheric haze as we look into the distance. Details become less distinct, contrast is reduced, and colors become less intense (desaturated) and sometimes bluer. These differences support the illusion that one object is farther away than another.

Visual perspective is the term sometimes used to describe the illusion of depth created when objects overlap or when diminishing size is used to create distance.

Linear perspective imitates what happens to straight edges, shapes, and sizes depending on the observer's viewing angle and distance from the object. In a drawing that employs linear perspective, parallel edges seem to converge in the distance. The eye level

In Lake Louise, *shown on page 123, visual and aerial perspective are used as the trees overlap and become smaller, less detailed, less intense in color, and bluer with distance. The sides of the path converge to a single vanishing point, using one-point linear perspective.*

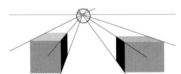

In one-point perspective, all objects share the same vanishing point on the horizon.

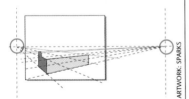

Two-point perspective can be established by using the Add Perspective command or by setting up two vanishing points on the horizon, drawing lines that pass through these points and the corners of the frontmost vertical edge in the drawing, and adjusting the other corner points with the Shape tool. Other objects can then be put into perspective with the Effects, Copy Perspective From command or by drawing more guidelines and adjusting more corners. These techniques are described in "Putting Things into Perspective" on page 171.

that the artist establishes for the viewer determines which surfaces and edges of a three-dimensional object are visible. Artists commonly use three kinds of linear perspective in their drawings:

- In **one-point perspective** the viewer is looking directly at *one of the surfaces* of the subject. The parallel edges of that surface don't recede in the distance, but the horizontal parallel edges of other visible surfaces recede toward a single vanishing point on the horizon. All the other objects in the drawing typically share the same vanishing point. (In CorelDRAW, the Extrude command from the Effects menu creates one-point perspective for the "side walls" it creates, as described in step 4 on page 178.)

- In **two-point perspective** the viewer doesn't look directly at any surface of the subject, and all parallel horizontal edges recede toward one of two vanishing points on the horizon. Other objects in the scene also share these two vanishing points. The Add Perspective command from the Effects menu can be used to establish two-point perspective, or you can do it by drawing two vanishing points and then drawing guidelines from these points to the corners of your objects, as described in "Putting Things into Perspective" on page 171.

- In **three-point perspective** the vertical parallel edges also recede into the distance, typically either directly above or directly below the subject. If there are several objects in the drawing, the vertical vanishing point is typically above or below the middle object. To create three-point perspective in Corel-DRAW, you can use the Add Perspective command to establish the two vanishing points on the horizon and then add the vertical vanishing point and guidelines for adjusting the top corners of your objects.

True linear perspective employs a complex geometry that can account not only for rectangular solids like boxes or buildings, but also for curved surfaces like spheres and cylinders, and for inclined planes like ramps or pitched roofs. If the drawing you want to make includes these complexities, you might want to consult a book that treats perspective drawing in depth, or construct and render your scene in a true 3D program such as CorelDREAM.

Perspective — atmospheric, visual, or linear — isn't strictly for making a drawing look more realistic. It can also be used to create a feeling or mood. For instance, a large amount of atmospheric perspective can create a mist or murkiness that heightens a sense of

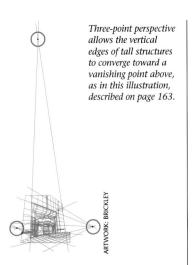

Three-point perspective allows the vertical edges of tall structures to converge toward a vanishing point above, as in this illustration, described on page 163.

ARTWORK: BRICKLEY

SMITH

For some kinds of technical drawings, true perspective techniques are not used (see "3D Projections from 2D Layouts" on page 187 for some examples). David Smith used CorelDRAW's Grid and the Snap To Grid commands to draw the PTI PowerArc, *an illustration for a catalog. The grid made it easy to draw the squares and rectangles he needed and then reposition their corners to produce the projection he wanted.*

Sweeping an imported shape into a solid object in CorelDREAM 3D

Using the Torus preset to "lathe" a shape into a solid form

mystery. And an exaggerated three-point perspective can create the impression of an environment that towers or looms over the observer.

A BRIEF INTRODUCTION TO CORELDREAM 3D

You can team up CorelDRAW, where you can create two-dimensional shapes, with CorelDREAM 3D, where you can turn those shapes into 3D models, assemble them into a scene, and render the scene from as many camera angles as you like. This book doesn't attempt to present a complete treatment of CorelDREAM, but here are some tips for modeling with shapes you create in CorelDRAW.

Adding Depth with Sweep

The **Sweep** function in CorelDREAM adds thickness to a flat shape. First prepare your shape in CorelDRAW; the fill and outline aren't important because only the "wireframe" path will be carried into CorelDREAM. Select the curve; choose File, Export; change the Save As Type option to Adobe Illustrator (**.ai**) and click the Export or OK button.

Switch to CorelDREAM and drag with the Free Form tool to start a new object on the screen. When you release the mouse button, you'll see the Set Name dialog box, where you can name the object you're about to make, and click OK. Choose File, Import to bring in the shape you created in CorelDRAW. CorelDREAM will automatically "sweep" it into a 3D shape as it comes in. Then you can use the Selection tool to drag on the sweep path (the pink line on the back right wall) to control the size of the sweep. Click the Done button when the model is finished.

Extruding Around an Axis, or Lathing

The **Extrusion** presets, in CorelDREAM's Geometry menu, can transform flat shapes into 3D objects by moving a shape through space on a path more complex than the straight line used by the Sweep function. The Spiral preset makes springs or coils, but the **Torus** preset is generally more useful. With it you can make a solid, with a hole in the middle if you like, by extruding a shape around an axis. You can make a thick-walled shape (like a doughnut) or a thin-walled shape (like a vase) or a completely solid shape (like a lathed bedpost).

First create a closed shape in CorelDRAW that's the "half cross-section" that you want to spin around an axis to make your solid shape. Export the shape as an Adobe Illustrator (**.ai**) file. In CorelDREAM, drag with the Free Form tool in the Perspective window and name the new object. Import the **.ai** file you saved, and it will automatically extrude itself along a straight path. To change its form, choose Geometry, Extrusion Preset, Torus. This will open the Torus dialog box, where you can key in a Distance To Axis value and click OK. If you're not satisfied with the result (for instance, if the Distance To Axis value is too big), you can reopen the Torus dialog box from the Geometry menu and try again.

A rectangular bitmap exported from CorelDRAW can be imported into CorelDREAM as a Shader and applied as a Texture Map with the Paint Rectangular Shading Shape tool to make a label.

HUNT

3D REFERENCES

There's a lot more to learn about CorelDREAM 3D. Some references you might find useful are *Ray Dream Studio for Windows and Macintosh: Visual QuickStart Guide* and *Getting Started with 3D* (both from Peachpit Press).

Applying Labels

CorelDREAM's **Shaders** let you apply color and texture to the surface of a modelled object. The Shaders are bitmaps that are "wrapped around" the model. Besides developing overall Shaders from Texture fills or patterns generated in CorelDRAW, you can also turn a fairly complex CorelDRAW graphic into a "label" that covers just part of the surface of a CorelDREAM model.

First design your label in CorelDRAW. Then export the image from CorelDRAW as a Windows Bitmap (**.bmp** format) or TIFF (**.tif**). Open the CorelDREAM file that includes your model, locate the Shaders browser (a window with a collection of colored spheres, which can be opened by choosing Window, Shaders Browser), and select Shaders, New. This will create a new Shader sphere in the default red color. Double-click on the new sphere to open the Shader Editor dialog box. From its View menu select Flat Preview, and from the Type menu, select Texture Map. Now locate the **.bmp** or **.tif** file you exported from CorelDRAW and click Open to bring it in as a Shader.

If you simply apply the new Shader to a model by dragging the Shader from the Shaders Browser or Shader Editor onto the model, it will cover the entire model. To apply it as a label instead, you can use the Paint Rectangular Shading Shape tool. Choose the Shader and then drag the tool on the target model to define the label size. The Shader will fill the area you've drawn.

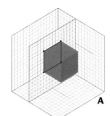

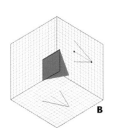

FORCIER

Inspired by art deco lions at the foot of a bridge, Rémi Forcier combined 3D effects he could achieve in CorelDRAW 8 with the 3D modeling of CorelDREAM. A pyramid was made in CorelDREAM by creating a new object with the Free Form tool, then drawing a square with the Draw Rectangle tool. The square was automatically extruded into a solid (A), and then choosing Geometry, Extrusion Envelope, Symmetrical and dragging the node of the top control line with the Selection tool shrank the front surface to a point (B). The pyramid was rotated with the One Axis Rotation tool and duplicated several times, and a scene was created to help work out the angles of the pyramids. The scene was rendered as a TIFF, imported into CorelDRAW, and traced to make the shapes that were then Texture-filled and modified with the Interactive Transparency tool for the final image (C). The lion was drawn entirely in CorelDRAW; Fountain fills gave most of the objects their shading, while Blend groups added more detail to the face.

Putting Things into Perspective

Overview *Draw a horizon and two vanishing points; draw perspective guidelines from the vanishing points through stationary corners of the most prominent component of your picture; adjust its shape to the perspective guides; use the reshaped component to align more guides; draw and reshape more components.*

3•4•5•6•7•8

Since CorelDRAW versions 3 through 8 all have a Guides layer, a Pencil tool and an Add Perspective command, this kind of drawing can be done in any of these versions of the program.

JOHN SPARKS

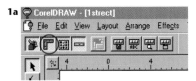

Turning on the rulers in CorelDRAW 6

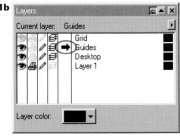

Activating the Guides layer in CorelDRAW 6

JOHN SPARKS USED LINEAR PERSPECTIVE to create the 3D space in his illustration *In-Line Process Machine,* an 8.5 x 11-inch drawing for a machine design proposal. You can use the same procedure to draw the buildings in a street scene or to arrange flat layouts for a package design into a mock-up of the finished box.

1 Establishing the vanishing points. Sparks used two-point perspective for his drawing. (One-, two-, and three-point perspective are defined in "Perspective Basics" at the start of the chapter.)

To set up two-point perspective, you'll need to display the rulers and open the Layers list: To toggle the rulers on and off, find a Rulers command under View (version 5 or later) or Display (version 3 or 4). Open the Layers list (Layout, Object Manager in Windows v.8; Ctrl-F3 in version 4, 5, 6, or 7; Ctrl-1 in version 3; ⌘-F3 in Mac v.6; Window, Palettes, Object Manager in Mac v.8), and make Guides the active layer: In version 6 or 7 click in the column to the left of the layer name; in other versions click on the name itself. Then pull down a guideline from the horizontal ruler to serve as your horizon. Drag two guidelines in from the vertical ruler so they intersect the horizon line at the places where you want your vanishing points. All the lines in your drawing that are supposed to be disappearing toward the horizon — the top and bottom edges of buildings in a street scene, for example, or of Sparks's machine housing — will run toward these two points. And this will make your objects appear three-dimensional.

2 Drawing the front. In the Layout (or Display) menu, turn on Snap To Guidelines. This will make your vanishing points act like magnets, attracting the perspective lines you draw. You can also turn on Snap To Objects to help the surfaces you draw fit together precisely.

Activate Layer 1 and start your illustration by drawing the front surface of your largest object. Sparks started with the front panel of the row of machines. He drew one surface of a box using the Rectangle tool, and converted it to curves (Arrange, Convert To Curves).

Now construct your first set of perspective guidelines: Activate the Guides layer again and click the Freehand tool on the right vanishing point; move the cursor so the "rubber band" line extends

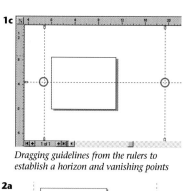

1c

Dragging guidelines from the rulers to establish a horizon and vanishing points

2a

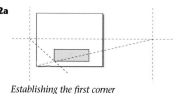

Establishing the first corner

2b

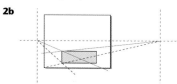

Drawing the second set of guidelines

2c

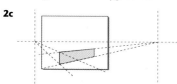

Reshaping the object to fit within the perspective guidelines

3a

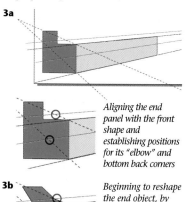

Aligning the end panel with the front shape and establishing positions for its "elbow" and bottom back corners

3b

Beginning to reshape the end object, by moving its "elbow" and bottom back corner

through the bottom left corner of your object, and click again. Draw another guideline from the left vanishing point through the same corner.

To make the second set of guides, Shift-select the first set with the Pick tool and duplicate them in place (press "+" on the numeric keypad). Using the Shape tool, move the near endpoints of these new lines up, so the new guidelines cross the top left corner of your object. Already you can begin to see how the guidelines will shape your image.

Now activate Layer 1 again. Using the Shape tool, grab the top right node of your rectangle and move it directly upward until it falls into place where you want it on top of the new guideline. In the same way move the bottom right corner up to the old, lower guideline, aligning it directly below the top point, and the first surface is finished!

3 Adding other surfaces. The end panel of Sparks's row of machinery started as a large "L" shape. The piece was dragged until it snapped into position beside the front panel. Guidelines from the right vanishing point were positioned to establish intersections where the bottom back node and the "elbow" node of this "L"-shaped end panel would go, and these nodes were dragged onto the intersections. Another guideline was drawn from the left vanishing point to establish the upper edge of the "L," and the two remaining corners were dragged into position.

To make the shape or shapes for a top surface for your object, draw guidelines from each vanishing point to the top corner on the opposite side. This will define the shape of the surface, and you can draw and reshape a rectangle to fit, or use the Bezier tool to click from point to point on the perspective guides to form a shape in place. Proceed in this way to finish your drawing: Each time you complete a step of your illustration, use the new pieces to draw more guidelines. Then use the guidelines to draw more pieces.

4 Lighting the scene. As your picture comes together, use color variations to enhance the illusion of depth. Imagine a light source, and then color the image accordingly: Surfaces facing the light and near it will be brighter than surfaces hidden from the light or farther away. Sparks's light source was above on the right. He used Linear Fountain fills (F11) to create subtle light-to-dark transitions. (For more about setting up Fountain fills, see Chapter 3.)

3c

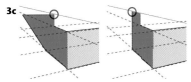

Reshaping the top of the end plate: The front corner is positioned directly over the corner below it. Then a perspective guide is drawn through that point, and the back top corner is moved onto and along the new guide until the back edge is vertical.

3d

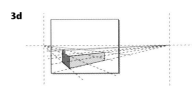

Perspective guides drawn through the top corners of the existing shapes outline where the top surfaces of the machine will go.

4

The in-line process machine with all panels in place

5a

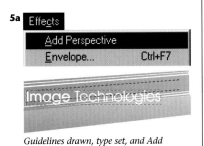

Guidelines drawn, type set, and Add Perspective chosen

5b

Perspective box corners and vanishing point adjusted to fit type within the hand-drawn perspective guides while keeping the characters vertical

5 Adding type. Lettering and other details on an object in a three-dimensional illustration need to follow the same perspective as the main elements of the illustration. To make lettering guides, draw two new guidelines, dragging the front endpoints into position to make guides for the baseline the type sits on and the height of capital letters. To set the lettering, choose the Artistic Text tool, activate Layer 1, click where you want the type to start, and type; the characters won't follow the guides, but you can fix that shortly. Next open the dialog box for formatting type (you can use the keyboard shortcut: Ctrl-T in Windows; ⌘-*T on the Mac*) and choose a typestyle and size.

Select the type by clicking it with the Pick tool. Then choose Add Perspective from the Effects menu (in CorelDRAW 3 it's Add New Perspective). Now use the Shape tool to drag the individual nodes of the dashed-line Perspective box to line up with the lettering guides you made, making sure to keep the two handles on each end of the box aligned vertically. When you finish, you should have one vanishing point (an "X") close to the original vanishing point you made for the drawing. Drag the "X" onto the original vanishing point.

6 Adding details. The details of Sparks's illustrations aren't meant to be photorealistic — just suggestions. He added the logos and knobs (including the type outlines arranged around them) from other machinery designs he had done, putting them into perspective as described for the type.

Each of the breaks between panels in the machine cabinet was drawn with the Bezier tool as two lines side by side, one black to suggest shadow, and another white — a duplicate of the first one ("+") — moved slightly to the side to make a highlight.

Each knob element is composed of three circles, a red-filled one for the face, a dark-green-filled one for the side surface, and a no-fill, no-line one for fitting the type (for more about fitting type to curves, see Chapter 6). The red one is offset to the right to make the knob look three-dimensional. The knob parts were selected and grouped (Arrange, Group), and the entire group was duplicated (Ctrl-D). The duplicate was selected and dragged into place with the Pick tool, then resized by dragging inward on a corner handle.

Two rectangles, one inside the other, suggest a monitor in the center of the top of the machine. If you draw a rectangle with the Rectangle tool and then drag one of its nodes with the Shape tool, you can round out the corners. Sparks opened the Fountain Fill dialog box (F11), where he set up a Radial fill and offset it by dragging on the center of the fill in the dialog box's preview window. The back rectangle was filled with an angled Linear gradient.

The conveyor belt at the left end of the cabinet is made up of several simple shapes, shaded with Fountain fills to suggest depth. The body of the roller is an ellipse, extruded by opening the

6a

Sparks drew a series of white lines to highlight grooves between panels. Black copies of the lines, offset slightly, made the shadows.

6b

Emergency shut-off knobs were drawn as overlapping circles, the back one a dark green to suggest depth and shading.

6c

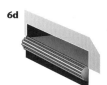

The monitor screen is suggested by Fountain-filled rectangles, the smaller one with rounded corners.

6d

Simple solid- and Fountain-filled shapes suggest the roller mechanism.

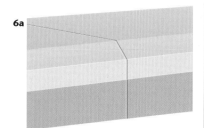

Extrude roll-up and using Arches, Small Back, and no lighting. The ridges on the roller are rectangles, rotated by double-clicking with the Pick tool and dragging on a corner handle.

WHY NOT JUST USE AN ENVELOPE?

If you want to apply a drawing or type as if it were a "decal" on a 3D-looking object, CorelDRAW's Add Perspective (from the Effects menu) can be frustrating if you just jump right in and begin experimenting. As an alternative the default Single Arc envelope distortion can be a lot easier to manipulate, so it's tempting to use it to fake perspective. If your decal is very small and the perspective distortion of the surface you want to apply it to is not too great, Add Envelope may work. But in other cases, Add Perspective really looks better.

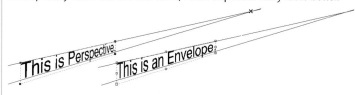

It's easy to get wild and weird effects just by playing around with Add Perspective, but to get a realistic perspective effect you need to understand how the Perspective controls work. There are **four independently operated corner control handles** and up to **two vanishing points.** One of these vanishing points marks the spot where the top and bottom edges of the Perspective box would meet if they were extended into the distance, and the other marks where the extended left and right sides would meet in the distance.

When you first choose Add Perspective, a Perspective box surrounds the object but no vanishing points appear. That's because the two sides of the box are parallel to each other, and so are the top and bottom edges. If these edges were extended, they would remain parallel and would never meet, so there are no vanishing points. But as soon as you drag one of the four handles of the box, the lines are no longer parallel, and at least one vanishing point shows up. Here are some practical tips for positioning the handles and using Add Perspective in this way:

• **To apply an object to a vertical surface,** you need to make sure the Perspective handles on each end are aligned straight above and below each other so a vertical line would pass through both. When the effect is complete, there will be only one Perspective vanishing point, to one side of the object, as shown above.

• **To keep the top and bottom of an object in parallel as the sides recede, as if the object were applied to a horizontal or tilted surface straight in front of you,** align the two top handles of the Perspective box with each other on a horizontal guide, and align the bottom handles on another. Again, there will be only one vanishing point, this time above the center of the object.

• **To apply an object to a surface that recedes in both directions** (such as top surface of the Inline Process machine in "Putting Things into Perspective") move the four corner handles of the Perspective box so they align parallel to the edges of the surface. The two Perspective vanishing points should coincide with the your original vanishing points for the surface itself.

Modelling Space

Overview *Create planets and stars; extrude 3D spaceship parts; copy the extrusion for subsequent objects; generate a bitmap and use bitmap editing features to fine-tune your design.*

5•6•7•8

The PowerClipping in this design will not work in CorelDRAW 3 or 4. But the extruding and exporting functions work in all versions. Versions 7 and 8 have bitmap-manipulation capabilities directly within CorelDRAW, so you don't have to export the bitmap in order to use filter effects typically found in Adobe Photoshop or Corel PHOTO-PAINT.

1a

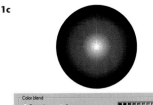

A Star symbol is welded to a rectangle to create the pulsar shape. This is filled with a Custom Fountain fill.

1b

Duplicate and rotate the original shape to create the star. Constrain the rotation to 45° and 90°.

1c

To finish the star, add a circle with a Custom Radial Fountain fill.

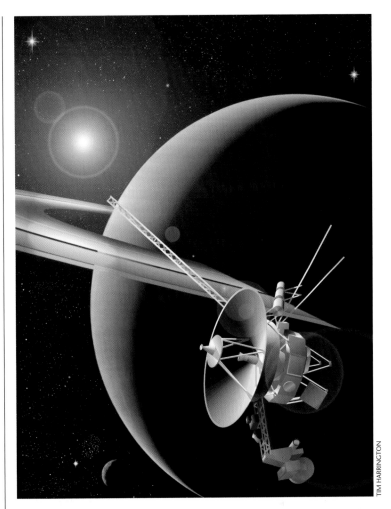

TIM HARRINGTON

IN THIS *VOYAGER* COMPOSITION, Tim Harrington used CorelDRAW's Extrude function and blending techniques to create the elaborate space scene. When the design was finished in CorelDRAW, he exported it in a bitmap format and added the sun flare in Adobe Photoshop. He used MetaCreations Painter to produce the sun's reflections in the rings.

1 Making the starfield. Starting with a black-filled rectangle, add the details of a starry sky. Harrington created the bright sun and starbursts first. The sun is a Fountain-filled circle with other detail shapes on top of it, made as follows: With the Rectangle tool, draw a long, thin bar. To add a star shape to this bar from the Symbols library, open the Symbols roll-up (Ctrl-F11, ⌘-*F11 on the Mac*), and find a simple four-pointed star (the Stars1 library comes with versions 5 and later, but you have to install it for it to show up on the roll-up; see the tip "A Wealth of Symbols" on page 146 for directions). Drag the star to the desktop. Shrink the Star symmetrically

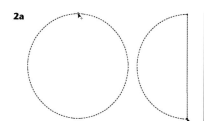

2a

Draw a perfect circle with the Ellipse tool. Then use the Shape tool to change it to a half-circle by dragging the control node inside the circle.

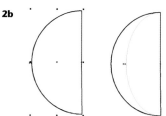

2b

Convert the ellipse to a curve, duplicate it, and shrink the copy.

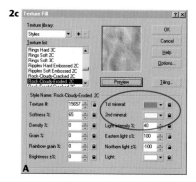

2c

Select both "planet" objects and give them the same Texture fill (A). Then select only the front object and change the Texture fill's colors to black (B). Now you can select both objects and use the Blend function to create the shaded planet (C).

by dragging a corner handle inward with the Pick tool, and then squash it horizontally by dragging the top center handle down. Shift-select the rectangle, and align the two pieces horizontally and vertically (Arrange, Align, Center, Center). Finally, merge them together with the Arrange, Weld command.

Duplicate this piece (press "+" on the numeric keypad) and rotate the copy 90°, holding down the Ctrl key (*Shift in Mac v.6, ⌘ in v.8*) to constrain the object to 15° increments while rotating. Select both objects, duplicate ("+"), and rotate them 45°. Then select all four objects, and open the Fountain Fill dialog box so you can add a Radial Fountain fill. Harrington used an 8% Vertical Center Offset, a 10% Edge Pad, and a Custom color blend from black to a custom tan color (C-8, M-23, Y-32, K-4) to white. (For tips on producing a "stair-stepped" color transition rather than the smooth blend you usually want from a Fountain fill, see the "Stripes" tip on page 79.) Draw a circle around the star with the Ellipse tool by placing the cursor in the center of the star and holding down the Ctrl and Shift keys while you drag to create a circle from the center out (*use the Shift and ⌘ keys in Mac v.6, the Option and ⌘ keys in v.8*). Give this circle a Custom Radial fill also, similar to the starburst; Harrington used more black in this color blend and a 15% Edge Pad.

To create other stars on the horizon, drag-select the elements of the star and group them (Ctrl-G; ⌘-G *on the Mac*), duplicate ("+"), and shrink. To keep the big star shape within the frame of the illustration, it was placed into a rectangle using the PowerClip command. To do this, draw a rectangle with the Rectangle tool, then select the star group, and choose Effects, PowerClip, Place Inside Container. With the resulting arrow, click on your rectangle to mask the star group inside it. (For tips on the placement of objects inside a PowerClip, see the "Turning Off Centering" tip on page 159.)

2 Constructing the planet. To show the swirling gases on the surface of Saturn, Harrington

CIRCLES, CURVES, AND SIZE

After you modify an ellipse with the Shape tool, as in creating a half-moon shape, you'll probably want to convert it to curves (Arrange, Convert To Curves) so CorelDRAW will recognize its new size. If you don't convert it, the program remembers the original ellipse size, and not the new object size. This can be important. For instance, if you want to align an object to this new shape, unless you've converted it, your object will be offset and aligned to the original ellipse dimensions.

BUILD FIRST, ROTATE LATER

When building an object that will be rotated, it's wise to wait until you finish building to perform the rotation. It's always easier to get predictable results with CorelDRAW's tools in the horizontal or vertical plane, rather than at an angle. For example, if you first rotate the original half-moon and then attempt to shrink it (A), you won't get the same result as if you shrink first and then rotate (B).

3a

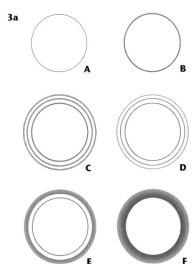

Harrington drew two concentric circles and combined them to make a ring (A, B), then duplicated the ring twice and resized the copies (C). These rings were then colored (D) and blended in two blends (outer to middle, E; and middle to inner, F) to create the color transition. The middle ring of the three was a blend control object for both blends.

3b

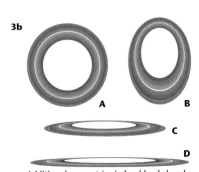

Additional concentric circles, blended and with gaps in between the blend groups, provide the coloring of the Saturn-like rings (A). All of the rings were grouped, so they could be distorted using the Add Perspective command from the Effects menu (B, C). The result was then "squashed" (D).

3c

To make the rings "disappear" behind the planet and also into the shadow, Harrington drew a shape with no outline or fill (shown here in pink) and used it to Power-Clip the rings.

blended two Texture-filled objects. You can use a whole circle as the basis for your planet, but Harrington used a half-circle since the right side of the planet would be completely hidden in shadow. Here's how to do it: First draw a perfect circle with the Ellipse tool. Then, using the Shape tool and keeping the cursor inside the circle, grab the circle's node and drag around to create a solid half-moon shape. (If you drag the pointer outside the circle by mistake, you'll make an open arc instead, which is not what you want.) When finished, convert the shape to curves (Arrange, Convert To Curves) so CorelDRAW no longer thinks of it as a circle. Duplicate this half-moon ("+"), and shrink the copy by dragging inward on the center side handle of the bounding box — the handle on the curved side of the object — to make the shadow shape.

Harrington made clever use of Texture fills and a blend to put his planet into shadow. First give both half-moon shapes the same fill by Shift-selecting them with the Pick tool, opening the Texture Fill dialog from the Fill tool fly-out, and choosing a Texture. Here Harrington modified the Rock-Cloudy-Eroded 2C entry in the Styles library. He changed the first mineral color to an orangey-red, and the second to a creamy yellow. He also clicked on the Preview button until a variant of the Texture appeared that he was happy with. Click OK when you've finished assigning a Texture.

Finally, select just the front, smaller half-moon, and again open the Texture Fill dialog. Change all of the colors in the pattern to black by clicking on the color swatches. Harrington changed the 1st and 2nd Mineral settings to black.

Now select both half-moon shapes again, make sure they have no outline (right-click the X in the on-screen palette, *Control-click on the Mac*), and perform a 30-step blend between them (Effects, Blend). Because only the color and lighting of the Texture fill were changed to make the black fill, and not the density or pattern, the resulting blend changes in coloring only. This results in the ever darkening transition pieces, which make the blend look like a shaded, round planet.

3 Making the rings. The rings around Saturn are a collection of blended "doughnuts" (circles combined together to make a ring), constrained within a container using the PowerClip function. Start by drawing a perfect circle by dragging the Ellipse tool while holding down the Ctrl key (*the Shift key in Mac v.6, ⌘ key in v.8*). Duplicate the circle ("+") and shrink it inward by dragging a corner handle while holding down the Shift key (⌘ *in Mac v.6, Option in v.8*). This will create a smaller circle within the original. Shift-select both circles with the Pick tool, and combine them (Arrange, Combine) to create the ring shape. Duplicate and scale the ring, and again once more. This should result in three evenly spaced, shrinking rings. Select the outer ring, and assign a light tan fill from the on-screen palette or the Uniform Fill dialog box (Shift-F11). Right-

4a

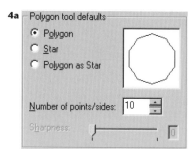

The Polygon tool introduced in version 6 lets you create polygons or stars. Double-click on the tool to open the Polygon tool's properties dialog, and then key in the desired number of sides.

4b

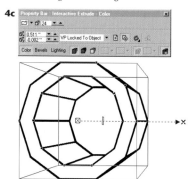

The polygon was duplicated, the copy was sized down, and the two were combined to make a ring. Then the ring was extruded.

4c

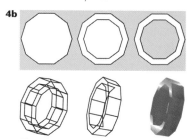

With CorelDRAW 8's interactive Extrude tool (found on the Interactive Blend tool fly-out), you can control the orientation and depth of the Extrude by dragging on-screen, with more options available on the Property bar. The Rotation values must be keyed in, however, so you may prefer the Extrude roll-up's 3D interface (see the "3D Rotation Interface" tip on the next page).

BEYOND EXTRUSION

To "freeze" an extrusion made with the Effects, Extrude command, so you can color the parts separately, or for trouble-free output or export, choose Arrange, Separate.

click on the X in the on-screen palette to remove any outline (*Control-click on the Mac*). Select the outer ring and assign a dark brown color, and no outline. Then select the middle ring and assign a medium brown tone, and again no outline.

Select the outermost ring, then Shift-select the middle ring, and open the Blend roll-up (Effects, Blend). Set up a 20-step blend between the two shapes and click Apply for a very smooth transition. Now select the middle ring again (first click the pointer on a blank spot to deselect the blend group). Shift-select the center ring, and again perform a 20-step blend. The end result is a blend from the outer ring to the middle ring and another blend from the middle ring to the center ring. This process was repeated with a variety of ring sizes and colors to result in the final Saturn ring collection.

The rings were grouped (Ctrl-G, ⌘-G), and given depth with the Perspective command, found in the Effects menu. Grab the bottom right node on the perspective envelope and drag right while holding down the Shift and Ctrl keys (⌘ *and Shift on the Mac*). This will move the bottom left node in the opposite direction, resulting in a flattened, foreshortened view. Rotate the rings by double-clicking with the Pick tool to activate the rotation arrows and dragging a corner arrow. Harrington constrained his rings within a container using the PowerClip command, both to fit the rings to the bounding rectangle of the illustration and to give the illusion of the rings going behind the planet and also into the shadow. Create the shape you want to use as your mask, select the ring group, and choose Effects, PowerClip, Place Inside Container. Now click on the mask shape, and the rings will be placed inside. Remove any outline or fill attribute from your "container" object to keep it invisible.

4 Starting the spaceship.

Working from a photo of the Voyager probe as reference, Harrington used the Extrude function to create 3D images from flat objects. Once a vanishing point and other characteristics of the extrusion are established for one object, you can copy them to other objects, with the result that many objects will share the same vanishing point. Although constructing the Voyager spacecraft involved many steps, the basic principle is easy to understand.

Start with a 10-sided polygon, made with the Polygon tool in version 6, 7, or 8. Duplicate the polygon ("+") and shrink the copy toward the center by holding down the Shift key (⌘ *in Mac v.6, Option in v.8*) while dragging a corner control handle inward. Shift-select the two polygons and combine (Arrange, Combine). With the object still selected, choose Effects, Extrude. Blue dotted lines

5

In version 5, without the Polygon tool, you can use a Symbol from the Shapes2 library, breaking it apart so that the back pieces can be selected and deleted.

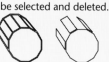

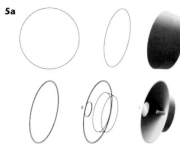

5a

To put a set of objects into the same orientation as an already extruded object, use the Copy, Extrude From command from the Effects menu. Then you can break apart the Extrude group and remove any extrusion pieces you don't want. After removing these pieces, the basic satellite dish shape can be duplicated to add thickness and to make additional dishes.

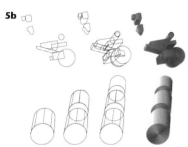

5b

Extruding one shape, then copying the Extrude settings to other shapes, results in a believable assemblage of 3D objects.

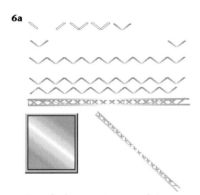

6a

To make the antenna, a rectangle is rotated, duplicated, and welded to create a "v." This is then duplicated and blended. The resulting shape is also duplicated, and flipped, and the two are positioned between bars, and details are added. Metallic-looking Custom Linear Fountain fills make the objects look shiny.

should appear on the screen, indicating where the default extrusion will build.

Harrington first dragged the crosshair vanishing point to the far right of the object. This would produce the angles for the extrusions he wanted. Then the Depth was set to 1. This is the smallest setting in the Extrude options, but it still produces a fairly deep object. Next the object was rotated. Open the Rotation menu and drag the 3D interface tool around until it's in the desired position, or click the little page icon and key in the angles you want. The dotted red and blue lines show you where the extrude will be. In version 5 you'll have to click on the movement arrows to rotate the object (or click the little page icon and key in the values you want). The shading attributes were not important here, as this extrusion group was broken apart with the Arrange, Separate command and each piece was given its own Fountain fill. Before it was broken apart, however, the other shapes that share the same vanishing point, such as the radar dish, were created. This process was made easy by the ability to copy the Extrude features of one object to another.

5 Making the radar dish and other elements. Harrington needed to orient the radar dish at the same angle as the Voyager body. He didn't want to use an extruded shape for the dish, but the Extrude command was helpful anyway. He created a circle for the dish by Ctrl-dragging the Ellipse tool (*Shift-drag in Mac v. 6, ⌘-drag in v.8*). Then, with the circle selected, Harrington chose Effects, Copy, Extrude From and clicked on the extrusion group of the Voyager body. This copied the extrusion values to the new object, which produced the correct orientation for the dish. He selected the extruded dish and chose Arrange, Separate to free the dish from the extrusion pieces, and deleted the extra extrusion objects. This left just the dish, in the correct alignment with the Voyager body pieces. To give the dish some thickness, he duplicated it and reduced the copy slightly toward the center. The two dish elements were again duplicated, and the pair was reduced to become the smaller dish; another copy became the tiny dish element. The smaller dishes were given a gray-to-white-to-gray Custom Linear Fountain fill. The large dish has a Custom Conical Fountain fill,

SUBTLE EXTRUSIONS

If you want a more subtle Extrusion depth than the lowest setting in the Extrude roll-up will produce, try building at a larger scale, extruding, and then shrinking the extruded object. This will give you a broader range of depth possibilities.

3D ROTATION INTERFACE

CorelDRAW 6, 7, and 8 have a very powerful 3D rotation interface in the Extrude roll-up. You can extrude an object by dragging and twisting the 3D "C" icon, with the blue-dotted lines on-screen providing a preview of the new extrusion whenever you release the mouse button. This makes extrusions more interactive than keying in numbers for the rotation values.

6b

Lens
shape

The finished spacecraft with the main antenna and smaller duplicates in place. Since the spaceship was placed over a solid black area, Harrington could apply a Brighten Lens set at –20 to a simple shape to create a shadow effect on the arm objects behind the dish.

7

Once CorelDRAW object-based artwork is converted to a bitmap, you can change the look easily using filter effects. If you're working with version 5 or 6 you'll need a program like Adobe Photoshop (used for the opening image) or Corel PHOTO-PAINT. But in versions 7 and 8 you can find filters in CorelDRAW's Bitmaps menu. The top image is the result of choosing Bitmaps, Color Transform, Psychedelic and applying the filter, while the bottom was transformed by choosing Bitmaps, Plug-Ins, PhotoLab, CSI GradTone, Electric Fire.

with a –28.7° Angle and the Center Offset 30% horizontally and –2% vertically. The Custom color blend is from black to gray to white to white, to produce a larger, sharper gleam area than a direct black-to-white color blend would produce. Many groups of extruded objects were assembled to become the final Voyager spacecraft illustration.

6 Extending the antenna. The intricate lattice work of the extended antenna started with a long thin rectangle. It was duplicated ("+"), and the copy was moved down, with the two pieces becoming the top and bottom rails. The bottom rail was duplicated and shrunk down horizontally by dragging the right center control handle. This small piece became the building block for the lattice work. The piece was rotated 36° by double-clicking with the Pick tool to bring up the rotation handles, and then dragging one of them. The piece was then duplicated and flipped horizontally by dragging a center control handle while holding down the Ctrl key (*the Shift key in Mac v.6, ⌘ key in v.8*). This copy was moved to overlap slightly on the original, and then the two pieces were selected and merged (Arrange, Weld). The Weld did not produce the perfect shape, so with the Shape tool Harrington edited it by pulling the center bottom node down more. The resulting "v" was duplicated, and the copy was moved to the opposite end of the antenna bar. The two "v" shapes were selected and blended in 7 steps to produce the first lattice. Duplicate this, flip, separate, and ungroup so that one of the "v"s can be selected and deleted. Two additional copies of the top rail, shrunk and rotated, along with smaller support rectangles, provide the finishing touches. All of the pieces were drag-selected and a three-color Fountain fill was assigned (F-11) to give a metallic, glistening look. (A Cylinder preset, like Cylinder - Gold 01, would also work well.)

7 Adding final effects. In order to further modify his image with filter effects, Harrington needed to generate a bitmap from his CorelDRAW art. All versions of the program have export functions to perform this process, and versions 7 and 8 even let you perform the conversion within the program using the Convert To Bitmap command, found in the new Bitmap menu. Since Harrington wanted to use Photoshop, he exported the artwork (File, Export, TIFF Bitmap). He set the Colors option to CMYK, the Image Size at 1 to 1, and the Resolution to 300 dpi. He then used the specialized bitmap-editing tools, such as the Blur and Lens Flare filters, and other effects to customize his image. *WOW!*

Beveling a Logo

Overview *Draw a logo; create an outside contour to make a bevel; divide the bevel into highlight and shadow shapes; color those shapes; add a drop shadow.*

TIM HARRINGTON

4•5•6•7•8

This approach to beveling requires the Contour function, not present in CorelDRAW 3. Version 4 has Contour but lacks the Trim and Intersect functions, so bevel shapes have to be made by node-editing, which is quite a bit more difficult.

1a

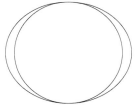

To start the border of the logo, an oval was drawn with the Ellipse tool and duplicated in place.

1b

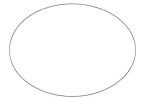

The copy was made narrower by holding down the Shift key and dragging inward on one of the side handles of the highlight box (on the Mac use the ⌘ key in v.6, the Option key in v.8). The two rings were Shift-selected and combined into a single ring object (Arrange, Combine).

SETTING THE OFFSET

When you use Contour, the Offset setting is expressed in inches. The size of the Offset will depend on how large your original object is and how wide you want the bevel to be relative to the object.

WHEN TIM HARRINGTON SET OUT to make a dimensional version of the PDA logo, he knew he wanted the top face of the logo smaller, with the side edges angling away to a larger back shape — in other words, a bevel — as if a carpenter had chiseled away the sides of the logo at a 45° angle. In some versions of CorelDRAW the Extrude function can bevel symmetrical shapes relatively easily and successfully, but beveling shapes like letters is tricky. Harrington decided to use the Contour function, followed up with the hand-trimming needed to divide the contour into the various surfaces he would need for applying lighting to the bevel.

1 Drawing the logo. The PDA logo had originated as type, which was converted to curves (Arrange, Convert To Curves) and node-edited to produce the final modified characters (for tips on node-editing, see "Node-Editing" on page 27). The surrounding oval was made by combining two ellipses and then trimming the resulting shape to accommodate the modified "P" and "A."

2 Starting a bevel. To begin to shape the bevel, Harrington needed to make a slightly expanded copy of the logo. The Contour function lets you to create new objects from your original, much like a blend, but with only one source object. So Harrington selected the flat logo (Edit, Select All) and combined its parts (Arrange, Combine). Then he activated the Contour roll-up from the Effects menu. He set the number of Steps to 1, set the Offset distance, specified that the contour should be Outside the original, and then clicked Apply. This created a larger shape that he could now use to build the edge for the bevel.

To make the Contour into the bevel edge shapes for all the parts of the logo, Harrington first separated the contour from the original object (Arrange, Separate). He stored a copy of this larger shape (for later use in making the shadow) by selecting it with the Pick tool, pressing "+" on the numeric keypad, and dragging the copy off to the side. Back in the work area he selected and ungrouped the original contour (Ctrl-U; ⌘-*U on the Mac*) and broke it into separate pieces (Arrange, Break Apart).

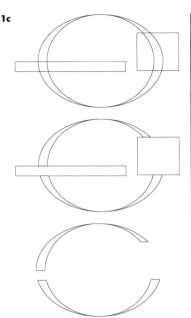

1c

Two boxes, drawn with the rectangle tool, were used to cut away parts of the border: To make each cut a box was selected, the ring was Shift-selected, and Arrange, Trim was chosen. (In versions of CorelDRAW without the Trim command, use node-editing procedures to remove part of an object.)

1d

The lettering was added to complete the logo.

2

The Contour command produced a larger outer object behind the original logo. Bevel shapes were built by combining each part of the logo with its corresponding Contour shape. (The bottom piece of the "P" was an exception; for a simple rectangle like this, you can use the Contour shape alone, as you'll see in steps 3 and 4).

He selected the original logo with the Pick tool and duplicated it in place ("+"). He dragged one copy off to the side and left the other in place so he could use it, along with the Contour shapes, to make the bevel pieces. To make a bevel for each part of the logo, he worked in Wireframe mode. He broke apart his duplicate (Arrange, Break Apart). Then he could select each part of it, Shift-select the corresponding Contour shape, and combine the two (Arrange, Combine) to produce a separate edge object.

3 Producing separate bevel shapes for lighting and shading. The next step is to determine where the light will come from; Harrington imagined the light source at the upper right. On a beveled edge, the bevel shapes facing the light source are highlighted, while those facing away are shaded. So to give the illusion of depth and beveling, Harrington had to break each edge piece into different shapes for the light and dark areas.

He began with the bevel for the upper arc, above the "PDA." He duplicated this object in place ("+"), so he would have two copies that he could edit and color — one for the top-left piece of the bevel and one for the bottom-right.

He began the editing by dividing up the top copy in his two-copy stack to make the top-left piece. In CorelDRAW 5 or later you can use the Trim command, as described next. In earlier versions, you'll need to do some tedious node-editing (for pointers on editing curves, see "Node-Editing" on page 27).

Here's one way to do the trimming: Use the Freehand or Bezier tool to draw a shape that surrounds the bottom part of the bevel shape (see "The Path-Drawing Tools" on page 25 for pointers on using these drawing tools). For a shape with narrow "passages" like the top of the oval in the PDA logo, you'll need to work at a high magnification to place the points with the Freehand or Bezier tool (click the Zoom tool on the spot where you want to work; to zoom back out, press F3).

When you've finished drawing this new shape (it will be the "trimmer" shape), use the Trim command: In versions 6, 7, and

SEPARATE BEFORE RESIZING

Like a blend, a Contour group remains "live" until you separate it. This means that if you enlarge or reduce an active Contour group, the contour(s) will grow or shrink along with the original. But the Offset setting stays the same! This can generate some strange results, with your Contour becoming disproportionately large if you shrink your object, or too small to have an effect when you enlarge it. Be sure to separate a Contour group (Arrange, Separate) before resizing.

Scaled down without separating

Separated and then scaled down

3a

A "trimmer" shape (shown in pink) can be drawn as the first step in producing the bevel pieces for the top of the arc.

3b

Finished bevel pieces of the entire logo, exploded to show the individual shapes

4a

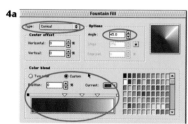

Setting up the Custom Conical fill

4b

All the bevel components were given the same Custom Conical fill, but with the Angle changed to fit with the imaginary lighting scheme.

5

The shadow started with a copy of the large outer shape of the contour group made in step 2. This copy was filled with 20% Black (left). Then the shadow was softened with a 6-step Contour, fading to white.

Windows 8, select the trimmer shape; then choose Arrange, Trim to open the Trim interface; if you are offered the opportunity to Leave Other Objects, be sure to choose this option; then click the Trim button; and click on the "trimmee" shape. (In CorelDRAW 4 or 5 or Mac v.8 select the trimmer; Shift-select the trimmee; and choose Arrange, Trim.) The result is a unique bevel shape — in Harrington's case a top-left piece for the top of the arc.

To produce the opposite piece of the bevel (for the "PDA" logo this would be the bottom-right piece for the top arc), you can use your trimmer shape again, this time with the Intersect command: Select the trimmer shape and Shift-click on the bottom of the bevel to select it also; then choose Arrange, Intersect. This should leave you with a bottom piece that fits exactly with the top piece

---

4

Even without the Trim and Intersect commands, you may be able to avoid node-editing to produce the second piece of the bevel. To save yourself some work, just leave the first bevel piece in place, covering up the top of the whole bevel copy underneath. When you apply Custom Fountain fills (in step 4), try filling the one bevel piece as described, and then fill the underlying bevel whole as described for the other bevel piece. You may find that the lighting illusion works fine without the additional trimming required to make a unique second bevel.

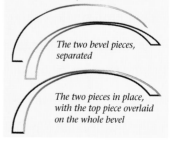

The two bevel pieces, separated

The two pieces in place, with the top piece overlaid on the whole bevel

Generally, the closer to the object a shadow is, the darker and crisper the shadow will appear. So a lighter, more diffuse shadow can make an object seem farther above the page (A). To make the light source appear more directly overhead, like the sun at noon, move the shadow closer under the object, and for side lighting, move the shadow farther out (B). And to simulate dim or diffuse light (like sky light on a cloudy day) (C), shadows should be less crisp than they are for brighter, more focussed light (like bright sunlight or a spotlight).

The two 3D versions of the logo shown here were assigned different surface textures for color and pattern, different bump maps to make the background look textured, and different lighting in a 3D program, and were rendered from different points of view.

you just made. (When you've completed the pieces for a bevel, there may be extra pieces hanging around from the Trim and Intersect commands; if so, select and delete them.) Harrington produced bevel pieces for the other parts of the PDA logo the same way as for the top arc.

4 Adding the light. To create subtle highlighting and shading effects, Harrington used the Custom Fountain fill feature found in CorelDRAW versions 4 and later. His Custom fill is from a large black area, to dark red, to white. To make a highlighting fill, open the Fountain Fill dialog box (F11). Click the Custom button, then double-click above the Fountain bar at every point where you want to add a color to the gradient. If you click any of the indicators that appear above the bar, you can choose a new color for that part of the gradient. Or drag one of these markers sideways to change how fast the color shifts in the gradient.

Harrington changed the Type of fill from Linear to Conical so there would be a specular highlight, characteristic of shiny, polished surfaces, with a light side and a dark side. The angle of the Conical fill was altered depending on the need of each bevel piece. The top-left bevel of Harrington's top arc, for example, has a 45° Angle on the Conical fill, while the bottom bevel of the same arc has the opposite Angle, –135°. This places the highlight in the correct position in relation to the imaginary light source.

The filling process was repeated until every piece of the bevel was highlighted. (If you've hidden or removed the shapes for the original flat surfaces of the logo as described in "Keeping Things in Position" at step 3, now is the time to bring them back and color them.) Then all pieces were given a dark red outline and the original logo was given a Uniform fill of dark red (Shift-F11). The dimensional effect was complete.

5 Adding a drop shadow. Harrington took the depth illusion one more step with the addition of a drop shadow. With the imaginary light source at the top right, the shadow would be cast to the left and down. Knowing where he wanted the shadow, Harrington put the Contour effect to work again. Working with the original logo he had stored off to the side, he applied the same Contour as he had in step 2, then separated the Contour group (Arrange, Separate) and used the new larger shape to develop the shadow: He gave the shadow a 20% Black fill (Shift-F11) with no outline (right-click the X in the on-screen color palette; *on the Mac, Control-click*). To soften the shadow's edge, he chose Arrange, Contour and entered settings for 6 Steps, an Outside Offset, a White Outline, and a White Fill, and clicked Apply, creating the effect of fading the gray softly to white. He selected the shadow and moved it into position behind the beveled logo.

Variations. After adding "Inc.," to the logo, Harrington exported a no-fill version of it from CorelDRAW in **.ai** format and imported it into a 3D modeling package similar to CorelDREAM. *WOW!*

From Plan to 3D

Overview *Import 2D AutoCad illustrations; skew the pieces into a 3D orientation; organize the illustration in layers to allow for "tear-away" viewing.*

3•4•5•6•7•8

All versions support skewing and layering.

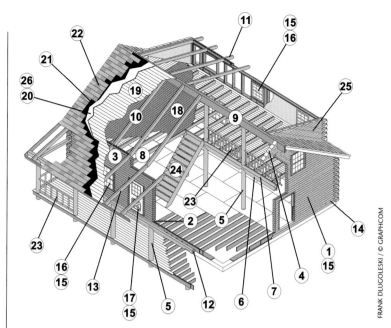

*The original illustrations were available as AutoCad (**.dxf**) files. These drawings were imported individually into CorelDRAW, where they translated into lines only — the fills disappeared.*

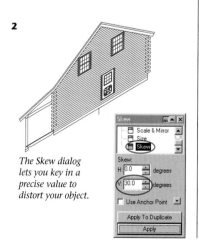

The Skew dialog lets you key in a precise value to distort your object.

FRANK DLUGOLESKI CONVERTED FLAT architectural renderings into *Log Home Construction,* a 3D cutaway view of the Hayes Log Home. Building the drawing in many layers made the drawing task more manageable and also made it easy to adapt the artwork for a touch-screen information kiosk showcasing the features of the building. This illustration was also used in promotional literature for Ashley Falls, Massachusetts–based Courtesy Country Log Homes.

1 Importing the files. For reference Dlugoleski was given a set of AutoCad files that had been used for creating the technical specifications for the building. When the vector-based drawings produced by this popular computer-aided drafting package were imported into CorelDRAW, the lines became disconnected. This meant that there were no closed objects that could be filled with color. So Dlugoleski used the imported files mainly as sizing guides to aid in rebuilding the image entirely within CorelDRAW. To import an AutoCad file, from the File menu, choose Import, and then change the Files Of Type to AutoCad (DXF), and double-click on the file name. (In CorelDRAW 8, you have the option to drag the relative size of the import on the screen, or just click without dragging for the file to import at its original size.) Dlugoleski imported four files, one for each side of the house, all at the same scale and dimensioned correctly. To make it easy to work with these multipart drawings, he drag-selected and grouped (Ctrl-G; ⌘-G on the Mac) all the parts of each side as soon as he imported it.

2 Skewing the sides. Many technical illustration methods don't follow the rules of perspective drawing. Instead of converging at one or more vanishing points, parallel lines remain parallel. Dlugoleski took one such approach to make his cutaway

3

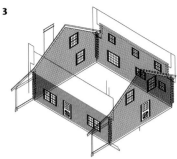

The left and right sides were skewed 30°, and the front and back –30°. Lining the four sides up at the corners of the building created the "box."

4

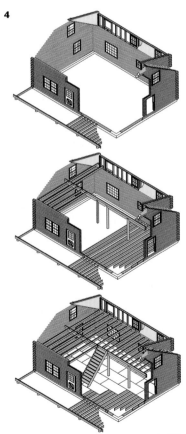

The skewed AutoCad drawings served as reference images for redrawing objects in CorelDRAW to add layers of color and detail to the illustration.

illustration, skewing the sides to produce a sort of bird's eye view. (Another standard approach to technical drawings is to use a projection in which an object is drawn with its horizontal and vertical lines kept in parallel, while curves and diagonals are optically distorted. "3D Projections from 2D Layouts" on the following page shows how to make several kinds of projections.)

To position the flat AutoCad illustrations into a 3D orientation, Dlugoleski used the Skew function. He selected the Near Side view, and opened the Skew interface (from the Transform or Effects or Arrange, Transform menu). Then he keyed in 30 for the number of degrees vertical (V), and clicked Apply. He selected the other side and clicked Apply again. Dlugoleski repeated the process for the front and back views, changing the V value to –30.

3 Aligning and locking. Dlugoleski dragged the sides into place to align at the corners. To ensure that these reference AutoCad illustrations would not accidentally be moved, each of the four pieces was selected and locked, each on its own layer. To lock an object or group onto a layer of its own, first select it with the Pick tool. Then open the Layers list (use the Object Manager in CorelDRAW 8, the Layer[s] Manager or Layers roll-up from the Layout or Arrange menu in earlier versions). From the Layers list's popout menu choose New, and then type in a name for the layer. Then again from the popout menu, choose Move To, and click on the new layer's name to move the selected objects to that layer. Now lock the objects on that layer: (in versions 5 and earlier, double-click on the layer name to open a dialog box that lets you choose Locked; then click OK; in versions 6 or later you can lock the layer by simply clicking in the Layers list to turn on or off the pencil icon).

4 Redrawing the details. Using the imported images as size and location reference guides, Dlugoleski carefully created a Corel-DRAW object for each piece of the illustration that needed to be solid, making a new layer for each feature.

Where he needed a number of boards to make a floor or wall, he first used the Rectangle tool to draw a rectangle of the correct width for a board, putting the bottom left corner in position in relation to the imported reference. Then he converted it to curves (Arrange, Convert To Curves). Next, using the Shape tool, he selected the two nodes at the right end and dragged them up or down until the right side was at the correct angle and in the proper position. This board was duplicated (press "+" on the numeric keypad) and the duplicate was moved up to the correct position at the top of the wall. He then Shift-selected the two boards, counted the number of boards between the two in the DXF image, and used the Blend function (from the Effects menu, or the Interactive Blend tool in version 7 or 8) to create the in-between boards, keying in the number of boards as the number of Steps in the Blend roll-up or

5a **5b**

Grouping the circle and type prevents them from getting accidentally nudged out of alignment. The type can be selected from the group by Ctrl-clicking (⌘-clicking) with the Pick tool.

The Wireframe view shows that the leader line passes through the approximate center of the circle, to make a consistent and pleasing angle between the line and the bullet.

6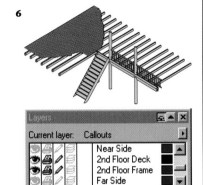

Layering made it easy to export the building's components as separate bitmaps.

Property bar), and then clicked Apply to build the wall or floor. The blends were separated (Arrange, Separate) and the pieces ungrouped (Ctrl-U; ⌘-U), so that Dlugoleski could use the Shape tool to further modify individual boards as needed for the cutaway views.

5 Labelling the components. Dlugoleski made a series of number bullets: Ctrl-drag the Ellipse tool (*Shift-drag in Mac v.6, ⌘-drag in v.8*) to make a small circle, big enough to accommodate the widest number you need. Give it a thin black outline and a white fill. The fill will help the numbers show up on busy areas of the illustration and will also hide the end of the leader line underneath the bullet. (Draw the leader line by clicking with the Freehand tool.)

Add type (Dlugoleski used Arial) by clicking inside the circle with the Text tool and typing a number. In the dialog box used for setting type characteristics (Ctrl-T; ⌘-T), make the type Bold and choose Center alignment. Drag-select the circle and number and group them (Ctrl-G; ⌘-G).

To make more bullets you can copy your first one (Edit, Copy), then paste it (Edit, Paste) as many times as you need bullets. In each bullet, select the type component of the group by Ctrl-clicking it (⌘-*clicking*) with the Pick tool. Then choose the Text tool, press Backspace to remove the existing numerals, and type in the new ones.

6 Exporting individual features. Because every sales feature was isolated to a unique layer, Dlugoleski could export each one as an individual bitmap using the File, Export command with the Visibility and Print attributes enabled only for that particular layer. These bitmaps were then imported into a multimedia program that displays a specific feature when the user touches the corresponding number in the opening graphic. *WOW!*

3D PROJECTIONS FROM 2D LAYOUTS

This chart shows the steps used in CorelDRAW to create several common 3D views from 2D layouts such as package designs. The order of the steps for each face of the box is all-important: Scale first, then skew, then rotate, if necessary, centering each operation around the common corner point. The Scale, Skew, and Rotation commands can be found in the Arrange, Transform, or Effects menu; in later versions choosing any of these commands opens a dialog box that includes all of them.

2D layout; the common corner is used as the anchor point and center of rotation.

		45° 45°	30° 30°	30° 60°	15° 30°
FRONT	H. Scale	70.711%	86.602%	96.592%	96.592%
	V. Skew	−45°	−30°	−15°	−15°
SIDE	H. Scale	70.711%	86.602%	50%	86.602%
	V. Skew	45°	30°	60°	30°
TOP	H. Scale	100%	86.602%	96.592%	70.711%
	V. Skew	0°	30°	15°	45°
	Rotate	−45°	−60°	−30°	−60°

Animating with Blends

Overview *Use Cylinder Fountain fills to color elliptical objects; draw control paths; use high numbers of steps to blend along the paths to create tubular objects.*

*The **biliary.cdr** and **electric** animation files are included on the Wow! CD-ROM so you can examine the structure and see the animation.*

3•4•5•6•7•8

All versions will blend along a path. Version 8 does not display objects in the order of creation, which allows for faster screen refresh but kills the "animation" phenomenon that allowed Boso to record the screen display on videotape for his training movies.

MARTIN BOSO

1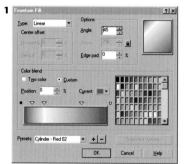

The Cylinder family of Fountain fill presets have the specialized shading necessary for Boso's blending technique. (See "Fountain Fill Presets" on page 84 for a complete catalog of the Cylinder options.)

SERENDIPITY PLAYED A ROLE when medical illustrator Martin Boso discovered that the drawing technique he had developed to show tubular structures resulted in a screen preview that made the structures seem to form from nothing, right before the viewer's eyes. He exploited this discovery to develop *The Body Electric*, a CorelDRAW file in which the structures of the human abdomen slowly form on the screen, from the backmost structures to the ones closest to the viewer. Building each organ group on its own layer within Corel-DRAW, Boso transformed his illustrations into a powerful training tool by videotaping the developing screen display. Because each layer can be turned on or off, Boso was able to "animate" or export an illustration for each anatomical focus.

The image above is just one layer from the many in *The Body Electric*. This section of the file is on the Wow! CD-ROM in the **\Boso** subdirectory (**biliary3.cdr** will load in version 3 or 4, **biliary5.cdr** in 5, 6, or 7; **biliary5.cdr** will also load in version 8, but it won't "animate," since CorelDRAW 8's screen refresh engine was updated to build everything at once). To watch the file build, open the file and then activate the Full-screen Preview (F9). Except in CorelDRAW 8 the file will build from back to front, "animating" the blend groups (the branching arteries, veins, and bile ducts) one by one.

SLOWING DOWN THE ACTION

The time it takes for a blend to build on-screen depends on how speedy your computer's graphics card is. If your "animated" blends seem to build too fast, you can slow the process down by increasing the number of steps in each blend: Click on the blend with the Pick tool to select it, then open the blend roll-up and enter a higher number of Steps. The maximum is 999.

2a

In versions 7 and 8, the Interactive Fill tool makes it easy to define Custom Fountain fills. Drag the tool across your object to establish a two-color Linear Fountain fill. Then simply drag a color from the on-screen palette to the control line and release to set a new color point. Add more colors in the same way. Or release a dragged color over an existing one to change it.

2b

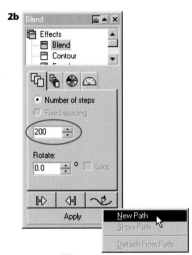

A many-step blend along a path builds a group of objects from back to front, and the cylindrical shading appears to create a three-dimensional tube. Either Custom fills like the one used here or Two Color Linear fills can produce convincing "tentacles."

1 Coloring the shapes. One of the keys to Boso's illusion is coloring the objects with a Fountain fill to suggest a strong highlight. First, draw a circle, then open the Fountain Fill dialog (F11) and create a Two Color or Custom fill or select one of the Cylinder presets. If you create your own Custom fill, try making the starting and ending colors (at positions 0 and 100) the same or very similar, with a highlight color somewhere in the middle, at a position between 35 and 65. (For the example shown here we chose Cylinder - Red 02 as the fill, and changed the angle to –45°.) Set the outline to none by right-clicking the X in the on-screen palette (*Control-click on the Mac*).

2 Building a tube. Use the Freehand or Bezier tool to draw a path where you would like your "tentacle" to grow. Duplicate your circle (press the "+" key on the numeric key pad), drag-select both circles, and open the Blend roll-up (Effects, Blend). At this stage, just click Apply to create an active blend. Then increase the number of steps (we used 200 for the smooth blend example shown at the left, but the number will vary with the length of the curve). Click on the Blend Along A Path icon (the arrow and curve) on the Blend roll-up and select New Path from the pop-out menu. Now click on your control path, enable the Full Path option in the Blend roll-up, and finally click Apply again. You can change the shape of the control path by moving nodes or curves with the Shape tool to make your tentacle twist and contort to your liking (to select the path so you can alter it, see "Pinpointing the Parts of a Blend" on the next page). When you have the shape you want, remove any outline attribute to make the path invisible (right-click the X in the on-screen palette).

If you want to change the way the loose end of a tube looks, select the blend control object at that end, duplicate it ("+"), and assign the duplicate a new fill. You can Shift-drag inward with the Pick tool (⌘-*drag in Mac v.6, Option-drag in v.8*) to shrink the new shape slightly until it looks right.

3 Branching out. The Split option from the Blend roll-up allowed Boso to divide up his tubes to branch off into many different directions. In versions that have a Miscellaneous Options page in the Blend roll-up (it looks like an old-fashioned elevator dial), select the blend, click the elevator dial, and click Split. (If the version you're using doesn't have the elevator dial, follow the directions in the next paragraph to make the branch.) With the resulting arrow, click on the blend where you would like to branch off. This will

3

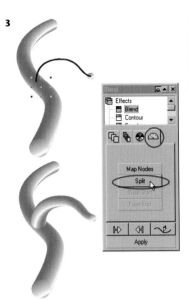

For the first branch from a tube, the Split command from the Miscellaneous Options page on the Blend roll-up in the versions that have it lets you isolate a single step in a blend so you can duplicate it to start another blend to make a branch.

4

Boso's abdomen illustration as it builds from one layer (top left) to six layers (bottom right). In an interactive presentation, the user can start with all layers in place and "remove" them one by one to see what's underneath.

isolate a single shape from that blend, which you can now duplicate (press "+") to make a blend control object for a "branch." Duplicate this blend control object (press "+" again), move it into position where you want the end of the branch, and make a new blend, along a path if you like, as described in step 2.

If you want to make more branches, you won't be able to split out another step from your original blend. But you can start a new branch by duplicating one of your existing blend control objects, duplicating this copy again, blending between the two copies, and assigning the blend to a path that you draw to make the branch.

4 Animating. To fully appreciate Boso's "living branches," view the **electric.avi** (Windows) or **electric.mov** (Mac) file included on the Wow! CD-ROM, found in the **\Boso** subdirectory. Boso used the video-out port of his computer to record each of the layers of his CorelDRAW file as it opened on-screen. He also exported bitmaps of the elements in his final illustration and used a multimedia program (like MacroMind Director) to incorporate these images into an interactive application, in which a user can literally peel away layers of organs, exploring through the human body.

PINPOINTING THE PARTS OF A BLEND

With several overlapping blends on a page, especially if each is bound to its own path that controls how it curves, it can be difficult to select one of the blend control objects or the control curve so you can change the shape or color. Here are some tips for getting to the parts:

• To select the whole blend so you can move it around, resize it, or otherwise manipulate it, click it with the Pick tool.

Normal view

• To select the second (forward) blend control object, click the blend and press the Tab key.

• To select the first (back) blend control object, click the blend, press Tab, and then press Tab again.

• To select the control path — even if you've made the path invisible — first click on the blend, then press Tab three times. The path will be selected and you'll be able to use the Shape tool to reshape the curve.

Wireframe

• Versions 7 and 8 have the Simple Wireframe option in the View menu. For a simple blend it displays only the two blend control objects; for a blend along a path, it also shows the path itself. This makes it simple to select and modify these objects, even within a drawing with several complex multistep blends, such as the example at the right, which consists of 18 non-path blends.

Simple Wireframe (versions 7 and 8)

*The **star.cdr** file (shown here) is included on the Wow! CD-ROM so you can examine it.*

Tom Graney's presentation artwork for the *LogoWorks box* also worked its way into ads for the product. The original artwork was laid out so it could be printed and die-cut from a single piece of cardboard. Before the project got that far, Graney mocked up and presented to the client a simulated 3D version. Starting with a copy of the art, he used the Perspective tool to skew the front panel (shown at the right) and side panel. He then drew in a box-shaped bottom and added a duplicate of the figure to hold up the box comp, as shown above.

Graney selected and duplicated the main shapes (with the Pick tool active press "+" on the numeric keypad), grouped them (Ctrl-G; ⌘-G on the Mac), filled the copy with gray and sent it behind the original as a drop shadow (Arrange [Order], To Back). To soften the shadow, the gray-filled group was duplicated (Ctrl-D; ⌘-D on the Mac), the copy was sent to the back, and the two groups were selected and blended, using enough steps to make a smooth, soft transition (Effects, Blend).
▶ *In CorelDRAW 8 you can create shadows with the Interactive Drop-Shadow tool. By* dragging to form the shadow and then adjusting the midpoint slider, you can easily control the color, placement, opacity and "fuzziness" of a drop shadow, for realistic results.

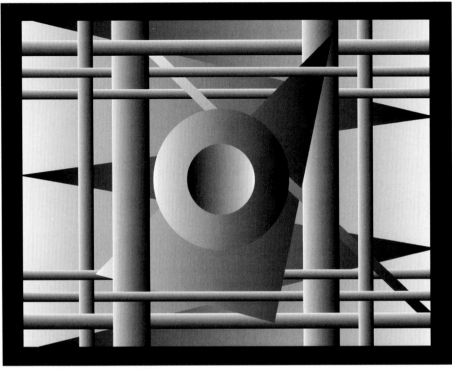

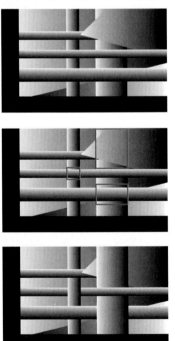

John **Sparks's** *Grid* challenges the viewer to resolve the conflicting visual messages about whether its components are flat or rounded, and where they are in space. Linear Fountain fills turn slim rectangles into rounded bars. Sparks used black-to-white Fountain fills at 180° for the vertical bars, and at 90° for the horizontal ones, to make the bars appear to be lit from the left and top. The two right-pointing triangles in the midground show the same lighting scheme.

In this starkly lit optical illusion, the rounded bars weave together, but without bending or casting shadows. To accomplish the intertwining, Sparks duplicated individual rods (choosing the Pick tool and pressing the "+" key on the numeric keypad to copy them in place). Then he dragged the top or bottom center handle inward to shorten the vertical rods, or dragged the right or left center handle inward for the horizontal ones. Finally, he brought these patches to the front (Arrange [Order], To Front) to cover parts of the criss-crossing bars, the tilted triangle, and the flat band that runs diagonally.

Sparks reversed the direction of the light in the background rectangle, which adds to the illusion of depth: This "wall" must be far enough back so it's lit by a completely different light source than the other objects in the image, or maybe it curves forward on the right.

The disc in the center foreground appears to have a dish scooped out of it. This figure illustrates a simple way to sculpt depressions and beveled edges: The two circles were formed by dragging with the Ellipse tool while holding down the Ctrl key to constrain the ellipses to circles (*the Shift key in Mac v.6, ⌘ in v.8*) and the Shift key (*⌘ key in v.6, Option in v.8*) to draw the circles out from a common center point. They were filled with simple two-color Fountains in opposite directions. Because the lighting is directly from the left, though, with no component from the top, the figure won't quite resolve itself in its surroundings, contributing to the dynamism of the image.

Rick Smith drew the *Celtic knot* design below by overlaying blue lines on thicker black ones and then adding small, thin segments of black to create the woven effect. He started with a circle, made by Ctrl-dragging with the Ellipse tool, and used the Shape tool with the Ctrl key to drag the circle's node on the inside to make a quarter-circle wedge (*use the Shift key in Mac v.6; ⌘ in v.8*).

He converted the circle to curves (Arrange, Convert To Curves). Then he selected the corner node and opened the Node Edit roll-up (in most versions this can be done by double-clicking on the node with the Shape tool; in version 8 double-click the Shape tool in the Toolbox). He clicked the Break button in the roll-up to split the node in two and used the Shape tool with the Ctrl key (*Shift or ⌘ on the Mac*) to extend the two lines out from the corner.

Next he made the inner part of the element (select the modified quarter circle with the Pick tool, press "+," and drag inward on a corner handle to shrink the copy). The small element was moved into position and its lines were extended. All four elements were Shift-selected and assigned a 14.5-point black outline (F12), then duplicated in place, and the duplicate was given a thinner blue outline (9.5 points).

Smith selected, duplicated, and flipped these layered lines to complete the circular design. To accomplish the "weaving," he drew a series of thin black lines (2.5 points, which is half the 5-point difference between the weights of the blue and the thick black lines). He worked in Wireframe mode to precisely align these "repair" pieces.

To "tie" her *Celtic knot* (above), **Alice Mininch McLean** started by using the Rectangle, Ellipse, and Freehand tools to draw a set of guidelines — a square with circles inside it and diagonal lines from corner to corner (for tips on drawing squares and circles, see "Starting with a Shape" on page 29). She used the guides to draw a series of objects that made up a knot group that filled one quadrant. (If you wanted to make smooth, precise, geometric curves, the Bezier tool would work well; McLean used the Freehand tool, which produced the more "organic" look.)

McLean drag-selected all the objects with the Pick tool and grouped them (Ctrl-G; ⌘-G). She duplicated the group (press "+" on the numeric keypad) and clicked the new group with the Pick tool to bring up the rotation handles. After dragging the center of rotation to the center of the guide circle, she Ctrl-dragged a corner handle to rotate the copy 90° (*Shift-drag in Mac v.6; ⌘-drag in v.8*). She repeated the duplicate-and-rotate process to make two more quadrants.

The outward-projecting end of the first group (shown in pink above) was then Ctrl-clicked to select it from the group (⌘-click on the Mac) so it could be brought forward to cover the edge of the fourth group (Arrange [Order], To Front). The inner ends were "tucked in" by selecting them and sending them to the back Arrange [Order], To Back). McLean masked and welded some of the center pieces and trimmed off the projecting outer ends to finish the circular knot. Finally, she drew a corner section to square off the knot and duplicated it to all four corners.

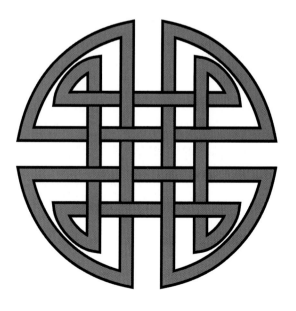

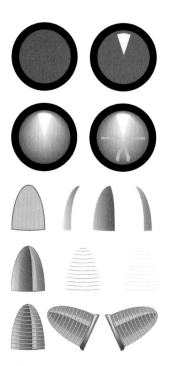

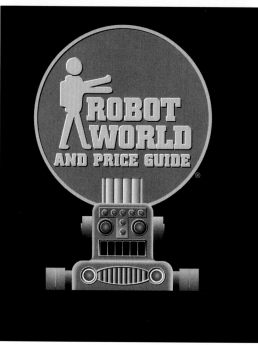

In his *Robot World catalog covers,* **Bruce Baryla** used shading techniques to add depth and life to his mechanical creations. Limited to a single color of ink, he made use of the wide range of grays that "black-and-white" offers. For example, he started with the logo filled with 20% black, a good light gray that lets highlights bounce and also stands out from a 100% black shadow. He made white and black duplicates for highlight and shadow, offsetting them to indicate lighting from the upper left and sending them behind the gray type. In the bottom illustration Linear Fountain fills suggest cylindrical shapes, again lighter on the top and left side, while Radial Fountains turn circles into half-spheres.

In the top illustration, Baryla used blends rather than Fountain fills to shape the more complex parts of the robot. For instance, the 16 glass tubes on the front of the robot each started with a black circle made by Ctrl-dragging with the Ellipse tool (*Shift-drag in Mac v.6; ⌘-drag in v.8*). The circle was duplicated, and the copy was reduced and filled with 50% black. Then this gray circle was duplicated in place ("+" on the numeric keypad) and the new copy was reduced and filled with white. Choosing the Shape tool made the single node of the white ellipse visible, and dragging it around within the circle turned the circle into a "pizza slice" shape. A 20-step blend between the slice and the gray circle produced the gleam. The other highlights were made by duplicating the slice, reducing it, and filling with 20% black. Because the light gray elements cross a gradient of gray tones, they also seem to change in tone.

The ceramic-looking transformers are simply stacked shapes with different fill attributes to suggest lighting. The original dome shape was duplicated and node-edited into three other elements that were then given Fountain fills. The rings give the most depth to the illustration. The bottom and top arcs were drawn in 50% black with the Bezier tool and an 11-step blend made intermediate lines. These arcs were node-edited to fit the dome shape and then grouped and duplicated at 10% black, and the duplicate was moved up slightly.

A black rectangle placed over the bottom of each robot made space for the volume number and date of the catalog.

Working with tight time and budget constraints forces **Marla Shelasky** to invent efficient shortcuts for working in CorelDRAW. These images, used to illustrate a black-and-white newspaper-style *electronic buyer's guide* for a cost-conscious client, are perfect examples. Shelasky started with flat objects and used Fountain fills to create a lighting scheme. Then she used the Add Perspective feature from the Effects menu to solidify the three-dimensional look. This command assigns an object (or a group of objects) a vanishing point and distorts the object accordingly. Shelasky used the Shape tool to manipulate the Perspective grid or vanishing point to get the orientation she wanted. ▶ *Once you have the Perspective set for one object, you can assign it to others by selecting the other objects, then choosing Effects, Copy, Perspective From and then clicking on the object with the desired Perspective settings.*

Once the main components of the drawing were in place, Shelasky drew in the finishing objects, "eyeballing" the perspective to finish things off. She also added shadows, either dark-filled objects blended to larger white shapes for a soft look (top) or Fountain-filled hard-edged shapes (bottom).

Butterfly Valve

Nelson Crabill uses CorelDRAW to create very detailed and accurately scaled illustrations, such as this *Butterfly Valve*, a cutaway drawing of a specialized component used in the oil-drilling industry. These illustrations appear in sales catalogs and also in the plans used for the construction of the components. Crabill's specialized technique of converting two-dimensional AutoCAD drawings into detailed CorelDRAW files is so accurate that he has at times found and helped correct engineering flaws, and his rendering skills are now employed much earlier in the design process than before, to work out mechanical problems.

When imported, the DXF "blueprint" files saved from AutoCAD come in with every line segment as a separate object, so Crabill simply uses them as a guide for remaking the artwork in CorelDRAW. To help organize the many sections of an illustration, Crabill creates each item on its own layer, which can then be locked and made invisible to speed up the drawing process as he works on another part of the drawing.

An accomplished airbrush artist, Crabill set out to achieve the look or an airbrushed rendering in CorelDRAW. He first blended two main shapes together, using only a few steps in the blend. Then he separated

the group of blend steps from the two original blend control objects (Arrange, Separate), selected the group of new steps and ungrouped it (Ctrl-G; ⌘-*G on the Mac*). Some of these pieces were deleted, leaving a few critical intermediate shapes for creating multistep blends. Using each of these new intermediate pieces as the end of one blend and the beginning of another, Crabill made a series of blends to create highlight and shadow elements to round the surfaces of the valve.

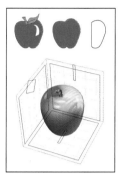

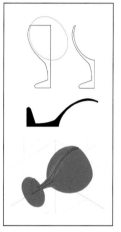

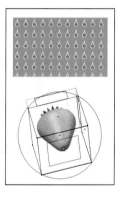

In **Rémi Forcier's** *Still Life*, the artist used objects made in CorelDRAW as the basis for many of the three-dimensional models he created in CorelDREAM 3D, which is packaged with CorelDRAW versions 6 and later. The table started as a 12-sided figure created by dragging the Polygon tool with the Ctrl key held down (*in Mac v.6 use the Shift key; in v.8 use ⌘*). Forcier filled the shape with black and saved the file in **.cdr** format. (You can export from Corel-DRAW in the **.ai** format if your version of CorelDREAM doesn't import **.cdr** files.)

He dragged CorelDREAM's Free Form tool in the workspace to create a new object, named it "Table," and clicked OK in the Set Name dialog box. Then he chose File, Import. CorelDREAM imported the polygon and automatically "swept" it through space on a path perpendicular to its surface. By dragging the control nodes on the pink line along the back wall of the Corel-DREAM workspace, Forcier could reduce or increase the depth of the sweep.

A goblet profile was started with the Bezier tool in CorelDRAW, then an ellipse on a slant was used to trim away the inside of the shape so the glass could be hollow rather than solid. The profile was rotated onto its side, filled with black, and exported. In CorelDREAM Forcier created another Free Form object, named it "goblet," and clicked OK. Then he imported the shape. This time, instead of adjusting the sweep path, he chose Torus from the Extrusion Preset fly-out in the Geometry menu. This lathed the curve into a 3D object, and Forcier assigned it a glass surface texture. ▶ *For a convincing glass look, assign an object a semi-transparent Shader from the Glass family by dragging it from the Shaders browser onto the object.*

The same Torus lathing technique was used to create the strawberries and apples. For the apple Forcier started with clip art, reducing the apple to a simple outline curve and cutting that in half. For a more realistic apple skin, Forcier created a red and yellow color mix in the Shader Editor, opened via the Windows menu.

For the strawberry, he created the seed pattern in CorelDRAW and exported it as a **.bmp** file for use as a Shader in CorelDREAM. To make it into a Shader, he opened the Shaders Browser from the Windows menu, chose New from the Shader menu, and named the shader "strawberry." This produced a new shader in the default red. He double-clicked on it to open the Shader Editor, where he chose Flat Preview from the View menu and those chose Texture Map from the Type menu. He opened the **.bmp** file he had created in CorelDRAW and enabled the Tile option, increasing the number of vertical and horizontal repetitions to make the seeds smaller.

Finally, Forcier arranged his models into his still life scene in CorelDREAM's Perspective window. He set up the lighting and the camera, and rendered the scene by choosing Windows, Render.

*The CorelDREAM **Fruit** file is included on the Wow! CD-ROM so you can examine it.*

6

WORKING WITH TYPE

IGNACIO-SKAGGS

IGNACIO-SKAGGS

Donna Ignacio-Skaggs' covers for contract-winning technical proposals are examples of the kind of graphics-intensive page layouts that CorelDRAW is so appropriate for. In the Jacksonville Multi-Modal System Linkage *design the type in the flowing arrows was shaped with the Envelope effect.*

TYPE, OR IN CORELDRAW PARLANCE *TEXT,* is the medium by which we communicate the written word, both in print and more recently on the computer screen. Whether the words compose a single bold headline or several paragraphs, the *typography,* which is the arrangement and appearance of type, can make an impression on the reader even before the words are read. Most of the techniques presented in this chapter involve applying special effects to small amounts of type — a few letters or words. These techniques barely touch on CorelDRAW's type capabilities, so the next three pages discuss typography. "Artistic Text" (page 201) and "Paragraph Text" (page 202) cover the basics of the two ways CorelDRAW handles type.

POINTERS FOR CHOOSING AND SETTING TYPE

Typography is determined partly by the typeface (or in computer parlance the *font*) that the designer chooses and partly by how he or she puts it to use. CorelDRAW comes with hundreds of typefaces, and the more fonts you have available, the more damage you can do by choosing a poorly made one or sometimes by bending, squeezing, and extruding a perfectly good one. So it follows that an understanding of type basics will be helpful in using CorelDRAW's type functions.

To get its message across, type has to catch and hold the reader's attention. Catching the attention usually depends heavily on the ***aesthetic content*** of the type — is it beautiful? scriptlike and flowing? playful? distinguished? grungey?

Once the type catches the reader's attention, then legibility and readability come into play. ***Legibility*** is what makes it possible to recognize characters quickly — to distinguish instantly whether a character is a "c" or an "e," or a "5" or a "6." ***Readability*** is the relative ease with which text can be read. Is it easy to see the words as units? to follow a line of type across the page? to make the leap from one line of type to the next? If it takes too much effort to distinguish the characters or to move the eye from one word or line to the next, you may lose the reader before the message is delivered.

Aesthetic content and legibility are built into the typeface. Certain built-in characteristics also affect readability, but here the typesetting itself can make a big difference. There are certain "defaults," or rules,

L'art du partenariat fructueux
Plus qu'une bonne idée!

Marketing social, marketing non lucratif, marketing de produits et services pour le gouv.

CASSELMAN

Roger Casselman's Successful Partnerships *poster was made by setting black headline type with the Artistic Text tool on a black-on-white illustration, then drawing a black-filled rectangle over the right side, selecting all, and choosing Arrange, Combine so the type on the right side became a series of "holes" in the black, allowing the white background to show through. Red detail shapes were added.*

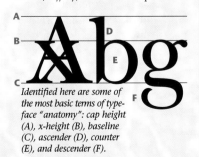

Typefaces come in all shapes and sizes. The letter "G," both capital and lowercase, are two of the most distinctive letters in a typeface. Shown left to right are "G's" from Galliard, Garden Hollow (on the Wow! CD-ROM), Optima, Caxton, and Oak Blow (also on the CD); the "g's" are from Prestige Elite, Remedy (from Emigre), Korinna, Belwe, Tiffany, and Lubalin Graph.

Identified here are some of the most basic terms of typeface "anatomy": cap height (A), x-height (B), baseline (C), ascender (D), counter (E), and descender (F).

of typography that can be helpful to a designer unless there's a good reason to do something else. ("Everybody's doing it" is not necessarily a good reason.) The defaults are these: white paper; one typeface — possibly with several weights (for instance, regular and bold) and several styles (roman and italic, for example); legible, black, undistorted type; a simple, logical format. It's likely that you'll violate these restrictive rules often for display type. They're more important for body copy — larger amounts of type set at fairly small sizes.

What makes a good typeface? Here are some things to look at when you evaluate a typeface:

- **Well-designed fonts** generally have characters made up of **smooth curves** with relatively few nodes, so there's less chance for unwanted distortion when the characters are resized. You can learn something about the construction of a typeface by setting a sample with the Artistic Text tool (as described on page 201) and then choosing Arrange, Convert To Curves so you can see how many nodes there are and where they are placed.

- Fonts have built-in spacing controls — ***letterspacing*** (the amount of space on the left and right of each letter), ***kerning*** (the way spacing is automatically adjusted when certain pairs of letters occur together), and ***word spacing*** (the size of the space character). CorelDRAW lets you adjust spacing, but it's better to reserve this option for special cases rather than to have to tweak every piece of type you set in order to compensate for the problems of a poorly designed typeface.

Serif or sans serif? Two distinguishing aspects of type "anatomy" are variation in stroke thickness and how the strokes end. Some fonts have strokes of uniform thickness, and others are thick-and-thin. Some have vertical strokes that simply come to a halt at the baseline (*sans serif* fonts) and others have "feet" (*serifs*) that provide a finish to the strokes. When do you use serif and when sans serif? It's up to you, of course, but here are some traditional rules:

- For **display type** — a few words set large — you'll make your choice based on the design of your page.

- For **text in print, serif faces** are generally considered more readable than sans serif. Maybe it's because the serifs form a kind of visible baseline that guides the eye across the line of type, or maybe it's because we have years of experience reading books and magazines set in serif faces and we're used to them.

- If you're planning to **stretch or compress** the type more than about 10% horizontally or vertically, it's usually better to **use a serif face.** In general, serif faces are built with obviously thick-and-thin strokes, which are more amenable to reshaping

Not all typefaces are visually the same size at the same point size. Even in typefaces whose visual overall heights are the same, there may be differences in x-height. The examples shown here were set at 36 points. Left to right they are Antique Olive, Glypha, Life, Garamond, New Caledonia, and Cochin.

DAVIS

A   B

CorelDRAW's ability to set type on a path makes it possible to make circular logos like the one above. Use the Artistic Text tool to set the type for the top of the circle, and use it again to set the type for the bottom. Draw the circle. (In CorelDRAW 8 you can set more than one piece of type on a single path, so both top and bottom type in the logo above can be fitted to the same circle. In earlier versions, with only one piece of text allowed per path, the bottom type can be fitted to a copy of the circle used for the top text and the two can be aligned in Wireframe view.) To fit each piece of type to the circle, select type and circle with the Pick tool and choose Text, Fit Text To Path. Open the Fit Text To Path roll-up or Property bar (in some versions it opens automatically; in others you have to choose it from View, Roll-ups). For the top type (A), accept the default settings by clicking Apply. For the bottom type, make choices that put the type below the baseline, in the bottom sector, with Place On Other Side selected.

without getting ugly than are the nearly single-weight strokes of most sans serif faces.

- For **on-screen display,** it's generally better to set text in a **sans serif** font. Since the screen display has only 72 pixels per inch to work with, it's very hard to get pleasing thick-and-thin strokes and nice-looking serifs on text-size type.

Size and leading. Type size is expressed in units called *points.* Here are some general rules on point sizes for body copy:

- **Nine to 12 points** is the usual size for text.
- *Leading* is the height of the typeface plus any extra space added between the lines of type. Leading can make a difference in readability. Somewhere around 120% of the type size can be a good place to start when experimenting with leading. The goal of leading in body copy is to make the lines of type distinct so the eye can follow them easily, but not to make them so far apart that it takes a conscious effort to get from the end of one line to the beginning of the next.
- Leading is related not only to the overall point size of a typeface, but also to the **x-height,** which is the height of lowercase letters. In large x-height fonts the lowercase letters are bigger in relation to the height of the capital letters (*cap height*). **Large x-height fonts** can be more legible, and they typically require **more leading** than small x-height fonts.

Column width. You can set what would otherwise be easily readable type — say 10-point type on 12-point leading — and it can still be hard to read if the line length is wrong. A rule of thumb for **line length** is that columns of text should be **40 to 70 characters** wide. Any wider and the reader's eye has to make too many jumps to get across it. Any shorter and the frequent "returns" from one line to the next become bothersome.

Alignment. Long bodies of text are usually aligned either *flush left, ragged right* (this is called *Left* alignment in CorelDRAW) or *justified* (called *Full justification*).

- **Left alignment,** in which the left margin is straight and the line ends wherever the word breaks dictate, results in **consistent *color,*** or overall evenness of tone in a block of type.
- **Left-aligned** text is also **easier to read** (and easier to set) than justified text, in which the type is spaced across the line so that both left and right margins are straight. When type is justified, the process of making the margins straight requires adjusting the letterspacing and word spacing, sometimes with unlovely, hard-to-read results, especially if the column width is narrow or if you try to wrap text around a graphic in too narrow a space.

A B

C D

CorelDRAW's Extrude creates a set of objects to simulate depth. When you add shading, lighting, and in version 7 or 8 a bevel, the type takes on a convincing third dimension. Both the type and the Extrude remain changeable until the type is converted to curves (Arrange, Convert To Curves) or the Extrude is "frozen" (Arrange, Separate). Shown here are the original type (A), with the Extrude command applied (B), recolored and with a bevel added via the Extrude rollup (C), and with the extrusion objects deleted but the bevel effect retained (D). For more about Extrude, see "Generating New Shapes" on page 138.

ARTISTIC TEXT

CorelDRAW has two ways of dealing with type: as Artistic Text and as Paragraph Text. Type set with the **Artistic Text** tool is good for low word-count applications such as headlines, logos, or any other instance of "type as a graphic." (CorelDRAW 3, 7 and 8 have only one text tool.) You can set Artistic text by clicking the tool anywhere in the workspace and typing. The font will be the default Avalon or AvantGarde unless you've changed it. You can make changes to the font, size, leading, spacing, or alignment by choosing Text, Character or pressing Ctrl/⌘-T.

After you've set Artistic text, besides making changes inside the text-formatting dialog box, you can edit the type by dragging over it with the Artistic Text tool and retyping. The type remains editable unless you apply a command (such as Arrange, Combine or Arrange, Convert To Curves) that changes the Text into standard vector objects made up of curves and nodes.

You can also make changes to the type with the Pick or Shape tool:

- To **change the type characteristics of a single letter,** double-click its node with the Shape tool to open the character-formatting dialog box.

- To **stretch, rotate, or skew** the type, click or double-click the type block with the Pick tool and drag, just as you would for any CorelDRAW object.

- To **reduce or increase the letterspace** between all characters, click the type block with the Shape tool and then drag the right-facing arrow left or right.

- To **reduce or increase word space,** use the Shape tool to Ctrl/⌘-drag the right-facing arrow.

- To **move a single character,** use the Shape tool to drag on the node that appears at the bottom left of the character.

- To **move more than one character** at once, Shift-select their nodes with the Shape tool and drag one of the nodes.

- To **color the entire type block,** click it with the Pick tool and choose a fill just as you would for an object (for more about coloring, see "Fills" on page 78).

- To **change the color** of one character (or more), select (or Shift-select) the node(s) with the Shape tool and assign a fill.

- In versions that allow you to set more than one line of type in an Artistic Text block, pull on the down-arrow cluster **to increase or decrease the space between lines.**

SPECIAL EFFECTS

In CorelDRAW almost anything you can do to any other object you can do to type and still have the ability to edit or restyle the text. You can also set Artistic Text on a path. In CorelDRAW 8 you can

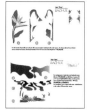

Gustavo Ortiz uses CorelDRAW to lay out the pages of his how-to newsletter, Como!. *The inside pages of each issue show how the cover illustration was constructed. Type is limited to a few paragraphs per page.*

even set Paragraph text on a path, so you can make type flow from one block, then along a path, then to another block if you like. You can also shape Artistic or Paragraph Text within an Envelope (see "Using Envelopes" on page 132 for more about the Envelope); this can be useful for wrapping Paragraph Text around a graphic on the page. Through all these changes the type can remain live and editable.

PARAGRAPH TEXT

For projects that involve text that flows over several pages, you're better off using a full-fledged page layout program, even though CorelDRAW provides some of the tools commonly found in these programs; for instance, every version has a spelling checker and thesaurus, available from the Text menu. But for single-page jobs or page spreads that consist largely of graphics, CorelDRAW's Paragraph Text can be ideal.

Dragging with the Text tool in version 3, 7, or 8 or the Paragraph Text tool in other versions allows you to define the size and shape of a block. Then when you type, the text flows inside the block. In CorelDRAW 4 and later you can also flow text from one block to another, and even to multiple pages. If you have the Edit Text On Screen option enabled, you can type your text directly onto the page. Otherwise, a dialog box will appear and you can enter the text there. Once you have the text in place, here are some things you can do to make changes:

- To **enlarge or shrink the paragraph box,** changing line length but not text size, drag on one of the side or corner resizing handles of the text box.

- In version 7 or 8 you can **scale the font** as you scale the box: Hold down the Alt/Option key while you drag a corner sizing handle with the Pick tool.

- To **continue the text in another box,** even on another page, choose the Pick tool, select your paragraph text, click on the bottom flow icon (it looks like a down arrow in a box). The drag a new, linked box for the text to flow into.

- To **edit Paragraph Text** at any time, select the text box with the Paragraph Text tool and choose Text, Edit Text if your version of CorelDRAW has this choice; in other versions press Ctrl/⌘-T.

If you want **to import text** from another source, such as a word processor package, choose File, Import and select the document to import. If you're running CorelDRAW on a version of Windows before 95, be sure to change the Files Of Type setting to the format of the file you want to import — for instance, MS Word For Window. CorelDRAW will usually assign the imported text an "unnamed" RGB color. Be sure to convert this to a true black by clicking the black swatch (100K) on the on-screen color palette. 〔WOW!〕

Designing a Label

Overview *Import or create artwork; set type; expand the letterspacing; change the attributes of individual letters; add background art.*

3•4•5•6•7•8

The Shape tool can change the letterspacing and individual letter attributes in all versions of Corel-DRAW.

1

An ink drawing was scanned and converted with CorelTRACE.

2a

Drag the spacing arrow with the Shape tool to change the spacing between letters set with the Artistic Text tool. This interactive method is faster than keying in a value in the text-formatting dialog box.

2b

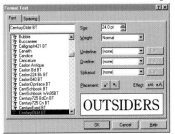

With a letter or letters individually selected, you can change the font, size, and other attributes, or move the letters around, without affecting the nonselected letters.

3

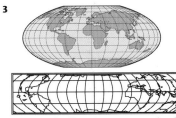

Elements of a clip-art map were moved and framed within a rectangle.

EDWARD CRISTINA CREATED THE *Outsiders* logo for an outdoor clothing line and then duplicated it, making both black-and-white and color versions. Relying mainly on type and an image of mountains, he used a world map image in the background, subtly colored to look like a spot varnish on documents that were generated on the computer and printed in-house on the client's inkjet printer.

1 Making mountains. The main artwork for the logo was an ink drawing of mountains, scanned, traced with CorelTRACE, and colored in CorelDRAW. ("Updating a Logo" on page 59 has tips on tracing.)

2 Setting and styling the type. Starting with the text tool in Artistic mode, Cristina clicked on the screen and typed "OUTSIDERS." Then he changed to the Pick tool and opened the dialog for formatting type (Ctrl-T; ⌘-*T*). Scrolling through the font list and viewing the type in the sample area, Cristina stopped when he got to Century Oldstyle, changed the size to 8 points, and then clicked OK. (In versions 5 and later you can use the up and down arrow keys to scroll through the list.)

When Cristina changed to the Shape tool, arrow assemblies appeared below the left and right ends of his text. He dragged on the array of lines in the bottom right arrow, dragging to the right to increase the letterspacing to fit the type to the artwork.

Next, he clicked on the first node (for the letter "O") to select it and Shift-double-clicked the last node (for the letter "S") to add it to the selection and open the text-formatting dialog. He changed the Size to 24 points and clicked OK. This enlarged the two selected letters. While they were still selected, Cristina then dragged one of the nodes downward so these letters moved down to frame the mountains.

3 Adding a map. From the **Map** directory on the CorelDRAW clip-art CD-ROM, Cristina imported **world3.cmx**. He ungrouped this artwork (Ctrl-U; ⌘-*U*) and used the Pick tool to move the continents so they wouldn't be hidden by the mountains. To define the shape of the logo, he used the Rectangle tool. In versions 5 and later the Effects, PowerClip command can be used to mask selected objects inside a bounding shape. In earlier versions you can use the method described in "Masking To Make a Logo" on page 41.

Puffed-Up, Popped-Out Type

Overview *Create a "rich" black text object using a rounded typeface and blend it to a lighter, offset duplicate for depth; create a highlight shape with the Trim function; add a shadow.*

*Finished **.cdr** files for Spooky, Wet, and Wingding are on the Wow! CD-ROM.*

3•4•5•6•7•8

CorelDRAW 3 doesn't have the Trim function, but you can make the highlight by exporting the shapes that make the highlight as a bitmap and then reimporting them, as described in the workaround provided at step 3. Or offset a light-colored copy of the text behind the front copy.

1a

Setting the type

1b

Deforming the text with the envelope tool

2a

Filling and stroking the type with rich black

USING A BLEND TO ADD THICKNESS to type or clip art is a great way to get the words or images to pop out. For the "Spooky" type, blending between black type in back and an offset color-filled copy in front creates a forced perspective effect to thicken and round the edges. This technique will work to thicken the letters of any font, but the round-edged look depends on the letters having no sharp corners. Distorting the type and adding a drop shadow, stretched a bit, makes the effect more dynamic — the right end of the text looks farther away from the viewer and closer to the page.

1 Creating the text. The 1.5-inch high type was set in a font called Horror (from the MasterPiece True Type Font library by Attitude, Inc.). Press Ctrl-T (⌘-*T on the Mac*) to open the dialog box for setting the font and size. Then click with the Artistic Text tool and type the word.

At this point we converted the type to curves (Arrange, Convert To Curves), though it wasn't essential. We used an envelope to change the shape: With the text selected, in version 8 click with the Interactive Envelope tool; in other versions choose Effects, Envelope Roll-Up (in CorelDRAW 3 it's Effects, Add New Envelope and then Effects, Edit Envelope). Select the Single Arc envelope (it's the second button); in CorelDRAW 4 or later press the Add New button.

Then edit the envelope: We moved the bottom left node way down, the top left node down a little, and the top center node up to make the left end bigger so the right end would look farther away. In versions where it's necessary, click on Apply to deform your text.

2 Adding thickness. Give the reshaped type a rich black fill (press Shift-F11 to open the Uniform Fill dialog box, and in the CMYK Model, enter 100K and the C, M, and Y values of the color you want to use for the face of the type). Add a relatively thick outline in the same color; ours was 2.75 points. This black type will become the back control object for the blend that rounds the edges of the type and adds thickness. With the rich black, the blend you'll do next will produce a smooth color gradient.

Select the type with the Pick tool, duplicate it (press "+" in the numeric keypad), and move it to the top and right. This piece should be assigned a fill and thin outline (ours was 0.216 points) in the main color.

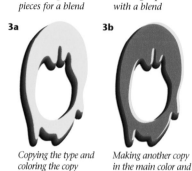

2b   **2c**

Positioning the pieces for a blend   Gaining depth with a blend

3a   **3b**

Copying the type and coloring the copy   Making another copy in the main color and offsetting it.

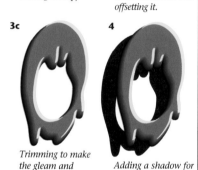

3c   **4**

Trimming to make the gleam and removing the green trimmer   Adding a shadow for contrast and depth.

Type was set in the Glacier font (supplied with all versions of CorelDRAW from 3). The front blend control object was given a Linear Fountain fill (F11) and no outline, and the back blend control object was given a Uniform fill of a darker blue and no outline. Light blue was used for the highlight and medium gray for the shadow.

Here the effect is applied to Wingdings from the Symbols roll-up, using a rich black (100M, 100Y, 100K) and red, with a yellow highlight and a light gray shadow.

Drag- or Shift-select both objects with the Pick tool and choose Effects, Blend Roll-up and enter the number of Steps (we used 10); click the Apply button. With the dark back object to the left and down, the blend creates shadowed lower left edges to make the type appear three-dimensional. At this point you can drag the top control object to cause a reblending to increase or decrease the edge thickness, or increase the number of Steps if necessary to make the rounding look smooth.

3 Adding a gleam. Select the front piece of your type with the Pick tool and duplicate it ("+") twice, using your gleam color for the fill and outline of the first copy and the main color for the top copy. Move the top copy just a hair to the left and down from the original; the distance you move it will determine the width of the gleam. Now you'll use the top copy (the one you just moved) to trim the next one down (the gleam); you may want to use a close view for this part (press F2 and drag-select the area you want to see up close): In CorelDRAW 4 or 5, select the "trimmer" shape, then Shift-select the "trimmee" shape, and choose Arrange, Trim, and then select and delete the trimmer; in version 6 or later select the "trimmer," choose Arrange, Trim, turn off the Leave Original options, click the Trim button, and click on the "trimmee."

4 Adding the shadow. To make this spooky type hover in front of the page, we added a drop shadow and distorted it to make the illusion more dynamic. Select your front text piece with the Pick tool, duplicate it ("+"), give it a black outline and fill, and then send it to the back (Shift-PgDn). Then you may wish to stretch it by dragging the middle control handle on the left side of its highlight box to the left a tad. This will give the illusion that the leftmost text is farther away from the page than the right — it makes the words jump off the page!

Variations. You can try the effect with other typefaces, objects, symbols, or clip art, altering the lighting effect by changing the position of the highlight and the position and color of the shadow. WOW!

3•4

CorelDRAW 3 and 4 don't have a Trim function. Sometimes node-editing is the best alternative for cutting away part of an object, but for a project like this it would mean a lot of hand work. Instead you can get the gleam with Export and Import: Duplicate and offset your artwork as if you were going to trim it. Give the front piece a white fill, and the back a black fill. Select these two objects with the Pick tool, and choose File, Export, Selected Only, Tiff Bitmap. Make the bitmap Black and White, 1 to 1, at 300 dpi resolution or higher so the edges will look fairly smooth. When you import this bitmap back into your design (File, Import), the white will be transparent. Assign the black part an outline color and move it into place as your gleam.

14-Carat Type

Overview *Create a text object; add a bevel with a Contour and custom fills; add depth with a shadow.*

3•4•5•6•7•8

CorelDRAW 3 lacks the Contour and the Custom Fountain fill needed for this effect. But if you need to fake it in version 3, try the workaround at the end of this section.

CHANGING THE DEFAULT FONT

You can have any font as your *default* typeface — the one that appears when you start to type without first choosing a font in the Character Attributes dialog box. To change the default, first make sure you don't have any type selected, not even an active type cursor — in other words, don't click the Artistic Text or Paragraph Text tool on the page. Then choose Text, Character (or press Ctrl/⌘-T in CorelDRAW 5 or later). With nothing selected, CorelDRAW will remind you that you are about to change the default. Choose whether you want the default changed for Artistic or Paragraph Text or both, and click OK to open the dialog box where you can set the type specs. Select a new Font name from the list and make any other style changes you want, then click OK. This new font will be the default until you follow the same procedure to change it again.

YOU CAN TAKE A HEADLINE FROM RAGS TO RICHES, converting your plain text into golden opportunities with a beveled type effect. Make your display type stand up and demand attention with the Contour effect, a Custom Fountain fill, and a cast shadow. (For a more sophisticated lighting effect, see "Beveling a Logo" in Chapter 5.)

1 Setting the type. Select the Artistic Text tool, click it on the page, and start typing. The text will appear in the default typeface, usually a multi-purpose font like Avant Garde. To change the font, drag the Text tool over the type to select it, choose Text, Character (in CorelDRAW 5 or later, you can press Ctrl/⌘-T) to bring up a dialog box for setting type specs, and click on a new name in the Fonts list. A preview will show how your text will look. For some fonts you can also change the style from Normal to Bold, and you can change the size. When finished, click OK. We used a version of Swiss, Corel's equivalent of Helvetica Bold (it's called Switzerland in some versions). We set the type at 57 points, which is about ¾-inch tall (it's enlarged above). We also changed the Spacing from 0% to 26%, to make room for the bevel. (If your first guess at spacing doesn't work, you can adjust the spacing again in step 2.)

2 Adding the contour. To give the text a beveled look, a second, slightly larger version is needed. With your text selected, in version 4 or later choose Effects, Contour. Apply a 1-Step, Outside contour to create the bevel shape, wide enough to add the depth of a bevel, but not so wide that it deforms the outline of the text in critical areas such as in the inside corners of the "G." (For CorelDRAW 3, see the workaround at the end of this section.) If you need to adjust the spacing after you apply the bevel, use the Shape tool to drag the right control handle of the text to the right for more letterspace; Ctrl/⌘-drag for space between words.

3 Applying Fountain fills. To give the shapes a shiny, metallic look, Custom Fountain fills were assigned to both the main shapes and the bevels. The text has a dark-to-light-to-dark look, while the bevel has a darker, more com-

TYPE ON THE SPOT

In CorelDRAW 5 or later, if the Edit Text dialog box opens when you click the Artistic Text tool on the page, click Cancel to get out of the box and then reset the preferences for the tool: Open the Preferences (or Options) dialog (Ctrl-J; ⌘-*J* on *the Mac*), and in the Text section turn on Edit Text On Screen.

1

Type was set in 57-point Swiss721 Hv BT for a bold, solid "investment" feel, with letter space increased to make room for the bevel that would be added.

2

We used a 0.025-inch Offset for the Outside Contour for our 57-point type.

3

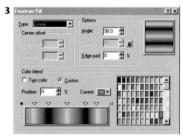

The contour was assigned a seven-color Custom Fountain fill with light and dark colors alternating (top) and a 2.1-point gold outline. The type was filled with a six-color dark-light-dark Fountain.

4

A skewed shadow adds depth

---

plicated scheme that helps make it look like the edge is receding. The combination mimics a reflective, shiny surface.

Choose the Pick tool and drag-select your text, which is still a Contour group, and from the Arrange menu, Separate the bevel from the type. Click on the bevel object and then open the Fountain Fill dialog box (F11). Set the fill Type to Linear and the Angle to 90° for vertical banding.

Before leaving the Fountain Fill dialog box, you'll need to make some other choices to set up your multibanded Custom gradient: In CorelDRAW 4 or later choose Custom for the type of Color Blend. For the bevel shape you'll want a light-dark-light-dark-light color scheme. Click on a medium brown color from the color selection box to assign it to the left end of the Fountain. Then click on the tiny box above the right end of the Fountain and select the same brown. Now double-click above the center of the Fountain bar to add a new color point. Click on a gold color from the selection palette.

Now add more bands — two black near the center and two gold near the ends — by double-clicking above the bar to make new color points and then choosing colors. This finished Custom color blend will give the illusion of reflected light and dark that a gold or bronze metallic surface produces. When finished, click OK. To add a dark-gold outline, open the Outline Pen dialog box (F12) and assign a stroke Width (we used 2 points for our 57-point type) and color.

For the text shape, the procedure is similar, but this shape has only a single light band, not three as in the bevel. First, start a Custom Linear Fountain fill as before, from black to black. Then add a white color stripe slightly off center to make the brightest gleam. Add a bright gold band just to the right of this white one. Finally, gold bands at 19% and 77% finish the gold/bronze color range. Right-click the X in the on-screen palette to remove any outline.

4 Adding a shadow. To make a shadow so your text appears to be standing solidly on the page, duplicate the bevel shape (a shadow made from the largest piece will look more realistic) by selecting it with the Pick tool and pressing the "+" key in the numeric keypad. Drag down on the top center handle to reduce the height of the shadow to about half the height of the type. Then click the Pick tool on the shadow again to get the rotation and skew arrows and drag the top center arrow to the right to slant your shadow. Give this object a dark gray or black fill and no outline, and send it to the back (Arrange [Order], To Back). A shadow falling to the right behind the type indicates a strong light from the left, above and to the front.

Variations. Here are two more sets of Custom Fountain fills that simulate metal. The bronze has duller highlights and fewer highlight bands in the bevel than the silver or gold. *WOW*

Fountains of black, white, and shades of gray simulate silver face (left) and bevel.

Fountain fills built around yellow-gold and light brown produce a brass or bronze look.

3

In CorelDRAW 3, with no Contour effect and no multicolor Fountain fills, you can make beveled edges by exporting, tracing, and importing, and then use off-center Radial fills in opposite directions to get the look of reflective metal.

A Set the type as in step 1 of "14-Carat Type." So that you can fill each letter with its own Radial Fountain, convert the type to curves (Arrange, Convert To Curves), separate the letters (Arrange, Break Apart), and then put the individual letters and their holes back together: Drag-select a letter and its counter (like the "o" or the "d" in "Gold") and choose Arrange, Combine (Ctrl-C). When the letters are ready, drag-select all of them and group them (Ctrl-G). (Grouping lets you fill all the individual letters in one step, without spreading a single Fountain over the entire block.) Then press F11 and set up a dark-brown-to-bright-gold Radial fill; drag in the preview box to offset the center to the top and right, and click OK.

B To make the contour, start by selecting the type group with the Pick tool and duplicating it in place (press "+" on the numeric keypad). Add a black fill (click the black swatch in the on-screen palette), and open the Outline Pen dialog box (F12) and assign it a heavy black outline (twice the width of the bevel you want) with flat corners. Use the Rectangle tool to draw a no-outline, no-fill rectangle around the type. This will protect the thick outline when you export the type — otherwise it will be trimmed to the wireframe; it will also help with alignment in step D below. Add the type to the selection by Shift-clicking, and export both box and type (File, Export, Selected Only, TIFF, Black And White, 1 to 1, 300 dpi). Now you have a bitmap you can trace to get the expanded letters. Click on nothing and then click on the fat black type and delete it from the CorelDRAW file at this point, leaving the rectangle and the Fountain-filled type.

C In CorelTRACE, open the TIFF you just made. Choose Tracing Options, Normal Outline, and click the Trace All button. Save the trace in **.eps** format.

D Import the trace into CorelDRAW (File, Import) and ungroup it (Ctrl-U). To set up the fat letters for filling (just like you did for the thin ones in step A, use the Pick tool to drag-select each individual imported letter that has a hole, and combine the letter body and the hole (Ctrl-C). Shift-select all the fat letters and group them (Ctrl-G). Then drag-select both sets of letters and rectangles and choose Arrange, Align, Center, Center. The fatter letters will now be on top, so select them and press Shift-PgDn to move them to the back.

E With the fat letters in back and still selected, choose Edit, Copy Style From and click on the Fountain-filled set. Then open the Fountain Fill dialog box (F11) and drag in the preview box to offset the center of the fill to the diagonally opposite corner (bottom left). This finishes the beveled metal effect.

A Radial fill was applied to converted, grouped letters.

A black fill and thick black stroke were applied to a duplicate of the letters and they were exported as a TIFF.

The black lettering was traced in Corel-TRACE, imported, and sent to the back.

A diagonally opposite Radial fill was applied to the imported, grouped "fat" letter shapes.

Adding Character to Your Characters

Overview *Create a text element; duplicate it, and use varying line weights to add a triple-outline effect; add a blend for a soft shadow effect.*

3•4•5•6•7•8

The inline-outline effect relies on stacked copies of type with different line weights, which can be done in all versions of CorelDRAW.

A Cylinder or Custom Fountain fill can help to round the type, especially for fonts that have slightly rounded characters already, like Stubby (above) or Cancun (also called Signboard), which comes with CorelDRAW (below).

Multicolor Fountain fills like the one used here aren't available in CorelDRAW 3, but you can use a customized Radial fill as shown in the workaround for step 3.

DUPLICATING A SHAPE TWICE and assigning a different outline weight to each of the three copies creates an inline-outline effect, as in this comic book headline. The drop shadow that fades into the background adds depth. It's a bold look, and easily accomplished!

1 Setting the type. Set type on the page with the Artistic Text tool. To change the font or size, drag the Text tool to select the type and open the dialog box for setting type attributes (Text, Character). We used the Stubby font (from the MasterPiece TrueType Font Library by Attitude, Inc.). If you want to loosen the spacing to make room for the outlines you'll add, you can use the Shape tool to grab the right arrow marker and drag to increase until you get the letterspacing you want. If you have more than one word, you can Ctrl-drag (⌘-*drag on the Mac*) to increase word spacing.

2 Setting the outlines. As you make copies in the next few steps, the original type will stay on the bottom of the stack, so it will need to have the heaviest outline. Assign this object a solid black fill (click the black swatch in the on-screen palette), and a thick black outline (press F12 to open the Outline Pen dialog box, and set the line Width). Turn on Scale With Image to ensure that line-weight effects will scale properly if you change the size of the artwork.

Now select the type with the Pick tool and duplicate it in place (press "+" on the numeric keypad) to create another type object on top of it. Give this new object a thinner, white outline, and again turn on Scale With Image. Notice that the object behind it is now partially obscured, leaving a thinner black outline than before. (Since half the outline width extends outward from the wireframe of the type, the white outline covers up part of the black outline.

Now duplicate once more ("+"), and assign a thinner black outline and Scale With Image.

3 Filling the type. To accentuate the rounded look of this type, we added a Custom Fountain fill

AUTOMATIC SCALING

When creating objects that depend on outline weights for the design, be sure to select Scale With Image in the Outline Pen dialog box (F12). Otherwise, your outline won't stay proportional to your objects when you enlarge or reduce them. It's a nuisance to have to go back after you've finished your artwork and pick out individual objects so you can assign the Scale With Image characteristic, so it's a good idea to set it when you first set the outline.

1

Type was set at 52 points in the Stubby font, with letterspace expanded by 40%.

2a

An 8-point black outline thickened the letters. Scale With Image was turned on in the Outline Pen dialog box so the finished type could be scaled up or down without ruining the inline-outline effect.

2b

A duplicate of the type was given a 4.3-point white outline.

3

Duplicating the white-outlined type and assigning this last copy a 1.7-point black outline completed the inline-outline, and a Custom Fountain fill enhanced the rounding already built into the shapes of the letters.

4a

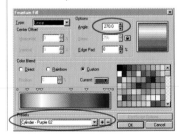

Blending gray type with a very thin outline to white type with a thick outline (shown here outlined in pink, top) made a soft shadow (bottom).

4b

The shadow was offset down and a little to the left.

from black, to purple, to white, to blue. The white highlight helps make the center look closer than the darker-colored edges. To set up a Custom Fountain fill in Corel-DRAW 4 or later, press F11 to open the Fountain Fill dialog box. Set the Type to Linear and the Angle to 90° for horizontal bands. Before leaving the Fountain Fill dialog box, you'll need to make some other choices to set up your multibanded custom gradient (for more about setting up such a gradient, see step 3 in "14-Carat Type," earlier in this chapter).

4 Adding a soft shadow. In contrast to the dark, sharp-edged shadows used in "14-Carat Type" and "Puffed-Up, Popped-Out Type" (also earlier in this chapter), a lighter, soft-edged shadow suggests a more diffuse light source. To make the shadow, the text object was duplicated again ("+") and given an 8-point outline (so it would be the size of the largest layered letter). This duplicate was dragged to one side and made white, the color of the background (so the soft edge of the shadow would appear to dissipate to nothing). This copy was duplicated again, this time with a very light-weight medium gray outline and fill (using no outline would also work). A 20-step blend was set up between these two copies (drag-select the two objects with the Pick tool; choose Effects, Blend; enter the number of Steps; and click Apply).

When the shadow is complete, drag-select it with the Pick tool and group it (Ctrl-G; ⌘-G). Then drag it back to the type, send it to the back (Arrange, [Order], Send To Back), and drag it into place, offsetting it a little. A larger offset makes it look like the type is floating higher above the page or like the light is coming from a shallower angle.

Adding more type. "EXTRAVA-GANZA!" was set in the Nervous font.

3

In CorelDRAW 3, without the multicolor Fountain fill, you can get a somewhat rounded look by converting the type to curves and using individual radial fills as in the "Metallic Type in Version 3" workaround in "14-Carat Type," earlier in this chapter. The example shown below, a purple-to-white radial fill with its center offset to the upper left and a 10% Edge Pad, adds to the rounded look.

FOUNTAIN FILLS FOR ROUNDING

The Presets list in the Fountain Fill dialog box (F11) in CorelDRAW 5 and later includes several prefab fountains that create a rounded look. Try the Cylinder settings, especially the ones that include color names. For a catalog of all the Preset fountains, see "Fountain Fill Presets" in Chapter 3.

Contouring for Colorful Type

Overview *Set type; use the Contour roll-up to generate larger and smaller shapes from the type; separate the contour elements and assign outline and color attributes; weld border elements together to make a frame; set supporting type elements.*

*The **Candy.cdr** file is provided on the Wow! CD-ROM so you can examine it.*

4•5•6•7•8

CorelDRAW 3 doesn't have the Contour and Weld functions.

1

Type was set in the Victorian font.

2a

The Contour roll-up (from the Effects menu) was used to create the inner and outer shapes around the type.

THIS DESIGN IS ONE IN A SERIES of retro-style country fair showcards and labels designed by William Mogensen. CorelDRAW's Contour feature was important in developing this multiple-outline type treatment. The addition of a shadow and a banner element created the illusion of depth: The "Candy" type is in front of the back folds of the banner, while the central part that holds the word "COTTON" floats forward. And the "CONFECTIONS" type is in the foreground, floating in front of the "Candy" shadow.

1 Setting the type. Mogensen chose the Artistic Text tool, clicked on the page, and typed out the word "Candy." From the Format Text dialog (Ctrl-T, ⌘-T on the Mac) he selected a font called "Victorian" and clicked OK. At this point you can either select the type and convert it to curves (Arrange, Convert To Curves) or leave it as type. Mogensen converted the text to curves. He used the Shape tool, adjusting the spacing overall and repositioning individual letters (for tips on spacing type, see "Designing a Label" earlier in this chapter).

2 Creating contours. With the type selected, open the Contour roll-up (Ctrl-F9; ⌘-Shift-C in Mac v.6, ⌘-F9 in v.8). From there Mogensen selected Inside, an Offset of .008 inch, and 4 Steps, and then clicked Apply. This created shapes inside the type, but Mogensen also wanted to build the letters outward. He selected Separate from the Arrange menu so he could then select the main type again and perform another Contour. This time he changed the Contour option from Inside to Outside, then clicked Apply again to create more shapes.

Before the pieces created by the Contour command can be worked on individually, the Contour group must be separated from the original type or object (Arrange, Separate) and then ungrouped (Ctrl-U, ⌘-U). Mogensen deleted some of the shapes and recontoured others. Then he gave them various Uniform and Fountain fills using colors true to his old-fashioned carnival theme. The largest Contour shape was duplicated ("+" key on the numeric keypad) and sent behind the others (Arrange [Order], To Back). A duplicate

2b

After making contours and experimenting with colors, Mogensen kept the original type (solid red) and two inside and three outside contours, arranged in the order shown here.

2c

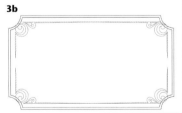

A duplicate of the largest contour shape was filled with dark red (top) and was blended to a slightly enlarged copy in the background color to make a soft shadow.

of this shape was enlarged slightly by selecting it with the Pick tool and dragging out on the lower right corner handle. This shape was filled with the red background color and sent behind the darker one (Arrange [Order], Back One). The two were selected and blended (Effects, Blend) to fade the shadow into the background.

3 Framing the composition. To make a frame for the type, Mogensen drew a corner element in ink, scanned it, and traced the scan in CorelTRACE in Outline mode to produce a fillable object. (For tips about working with CorelTRACE objects, see "Tracing" on page 32.)

He duplicated the corner three times, flipping the copies into place to make the other corners. To duplicate and flip a corner object like Mogensen's, select it with the Pick tool, press "+" on the numeric keypad, and Ctrl-drag a side handle of the new copy's highlight box across the object until it flips to make a mirror image of the original object (*Shift-drag in Mac v.6; ⌘-drag in v.8*). Once the second corner is made, you can drag-select the two corners with the Pick tool and repeat the copying and flipping process, this time Ctrl-dragging the top handle downward to flip the two-corner copy to make the bottom pair of corners.

Setting more type. Mogensen set the word "COTTON" in the Thunderbird font. He applied a heavy outline in a color that contrasted with the fill of the type and with the fill of the banner on which it would sit. He used the Fit Text To Path command from the Text menu to place it on an invisible (no-outline) wavy path. To put

3a

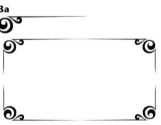

A decorative corner was hand-drawn, scanned, and traced with CorelTRACE, and the result was imported into CorelDRAW. The corner was duplicated to make the other three corners, and the four were combined to make a single object.

3b

Welding the corners to a clip-art border completed the shape to frame the type. It was given a Radial Fountain fill with the center slightly offset.

type on a path, set the type and draw a path, then select them both with the Pick tool and choose Text, Fit Text To Path. The type will now follow the path. (In some versions of Corel-DRAW you select the type first and then choose the command and then click on the path. In CorelDRAW 8 you can just click the Text tool on the path and start typing.)

For "CONFECTIONS" Mogensen set the type, increasing the letterspace by dragging the righthand arrow to the right with the Shape tool. He used the Behind Fill option, set in the Outline Pen dialog (F12), to make a bold outline behind the type without reducing the area for the fill color. *WOW*

Shaping and Framing Type

Overview *Set type; arch the tops or bottoms of the type with the Envelope; extrude the type; create a frame.*

*The **Icecream.cdr** file is provided on the Wow! CD-ROM so you can examine it.*

3•4•5•6•7•8

All versions have Envelope and Extrude; Weld is missing from version 3, so node-editing is required in step 3.

1a

A dark blue copy of the type made an appropriately colored drop shadow on the blue panel behind it.

1b

Dragging the top center node of the envelope in Single Arc mode rounded the top of the type.

1c
Ice Cream

Mogensen set the "Ice Cream" type, stretched it vertically and then rounded the baseline with a Single Arc envelope.

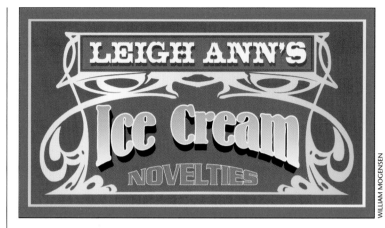

WILLIAM MOGENSEN USED CORELDRAW'S Envelope and Extrude functions to bring his type elements to life for this "retro" design for a series of country fair labels and show cards. The Weld command helped him put the frame together. (In CorelDRAW 3, without the Weld command, you can do the job with node-editing.)

1 Setting and bending the type. Mogensen used the Artistic Text tool to set "LEIGH ANN'S," "NOVELTIES," and "Ice Cream" as three separate type objects, clicking the Text tool on the page to start each one and then opening the dialog box to choose the font and size. He selected "LEIGH ANN'S" with the Pick tool, duplicated it (Ctrl-D), and moved the duplicate aside slightly. To "pop" the type, he gave the top copy a light yellow Uniform fill (Shift-F11) and an outline (F12). The bottom copy was given no outline (X from the on-screen palette) and a Uniform fill in a darker blue than he used for the rectangular panel behind it.

Mogensen selected "NOVELTIES" with the Pick tool, opened the Envelope roll-up (Ctrl-F7 in Windows versions 4 and later; ⌘-Shift-N in Mac v.6). He chose the Single Arc envelope and clicked Add New. (Version 3 doesn't have a roll-up, so you can use Effects, Edit Envelope; version 8 adds the Interactive Envelope tool with controls in the Property bar.) Dragging the top-center envelope node upward created an arc, and clicking Apply "enveloped" the type.

CONVERTING TYPE

CorelDRAW's Envelope and many of its other effects can be applied directly to type, and the type stays editable even after it's distorted. This makes last-minute changes easy to do. Nevertheless, it's often a good idea to make a copy of the file when it's finished (File, Duplicate) and convert the type to curves before you pass the copy on to another person or send it for remote printing. Select the type with the Pick tool and choose Arrange, Convert To Curves. That way you won't need to send the fonts along with the file, and you can be confident that the artwork will print right, even if the recipient doesn't have the fonts you used to create it. Meanwhile, you'll still have the editable file in case you decide to modify it.

The Extrude command added dimension to the type.

2b

An orange-to-cream Fountain fill (F11) and a thick cream outline (F12) colored the face of the type and made the black extrusion seem to be shadowed.

3a

In CorelDRAW Mogensen duplicated the half-frame artwork and flipped the copy.

3b

Welding the two halves together made a shape that could be filled with a Radial Fountain (F11).

3c

Creating a duplicate of the welded art and then breaking the duplicate apart yielded a center object that could be filled with color.

With "Ice Cream" selected, Mogensen stretched the type taller by dragging the bottom-center sizing handle downward. Then he applied a Single Arc envelope and dragged the bottom-center node upward to arch the baseline and "unstretch" the center letters.

2 Adding depth. The Extrude command can add depth to any object. Select the type with the Pick tool and open the Extrude roll-up (Effects, Extrude; or Ctrl-E in Windows versions, ⌘-*Shift-E in Mac v.6*). On the coloring page, select Solid fill, then the color Black, and click Apply. This will build the pieces for a 3D-looking extrusion. Adjust the extrusion by dragging the vanishing point (the X; you may have to zoom out to see it) or changing the Depth setting in the Extrude roll-up. To color the type, choose Arrange, Separate; then select only the top (original) type and assign a fill.

3 Making a frame. The elaborate frame started as an ink drawing of only one side, which was scanned and traced (for tips on tracing see "Tracing" on page 32).

3

The Weld command is missing from CorelDRAW 3, so it takes some node-editing to put the two halves of the frame together. In order to be able to join the matching nodes at each point where the two halves meet, both halves must be part of the same path. To make them into a single path, select them both with the Pick tool and choose Arrange, Combine. Now you can connect the nodes. For each overlapping pair that you want to connect, Shift- or drag-select them with the Shape tool and click the Join button (in versions before 8, double-clicking on a path opens the Node Edit roll-up, where you can find the Join button; in CorelDRAW 7 or 8 the Join button will appear on the Property bar when you select the overlapping nodes).

Mogensen duplicated the art in place (click it with the Pick tool and press "+" on the numeric keypad) and flipped the copy (Ctrl-drag the side handle across the artwork; *Shift-drag in Mac v.6, ⌘-drag in v.8*). He selected both halves of the frame, stretched them to fit the type, and welded the two halves together (Arrange, Weld). Then he could fill them with a Radial Fountain fill to simulate gilt paint.

To generate shapes for the panels behind the type, he duplicated the welded frame ("+"). Then he broke the copy apart (Arrange, Break Apart) so he could delete all of its parts except the internal shape that would make the background panel for the type. To set off the type, Mogensen filled the panel piece with an antique red. *WOW!*

TROUBLE-FREE EXTRUSIONS

To avoid output problems with files that include objects made with the Extrude command, first save a copy of the file with the extrusion still "live," in case you need to go back and make changes later. Then "freeze" the extrusion in the file you will send for output: Select the extruded object and choose Arrange, Separate to detach the extrusion objects from the original.

"Electrified" Type

Overview *Create a type or graphic object; create a blend from a thick-outlined white copy to a thin-outlined black copy; export the blend as a dithered black-and-white bitmap; reimport the bitmap to create a pixelated sparkle effect.*

 A .cdr file for Zap! is on the Wow! CD-ROM

3•4•5•6•7•8

All versions can create bitmaps with the Export feature and incorporate them into your design with the Import function.

1a

The text set in the Zap font

1b

Converting text to curves allowed the type to be modified.

2

A Single Arc Envelope further modified the artwork.

By using the Blend tool to create soft color transitions and then converting the blend as a dithered black-and-white bitmap, you can give your type an electric glow like the one above. The sparkling bits will be smaller or larger depending on the resolution you use in making the bitmap. And the bitmap can be made transparent to let objects behind it show through the sparkle.

1 Setting the type. Any font will work with this effect, but to exaggerate the "electric" feel, a font called Zap was used. Set the type on the screen with the Artistic Text tool.

If you want to manipulate the shapes of the letters, as we did, click the type with the Pick tool and choose Arrange, Convert To Curves, then Arrange, Break Apart. Next we Shift-clicked on the "Z" to deselect this one letter, then chose Arrange, Combine to turn the "AP!" into one object, restoring the counters (openings) in the "A" and "P," and leaving the "Z" as a separate object.

We clicked the "Z" with the Pick tool to select it, then enlarged it by dragging a corner control handle. We simplified the "Z" object by using the Shape tool to drag-select all of the nodes, then clicking on the Auto Reduce button in the Node Edit roll-up (opened by double-clicking the Shape tool in the Toolbox in version 8, or by double-clicking with the Shape tool anywhere on the path in other versions). To make all the angles sharp and crisp, with all nodes still selected we clicked on the To Line button, which eliminated any curves from the straight-line zig-zags of the "Z." We dragged the nodes of the base of the "Z" to the right to extend it under the other letters and moved the jaggy section to the center of the lengthened base. When satisfied with the placement and look of the "Z," we used the Pick tool to select all of the letter shapes, and combine them into one object (Arrange, Combine).

2 Warping with an envelope. To give the word "ZAP!" even more energy, we added a Single Arc Envelope: In version 8 you can click on the object with the Interactive Envelope tool. In other versions

3a

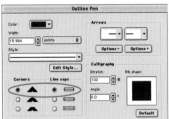

A duplicate of the type was given a thick white outline (shown here in pink, with Miter Limit set at 5°) and sent behind the original type. The default Corners and Line Caps settings produced the sharp points.

3b

The two copies of the type were blended in 20 Steps

4a

The blend and its bounding box were exported as a TIFF.

choose Effects, Envelope (Effects, Add Envelope in version 3), then press the Single Arc button (in version 3 choose Effects, Edit Envelope to see the button). In versions 4 through 7, click on Add New to activate a new envelope. Drag the top center node upward while holding down the Ctrl key to make an arch in the envelope (*use the Shift key in Mac v.6, the ⌘ key in v.8*). Click Apply if necessary to deform the object.

3 Making a blend. Now it's time to begin the glow. Duplicate the object (press "+" on the numeric keypad) and set it aside for later. Select the original and give it a thick outline and a white fill.

Duplicate this object in place ("+") give it a black fill and a hairline: Click on black in the on-screen palette to fill the object with black. Then right-click on the X in the on-screen palette to eliminate the outline, and right-click on the black swatch, which will assign the default hairline width to the outline, along with the black color. Drag select the fat white and thin black versions, and choose Effects, Blend. We applied a 20-Step blend to create a feathered black-to-white fade.

4 Converting the blend to a bitmap. To get the dithered, intermittent quality needed for the glow, turn a copy of the blend into bitmap: Using the Rectangle tool, draw a box around the perimeter of the blend group. Zoom in and Preview the image to be sure that your box is larger than the fattest outline of the blend group. Then give this box a white outline and a white fill, and choose Arrange, [Order], To Back. This boundary box is necessary for the export, because when CorelDRAW exports an object, it uses the path (wireframe) as a reference to define the extent of the object. For an object with a heavy outline, that means the bitmap wouldn't include the part of the outline outside the wireframe. Adding a boundary box ensures that the bitmap will contain all of the visual information you built into the artwork.

Drag-select the box and the blend pieces, and choose File, Export. In the Export dialog box, be sure that the Selected Only box is checked, and the Save As type is TIFF Bitmap. Type in a unique name, and click on Export. The Bitmap Export dialog will appear so you can set the options for the TIFF bitmap. Change the Color to Black And White, and check the Dithered box. Make the size 1 to 1 and the Resolution 300 dpi. Then click OK. When finished, you can delete the blend group.

Once the bitmap has been exported, you're ready to import it back into your CorelDRAW file. From the File menu, choose

The imported TIFF was assigned a yellow outline and a fill of None.

5

A Custom Fountain fill was used to color the type.

The result of applying Convert To Bitmap at 300 dpi, Dithererd

Import, then select the new bitmap file you just created. The black-and-white bitmap will appear in the center of your desktop.

Zoom in to see how the blend has resulted in a nicely dithered dot pattern. The black dots can be assigned any color with the Outline Pen: Press Shift-F11 or right-click on a color in the on-screen palette to make the dots that color; click on the X in the palette to make the white background of the bitmap transparent. Align this bitmap over the original text, and choose Arrange, [Order], To Back.

5 Coloring the type. Select the original type and assign an outline (F12) and fill. We increased the Width of the black outline to .051 inches and enabled the Behind Fill option; this meant that the fill would cover the part of the stroke that was inside the wireframe. We created a Custom Fountain fill for a three-color blend effect. In the Fountain Fill dialog box (F11) we scrolled through the Presets to Pink Neon, then we changed the Angle to 90° and clicked OK.

Adding depth. With the black-and-white bitmap changed to colorful dots on a clear background, it's easy to place this element on top of others to give the illusion of depth. For instance, you can place the text and sizzling bitmap on top of other design elements (such as a star shape from the Stars Symbols library), or over a photograph or illustration. If your design doesn't call for a clear bitmap for strategic reasons, you may wish to simply stick with the original blend concept and avoid the exporting process altogether.

Resizing. In order to make the large version of "ZAP!" shown at the beginning of this section, we had to rebuild the bitmapped element. We enlarged the blend and then assigned the white blend control object a thicker outline in order to get the same sparkly look for the bitmap as we had for the smaller versions shown on these three pages. Then we followed the export, import, and coloring procedures described in steps 4 and 5.

Chiseled Type

Overview *Set type; convert to curves and break each character apart; create a bisecting line for each stroke of each letter; use these lines to draw new bevel shapes for each letter; add depth with Fountain fills.*

3•4•5•6•7•8

All versions support this manual chiseling technique.

JOSEPH MCCOURT WANTED A HARD-EDGED, CHISELED LOOK for the type in his *IMAX movie poster* (shown in the "Gallery" section at the end of this chapter). The chiseling technique is rather involved, but for this job, with only four letters and no curved strokes, he decided it was worth the effort.

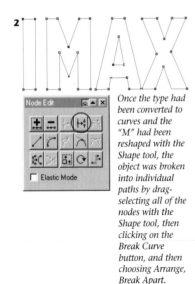

Type was set with the Artistic Text tool and was stretched with the Pick tool by dragging the top center sizing handle upward, and the right center handle inward.

Once the type had been converted to curves and the "M" had been reshaped with the Shape tool, the object was broken into individual paths by drag-selecting all of the nodes with the Shape tool, then clicking on the Break Curve button, and then choosing Arrange, Break Apart.

1 Setting the type. McCourt could not find the exact type style that he had in mind, so he started with Gothic725 BLK BT, and stretched it with the Pick tool by dragging the sizing handles. Then he converted the text to curves (Arrange, Convert To Curves) so that he could node-edit with the Shape tool to change the look of the letter "M," making the point smaller.

2 Breaking each stroke into two lines. McCourt drag-selected all of the nodes in the text object, and then clicked on the Break Curve button in the Node Edit roll-up (opened by double-clicking the Shape tool icon in the Toolbar or by double-clicking on a curve with the Shape tool, depending on which version of CorelDRAW you're using; in version 7 or 8 you have the option of using the Property bar instead). This converted each line in the letters to a separate subpath. Then choosing Arrange, Break Apart converted the subpaths into individual paths, so they could be used for blending, as described in the next step.

3 Generating the ridges. To make a center ridge, select an opposing line pair, such as the verticals in one of the legs in the letter "M." Now open the Blend roll-up (Effects, Blend), and perform a single-step blend to create a line bisecting the two. If the top node in the first line is blending to the bottom node in the second, your blend will look odd. To fix this, click on the Miscellaneous Options tab on the Blend roll-up (it looks like and old-fashioned elevator dial), then click the Map Nodes button. With the resulting arrow icon, click on the top node of the first line, then click on the top

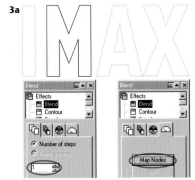

3a

A single-step Blend between two lines results a bisecting line. Use the Map Nodes feature to ensure that the lines blend together smoothly.

3b

Line pairs were blended to create a bisecting line between them.

4a

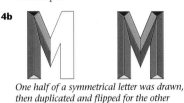

After the blend was broken apart, moving the endpoints of the bisecting lines until they met produced a guide for drawing the bevel shapes.

4b

One half of a symmetrical letter was drawn, then duplicated and flipped for the other half.

5

Two-color Radial Fountain fills in all the shapes give the illusion of depth by emphasizing highlight or shadow.

node of the second line. Click Apply again, if necessary, and the blend will happen correctly, resulting in a new line halfway between the two parent lines. So that you can node-edit the in-between line, separate it from the original blend control objects (Arrange, Separate; you may also have to choose Arrange, Ungroup). McCourt repeated this process to find a mid-point for each stroke of each letter.

4 Drawing the bevels. Using the original lines and the new in-between lines as guides and drawing with the Bezier tool, McCourt drew the pieces for each of the chiseled letters. He could easily click from point to point to create a solid, straight-lined, four-sided bevel face.

To save time symmetrical components (such as the left and right halves of the "M") were drawn once, then duplicated and flipped: Select the object, duplicate it in place (press "+" on the numeric keypad), then drag the left center sizing handle with the Pick tool to the right while holding down the Ctrl key (*Shift key in Mac v.6; ⌘ in v.8*) to flip the duplicate horizontally. McCourt took advantage of this shortcut for the "M," for the legs of the "A," and for the "X."

5 Coloring. Although the shapes for the symmetrical halves are identical, the shading is not. Using Twilight Blue as the base color, each chisel object was shaded using a Radial Fountain fill either as a highlight or shadow, based upon its orientation to an imaginary light source to the top and left. For highlight objects, McCourt used a Radial fill from Twilight Blue at the edge to White in the center. For shadow shapes, the fill was either from Black to Twilight Blue or vice versa. The mid-point of a Radial Fountain fill can be changed by dragging it around in the preview window of the Fountain Fill dialog (F11), or on-screen with the Interactive Fill tool in version 7 or 8.

CHISELING CURVY LETTERS

Some letters are more difficult to "chisel." Blending the curves in an "S" shape, for example, may not result in a smooth bisecting line. Use the Shape tool to smooth out the center line, and then duplicate it. With the Freehand tool, draw lines connecting the open ends, then use the Pick tool to drag-select all parts of the shape you've made and choose Arrange, Combine. Use the Shape tool to drag-select each "joint" in the shape and use the Node-edit roll-up or the Property bar to join any that aren't already joined. For more flexibility in shading, use a Custom Fountain fill, which allows you to use more color changes to suggest highlights and gleams across these objects.

(If you're looking for thorough instructions for chiseled effects on letters of all forms, check out Corel-DRAW Design Workshop by J. Scott Hamlin and Barry Meyer, published by Sybex.)

Transparent Type

Overview *Set two lines of type and assign both a "calligraphic" outline; create a gradient of transparency in each line of type.*

JOSEPH MCCOURT

7•8

Versions 7 and 8 have the Interactive Transparency tool, which can create a smooth transparency gradient.

3•4•5•6

In these earlier versions, you can create semitransparent type using one of the workarounds described on page 221. But neither approach produces the smooth gradient that's possible with the Interactive Transparency tool of later versions.

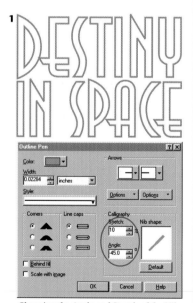

Changing the Angle and Stretch of the Nib in the Outline Pen dialog (F12) produced a calligraphic outline for the type.

JOSEPH MCCOURT'S UPDATED *IMAX POSTER* (shown in the "Gallery" section at the end of this chapter) includes type outlined with calligraphic strokes and "colored" with the Interactive Transparency tool. (Converting a copy of the type to a black-and-white bitmap or using the Transparency Lens can create similar transparency effects, as described on the next page, although the results aren't quite as elegant as those you can achieve with the Transparency tool.)

1 Setting the type and adding calligraphic strokes.

McCourt used the Artistic Text tool to set type in the Asian font. He created "DESTINY" and "IN SPACE" as two separate text elements. He then manipulated the letterspacing and word spacing to get the kerning he liked and to make the two pieces of type the same width. To adjust the position of an individual character in a block of type, use the Shape tool with the Ctrl key held down to drag the control node for that character along the baseline for the type (*in Mac v.6 use the Shift key; in v.8 use ⌘*). To adjust the space between words, hold down the Ctrl key (*the ⌘ key on the Mac*) as you drag the type block's righthand arrow assembly.

With both text blocks selected with the Pick tool, open the Outline Pen dialog box (F12). In the Calligraphy area, change the Stretch value and the Angle (McCourt used 10% and –45°). Click the color chip to open the palette and choose a color (McCourt used a light blue). Click OK to close the dialog box.

3•4•5•6

To accomplish the transparency gradient in a version of Corel-DRAW before 7, you'll need to make a duplicate of the type at this point, since the outline and faded fill have to be made as separate pieces. Shift-select the two blocks of type with the Pick tool and press "+" on the numeric keypad. Move the new copy off to the side until you need it later.

2

The Interactive Transparency tool created a gradual fade from blue to transparent. By repositioning the black and white control points you can experiment with the start and end points of the fade.

2 Adding transparency. Now you can use the Interactive Transparency tool in CorelDRAW 7 or 8 to make the fill of the type partially transparent. Select one of the text objects (the "DESTINY" in this case) and fill it with a solid color. Next choose the Interactive Transparency tool from the Toolbar and click on the point in your type at the highest level where you want the type to be fully opaque; then drag up to a point at the lowest level where you want the type to be fully transparent and release the mouse button. You'll see the background show through as the fill fades to transparent.

You can adjust the position of the two end points by dragging, or use the Property bar to change the opacity of either point, or to change the type of Fountain in the fade (McCourt used the default, Linear, but Radial, Conical, and Square are also available).

5•6

CorelDRAW 5 and 6 lack the fade-out effect of the Interactive Transparency tool, but you *can* make your type (or any other object) transparent *at the same opacity throughout.* Select the type object(s) with the Pick tool. Then open the Lens roll-up (from the Effects menu) and scroll through the options with the down arrow until you find the Transparency Lens. Pick a color (in this case a light blue) and enter a percentage

(Rate) for the transparency; the higher the setting, the more transparent. When you click Apply, the fill of the type will become partially transparent, allowing the background to show through.

3•4

In CorelDRAW 3 and 4 you can get a transparent (if somewhat dithered) effect by using a second copy of your type object. Give the copy no outline (right-click the X in the on-screen palette; *Control-click on the Mac*) and a black-to-white Linear Fountain fill (F11), changing the Angle setting in the Fountain Fill dialog box to put the black where you want the type to be opaque and white where you want it to be transparent (an Angle setting of 90° was used to put the black at the bottom of each of the two blocks of type). Then Shift-select the two blocks with the Pick tool and choose File, Export, choosing the TIFF (.**tif**) or Windows Bitmap (.**bmp**) format, assigning a file name, clicking Selected Only, and clicking OK to open the Bitmap Export dialog. Set the color to Black And White, enable the Dithered option if it's available, and set the Size at 1 To 1 and the Resolution to 300 dpi for a fairly smooth dither pattern. Then click OK to complete the export.

Now you can import the bitmap file you just made (File, Import) and assign a light blue (or any other replacement color) to the black dots in the bitmap by right-clicking a color in the on-screen palette (*Control-click on the Mac*) or choosing a color from the Outline Pen dialog box (F12). The white dots will be clear, revealing anything below.

When the coloring is complete, bring the outline type element forward (Arrange, To Front) and work in Wireframe mode (chosen from the View menu) to line up the bitmap and the original calligraphic outline of the type.

COLORING IMPORTED BITMAPS

When you import a black-and-white bitmap, the clear dots (in some versions they're white) can be assigned any fill, including a Fountain fill (as shown here) or a Texture fill or no fill (for a transparent look). And you can color the black dots with any outline color you want.

To color this imported black-and-white bitmap, a Two Color Linear Fountain was assigned as the fill (F11) and a green was used for the Outline color.

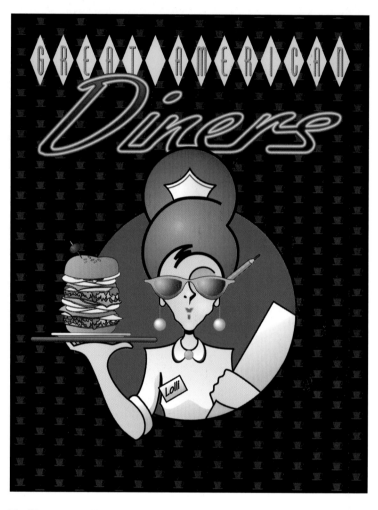

To create the neon for *Great American Diners*, **Joseph McCourt** set type in the Freeport font, converted it to curves, and then modified it with node-editing into a single flowing object. When "Diners" was assigned an outline and no fill, he had the basic shapes he needed to create his neon tubes.

Using a method like that described in "Repeating Yourself" on page 118 in Chapter 3, he layered a thin white outline on top of a thicker colored one and blended to light the neon. For the glow, instead of creating a white-to-black blend behind the neon object, he used a no-outline Fountain-filled copy that emphasized the tops of the letters, placing this copy of "Diners" behind the neon.

The "Great American" type was set in the RS Phoenix font from Reasonable Solutions' "100 Fonts for a Nickel" collection. The type was converted to curves, and each letter was centered on one of the diamonds in a row that McCourt had created by blending between two copies of a shape drawn with the Rectangle tool and then rotated and squashed sideways with the Pick tool.

The drawing of the waitress was assembled largely from objects made with CorelDRAW's Rectangle and Ellipse tools and combined. (In versions with the Weld command, it's easy to assemble shapes from parts; in earlier versions you can achieve the same result by using the Combine command and then node-

editing to remove the "holes" and make the shapes solid.)

For the sandwich ingredients, McCourt started by drawing with the Freehand tool, then offset a duplicate behind and below to give depth to the "slices." The original pieces were duplicated and deformed with the Envelope command to make each ingredient unique.

The coffee cup "wallpaper" behind the waitress is a bitmap pattern drawn with CorelDRAW's Two Color Pattern editor. (For more about making and applying patterns, see "Patterning" on page 96.)

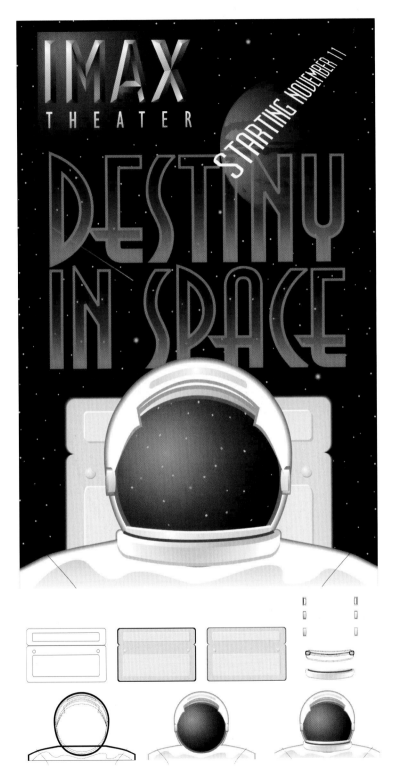

To put together this *IMAX Theater poster*, **Joseph McCourt** first sketched his concept on paper. Then he built each piece of the composition separately, to cut redrawing time, and finally assembled all the pieces. Using a hand-held scanner, McCourt scanned a photo of Mars, enhanced its contrast in Adobe Photoshop, and traced the color areas. The process of coloring the planet to simulate strong directional lighting is described in "Lighting a Planet" in Chapter 3. The transparent effect used for "Destiny in Space" is covered in "Transparent Type" on page 220, and the method used to create the "IMAX" type is described in "Chiseled Type" on page 218.

The type announcing the starting date was reshaped with CorelDRAW's Perspective function and then rotated. (Applying perspective to type is covered in the tip "Putting Type into Perspective" in Chapter 4.)

Breaking the spaceman down into basic geometric shapes, McCourt drew many of the elements with the Rectangle and Ellipse tools. To make the rocket backpack, the Shape tool was used to round the corners of objects drawn with the Rectangle tool. For backpack and helmet, duplicate shapes were created and the copies were sized by dragging inward on the center handles at the top, bottom and sides of the shapes. Then the copy-and-original pairs were Blended to round the edges and create shading using a method like that shown in "Modelling with Blends" on page 113.

For the star field in the background McCourt fostered the illusion of deep space by forming stars with different amounts of "detail." Most of the stars are small circles drawn with the Ellipse tool and assigned a Uniform fill; McCourt used white and several shades of blue to vary the brightness and distance of the stars. Blends from a large black circle to a smaller blue one made several rounded planets among the stars, and a Blend from a small black circle to a larger, offset blue one created a shooting star.

A Radial Fountain fill from Black (from the default CorelDRAW palette) to a 60% tint of Electric Blue, offset 19% Horizontally and 17% Vertically, gave the visor both a rounded look and a highlight. Star shapes on top of this fill add to the illusion of a curved, mirrored surface. Like most of the stars in the background, these were drawn as circles with white and light blue fills. Grouping the stars and applying a circular preset Envelope warped the field of stars as if they were being reflected by a rounded surface.

Nelson Crabill designed this *Black Ice logo* as brand-name identity for a specialty petroleum product for the oil industry. The product name and typeface had long since been trademarked by the client, but Crabill didn't have a digital font available to reproduce it. The client faxed an existing hard copy, which Crabill received on his computer. He imported this bitmap, just as you would a scan, and traced it by hand in CorelDRAW to make the shapes he needed for the letters, using the Freehand and Bezier tools and node-editing.

Then he selected all the letter shapes and used Effects, Contour with a 1-Step Offset Inside to create the shapes for the main bodies of the letters. (In a version of CorelDRAW without the Contour function, the bevel for a type treatment like this could be created by a heavy outline or as described in the version 3 workaround on page 208.) He Ungrouped the contoured type so he could work with the interior shapes and then selected and combined them (Arrange, Combine) so he could work with them as one object.

To create the illusion of a shiny metal surface reflecting the environment around it, Crabill first drew a shape that would create a horizon line across all the letters. As he dragged the Freehand tool through each letter, he created a slight "U" shape to suggest a curved chrome object. Once the shape was drawn, he Shift-selected the interior letter shapes object and the freehand shape and chose Arrange, Intersect, with the Leave Original options selected, to create the top (sky) halves of the letters. Then he used the freehand shape again to trim the letter shapes (Arrange, Trim) to create the bottoms of the letters. (For more about using the Intersect and Trim functions, see "Object Interaction" on page 137.)

After duplicating and flipping to create the reflection, Crabill changed its coloring. He deleted the "sky" shapes and filled the original traced shapes with a 30% to 70% black Fountain fill. The bottoms of the letters were dulled by reducing the contrast in the Fountain fill; Crabill again used a 30% to 70% black

Fountain but in the direction opposite the fill in the larger letter shapes.

The pool of oil was created with the Ellipse tool, converted to curves (Arrange, Convert To Curves), and edited with the Shape tool by adding nodes and moving them to reshape it around the "B" and "E." The large letters of the reflection were cropped within the pool with the Intersection command.

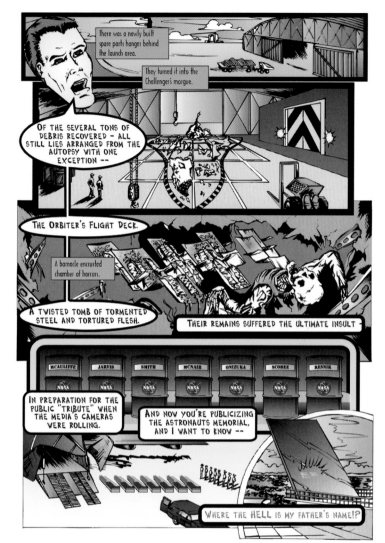

Starting from pencil sketches and inking strong black lines, **Joe King** drew the elements that would make up the pages of this *Men From Earth* comic book. Each element started as a unique illustration separate from the rest, and not necessarily to scale. The separate pieces were then scanned as line art, traced with CorelTRACE (Trace, Outline), and saved. King could then import the files (File, Import), ungroup the objects (Ctrl-U, ⌘-U), and manipulate them individually in CorelDRAW. This way he had flexibility in arranging the pieces and it was easy to color the artwork with the program's Fountain fills.

Although most of the elements were completely drawn by hand before being computerized, King did take occasional shortcuts. For instance, only one of the barrels near the bottom of the page shown above was drawn, traced, and colored. The remaining barrels are duplicates of the first, with the center-aligned text changed in the labels to make each one unique. After coloring and saving each element separately, King assembled the pieces into pages.

He added the dialog balloons on top of the other elements with CorelDRAW's standard shapes. In one case ellipses and rectangles were merged into a single balloon using Arrange, Weld (available in versions 4 and later). ▶ *A collection of ready-*made speech balloon shapes can be found in CorelDRAW's Balloons Symbols library.

King used the Shape tool to round the corners of rectangles and also to pull the speech balloons toward the speaker's mouth. ▶ *You can "point" a speech balloon by doing some node-editing: Add three nodes in a row where you want the point — the two outside nodes will anchor the point on the curve as you pull the middle node outward. Shape the point by turning one or more of the nodes into Cusps and converting one or both lines between the curve and the point into straight lines.*

King set center-aligned type to fit inside the speech balloons. To fit type inside a balloon, you can type it letter by letter, line by line, or in version 5 or later you can Envelope the type using the balloon as the shape. (If you use the Effects, Envelope command, it's a good idea to do so before adding the point to the balloon.)
▶ *To fit speech inside a balloon, set the type as Paragraph Text (either choose the appropriate Text tool in earlier versions or drag with the single tool in later versions to define a text box). Then open the dialog box where type specifications can be set (Text, Character or Text, Text Roll-up) and choose Center for both the Alignment and the Vertical Justification. Then choose Effects, Add Envelope (or choose the Interactive Envelope tool in version 8); click the Create From button (or eyedropper) in the Envelope roll-up, and click the arrow on the balloon shape. This will reshape the text, and all that's left is to drag the text block onto the balloon.*

CORELDRAW AND THE WEB

One site-building strategy is to design a web page entirely in CorelDRAW to help visualize how the site will look. Then export the graphics in web-appropriate pieces, such as the top frame background, left frame background, and middle frame background.

CorelDRAW's Brighten Lens (from the Effects menu) with a rate of –50%, and a type color change, creates the "at rest" and "selected" button variations.

The GIF89a format allows you to make one of the colors in your artwork transparent, so you can produce silhouetted images that look like they're floating free on your web page background.

ALTHOUGH CORELDRAW WAS ORIGINALLY DESIGNED with desktop publishing in mind, it has evolved along with the rest of the design community to support the World Wide Web. In versions 7 and 8, you can publish your graphics at the appropriate resolution and color depth and with HTML links established.

CorelDRAW is not only a great resource for generating web graphics, but also a good tool for organization. You can use it as a "sketch pad" to create a flowchart, mapping out your design and roughing out pages. You can also work out your navigation strategy and icons. Because of the object-oriented nature of CorelDRAW, you can later fine-tune your roughs to make your final graphics.

PREPARING ARTWORK FOR THE WEB

When you prepare art for the web, you want it to look good and download fast. You want the colors to be accurate and predictable — you want your graphics to look the same to web visitors as they look on your own computer. At the same time, you don't want visitors to give up and move on to another site because your graphics take too long to download. Although we can't provide a complete treatise on balancing color fidelity with transfer speed, here are some general tips.

Keeping Files Small

- Make the elements as **small** as you can and still create the impression you want.

- If you use Fountain fills, orient the color gradient top-to-bottom rather than side-to-side or diagonally. Because of the compression scheme used in GIF files, **vertical color gradients** compress much smaller than the others.

- Use web page backgrounds made of small **repeating tiles**. The small tile has to be downloaded only once to fill the entire background, which is a lot faster than downloading a large background image.

DESIGN'S THE THING

On-screen projects share many of the basic rules of design and composition that print projects do, but they also present their own unique design parameters. For design inspiration and practical pointers for planning, constructing, and promoting web sites, we recommend *The Web Design Wow! Book* (by Jack Davis and Susan Merritt, published by Peachpit Press).

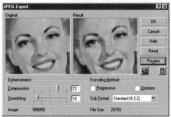

In the JPEG dialog box (File, Export, JPEG Bitmaps) you can view the image and the new File Size as you change the settings for Compression (larger numbers produce smaller files, but the color may suffer) and Smoothing (larger numbers blur the image to avoid a pixelated look). If you choose Progressive, your file will be saved in a format that appears quickly (though blurred) and then builds sharp detail. Not all browsers can handle Optimized JPEGs or the Optimal Sub-format, so it's usually best to leave these at their default settings.

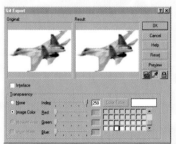

In the GIF Export dialog box the Interlace option builds the image in stages, from large chunks to a crisp image (downloading is faster, but not all browsers can handling Interlacing). Transparency sets a color in your artwork to "clear" (this will allow a background to show through); you can select the color by clicking in the palette (it shows all the colors in the file), by clicking with the eyedropper tool on the Original image, or by entering a number for the color's position in the palette (Index).

RESOLUTIONS FOR ALL

If you think you may need to create print ads or brochures to promote your new web site, try to work with high-resolution graphics from the beginning. Build your web page design in CorelDRAW at 300 dpi, then export the images at web resolution (72 dpi). If you build only the 72 dpi graphics, anything you try to print with them will look unacceptably grainy and pixelated.

File Formats

There are two file formats that CorelDRAW can produce that are compact and commonly used for preparing web graphics:

- Use **JPEG** (.jpg) for continuous-tone art such as photos or "paintings" — art that involves many subtle color or texture differences.
- Use **Compuserve GIF** (.gif) for flat-color, object-oriented artwork. If you're using a version of CorelDRAW that supports the GIF89a format, you may want to use **GIF for continuous-tone images** that aren't rectangular, because you can designate part of the image as transparent, which makes it easy to silhouette it against a background.

In CorelDRAW 8 the JPEG and GIF export dialog boxes give you a great deal of control over image size and quality, including on-screen previews that let you see in advance how your choices will affect your image. (These dialogs are also available in PHOTO-PAINT 8).

Resolution

Compared to CorelDRAW 8, earlier versions create fairly "chunky" bitmap graphics, especially at actual size for use on a web site (using the 75 dpi Resolution setting). One way to avoid this problem is to export it at twice actual size (150 dpi), and then use the Image, Resample command in PHOTO-PAINT, or choose Image, Image Size in Photoshop to reduce the resolution down to the 72 dpi used for web graphics. Photoshop and PHOTO-PAINT do a much better job of anti-aliasing bitmaps than the pre-8 CorelDRAW File, Export function.

Color

If you're creating web graphics using CorelDRAW 3, 4, 5, or 6, you'll need to use a utility such as Debabelizer to ensure that the color in your artwork is "browser-safe" — that is, to keep your graphics from changing color when viewed on various computers and to reduce the number of colors in your image to the ones you need, discarding any additional colors in the palette and thus shedding file size.

In CorelDRAW 7 and 8 you can start with a browser-specific palette, such as the Netscape or Internet Explorer palette, to ensure that you don't build your graphics with colors outside of the browser's capability (choose a palette from the View, Color Palette flyout). And the GIF 89a export function automatically reduces the number of colors to those used in your graphic.

CHOOSING GOOD ALTERNATIVES

There are some web graphics jobs that you *can* do in CorelDRAW but you probably *shouldn't*. CorelDRAW provides the capabilities you need to generate most web graphics, but it's better to use a web-page-specific application such as Microsoft's Front Page, Adobe PageMill, Net Objects Fusion, Macromedia Dreamweaver, or Adobe GoLive to assemble the actual web site.

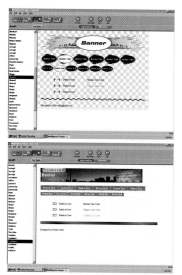

Net Objects Fusion, a tool for designing and managing web sites, lets you change the look and feel of your whole site by simply selecting a new Style Set of graphic components — such as buttons, banners and backgrounds — that are easy to create with CorelDRAW.

The CorelDRAW file exported as a 72 dpi GIF (top) loads faster and looks better than the same page saved and viewed using the Barista technology that ships with CorelDRAW 7 and 8 (bottom).

Image Maps, Not Web Sites

It's definitely possible to build an entire web site using CorelDRAW 8 alone, but it isn't recommended. CorelDRAW pages use cryptic file-naming conventions that defeat common caching strategies (for instance, the same graphic used on two different pages will download twice), and the code can be pretty vexing and confusing to interpret. Also, complex pages with many Internet links and complicated graphics have a tendency to crash when you export them as HTML. A more practical web-publishing tool is the image-mapping function found in versions 7 and 8, described step-by-step in "Creating Image Maps" later in this chapter. (An *image map* is a single bitmap that has live "hot spots" that link to other pages or web sites).

Things You Can Do Without

CorelDRAW 7 and 8 include a technology called *Barista* that lets you save your files directly in an HTML format that's viewable on the World Wide Web using a specialized Java applet. For a number of reasons, this technology isn't very practical to implement and is better avoided.

It's possible to include Corel Presentation Exchange (**.cmx**) files on your web site. Corel provides a filter that allows users to view CMX's directly from the web. You can get the CMX filter from Corel's web site: **http://www.corel.com/corelcmx/**. You can download and install the filter to view CMX files on other sites. But if you include CMX files on your own site, only people with the plug-in installed will be able to view them, so it's better to stick with GIF or JPEG.

ANIMATIONS

You can create animations in CorelDRAW by generating the art-work for each cel, then assembling the pieces using a third-party utility such as GIF Construction Set (Windows) or GIFBuilder (Mac), both of which are on the Wow! CD-ROM that comes with this book (see "Animating for the Web" on page 233 for animating instructions). Another alternative is to load movie files (**.mpg, .mov, .avi**) and manipulate them directly in PHOTO-PAINT to add effects, resize, and even change the resolution and color depth. **Note:** PHOTO-PAINT doesn't support sound, so if you change the size of your movie by adding or deleting frames, the sound track (if any) will be out of sync!

Vector-based web animation technologies such as Macromedia Flash, which is CorelDRAW-compatible, offer the appeal of small file sizes coupled with incredible animation capabilities.

Designing Seamless Tiles

Overview Use lines as guides to align and mask objects inside a rectangle; export the rectangle and its contents as a bitmap; use the exported bitmap as a repeating tile to make a background image for a web page.

5•6•7•8

All these versions of CorelDRAW have the drawing, alignment, PowerClipping, and export capabilities needed to make repeating tiles using this method.

1

 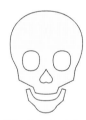

A skull object from the Wingdings Symbols library provided the pattern element.

2a

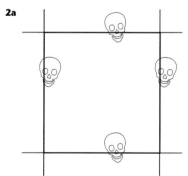

Four lines were aligned to the sides of a pink square that defined the physical size of the pattern tile. These lines allowed Hunt to align objects perfectly with the sides of the square. Perfectly aligned object pairs allow an element to exit one side of the tile and enter on the opposite side, creating a seamless pattern when multiple tiles are butted together.

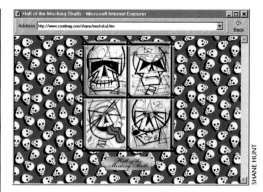

SHANE HUNT

USING ELEMENTS THAT CROSS THE EDGES OF A PATTERN TILE helped to hide the pattern repetition, making a seamless background for Shane Hunt's *Mocking Skull* web page. CorelDRAW's alignment tools allow you to position objects to create the seamless pattern. The PowerClip feature constrains the objects inside the tile shape, and then the Export function can be used to generate a bitmap tile.

1 Defining the pattern element. This patterning technique works well with small, repeating pattern elements such as the skulls used here or the footprints in *Chickens on the Electronic Highway,* shown on page 237. For this example Hunt used a skull-and-crossbones symbol from the Wingdings Symbols library (Ctrl-F11, ⌘-*F11 on the Mac*), deleting the crossbones and filling the skull with a very light yellow. Locate the symbol of your choice, and drag it onto the desktop.

2 Setting up the tile. The key to making a pattern is defining the tile size and then aligning complementary pairs of pattern elements that extend over the tile edges so that each element that extends off one edge of the tile has a mate that extends onto the tile from the opposite edge.

This step defines a square pattern tile and also makes a line to correspond to each side of the rectangle so that complementary pairs can be lined up exactly with the tile's edges. Here's how it works: Drag the Rectangle tool while holding down the Ctrl key (*Shift key in Mac v.6,* ⌘ *in v.8*) to draw a perfect square. Give this square no fill and a bright pink outline so it will be easy to see during the assembly process. Switching to the Freehand tool, draw a straight horizontal line longer than the width of the square. Select this line, Shift-select the square, and choose Arrange, Align [& Distribute] and click the buttons for aligning to the vertical Top, horizontal Center, and click OK.

Next duplicate the line (by selecting it with the Pick tool and pressing "+" on the numeric keypad), Shift-click the square again, and align to the Bottom, Center and click OK. To make guides for the sides of the square, Shift- select the two existing lines, press "+" to duplicate them, click them again with the Pick tool to bring up rotation handles, and then Ctrl-drag (*Shift-drag in Mac v.6,* ⌘-*drag in v.8*) to rotate the copy 90°.

2b

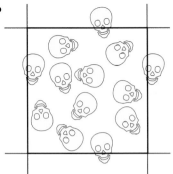

Each element that was fully enclosed within the tile area could be positioned without the need for a complementary element.

3

To add shadows, Hunt drag-selected all the skulls, duplicated them, filled the copy with black, and sent it behind the original skulls (Arrange, Order, To Back). Then he cropped all of the objects within the tile using the PowerClip function. The outline was removed from the square before export, to prevent lines from criss-crossing the pattern.

Select your pattern element (in this case the skull), Shift-click on the left guide to select it also, and align to the horizontal Center in the Align & Distribute dialog box, leaving all the Vertical buttons unselected. Now select and duplicate the pattern element ("+"), Shift-select the right guide, and again align to the horizontal Center. Now you have an object pair that are in perfect alignment, so that any overhang on the right is balanced on the left, which will make a seamless transition across the edges of the tile. You can now Shift-select the pair of elements and move the pieces in unison around the tile area, changing the amount of overlap at the edges, and they will still generate the seamless tile pattern, because they will remain in perfect alignment in relation to the tile width.

Hunt repeated the duplicate-and-align process with another skull, this time using the top and bottom lines and the Center button in the vertical section of the Align & Distribute dialog box. He now had skull pairs for both directions, horizontal and vertical.

Hunt added more elements — these unpaired — completely inside the tile boundaries. Then he added matched skulls at the four corners. First he put a skull at the upper left corner and aligned it to the horizontal Center of the left vertical line; then he aligned it to the vertical Center of the top horizontal line as well. He duplicated the skull ("+"), moved the copy to the top right corner, and aligned it to the top and right lines. Then he Shift-selected and duplicated the two corner skulls, Ctrl-dragged the copies straight down to the two bottom corners (*Shift-drag in Mac v.6, ⌘-drag in v.8*) and aligned the pair (vertical Center) with the bottom line. Once all four were in position, he could Shift-select and move them.

3 Cropping and exporting the tile. When all of your elements are aligned, you can select and delete the lines. Then make sure that CorelDRAW's Auto-Center New PowerClip Contents is turned off (press Ctrl/⌘-J and deselect this option under General or Advanced, or under Workspace, General or Edit, depending on which version of CorelDRAW you're using). Then drag-select all of the remaining objects — the tile square and all the pattern elements. Next, Shift-click the square to deselect it, leaving all the pattern elements selected. Then choose Effects, PowerClip, Place Inside Container and click on the square.

Now select the PowerClip object and remove the pink outline by right-clicking the X in the on-screen color palette (Control-click on the Mac), and assign any fill color you want for a background. To generate a tile bitmap for the web, export this object (File, Export) as a 72 dpi GIF image.

Applying the pattern to a web page. You'll need to add background="*filename.gif*" to the <body> section of your HTML file coding. Or use web-builder software such as Adobe PageMill to assign the bitmap as the background pattern. *WOW!*

Creating
Image Maps

Overview *Using a graphic created in or imported into CorelDRAW, define "hot links" areas and assign the link information; export the file as a GIF image and accompanying image map for use on the web.*

SHANE HUNT

7•8

Versions 7 and 8 provide the web tools needed for this method of creating an image map.

3•4•5•6

If you're using a Windows version of CorelDRAW other than 7 or 8, you can use the MapEdit utility on the Wow! CD-ROM to create an image map. After you start the program, choose Help, Contents to read about how to create an image map.

AN IMAGE MAP CAN TRANSFORM a static bitmap into a dynamic navigation tool for a web page. The image map assigns "hot spots" to your bitmap, and when a web-site visitor clicks on a hot spot, the linked page appears on-screen. Shane Hunt used the built-in image-mapping tools found in CorelDRAW 7 and 8 to create an image map for this opening graphic on the *USConnect Los Angeles* home page. This graphic started as basic components in CorelDRAW and was fine-tuned in Adobe Photoshop using plug-ins from Alien Skin (you can download demos of the plug-ins from **www.alienskin.com**).

1 Creating the navigation graphics. Shapes were drawn with the Rectangle, Ellipse, and Polygon tools to provide the basic size and colors for the buttons that would be developed in Photoshop. Type was set as Artistic Text for individual buttons and a navigation bar. The man and woman graphics, which were **.cmx** clip art supplied with CorelDRAW, were imported (File, Import), ungrouped (Ctrl/⌘-U), and the pieces modified and reassembled into a single graphic. When all of these basic elements were in place, the entire graphic was exported (Ctrl-H, ⌘-*E on the Mac*) as a 150 dpi, 16 million color (24-bit RGB) TIFF bitmap. This resolution allows for smoother special effects, such as bevels. The resolution and color can be reduced after these effects are applied.

In Photoshop (or you can do it in Corel PHOTO-PAINT, which also supports Photoshop-compatible filters) the bitmap image was enhanced using plug-in filters, as follows: First the simple, single-color shapes were selected with the magic wand and given the look and shading of raised buttons using Alien Skin's Inner Bevel 2.0 plug-in. While still selected, the buttons were moved into position, and the illusion of depth was created with Alien Skin's Drop Shadow filter. Once all of the effects were finished in Photoshop, the revised bitmap was saved again as a TIFF.

2 Defining hot spots. In CorelDRAW a new file was created (Ctrl/⌘-N) and the bitmap was imported (Ctrl/⌘-I). At this point

1a

Two clip-art images were taken apart and their pieces recombined for the main homepage graphic. The type blocks and button shapes were defined with the Rectangle, Ellipse, Polygon, and Artistic Text tools.

1b

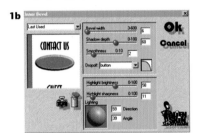

The Inner Bevel plug-in filter from Alien Skin transformed the simple shapes into three-dimensional buttons.

2

Using the Internet Objects toolbar, you can assign an internet address (URL) to each "hot spot."

3

The Publish To Internet feature generates both the bitmap and the appropriate HTML code to make the image map work.

the image was scaled to the size that it would appear on the web site. Bitmaps can be scaled by choosing Bitmaps, Resample; setting the Resolution to 72 dpi and turning on the Maintain Aspect Ratio option; then setting the Width of your web page (in Pixels) in the Image Size area of the Resample dialog box and clicking OK. Using the Rectangle tool, drag over an area that you wish to make a hot spot on the graphic — for instance over a type element or a button graphic. Choose View (*on the Mac choose Windows*), Toolbars, Internet Objects. This will open the Internet Objects toolbar, where you can key in the properties for your hot spot. In the Location area (version 7) or Internet Address (v.8), key in the web address that you would like your hot spot to link to. For a destination in the same host directory you need enter only the page name, such as **art.htm**, while an outside destination requires the entire Universal Resource Locator (URL) such as **http://usconnect.com**. In the Alternate Text area (v.7) or the Internet Bookmark (v.8) key in a brief description of the URL, such as "Corporate Headquarters." When you press Enter/Return these attributes will be associated with your rectangle. Repeat this process to add more hot spots anywhere on your graphic. Then make sure that the rectangles you create for the hot-spot objects have no outline and no fill attributes.

3 Publishing. With the Pick tool drag-select or Shift-select all of the hot-spot objects and the bitmap image, and from the File menu, choose Publish To Internet. In version 7 change the Save As Type to Corel Image Map (HTM), then click on Export. (**Note:** If you don't find a Corel Image Map (HTM) choice, you can install it from the CorelDRAW 7 CD-ROM: Choose the Custom Setup Option, turn off everything on the Components screen, press Next to get to the Filters screen, and turn off everything except Corel Image Map (HTM), which is under Internet Filters. Then proceed with the installation.) In the HTML Image Map Export dialog, choose either Gif or Jpeg (Hunt used Gif, since his artwork was mainly drawn graphics and text), and click OK. Now from the Bitmap Export dialog, make your Color choice 256 colors, Size 1 to 1, Resolution 72 DPI, and enable the Super-sampling Anti-aliasing feature. When you click OK the Gif89a options dialog will appear; click OK again to export the image and generate the HTML code with the image map information.

In version 8 choose File, Publish To Internet. To create an image map, choose the Single Image option, key in the desired destination information, choose a file format (GIF in this case), and click OK.

Loading the code. CorelDRAW creates an HTML file that associates the hot spots with the graphic image. This file can be run directly from a web browser such as Netscape or Internet Explorer, but you will probably want to copy and paste the code into your own HTML document. All of the text after the <MAP> tag and before the </MAP> tag is necessary for the image map to work properly.

Animating for the Web

Overview *Alter a CorelDRAW file and export different bitmaps to make animation "cels"; assemble the individual bitmaps into an animation file format.*

3•4•5•6•7•8

All versions can export the GIF (**.gif**) format suitable for animations on the World Wide Web. PHOTO-PAINT versions 7 and 8 can generate GIF animations, as well as other movie formats. For earlier versions, animation can be done with GIF Construction Set (Windows) or GIFBuilder (Mac).

PAUL KANTOREK

PAUL KANTOREK USES CORELDRAW to produce his single-panel comics (you can find examples on page 65). So when it came time to produce a web site to promote his work, the CorelDRAW files were the perfect starting point for creating a series of small animations. Starting with his original comic files, Kantorek made images one by one for the animation sequences. The object-based nature of Corel-DRAW coupled with a modular approach to the original illustration is a perfect combination for creating animations.

1 Drawing the character. Kantorek starts with an ink drawing and uses a modular design approach. This means hand-drawing separate pieces that can be assembled in a variety of character poses. In this example, the head and body are separate, so each object can be manipulated individually.

Kantorek's ink illustrations were scanned as line art, then converted to vector objects using CorelTRACE in Outline mode, and the files were saved in Adobe Illustrator (**.ai**) format. This format doesn't include all the layering information that saving the trace in Corel Presentation Exchange (**.cmx**) produces, which is unnecessary for these simple traces.

2 Colorizing the character. After the CorelTRACE file was imported into CorelDRAW and ungrouped (Ctrl-U, ⌘-U on the Mac) Kantorek added details and shapes to colorize the artwork. For instance, to create a two-node cigar-shape to make an orange stripe, he used the Bezier tool. The shapes he created were given an orange fill and no outline. Working on top of the black shapes, Kantorek could see exactly how the color shapes related to his imported "line art." When the shapes were done, he Shift-selected them with the Pick tool and sent them behind the black "outlines" (Arrange [Order], To Back).

1

An illustration drawn with the head, whiskers, and body separate was scanned and traced with CorelTRACE.

2

Once the character was imported into CorelDRAW, shapes were drawn to colorize it and add other details.

3

Kantorek had designed the character with separate head and body elements, making it easy to bring it to life by rotating or flip-flopping the head group, changing details like the eyes and mouth, and adding motion lines ("moovles").

4

Kantorek used the Pick tool to select and delete the irises and pupils, then modified the eyes with the Shape tool. The Bezier tool was used to draw a sweeping line across the eyes to make the cat blink. From the Outline Pen dialog (F12) a thick black outline (.027 inch) matched the width of the other black "lines."

3 Putting the art in motion. With these simple elements in place, Kantorek already had many animation possibilities. Because the head was a separate group of elements, it could be rotated or flip-flopped to make the kitty come to life. He drew a boundary box with the Rectangle tool to define the cel size, saved the kitty and box to disk under a new file name (File, Save As), and also exported the drawing and its box as a bitmap that he could later incorporate into an animation (File, Export, Compuserve Bitmap, Selected Only). For the export, he gave the image a uniqe numbered name, such as **CAT01.GIF** (see the "Storyboards and File Names" tip below).

The bounding box is important. The trick to convincing animation is continuity — the pieces should fit together seamlessly, with the static pieces as important as the moving ones. The stationary pieces need to be solidly anchored, so they don't hop arround during the animation. For this reason, these elements should be in the same relative positions from frame to frame, and each bitmap should be the same size. This is why Kantorek created a boundary box around the his first image and retained it for all subsequent cels, to make sure each bitmap was the same size at the time of export.

You can save each drawing as a **.cdr** file before you export it as a bitmap, thereby creating a library of animation cels to draw from. Or just modify the image on your page and freeze it in stages as exported bitmaps. But it's a good idea to save the **.cdr**'s, since some of the modifications take time, and it's nice to have the original editable files to go back to if you wish.

The CompuServe Bitmap (GIF) is the appropriate filter for creating animated images for the World Wide Web. (JPEG allows for more color depth, but not animation.) In the Bitmap Export options menu, which comes up when you click OK in the Export dialog box, select Paletted 8-bit (or 256 Colors) from the Palette/Color option, Size 1 to 1, and Resolution 75 DPI, and enable the Anti-Aliasing option (available in versions 6, 7, and 8). Click OK. If you have a choice, selecting the GIF 89a format will allow you to make your background transparent, so your

STORYBOARDS AND FILE NAMES

Even for a simple animation, the multiple file names and repeating images can get pretty confusing. It's a good idea to do what the pros do and create an animation worksheet, or storyboard, to plan the action and keep track of the files. You can list the file names of the images one by one as they are exported, and refer to the list later when you assemble the animation file.

5a

5b

The Shape tool was used to drag the nodes in the tail shape to reposition it. You can use the Node Edit roll-up or the Property bar to add or delete nodes as needed. You can also Shift-select more than one node at a time to drag them around, or use the Rotate button to spin selected nodes.

With the tail in the new position, Kantorek found it easiest to delete the old stripes and draw new ones with the Bezier tool.

objects can "float" over a background. Since the kitty graphic was designed to be on a white background, transparency was not necessary. Selecting OK finishes the export.

4 Adding details. Making the kitty blink her eyes was simple. First, the iris-and-pupil circles were deleted. Next Kantorek used the Shape tool to modify the whites of the eyes. Then, using the Bezier tool, he drew a line across the center of the eyes so they looked closed. This line was given a heavy weight to match the other black "line work."

5 Wagging the tail. Making the tail wag was more complicated than closing the eyes. The Shape tool was used to manipulate the nodes of the tail curve to reposition it in the first wagging pose. As a result of the CorelTRACE of the illustration, the tail actually consists of a path on the inside (for the white object) and a path on the outside (for the large black object). So both had to be manipulated carefully to maintain the proper "line weight" throughout.

More nodes could be added to make the shape look right by clicking on a point on the line, then clicking the "+" button on the Node Edit menu or Property bar (in version 8, simply double-clicking on a line adds a node at the click point). In modifying a drawing for motion, you may also want to "cusp" a node, which allows you to modify each Bezier control handle independently of the other one (see "Understanding Nodes and Control Handles" on page 25 for more about node types).

The original stripes were deleted, as it was easier to redraw than to reposition and tweak them. Kantorek used the Bezier tool again to draw in the three stripe shapes, and these were also sent behind the black outline shapes. The file was saved as a .cdr file with a new name, and the artwork and bounding box were also exported as a bitmap. This process was repeated to result in the second wag frame. In the second frame, more pieces were added for motion and a licking tongue.

Making a movie. Once you have repeated the process until you have the same size bitmap for every frame you need for your animation, the next step is to assemble the cels into an appropriate "movie" file. For the web, typically a multi-frame GIF file works well, and that's what Kantorek used to bring his kitty to life. You can do the animation in Corel PHOTO-PAINT 7 or 8. (If you don't have one of these versions of PHOTO-PAINT, see the workaround on the next page.)

Start PHOTO-PAINT and open the bitmap image that will start your "movie" (File, Open). Now, from the Movie menu, select Create From Document. To add another frame to your movie, from the Movie menu select Insert From File, then select your next image, enable the After option from the Insert File dialog, and click OK. Continue to use the Insert From File option until you have

The Freehand tool was used to draw a licking tongue and the loose, hand-drawn-looking motion lines.

3•4•5•6

You can assemble a series of GIF images generated from any version of CorelDRAW using the GIF Construction Set program (for Windows, a shareware program provided on the CorelDRAW Wow! companion CD-ROM) or GIFBuilder 0.5 (for Mac, a freeware program that developer Yves Piguet has allowed us to include on the Wow! CD-ROM).

GIF Construction Set: Start the Animation Wizard from the File menu, and follow the easy step-by-step instructions to assemble individual bitmaps into an animated GIF file.

GIFBuilder: Choose File, Add Frame and choose the image you want for your first frame. Import additional frames in the same way. In the Options menu you can set the characteristics you want for your animation. The Documentation file that comes with GIFBuilder tells what each menu choice means and suggests settings. When your Options are set, choose Window, Preview Window. Then choose Animation, Start to run the animation. If you want to change the timing or the order of frames, or if you want to remove or duplicate frames, choose Window, Frames Window, and double-click an entry.

populated your animation with all of the cels you created in the previous steps, in the correct order. At any time you can view your animation (Movie, Controls, Play Movie).

When you've finished assembling frames, check that the color depth is correct by selecting Image, Convert To, Paletted (8 bit). Other movie file formats can use RGB 24-bit color, but not GIF files, so choose the palette that's appropriate for your project — for example, the Microsoft Internet Explorer or Netscape Navigator palette. Save your file (File, Save As, GIF Animation).

Other movie formats. Besides creating animations for the web, you can use the process outlined here to create other kinds of movie files by exporting your artwork in a different bitmap format and then choosing a different movie file format when you save in PHOTO-PAINT. *WOW!*

ANIMATION RIGHT OUT OF THE BOX

Some versions of CorelDRAW ship with clip art that's just begging to be assembled into custom animations. For example, we found these flapping birds in the CorelDRAW 6 clip-art collection in a subdirectory called Images/Cartoons, with bitmap images perfect for animations. To create an animation from three bitmaps like these, create a bounding box, duplicate and arrange the images inside it, and save this as the master **.cdr** file. (The bounding box is shown here in pink, but you would use a box with no outline or fill in the actual steps.) Then one-by-one, create the cels for the animation. For the first frame, load the master file and delete all but the leftmost flapping bird. Then select the bird and and the bounding box and export them as a bitmap for assembly into a movie file format later. (Save as a GIF file if your animation is for the web). Revert to the master file, and repeat the delete-and-export process, this time leaving only the bounding box and the second bird. Repeat until you have a collection of images for your flying bird animation. (You can view this animation at **www.peachpit.com/wow**.)

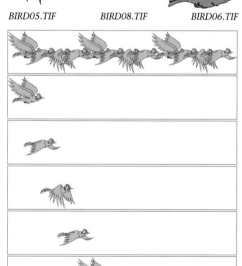

BIRD05.TIF   BIRD08.TIF   BIRD06.TIF

PHD-Piled Higher and Deeper

Physiognomy of Yer Average Hen

Hens are capable of displaying a wide range of emotions:

- Elation
- Jealousy
- Righteous Rage
- Curiosity
- Feigned Indifference

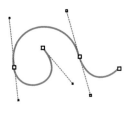

Mary Carter used CorelDRAW extensively to create the bright, whimsical graphics for her *Chickens on the Electronic Highway* web site. Her partner Gary Priester helped with the HTML programming, using HTML Assistant Pro software. (Priester's work appears in "Blasting Holes" in Chapter 4.)

After creating a flow chart to plan the entire web site, Carter set out to give each page a unique look but to keep an overall design consistency for the site as a whole. Another goal was to make the graphics interesting and appealing while keeping file size small in order to minimize download time for site visitors.

She used a seamlessly tiling pattern for the page background since Web browsers can download a tiled background more quickly than a single large graphic. Carter defined a shape for her square tile and then arranged chicken footprints to create the repeating pattern. She carefully aligned each footprint that extended off the right side of the square with one that extended off the left, and also lined up elements that extended off the top and bottom. Then the PowerClip function was used to trim the tile.

Carter set up a design template for the buttons, consisting of a gray square and a lighter gray triangle, stacked to give the button a beveled look, and the sunshine blend. For each button a unique graphic element was added to the template, either drawn in CorelDRAW or imported as a 1-bit bitmap (like the two hens at the top left).

The buttons and background tile were exported as GIF images (File, Export, CompuServe Bitmap [GIF]) for incorporation into web pages. ▶*The run-length encoding used in the compression scheme for GIF files starts at the top left corner of a graphic and reads across the first row of pixels, trying to store the color information in less file space without throwing away any color information. For instance, instead of storing "red, red, red, red, red, red, red, blue, blue . . ." it can store "7 red, 2 blue . . .," which takes less file space. When it finishes the top row, it goes on to the next one down, and so on. The fewer color changes there are across each row, the more the file size can be compressed. For this reason, solid-filled shapes can be compressed very effectively, and top-to-bottom gradients also compress much better than side-to-side gradients.*

In creating this home page for the Ingram Micro *IMageLink* project, **Shane Hunt** imported a TIFF background image created in Adobe Photoshop 4 (File, Import). Next he copied the imported image to the clipboard (Ctrl-C; ⌘-C *on the Mac*). Then he softened the original bitmap by choosing Bitmaps, Blur, Gaussian. He pasted the sharp copy from the clipboard back on top of the blurred original (Ctrl-V; ⌘-*V on the Mac*) and used the following method to create the illusion that the discs and other floating objects progressively fade out of focus toward the right: He chose the Interactive Transparency tool (found in versions 7 and 8), leaving it in its default Linear Fountain mode, and dragged it across the sharp image, which made a transition from the sharp to the blurred.

Hunt used a similar approach on the face, this time using two applications of the Interactive Transparency tool — one to fade the right edge and another in the opposite direction to fade the left edge. Then he used the Rectangle tool to draw an object that he could turn into a Lens to highlight the eye (Effects, Lens, Brighten).

The ever enlarging spiral that centers on the eye is a closed and filled path made by combining two spiraling open paths, as follows: Hunt drew one spiral by Ctrl-dragging lower-right-to-upper-left with the Spiral tool (*Shift-drag in Mac v.6;* ⌘-*drag in v.8*). Then, with the spiral selected with the Pick tool, he duplicated it in place by pressing "+" on the numeric keypad. He slightly enlarged this copy

from the center outward by Shift-dragging up and out on the upper left corner handle of the spiral's highlight box (⌘-*drag in Mac v.6; Option-drag in v.8*).

In order to join the ends of the two spirals to make a closed shape, he first had to Shift-select the two paths with the Pick tool and combine them into one object (Arrange, Combine). Then he could use the Shape tool to drag-select the two nodes at the outside of the spiral and click the Join button in the Property bar. He did the same to the two overlapping nodes at the center of the spiral. He dragged a color swatch from the on-screen palette

and dropped it on the spiral to fill the now solid object with brown. Then he made it 50% transparent (choose the interactive Transparency tool, choose Uniform in the Property bar, and set the transparency slider in the Property bar to 50; or use a Transparency Lens).

The finished artwork was exported as a TIFF (File, Export) and opened in Photoshop. The five photographic icons, with their exterior glows, were added in Photoshop using a method described in *The Photoshop 4 Wow! Book* for making a unified set of buttons from a number of unrelated photos.

Appendix A: Workarounds

On these two pages are alternative approaches to some of the steps in the drawing and coloring techniques presented in Chapters 2 and 3. They provide methods for getting things done in CorelDRAW 3 and 4, versions that don't have some of the commands that were added later. Even if you work with a later version of the program, if you like the fundamental "constructionist" approach to drawing, you may enjoy some of these methods.

Note 1: Making scalloped corners
FROM "BUILDING MEDALLIONS," STEP 2, PAGE 58

CorelDRAW 3 and 4 don't have the Trim command, but you can use circle-and-rectangle construction as a guide for drawing scallop-cornered rectangles like those in the "Yearn To Learn" border medallions, using the Freehand and Shape tools. For instance, starting at the top of the circle for the lower left corner, click with the Freehand tool to make the first point. Then, holding down the Ctrl key (*the Shift key in Mac v.6, ⌘ key in v.8*) to constrain drawing to vertical, pinpoint the bottom of the circle for the top left corner; double-click there, go on to the next critical point (at the point where the right side of the circle intersects the top of the rectangle) and double-click there. This will make a slanted line at the corner (A). Proceed around the rectangle, making three more slanted corners, and return to the starting point with a single click to close the shape. Now choose the Shape tool and double-click one of the slanted corners to open the Node Edit roll-up, click the To Curve button, and drag the resulting node control handles to straight horizontal and vertical positions that make the curve fit the circle (B). Repeat for the other corners, and delete the original rectangle and circles.

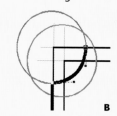

Note 2: Trimming in CorelDRAW 4
FROM "SHIMMERING COLOR," STEP 5, PAGE 106

Since the Trim command doesn't exist in CorelDRAW 4, the process of making an arc band similar to the one Purcell used to make his tower of rings (see step 5) is slightly more complicated: First draw an ellipse (A); then turn it into an arc by using the Shape tool to drag its single node inward and a little to the side; repeat the dragging, this time a little to the other side (B). Select the arc with the Pick tool; convert it to curves so it will stop thinking of itself as an ellipse (Arrange, Convert To Curves) and press keypad "+" to duplicate it. With the duplicate selected, use the down arrow key to move it straight down a little (C). Use the Shape tool on the end-points of the top arc to reshape the arc slightly, moving the end nodes down until they sit on top of the ends of the bottom arc (D). Select both arcs with the Pick tool and combine (Arrange, Combine); then use the Shape tool to drag-select one pair of overlapping nodes and join. Repeat for the nodes at the other end and join.

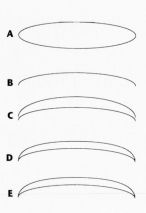

Appendix B: CorelDRAW-Friendly Service Bureaus

No matter which graphics programs you use, when it comes to getting professional-looking results in print, there's nothing that can be more helpful than a competent, supportive imagesetting service bureau. We know there are many out there, but we've listed on this page some of the service bureaus recommended by artists who have contributed to this book. These artists applaud the abilities and attitudes of the people who operate these businesses.

Adage Graphics
8632 South Sepulveda Blvd. #100
Los Angeles, CA 90045
(310) 216-2828

CBM Type
265 Sobrante Way #K
Sunnyvale, CA 94086
(408) 739-0460

Command-P
20028 State Road
Cerritos, CA 90703
(800) 426-8067
(310) 203-3185

Computer Generated Services
915 Adana Road
Baltimore, MD 21208
(410) 484-7515

Copy Craft
4418 82nd Street
Lubbock, Texas 79424
(800) 794-5594

CPF Imaging Services
2840 Dundas Streeet West
Toronto, Ontario M5P 1Y7
(416) 762-7158 or
(800) 361-6088
(416) 760-0052 (modem & fax)
Web Page: www.cpf.net

Digicolor Prepress
3939 S. Harvard
Tulsa, OK 74135
(918) 742-6567

Pacific Press
7250 Convoy Court
San Diego, CA 92111
(619) 278-3500

Page One
2372 Morse
Irvine, CA 92614
(714) 851-1530 (voice)
(714) 851-3947 (fax)
www.pageonenet.com

Quad Right
711 Amsterdam Ave.
New York, NY 10025
(212) 222-1220

Severn Graphics
7590 Ritchie Hwy.
Glen Burnie, MD 21061
(410) 768-6118
imaging@sevgraph.com
www.sevgraph.com

Station To Station
1741 Commerce Drive NW
Atlanta, GA 30318
(404) 609-7820

Appendix C: Production Notes

The CorelDRAW Wow! Book was produced in Adobe PageMaker 6.5 for the Mac and was printed on a web press using computer-to-plate technology. Type was set in the Stone family of fonts from Adobe, which has both serif and sans serif fonts in three weights and two styles (roman and italic).

Featured in the book is artwork created in every version of CorelDRAW from 3 to 8. Originally, our plan was to output color-separated film from our page layout files, reviewing Matchprints before printing plates were made. We made several test pages, placing CorelDRAW EPS files in PageMaker pages. Adage Graphics, one of the CorelDRAW–friendly service bureaus listed in Appendix B, ran film and Matchprints on the tests. The results were largely successful, and working with Adage, we were able to solve most of the problems we had encountered, and were on our way to solving the others.

Then our publisher persuaded us to take advantage of computer-to-plate technology, eliminating the time and hassles involved in producing, proofing, and storing film. The printer (Graphic Arts Center/Shepard Poorman in Indianapolis) would produce Iris prints for us to check — to verify that all artwork was in place and that no font substitution was occurring. But the files wouldn't be going through the same RIP (raster image processor) to make these soft proofs as they would when the printing plates were made. This meant we wouldn't see the results of the final RIP until the press was running. We didn't want to risk finding glitches in the output as the web press was running 10,000

sheets an hour, so we decided to rasterize all the CorelDRAW artwork ourselves before placing it in the PageMaker layouts.

We tried several different methods for producing the CMYK TIFF files that PageMaker handles so well. In the end we settled on the following: The CorelDRAW files were exported in EPS format, and then these EPS's were opened in Adobe Photoshop 5 at the approximate dimensions they would be used on the page and at 300 to 600 dpi. The Photoshop files were then saved as TIFFs.

Before arriving at this process, we tried outputting TIFFs from several versions of CorelDRAW, with and without Super-sampling turned on for antialiasing. Until version 8, the quality of CorelDRAW's TIFFs didn't come close to what we could get by rasterizing in Photoshop 5, largely because the antialiasing in CorelDRAW produced rough edges or light "halos" between colors. (It may be possible to use PHOTO-PAINT 8 the same way we used Photoshop 5, but being Photoshop users, we stuck with what we knew.) We had also tried rasterizing with Photoshop 4 and with a program called EPSConverter, but some of the artwork created in early versions of CorelDRAW "flew apart" when the EPS's were rasterized, creating some pretty wild graphics.

Here are some of the things we learned in processing the CorelDRAW files:

- To maintain the sharp points created by sharply mitered corners, we had to set the Miter Limit for CorelDRAW very low (for example, 6°) at the time we made the EPS. The Miter Limit setting doesn't travel with the **.cdr** file; it's set for the program generally and is built into the EPS when the encapsulated PostScript is generated.

- For some reason, some instances of blending on a path twisted around the path, until we used the Photoshop 5 method.

- The one thing that even Photoshop 5 had trouble with was not a blend within a blend or a PowerClip but the results of an Extrude command. To get good results when Extrude is used, it's a good idea to use the Arrange, Separate command to separate the objects created by the extrusion from the original object. (It's also wise to freeze any Lenses in your file.)

- Early versions of CorelDRAW produced banded color gradients (Fountain fills). We couldn't figure out how to prevent the banding when we generated the EPS's, so we dealt with it afterwards in Photoshop. Sometimes running the Add Noise filter on one of the color channels hid the banding. In other cases we sampled the lightest band and the darkest, selected the banded area by whatever means was appropriate, and applied the color using Photoshop's Gradient tool.

- Over the years CorelDRAW, like other vector-based drawing programs, has gotten better at writing PostScript, and rasterizing software has gotten better at interpreting it. Output to a film recorder was a method discovered by CorelDRAW pioneers to RIP files that choked imagesetters in the early days of computer art. This method also tends to reduce banding and soften color breaks. In some cases, at the artists' request, we reproduced artwork from early CorelDRAW versions by scanning color transparencies (35 mm or 4 x 5 inches) they provided, in order to be sure of predictable output.

- Some of the CorelDRAW files we received were created with RGB or Pantone colors. When these were converted to CMYK, the colors sometimes looked duller than what the artist expected, based on the way the artwork looked on-screen. One way to liven up dull colors is to apply a Hue/Saturation Adjustment layer in Photoshop, boosting the saturation and putting the Adjustment layer in Color mode to add life to the color without increasing the contrast.

Appendix D: Contributing Artists

Here's a list of the artists who have kindly allowed us to use their artwork as examples in this book. They have let us in on their "tricks of the trade" and in some cases have even given us permission to include their files on the Wow! CD-ROM so you can examine their construction.

Stephen Arscott
4291 Village Centre Ct
Mississauga, ONT
L4Z 1S2 CANADA
(905) 896-4664
atk@passport.ca

Bruce Baryla
1213 Avenue Z
Brooklyn, NY 11235
(718) 332-3877
bruce@ciociola.com

Martin Boso
Columbus, OH 43229
(614) 293-5483
(614) 885-4582

David Brickley
Shooting Brick Productions
3318 NE Peerless Pl.
Portland, OR 97232
(503) 236-4883
brickley@europa.com

Mary Carter
The Black Point Group
(415) 892-4392
themook@well.com
www.well.com/user/themook

Roger Casselman
554 De Bruyne Crescent
Aylmer, Quebec
Canada J9H 5N8
(819) 684-1591
roger_casselman@sympatico.ca
roger@indelta.com

John Corkery
1606 Dublin Dr.
Silver Spring, MD 20902
(301) 681-1641
artattack@smart.net

Nelson Crabill
5122 Mockingbird Lane
Katy, TX 77493-2128
(713) 391-6381

Edward Cristina
4-328 Mcleod
Ottawa, ONT
K2P 1A3 CANADA
(613) 237-0158
(613) 234-8468

Marin Darmonkow
Darmonkow Ellis
P.O. Box 23223
St. John's, NF
CANADA
(709) 747-0140
dedg@nfld.com

James D'Avanzo
(11/2/73–5/28/96)
Family of James D'Avanzo
1446 Jennings Rd.
Fairfield, CT 06430
(203) 255-6822

Jack Davis

Wil Dawson
11004 East 11th Place
Tulsa, OK 74128-4210
(918) 234-1362
wdawson@pobox.com
http://pobox.com/
~graphics.gallery

Antonio De Leo
Via Cimabue
Rome COLLEFERRO
40-00034 ITALY
39 6 970 0322

Frank Dlugoleski
GraphCom
P.O. Box 411
New Britain, CT 06050
(860) 225-6206

Reed Fisher
San Clemente, CA 92673
(714) 498-0634
rfisher@fea.net
www.fea.net/~rfisher/cyberfish

Rémi Forcier
410-40 Alexander St.
Toronto, ONT
M4Y 1B5 CANADA
(416) 921-4337
remi@aircastle.com
www.aircastle.com

Sharon George
2259 Dunlop St.
San Diego, CA 92111
(619) 292-0194
gorgeous@gorgeousgeorge.com
www.gorgeousgeorge.com

Tom Gould
2966 Dove St.
San Diego, CA 92103
(619) 298-8605

Tom Graney
Ideas at work!
7735 Pomeroy Ct.
Richmond, VA 23228
(804) 965-6280
TGraney388@aol.com

Tim Harrington
501 NW Woods Chapel Rd.
Blue Springs, MO 64015
(913) 469-8700 x4114
tim@pdainc.com

Donna Ignacio-Skaggs
6905 Barquera Street
Coral Gables, FL 33146
(305) 740-0563
d730@aol.com

Paul Kantorek
P.K. Productions
321 Chaplin Crescent Unit 210
Toronto, ONT
M5P 1B2 CANADA
(416) 482-2876
kantorek@acs.ryerson.ca

Joe King
P.O. Box 231
Seal Beach, CA 90740
(562) 670-1191
Thatjoeguy@aol.com
www.toonguy.com

Valerie Babb Krohn
3164 South Woodward Blvd.
Tulsa, OK 74105
(918) 743-8531

Dalia Levin
Laskov St. 44
Rehovot, ISRAEL
972 8 9353443
dilewin@shani.net

Ceri Lines

Kent Looft
2343 West Estrella Dr.
Chandler, AZ 85224
(602) 786-9411

Joseph T. McCourt
Bark@TheMoon Studio
1751 Indian Court
Hampstead, MD 21074
(410) 239-0667
JTMcCourt@aol.com

Robert McCoy
103 Somerset
Pontiac, IL 71764
(815) 844-3808

Alice Mininch McLean
6189 Heritage Park Crescent
Orleans, ONT
K1C7G8 CANADA
(613) 830-9455
hrdc-hrs@ottawa.net

Barry Meyer
1739 Cedar Rd.
Homewood, IL 60430
(708) 957-5962
76516.2135@compuserve.com

William Mogensen
Mogensen Design
Shadow Hills, CA 91040
(818) 352-4102
mogensen@wman.com
www.wman.com/~mogensen

Barry Monaco
1400 Cotton Court
Crownsville, MD 21032
(410) 923-2069
fmnw28a@prodigy.com

Gustavo A. Ortiz
2156 NW 82nd Ave.
Miami, FL 33122-1507
gustavo@mentecolectiva.com
www.club-como.com

Gary Priester
The Black Point Group
themook@slip.net
Http:www.slip.net/~themook

Christopher Purcell
Compaq Computer
Houston, TX 77070
(713) 514-4679
ChrisP@Bangate.compaq.com

Lance Ravella
Osborne/McGraw Hill
2600 10th St.
Berkeley, CA 94710
(510) 549-6632
ravellal@crl.com

Cecil Rice
5784 Salem Terrace
Acworth, GA 30102
(770) 974-0684
CGrahmR@aol.com

Jolanta Romanowska
ul. Sienna 55 m 8
Warsaw, POLAND 00-820
4822 24 38 69

Nicki Salvin-Wight
17215-195th Place NE
Woodinville, WA 98072
(206) 788-2415
(206) 788-9404

Marla Shelasky
1380 Filbert St #8
San Francisco, CA 94109
(415) 922-8426

David K. Smith
Photon Technology International
447 Silvia St.
West Trenton, NJ 08628

Rick Smith
The Valley Scribe
640 Sloan St.
Delta, CO 81416
(970) 249-0233

John Sparks
GRAFX Design
Louisville, KY 40217-1603
(502) 636-2790
grafx@mystique.net
http://members.xoom.com/jsparks/

Cher Threinen-Pendarvis
San Diego, CA
(619) 226-6050

Gerald Tooke
57 Gothic Ave.
Toronto, ONT
M6P 2V8 CANADA
(416) 766-1836
gtooke@inforamp.net

Theodor Ushev
Blvd. Samokov 78 Ap. 12
Sofia, BULGARIA 1113
359 2 65 88 51

Appendix E: Resources

Listed on this page is contact information for the software developers who have contributed resources to the Wow! CD-ROM.

The "GIF Construction Set Professional 2.0n" software included with this publication is provided as shareware for your evaluation. If you try this software and find it useful, you are requested to register it as discussed in its documentation and in the About screen of the application. The publisher of this book has not paid the registration fee for this shareware.

Adobe Systems, Inc.
345 Park Avenue
San Jose, CA 95110-2704
(408) 536-6000
www.adobe.com

Alchemy Mindworks Inc.
P.O. Box 500
Beeton, ONT
L0G 1A0 CANADA
(905) 936-9501
alchemy@mail.north.net
www.mindworkshop.com/
alchemy/alchemy.html

Bitstream Inc.
215 First St.
Cambridge, MA 02142
(800) 522-FONT
sales@bitstream.com
www.bitstream.com

Boutell.Com, Inc
MapEdit
P.O. Box 20837
Seattle, WA 98102
(206) 325-3009
mapedit@boutell.com
www.boutell.com

Cerious Software, Inc.
1515 Mockingbird Ln., Ste 209
Charlotte, NC 28209
(764) 529-0200
(704) 529-0497 (fax)
pc.eus@cerious.com
www.cerious.com

Corel Corporation
1600 Carling Avenue
Ottawa, ONT
K1Z 8R7 CANADA
(613) 728-0826
www.corel.com

FontLook
86-22 60th Rd.
Elmhurst, NY 11373
76044.747@compuserve.com

GarageFonts
P.O. Box 3101
Del Mar, CA 92014
(619) 755-4761
info@garagefonts.com
www.garagefonts.com

GIFBuilder
Yves Piguet
Av. de la Chabliere 35
Lausanne, CH-1004
piguet@ia.epfl.ch

Macromedia
600 Townsend Street
San Francisco, CA 94103
www.macromedia.com

Peachpit Press
1249 Eighth Street
Berkeley, CA 94710
(510) 524-2178
www.peachpit.com

Time Tunnel, Inc.
31316 42nd Place SW
Federal Way, WA 98023
(888) 650-6050
(253) 838-3377
ttunnel@halcyon.com
www.timetunnel.com

Ur-Text
Colin MacNeil
5234 Morris St. #41
Halifax, NS B3J1B4
http://tfts.i-us.com

Index